Torches of Light

Torches of Light

Georgia Teachers
& the Coming
of the Modern South

Ann Short Chirhart

The University of Georgia Press

Athens & London

© 2005 by the University of Georgia Press
Athens, Georgia 30602
All rights reserved
Set in Goudy Oldstyle by
Graphic Composition, Inc., Athens, GA
Printed and bound by Maple-Vail

The paper in this book meets the guidelines for
permanence and durability of the Committee on
Production Guidelines for Book Longevity of the
Council on Library Resources.

Printed in the United States of America
09 08 07 06 05 c 5 4 3 2 1
09 08 07 06 05 p 5 4 3 2 1

Library of Congress Cataloging-in-Publication Data

Chirhart, Ann Short
Torches of light : Georgia teachers and the coming
of the modern South / Ann Short Chirhart
p. cm.
Includes bibliographical references and index.
ISBN 0-8203-2446-9 (hardcover : alk. paper) —
ISBN 0-8203-2669-0 (pbk. : alk paper)
1. Women teachers—Georgia—History.
2. Women teachers—Georgia—Social conditions.
3. Discrimination in education—Southern
States—History.   I. Title.
LB2837.C5215 2004
371.1'0082'09758—dc22   2004021103

British Library Cataloging-in-Publication Data available

To the memory of my grandmothers,

Anna Marie Weber Short

and

Anna Marie Brandt Bannon;

the memory of my mother,

Marjorie Bannon Short;

and to my father,

James Short

Contents

Illustrations

Abbreviations

A & M	agricultural and mechanical
AMA	American Missionary Association
AUL	Atlanta Urban League
CIC	Commission on Interracial Cooperation
CIO	Congress of Industrial Organizations
FERA	Federal Emergency Relief Administration
GEA	Georgia Education Association
GEB	General Education Board
GERA	Georgia Emergency Relief Administration
GSIC	Georgia State Industrial College
GTEA	Georgia Teachers and Education Association
JRF	Julius Rosenwald Fund
MFPE	Minimum Foundation Program for Education
NAACP	National Association for the Advancement of Colored People
NYA	National Youth Administration
USDA	U.S. Department of Agriculture
WMU	Women's Missionary Union
WPA	Works Progress Administration

Acknowledgments

LIKE MOST SCHOLARS, I owe thanks to many people and institutions. Most suggestions and every bit of financial aid helped me complete this book. Without the staffs at archives, my work would have been considerably more difficult. Many thanks to Thomas Rosenbaum at the Rockefeller Archive Center, Beth Howse at Fisk University, Bill Sumners at the Southern Baptist Historical Library and Archives, David Moltke-Hansen at the Southern Historical Collection, Aloha South at the National Archives, and the archivists at Emory University, the Georgia Department of Archives and History, the University of Georgia Special Collections, Kennesaw State University, Savannah State College, Atlanta University, the Library of Congress, and the Franklin Delano Roosevelt Library.

Financial assistance encourages thorough scholarship, and I am truly grateful for the fellowships I have received. Funds from the Graduate Institute of the Liberal Arts and Institute of Women's Studies at Emory University, the Andrew W. Mellon Fellowship in Southern Studies, and the Southern Baptist Convention helped me to complete my dissertation at Emory University. A welcome postdoctoral fellowship from the National Museum of American History at the Smithsonian Institution assisted me as I began the process of writing a book. Indiana State University's Department of History and a provost's grant from Indiana State University's College of Arts and Sciences provided essential aid for travel and research. Indiana State University's Research Grant gave me the funds to complete the project when that one last trip became necessary.

From beginning to end, the editors and staff at the University of Georgia Press encouraged this project. Alison Waldenberg's enthusiasm for the manuscript assured me that the book would be published. Derek Krissoff more than adequately filled her position with his humor and grace about delays. Managing editor Jennifer Reichlin, project editor Jon Davies, and copyeditor Ellen Goldlust-Gingrich shepherded the manuscript through the final stages and made sure I said what I intended. The two anonymous readers offered insightful critiques that redirected my prose in some vital ways. I am truly grateful to have published with a terrific press.

Several historians graciously offered advice, suggestions, and a friendly ear. I thank James Anderson, Charles Banner-Haley, Ronald Butchart, Dan T. Carter, Mary Frederickson, Thavolia Glymph, Jacquelyn Dowd Hall, Jack Temple Kirby, John Inscoe, James Leloudis, William Link, Valinda Rogers Littlefield, Kate Rousmaniere, Mark Schultz, Stephanie Shaw, Melissa Walker, and Nan Woodruff for their encouragement and suggestions at various conference sessions and meetings.

I am honored to have worked with three remarkable scholars at Emory University. Allen Tullos contributed to the early days of this work by recommending that I get a tape recorder and find some retired teachers. His careful readings and frequent contributions enriched the development of my thinking. Mary Odem, with her knowledge of women, labor, and reform, shaped and clarified my arguments. Her firm belief in the importance of my topic convinced me to persevere to the end. My adviser and mentor, Elizabeth Fox-Genovese, gave me more than her skillful analysis and provocative acumen: she offered friendship and guidance that helped me believe I could complete this work; she stretched and challenged my ideas with insightful commentary and an astonishing breadth of knowledge. From the first day I attended Emory University to this manuscript's publication, she has encouraged me.

Fitz Brundage, Jonathan Bryant, Joan Cashin, Pete Daniel, Mary Frederickson, Robyn Muncy, and Ronald Walters read the entire manuscript and provided valuable comments. They gave me a broader perspective on the arguments and offered important suggestions for revisions. Pete Daniel read every draft I wrote and discussed changes with me. From him, I gained an appreciation for the complexities of southern history and southern humor. Joan Cashin, John Inscoe, and Elna Green accepted essays from this work for publication in their edited volumes. Their comments honed my prose and convinced me of the significance of this work. Portions of my article "Gardens of Education" are reprinted courtesy of the Georgia Historical Society. Peter Lang Press also granted permission to reprint portions of my article "Carrying the Torch."

Numerous friends and family members also shared their time and strength with me. Donna Kessler, Lee Polansky, and Rebecca Sharpless laughed and anguished with me over the weekly trials of graduate school and revising a manuscript. Lee spent hours discussing various ways of presenting information as we joked about our lives. Amy Rolleri and Ron Butchart welcomed me to their

Athens home while I read microfilm. At the University of Georgia, Jim Cobb, John Inscoe, and Bryant Simon helped to clarify my thinking. Rosemarie Sanderson and Peter Schadae gave me the gift of unending friendship and support. My colleagues in the Department of History at Indiana State University, notably Christopher and Jennifer Olsen, eased my transition into the world of academia. More Bannons, Shorts, and Chirharts than I can mention proved to me the meaning of family. My husband, Ken Chirhart, endured to the end and learned more than he ever wanted to know about Georgia and teachers. His humor and reminders about eating kept me grounded. Thanks also to Emma and the late and great Frieda.

More than any archive or individual, the Georgia women who taught during the twentieth century made this book possible. Former teachers opened their doors to this Yankee woman with grace and a spirit of cooperation that still amazes me. I especially thank Carrie Oliver Bailey, Jimmie Kate Sams Cole, Narvie Jordan Harris, Nelle Still Murphy, Dorothy Oliver Rucker, Florrie Still, Horace Tate, Ruth Smith Waters, Susie Weems Wheeler, Laura Mosley Whelchel, and Leona Clark Williams for tolerating repeated visits and phone calls and for sharing their photographs and stories. My greatest hope is that I have told their stories in a way that reflects their accomplishments and dignity.

The dedication of this volume addresses my debts to my grandmothers, Anna Weber Short and Anna Brandt Bannon, who demonstrated characteristic independence, strength, humor, and intelligence. As Anna Brandt Bannon knew all too well, the price of a lack of education is high. Her stories not only taught me the importance of higher education and the meaning of class distinctions but also instilled in me the belief that women can accomplish most tasks and can endure. My parents, Marjorie Ann Bannon and Jim Short, encouraged me at every stage and provided me with strength, wisdom, and laughter. From my mother, who handed me a book at every opportunity, I learned to love reading. She listened to every discussion about teachers, read most drafts, and suggested ideas based on her forty years of teaching. In some respects, this book draws on my past—the ways I attempted to understand my mother and to understand segregated schools. To my deepest regret, my mother died before this project was completed. My dad taught me to laugh at life and myself. His reminders to "finish that book" kept me writing. To each of these people, I owe a debt that can never be repaid.

DADE CATOOSA WHITFIELD MURRAY FANNIN TOWNS RABUN
WALKER GILMER UNION
CHATTOOGA GORDON PICKENS LUMPKIN WHITE HABERSHAM STEPHENS
DAWSON
• Rome FLOYD BARTOW CHEROKEE FORSYTH Gainesville • HALL BANKS FRANKLIN HART
Cartersville JACKSON MADISON ELBERT
POLK Marietta • Lawrenceville • BARROW Athens
PAULDING COBB GWINNETT CLARKE OGLETHORPE WILKES LINCOLN
HARALSON Atlanta • OCONEE
DE KALB WALTON
DOUGLAS ROCKDALE COLUMBIA
CARROLL FULTON CLAYTON NEWTON MORGAN Greensboro • GREENE TALIAFERRO MCDUFFIE
WARREN Augusta •
HEARD COWETA FAYETTE HENRY JASPER PUTNAM HANCOCK GLASCOCK RICHMOND
SPALDING
Griffin • BUTTS Milledgeville • JEFFERSON BURKE
TROUP MERIWETHER PIKE LAMAR MONROE JONES BALDWIN
UPSON WASHINGTON
HARRIS TALBOT CRAWFORD • Macon WILKINSON JOHNSON JENKINS SCREVEN
Columbus • BIBB
MUSCOGEE PEACH TWIGGS EMMANUEL
CHATTA- TAYLOR Fort LAURENS TREUTLEN CANDLER BULLOCH EFFINGHAM
HOOCHEE MARION MACON Valley • HOUSTON BLECKLEY Statesboro •
SCHLEY PULASKI MONTGOMERY TOOMBS EVANS Savannah
STEWART WEBSTER SUMTER DOOLY DODGE WHEELER TATTNALL BRYAN CHATHAM
CRISP WILCOX TELFAIR LIBERTY
QUITMAN RANDOLPH TERRELL LEE TURNER BEN HILL JEFF DAVIS LONG
CLAY Albany • IRWIN COFFEE APPLING WAYNE MCINTOSH
CALHOUN DOUGHERTY WORTH BACON
EARLY BAKER TIFT BERRIEN ATKINSON PIERCE GLYNN
MILLER MITCHELL COLQUITT COOK WARE BRANTLEY
SEMINOLE DECATUR GRADY THOMAS BROOKS LANIER CAMDEN
LOWNDES CLINCH CHARLTON
ECHOLS

0 Miles 50
0 Kilometers 80

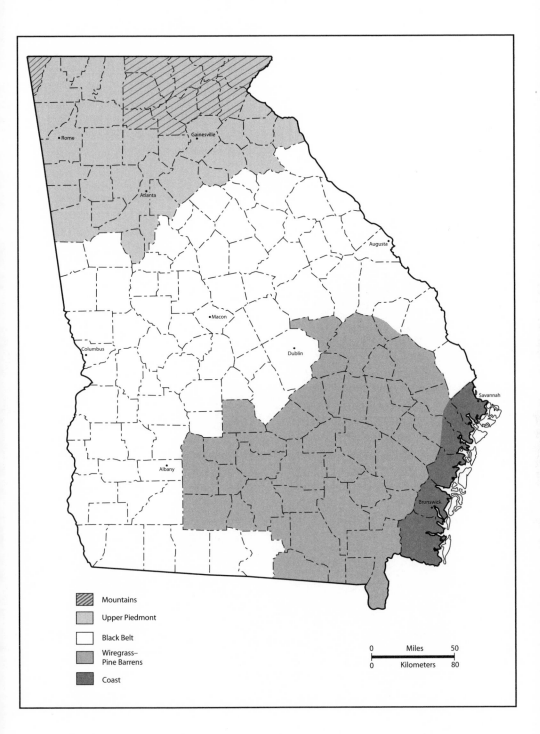

Mountains

Upper Piedmont

Black Belt

Wiregrass–
Pine Barrens

Coast

Introduction

To Light a Torch of Instruction

In 1936, in neighboring counties, Dorothy Oliver Rucker and Leona Clark Williams donned skirts, blouses, and stockings to prepare for their first day of teaching—Rucker at a black school and Williams at a white institution. Rucker and Williams arrived at their segregated public classrooms, opened with prayer and a devotion, checked attendance, and began lessons. During that year, Rucker might have taught one of James Weldon Johnson's poems, while Williams began listening to a group reading from basal readers. Rucker's students undoubtedly read from used books while sitting on benches. Although Williams's students had desks, several lacked books. Both classrooms were crowded with many children from impoverished homes. Because the cotton crop had collapsed during the Great Depression, some students came to school without breakfast. Other children might not have attended at all because they lacked shoes. When the day ended, Rucker and Williams remained at school, talking to students and parents and grading papers. Finally, between 4:30 and 5:00 P.M., both women headed home to prepare dinner. During the school year, they participated in church activities and attended teachers' organization meetings—also segregated. On Sundays, Rucker and Williams worshipped at segregated Baptist and Methodist churches and taught Sunday school classes.

Notwithstanding their common goals and beliefs, Rucker and Williams never talked to each other. Living in a society that legally and socially divided people according to their race, Rucker and Williams never met, nor did they have any occasion to do so. They belonged to separate teachers' organizations, so they never had the opportunity to discuss classroom procedures or state policies about education for black and white children. Rucker was prohibited from checking out books at the Gainesville Public Library, was forbidden to sit with whites at movie theaters, and sat in the back of city buses. If Rucker and Williams had entered a general store at the same time, Williams would have been served first, while Rucker waited. On election day, Williams proudly cast her vote, while Rucker waited to register until the 1940s. When paychecks were distributed, Rucker earned less money than Williams.[1]

Although both women discussed with friends and colleagues New Deal programs, Rucker and Williams perceived them differently. To Rucker, the New Deal and the new legal attack by the National Association for the Advancement of Colored People (NAACP) on educational inequality represented the possibility of revolutionary changes in African Americans' political, social, and economic lives. Federal programs and legal challenges gave hope for the fulfillment of the goals for which many African Americans had worked since Reconstruction. Still, Rucker feared the potential for violence against African Americans, which had abated to some extent during the 1930s. She always remembered the terrifying days in 1912 when her family had fled a white Forsyth County mob that torched and threatened blacks. Williams, in contrast, might well have been unaware of the NAACP strategy. Still, she had always noted inequalities between the black and white school systems and hoped for change. She welcomed New Deal programs that offered lunch programs for her students, job opportunities for her family, and electricity for rural homes.

Rucker and Williams became active participants in and witnesses to extraordinary changes sweeping across Georgia. Teachers fashioned public roles for black and white Georgia women. By redefining traditional values, teachers became vital to the creation of the modern liberal state, accentuating individualism and new skills. Rucker and Williams's generation not only carved out a professional status for women but also established a cultural space in which their authority prevailed—a classroom that stretched into the community. Because of these efforts, teaching became respectable work for both single and married women. Moreover, the push by black and white teachers for better education forced Georgians to heed reformers' pleas for improved educational facilities, increased funding, and qualified instructors. In some instances, African American educators' work forced white Georgians to implement changes in public schools. Teachers' efforts led to higher literacy rates and more wage-labor possibilities for many farmers' children. Rucker's involvement in her professional organization, the Georgia Teachers and Education Association (GTEA), brought her into contact with the nascent civil rights movement of the 1940s. Led by C. L. Harper, the GTEA became the leading civil rights advocacy group of the time, following the decline of the state's NAACP membership.

Rarely simple providers of knowledge or facts, female teachers—both black and white—served as cultural mediators who carried moral and spiritual values into their classrooms while working as agents of social and cultural change. No other profession spends as much time with individuals as teachers do. For approximately half the year, children's days are guided, managed, and directed by educators, most of whom—especially at the elementary level—are women. In some instances—notably in rural, one-room southern schoolhouses during the early twentieth century—teachers taught the same children for years and taught multiple generations of family members. It is little wonder, then, that teachers have become such dominant figures in family tales, individual remembrances, and national culture.

Because of the centrality of teachers to community life, many southern African American and white girls in the early 1900s dreamed of growing up to teach school. Yet historians have devoted little attention to who these teachers were and what they actually did.[2] Teachers did more than write lesson plans and follow established curriculum guidelines. For both blacks and whites, teaching represented a respectable, dignified career that offered women the chance to financially support themselves and their families as well as to serve the community and God, a strong concern for southern women raised in conservative Protestant evangelical churches.[3] For some women, teaching meant the difference between poverty and family survival.[4] For African American women, education held the promise of equality and formed the core of the idea of racial uplift. Because black and white women drew from inherited notions of duty, respectability, and self-sufficiency, they created a realm of authority that fell comfortably within gendered expectations for women.

Less obvious yet crucial to understanding teachers' work is the cultural and political content of their role.[5] Education lay at the core of every battle in Georgia about gendered identity, equality, individual rights, and industrial change, becoming the contested terrain on which fights for local control, church and family authority, white supremacy, and white male authority were fought. Serving as the flash point for contentious claims of traditional authority and modernity, teachers worked at the center of multiple debates. Public education, which had initially offered basic skills to most black and white children, became politicized because it held the potential to overturn inherited traditions. To white supremacists, African Americans' constant efforts to improve education threatened to lead to race mixing in schools.[6]

By the late 1930s, most Georgians saw education as an integral means for improving their lives, an understanding that led to confrontations with an entrenched hierarchy based on white supremacy and masculine authority. These confrontations, in turn, resulted in a modern—albeit segregated—school system that cut through the quagmire of cultural and social tensions dating from Reconstruction. On the one hand, education carried the potential to threaten decades of unequal traditions. Too much education could lead to opposition to white power brokers or could provide skills that would allow future generations to leave agricultural work for better jobs in urban areas. On the other hand, operating schools meant little if states lacked attendance laws, equal facilities for all children, and opportunities for graduates to use their knowledge. In the language of public education policies, some Georgians heard modernity's march— the possibility of changing the world through industrialization, secularization, and the expansion of individual rights.

Many Georgians clearly recognized education's potential to lead to change as well as the consequences of such change. Despite its status as one of the largest and most populated southern states in 1900, Georgia possessed only a rudimentary public school system. Yet by the 1920s, educational policy had become the most controversial and contentious of the state's transformations into the modern world for four reasons: (1) it created a means for women's public authority; (2) it threatened political and social patterns of localism; (3) it endangered Jim Crow standards of separate and unequal public facilities for African Americans; and (4) it blazed the path for modernity. Over the next two decades, the implementation of a public school system resulted in Georgia's worst political crises and social turmoil since the Civil War. Teachers taught for months without pay; counties battled over funding for white schools; African Americans fought for equal financial allocations; counties clashed with state authorities over control of education; and governors and local political officials almost came to blows in 1948 about who the governor should be as well as who should be educated and how education would be accomplished. At the same time, in the wake of violent attacks against African Americans during and after World War II, the GTEA initiated civil rights activism by fighting local battles against unequal funding. In 1951, black and white teachers' efforts led to legislation that attempted to equalize funding for black and white education, the Minimum Foundation Program for Education (MFPE). Despite these successes, notably those of black teachers, the state remained loath to provide unequivocal equal education. Furthermore, the state continued to ignore the needs of black schools and some rural white schools, and how to educate students and what they should be taught remained unsettled.

Examining teachers' lives reveals that African American and white educators shaped social policy and cultural beliefs as Georgia stumbled through the process of modern state building from 1910 to 1950. Analyzing these extraordinary events through the eyes of black and white teachers demonstrates that teachers constituted the core of the movement for change. Raised predominantly in agricultural regions that relied on cotton as a cash crop, teachers of both races drew from the cotton culture's values of self-sufficiency, interdependence, evangelical Protestantism, and localism to redefine women's public roles as leaders in a rapidly industrializing world. Starting from such traditional cultural sites as households, communities, churches, and schools, teachers increased their public roles, using familiar values for novel purposes. Even as teachers borrowed from inherited community beliefs, their ambition, combined with their parents' goals, church roles, kinship networks, and a degree of luck, impelled them to reach an achievement beyond most Georgians' expectations. African American women brought new meanings to the ideas of independence and interdependence while working for racial uplift and economic, political, and social justice. Black educators initiated challenges to racism that led to the civil rights movement. White female teachers used similar values to create a gendered professional identity for white women and to teach new skills required for industry. Pushing for policy reforms, educators of both races played a central role in the creation of a modern, centralized state. Becoming some of Georgia's most respected professionals, teachers linked their job to redefining what it meant to be men and women in the modern South.

During this transitional time, traditional beliefs rarely disappeared entirely, instead remaining to inform the new social order. This negotiation between tradition and modernity left intact some aspects of southern social hierarchies. Men and women understood gender relations in different ways. Elite whites dominated social and political terrain, but new professionals and industrialists challenged large landholders' claims to supremacy. In 1950 African Americans still lived without social, economic, and political equality, yet they were better educated and faced the post–World War II world determined to push for equality. Teachers' work in the classroom and beyond contributed to this preservation and realignment of older social relations. All in all, teachers sought to translate a core of traditional values such as interdependence and self-sufficiency into new beliefs in respectability and personal success that were believed to ensure students' accomplishments in the changing world.[7]

Teachers' work had mixed consequences for Georgia, its communities, and its students. Notwithstanding successes in privileging wage labor over the debilitating cotton culture, teachers undermined the roles of family, church, and community by redirecting authority to the state and to educators. Teaching students how to set a table, how to dress, or how to speak standard English may have facilitated students' admission to bourgeois culture while reinforcing self-sufficiency. Yet relying on wage labor to purchase dishes or clothing placed students at the mercy of an expanding consumer culture that sanctioned self-interest over community ties. Paths to consumption overwhelmed evangelical

Protestantism's lessons regarding duty and responsibility. Some historians have criticized black teachers' elitism and failure to galvanize a grassroots civil rights movement in Georgia, but such charges result from the disguised or overlooked nature of political actions by both black and white teachers.[8] Although some such criticisms are no doubt valid, as Narvie Jordan Harris, a prominent black reformer, said, "Teachers were never trained at public relations. We aren't supposed to talk about ourselves. That's one reason no one really knows what we did."[9]

Furthermore, drawing from political activism in the antebellum period, many African Americans realized that the road to equality required more than ideas about racial uplift and consequently shifted their efforts to race work within the black communities.[10] The movement toward state authority in social policies began to smash the power of local county politicians, providing an opening that the GTEA exploited in its work for social and political rights. At a time when membership in the NAACP could threaten teachers' employment and even their lives, black teachers managed extraordinary accomplishments through the GTEA. Pulled in different directions by their duty to their race, their ambitions, and their students, black professionals formed the vanguard of the civil rights movement. While their actions may not seem explicitly political, the fact that their organization's reach extended beyond that of the NAACP indicates that they formulated new means for political action.[11] Black and white teachers pushed for equal funding for segregated schools and professional benefits such as a teachers' retirement plan. Some black reformers also wanted voting rights and to challenge Jim Crow seating in public places, but these reformers saw all issues as inevitably centered on equal education for all Georgians.

Women's life stories and the ways they are told reveal how women define themselves within their history and culture. Personal narratives, whether written in autobiographical form or spoken in oral interviews, evoke women's experiences in specific moments and places, particularly as members of interlocking communities that included other women, men, and children of different classes, races, religions, and regions.[12] These communities provided modes of expression and concepts that helped female teachers define their place. Understanding how these women constructed their gendered identities requires examining their private and public lives in the context of Georgia's history and culture.[13]

Historians have recently come to rely increasingly on oral histories and/or personal narratives to depict the lives of farmers, tenants, industrial workers, and civil rights leaders.[14] At their best, personal narratives help to provide an understanding of the lives of people who seldom leave written records. Yet recollections often idealize circumstances or personal accomplishments—it would be foolish to believe that interviewees never embellish the truth or even simply misremember events long past. Many white teachers interviewed for this project claimed that "everyone was poor back then." But families' circumstances clearly differed according to variables such as property ownership, race, and access to consumer goods. Some African American women recalled their achievements as unparalleled individual gains with minimal intrusions by the Jim Crow system and white supremacist perspectives. Memory reconstructs positive and negative images of the past from the present perspective.[15] For these women, that perspective includes remarkable stories of individual triumph that demand admission into the best compilation of American success stories. The interviewees' points of view also include cultural beliefs that contain assumptions about what constitutes a moral and admirable person, including class, race, gender, and religious suppositions. Yet excluding personal narratives from historical studies risks ignoring those who have not left historical documents.

Black and white former teachers' narratives disclose the specific ways such women perceived and continue to perceive themselves in their region's history. Throughout early-twentieth-century Georgia, these women understood themselves as part of a constantly renegotiated and re-created cultural milieu. Their efforts underscore the ways in which American women experience and engage their regions. Numerous American historians have elaborated the ways in which women's identification with various interlocking yet diverse communities constructs personal identities, with these self-identifications often serving as means of division as well as interaction.[16] Women from disparate racial or ethnic groups occasionally find common ground, such as social or labor reform efforts, on which to join together and work cooperatively. At other, equally frequent times, women's ties and actions collide. Rather than being bound to a collective women's experience, gendered identities also contain elements of class and race that can divide women from each other—just like men.

Teachers, like many professionals, rarely leave diaries, possibly because of the obligations of work and family. Thus, oral histories provide telling information about such women's experiences and beliefs. Most of the women interviewed for this project taught in Georgia for between twenty and thirty years, remaining close to their native areas.[17] Others stayed in northern Georgia but chose to quit teaching after marrying and having children. As the interviewees—both black and white—pulled out photographs, newspaper clippings, and examples of their work, they beamed about their accomplishments. They bragged about students who had become professionals or who recognized their former instructors at restaurants. The women talked about their families and influences, eyes flashing their determination and frequent sacrifices required to complete an education and become a teacher. All of these women remained active members of evangelical Methodist or Baptist denominations. Finding time to talk about their teaching and childhood during busy schedules that included church and other volunteer work, the women dressed neatly and conservatively, as they had during their teaching years. With lives filled with visits from children and grandchildren and community work, they eagerly talked about their accomplishments and the importance of education.[18] Black and white teachers' stories also depict the legacy of Jim Crow, however. Raised in a world that consistently tried to keep blacks and whites apart, women of both races knew little about each other despite living in the same communities.

Teachers often unintentionally brought modernity to their communities. In this book, *modernization* means the process through which identity came to rely on an individual's occupation and material accomplishments rather than on kinship ties or church affiliation. A "modern" society relies on innovation, commercialization, and bureaucracies rather than on localism and consistency.[19] Throughout the early twentieth century, Georgia's history depicts the clash and synthesis of modernity with local traditions. Within this synthesis, diverse communities shaped Georgia's accommodation to modernity. As definitions of private and public roles modified and merged, as the state and the county vied for power, and as industrialists and planters argued about and came to a consensus on what Georgia should become, men and women understood their identities in similar yet new ways.

The meaning of *community* shifts over time. For example, in *I Know Why the Caged Bird Sings*, Maya Angelou identifies with various communities—her grandmother's household, her school, her church, African Americans, and Arkansans, among others. In this sense, *community* means shared values or attitudes. At the same time, each of these communities constitutes a portion of broader political, social, and economic structures. As a black woman, Angelou could not vote, check out books at the library, or attend the relatively well funded and equipped white schools. Communities, in other words, may best be understood as components of the larger social system, and the values and beliefs expressed within these components of society emerge and reappear in a variety of changing ways. The amount and extent of these values that each group may appropriate determines an individual's position, or "cultural capital," in his or her world.[20] Black women improved their positions by becoming teachers and avoiding sharecropping, yet their race perpetuated their inferior status within the Jim Crow South. White women brought new meanings to old values as a way of maintaining existing social arrangements, while black women used the same traditions to buttress arguments for racial uplift and equality.[21]

Many former teachers, both black and white, see themselves explicitly as having lit the way for the students, although they clearly intended not to limit their students to the same path. Beulah Rucker Oliver wrote in her brief 1953 autobiography, *The Rugged Pathway*, of having spent most of her life attempting "to light a torch of instruction" for her race.[22] GTEA members called the history of their organization *Rising in the Sun*. Funded by northern philanthropist Anna T. Jeanes, African American women teachers who worked as education supervisors in districts and became known as Jeanes teachers referred to themselves as the "guiding light of education." White teachers also identify education with light, in opposition to the darkness of ignorance. Teachers' metaphoric use of light derives from community and biblical narratives of freedom and self-sufficiency. African Americans' use of light recalls the shift from the darkness of enslavement to the light of freedom and literacy, from inferior status to the divine calling for racial improvement. To Oliver and countless other teachers of both races, "lighting a torch of instruction" meant religious redemption concomitant with learning. Black women used an existing cultural form of authority, evangelical Protestantism, to legitimate their public roles while challenging racist assumptions about black women's inferiority. White teachers saw their work as a means to claim individual public roles for women and to improve society.[23] As Christians, black and white women believed that their duty to God included maintaining and passing on their evangelical Protestant beliefs, spreading their light for the glory of God and the salvation of their people, however that group was defined.

Chapter 1 describes Georgia's cultural, social, and economic context from the late nineteenth century through the first decade of the twentieth century. These years saw the first stirrings of change as the region followed national economic trends and began to produce cotton for larger markets. Although a racist social hierarchy and patterns of localism preserved many traditions, African Americans and an expanding white middle class began to call for an improved educational system, thereby creating fissures in the social system. While some white Georgians had supported education for blacks in the aftermath of the Civil War, by the turn of the century, fear, white supremacist violence, and racism created the rigid segregation system as well as a decline in white support for African American education.

Chapter 2 takes a closer look at the women who became teachers. Personal narratives show that women absorbed gendered roles and social boundaries from their families, churches, and communities. Their descriptions of harsh punishments for breaking rules re-create a world in which disobedience and independent thought often were met with switches. Yet women learned to manipulate these rules, and family and community authority decreased during this time. As these women become adults, they looked for opportunities to improve their world by rejecting their parents' rural lifestyles, fulfilling personal ambitions, and becoming leaders. Work meant more than earning a salary: for black women, work meant finding means to challenge Jim Crow and to serve their communities; for white women, wage labor offered an escape from backbreaking agricultural labor and the chance to carve out independent lives. Black and white women discovered that teaching allowed them to fulfill their understandings of the possibilities of professional work.

But teachers had to cope with Georgia's convoluted educational system, the story told in chapter 3. From 1910 to 1930, the state debated who should be taught, who should teach, and what should be taught, putting a multitude of obstacles on the road to a public school system. Part of the tale of poorly funded black schools is known, but the state also ignored white rural schools without strong tax bases. Reformers, northern philanthropy from the General Education Board (GEB) and the Julius Rosenwald Fund (JRF), and the U.S. Department of Agriculture (USDA) sought to build a school system based on national models but met frequent opposition from the state and local authorities. The resulting hodgepodge of rules relied on local authorities to certify teachers and maintain schools. Nevertheless, even within this chaotic framework, teachers created a role as leaders and professionals.

Chapter 4 describes how women expanded cultural notions of respectability, duty, and self-sufficiency to devise professional careers as teachers.[24] With the support of northern philanthropic guidelines, the USDA's Extension Service, and state reformers, women constructed the modern profession of teaching by the 1930s. They insisted on higher standards and better training and established a gendered form of public authority in their classrooms. Black women thus attained coveted positions in their community as respectable individuals who understood how to negotiate the broader world and how to manipulate racism to their advantage. White women drew from national constructions of the "New Woman" but did so with a southern accent.

Although some efforts succeeded, Georgia's financial support for education was linked to cotton production, which collapsed before the 1929 stock market crash. Chapter 5 details how the Great Depression exacerbated the failures of localism. But Georgia's battles over New Deal programs such as the National Youth Administration (NYA) and the Federal Emergency Relief Administration (FERA) manifested themselves primarily in debates about education. Schooling became inextricably entwined with the morass of class, race, and gender definitions, portending new understandings of what it meant to be a Georgian in the post–World War II world. With pounding fists and inflated rhetoric, Governors Eugene Talmadge and Ellis Arnall and their supporters battled about what modern Georgia should be.

During World War II and Arnall's administration, the topic of chapter 6, educational improvements occurred for both races. Moderation seemed to prevail. Yet in the wake of the NAACP's legal attack on segregated education and the GTEA's activism, conflict again erupted over educational policy, ultimately resulting in the 1946 Three Governors Crisis. In 1948, Herman Talmadge became governor, violence against blacks escalated, and white moderation seemed to disappear. Although the actions of the GTEA and its white counterpart, the Georgia Education Association (GEA), resulted in the 1951 MFPE, which established minimum teacher salaries and a minimum level of funds for all schools, the early civil rights movement stalled in Georgia.[25] The GTEA became the state's dominant civil rights organization, yet its focus on local district efforts meant that the potential for a statewide grassroots movement waned. Black teachers thus formed the core of political action.

Working apart yet sharing some objectives, black and white teachers shaped the debate about what Georgians should become and how they could reach those goals. Schools, of course, remained divided by race and economic means. By 1950, however, the fabric that preserved these divisions had become tattered and faded. Most importantly, students, especially African Americans, had the means to face the challenges of the civil rights movement and of the new industrial economy over the next two decades.

1 · The Rugged Path

Foundations of Education

ON MAY 28, 1909, Beulah Rucker Oliver graduated with honors from the Knox Institute in Athens, Georgia. As she attended high school courses in her final year at the school run for African Americans by the American Missionary Association (AMA), she planned to "buy me a house and lot, horse and buggy to drive around and enjoy life."[1] Her graduation marked the culmination of years of deprivation and hard labor to complete her education. She would earn a salary, albeit a small one. She could achieve a bit of financial security—certainly more than her parents, who were sharecroppers, had.

Oliver, a devout Baptist, was nevertheless troubled. She began to have "dreams or visions that I would have to establish a school for my race. . . . I told [my landlady] I had to build a school for my people and the Bible must be taught therein. I prayed frequently. The dreams and visions continued to haunt me." Oliver eventually realized that her plans "for personal gain had to be canceled for the sake of fallen humanity." In the remaining months of 1909, she made and sold hats, gave music lessons, and taught at a local rural school to save money to open her school, one that would offer additional grades for black students. She then had another dream, this one telling her to build her school in Gainesville, Georgia, about forty miles to the northwest. So in 1910, Oliver loaded her belongings in a wagon and headed for Gainesville with her parents, a high school diploma, and a small sum of money. She had begun to fulfill her vision of operating a school for blacks, a task that would occupy her until her death in 1963. Combining her desire for middle-class success with her beliefs in racial uplift through education and evangelical Protestantism, she followed her calling as a teacher. Briefly, she stated that she chose to work "for the sake of fallen humanity," a possible reference to the whites' neglect of black schools in the Jim Crow South.[2]

Yet the reference to "fallen humanity" meant more than that. Oliver believed that the visions defining her mission came from God. Oliver was raised in a strict Baptist family for which faith structured the precarious rural world, and her religious beliefs undoubtedly framed the way she understood her future and its possibilities. Her use of "fallen humanity" marks the human condition as a descent from God's grace into sin, a construction of sin that derived from black Baptists' sense of wrongdoing as injustices or moral violations rather than original sin.[3] In this respect, Oliver indicted both blacks and whites for neglecting spiritual and physical needs and failing to use personal gain for the social, economic, and religious redemption of their communities. To Oliver, humanity's salvation lay in preserving diligent work habits, evangelical Protestantism, self-sufficiency, service to the community, and academic training. Drawing from her family, church, and community traditions, Oliver negotiated the tensions between modern middle-class success and the collective educational needs of her race by using her status as an educated woman to establish a school dedicated to racial uplift. Although Oliver framed her brief autobiography with stories of self-sacrifice and ceaseless labor, the intensity of her narrative derives from her audience's historical awareness of her struggle to obtain an education and to found a school within a rigidly racist hierarchical social system. Her story—told by her daughters, her former students, and her autobiography—presents an account of how she constructed her vision of education and thereby enables the definition of the process rural women used to reshape modern reforms for their traditional worlds during the Progressive and post–World War I eras.[4]

Not long after Oliver and her parents moved to Gainesville, Robin Clark and his wife, Sudie Bowman Clark, traveled with their baby daughter, Leona, born in 1911, in a wagon from North Carolina to northeastern Georgia in hopes of finding better farmland. The Clarks had never been anywhere outside of Macon County, North Carolina, and had never seen a black person. When the family's wagon ran off the road, Robin Clark went to get help, telling his wife, "If you see a black man coming toward you, get the pistol from the bread box and shoot him." Sudie Bowman soon saw a black man approaching the wagon. She had rolled Leona in a quilt and was aiming the pistol when the man suddenly turned and went down a different trail. Leona Clark Williams recalled the story to illustrate her parents' ignorance about the world and other people. Coming from the Appalachians, the Clarks knew little more of African Americans than the stories they had heard from neighbors or Georgians they met as they traveled. The Clarks accepted the popular racist caricatures of the black male beast. Growing up and becoming a teacher, Williams became more tolerant of cultural and racial differences, remembering her parents' beliefs as having been shaped by culture and lack of education.[5]

The Clarks returned to North Carolina after a few months, built a cabin on family land, and began a long and desperate struggle to succeed as farmers. In so doing, they presented their eleven children with a pattern of life to avoid if at all possible. Like Beulah Rucker Oliver, Leona Clark Williams changed her life by choosing education and a teaching career. Such decisions challenged inherited hierarchical boundaries. These women renegotiated notions of racism and gendered authority and worked for an increasing voice for an expanding middle class.

Oliver, Williams, and the other women interviewed about their years teaching in Georgia provide narratives of individual success that exclude many of the larger events of the first half of the twentieth century. Yet all these women understood their pasts as a context for the values and beliefs that shaped the decision to teach. Georgia's history and culture provide clues about Oliver's and Williams's lives and the choices that influenced their personal visions. At the same time that Oliver graduated from Knox Institute, Georgia had disenfranchised black voters; whites could lynch blacks and instigate race riots with impunity; W. E. B. Du Bois and others founded the National Association for the Advancement of Colored People (NAACP); young female garment workers struck in New York City for better working conditions; and Theodore Roosevelt began to wish he had never supported his friend William Howard Taft for the presidency. Black and white women looked for alternatives to lives as wives or spinster aunts, forming neighborhood reform associations and settlement houses across the nation.

In Georgia, education became the contested terrain on which women could publicly articulate and act on political issues such as the color line, health concerns, and working conditions for women and children. That so many women interviewed for this book rarely mentioned these topics marks how historical memory filters and shapes what the interviewees' understood as their accomplishments. The women interviewed centered their stories on state, county, religion, education, and family. This alone provides ample evidence regarding Georgia's history. Their stories, combined with historical events, indicate what their culture privileged and what it sought to deny.[6]

No other change created as much agitation, fear, and determination in Georgia as the development of a public school system. During Oliver's and Williams's lives, the state navigated a twisted and tormented fifty-year path to modernity, becoming industrialized and bureaucratized by 1950. Listening to African American and white women teachers' stories reveals a contrapuntal blend of public and private notions arising out of county and state political debates, family and community values, and modern reform. Public spaces from classrooms to streets as well as public discourse bore the marks of the challenges to inherited beliefs. These notions and the challenges to them originated in Georgia's households, which espoused self-sufficiency, evangelical Protestantism, interdependency, and localism.[7] Boundaries that seemed firm melted away and reemerged in different social, economic, and political issues, notably those of class, race, and gender. The tensions caused by differing interpretations of these beliefs erupted in late-nineteenth-century debates about education. Georgia's religious, geographical, political, race, class, and gender divisions defined and limited the public educational system that evolved. It reinforced the racist hierarchy and localism even as the state absorbed aspects of national trends by the Progressive era. Initially articulated by African Americans, calls for a state-supported and improved educational system were taken up by the expanding white middle class. Black and white reformers together began to crack the social system at the same time that white supremacists' challenges to equal education for black children began to escalate.

FIVE GEOGRAPHICAL REGIONS dominated Georgia's landscape: the mountains, the Upper Piedmont, the Lower Piedmont (the former Plantation Belt), the coastal area, and the Pine Barrens or wiregrass. The regions differed in agricultural emphasis yet shared religious, social, cultural, political, and economic characteristics. The turmoil of Reconstruction and populism positioned Georgians in certain patterns that persisted for decades. By the turn of the century, Georgia was dominated by a cash crop of cotton for national markets, conservative evangelical Protestantism, localism, interdependence within communities, self-sufficiency, divisions between blacks and whites, and gendered notions of masculinity and femininity that varied according to class and race.[8] Conceptions of power, race, and gender shifted as quickly as they were understood, making categorization complex, unstable, and even volatile.

Overall, rural women contributed labor to their households in three areas: by working to produce essential goods and services for household members, by making products for local exchange or sale in markets, and by earning money outside the household to aid in its support. Wives were indispensable to household survival because they provided essential services such as cooking and sewing, bore children, produced goods such as eggs or textiles for local exchange, and engaged in wage labor.[9] To supplement grains, vegetables, and cotton and other supplies raised on their farms, farmers organized in communities that included churches, gristmills, and country stores.[10] Each community produced most of the goods and services it consumed, creating a system of interdependency.[11]

Furthermore, rural women had rarely defined their productivity solely within the home. Apart from a brief time during Reconstruction, African American women had always worked outside their homes—either in the fields alongside other family members or in white women's homes—while retaining responsibility for household tasks such as child care and cooking. For white women, access to some manufactured products—for example, cloth and canned goods in local stores—reduced household duties but also required cash. White women gradually moved beyond their households into more public roles as teachers or organizers, roles that most of them regarded as extensions of their traditional tasks at home and at church, where they guided their children's moral and religious training.[12]

Both African American and white women hoped to lead pious lives that would lead to their and their families' salvation. In white congregations, men decided whose offenses should be punished, while women provided models of the behavior of those who were saved. Obituaries of Baptist women consistently describe devoted Christian mothers who raised their families in the church, supported church functions, and daily practiced their faith. Although women had little say in congregational policies, evangelical Protestantism provided a basis for perceiving the world from a gendered perspective. Given the responsibility to save and convert family and community, white women drew on the Protestant churches' evangelical message to carve a public means to convey their authority. Service to the church and personal and family salvation were essential goals for female and male members.

Local churches formed the core of each family's social life and each settlement's stability. The Baptist Church dominated the lives of Georgians of both races. Unlike other Protestant denominations, which formed synods or circuits, each Baptist congregation was responsible for the behavior of its members.[13] The Southern Baptist Convention could recommend certain practices but lacked the authority to enforce them. Moreover, some Baptist denominations, such as the Primitive Baptists, rejected any form of central religious authority.[14] What all Baptists shared were firm beliefs in local congregational autonomy, in the literal interpretation of the Bible, and in male authority. The white Baptist churches also generally closed themselves to African Americans. Although church records indicate that a few blacks joined up-country congregations after the Civil War, blacks had organized their own churches, predominantly Baptist, as early as the 1830s in Savannah, Gainesville, Marietta, Augusta, Macon, Rome, and Atlanta.[15]

During the antebellum period, male members of white congregations met monthly to discuss charges against other members. Most of the charges concerned nonattendance, but other offenses that could result in exclusion from the congregation included drinking alcohol, stealing, lying, gossiping, and disobeying congregational directives.[16] These proceedings reveal what most Baptists believed necessary for the preservation of order and stability. To neglect God, whose rules governed and preserved residents' lives, was tantamount to violating order in the community. With state governments distant and difficult to reach, congregational authority constituted an important means of preserving order. Each August, Methodists held camp meetings that reaffirmed members' religious commitments, while Baptists held tent revivals across Georgia. Most children never considered questioning church attendance.[17] Individual salvation was paramount in Baptist and Methodist congregations, but duties and obligations to neighbors and fellow church members were also valued, an indication of early tensions between individual rights and community responsibilities.[18]

Most Georgia rural families relied on their churches' interpretations of God's will to define life and the world. God could administer punishment for sins at any time and would answer prayers in his own way, forgive sins, and protect people in times of crisis and uncertainty. Both the Baptists and Methodists believed in original sin—that all people were by nature sinful and could be saved only through conversion. To be a Christian meant relying on an individual's public declaration of conversion and subsequent actions demonstrating salvation. Baptist and Methodist women across the South shuddered at the thought that their children might not experience conversion and thus would be consigned to eternal damnation. In contrast to northern evangelicals, who devotedly practiced good works or the Social Gospel to establish God's benevolence on earth, southern evangelicals privileged individual salvation over social reform and its attendant bureaucracy.[19] Rather than perceiving their Christian duty as charitable works for others in need, southern teachers, both black and white, constructed teaching as part of their duty to God.[20]

Thus were created the parameters of social relations in Georgia. People rarely traveled beyond their communities, very few of which had public schools before the twentieth century, although the planter elite diligently founded and sent their daughters to respectable female academies in Macon, Milledgeville, and Gainesville.[21] Sons attended the University of Georgia, military academies, or other southern universities. Whites seldom demanded public education because they believed that the essential knowledge for adulthood was acquired on the farm or in the church.[22] What children learned, when they learned it, and how they learned it rested entirely on parental desires. If parents failed in this responsibility, churches could enforce the rules by excommunicating individuals and teaching acceptable community morals. Construing education as largely a means of preserving rural self-sufficiency and personal salvation, cultural notions reflected local traditions. In the broadest sense, preserving local and family authority over the amount and kind of education confined future generations to the community and insured the perpetuation of cultural beliefs. Here lay a testament to the degree of white male authority in the form of God the Father and the male head of the household. Most Georgia residents were denied the opportunity to learn of the world beyond their communities. Religious, political, and economic beliefs overlapped, making it difficult to distinguish them.

GEORGIA'S POLITICAL ORGANIZATION underscored citizens' localized identities. In 1915, white men, predominantly landowners and businessmen, elected the governor and members of the General Assembly, but the state's 152 counties—the second-highest number in the South—decided most policies.[23] County authority, in turn, was divided according to communities. Each county rigorously guarded its autonomy, rarely cooperating with others in creating public improvements.[24] Residents who disagreed with local officials would petition the General Assembly to create a new county, a striking parallel with how Baptist congregations were formed. Consequently, as local officials sought to improve their positions relative to those of other counties, state legislators tended to represent their counties' interests over state policies, yielding chaotic disarray rather than cohesive government. For the most part, settlements and their residents maintained their independence, and the state legislature and governor had less power than local officials. Localism as understood by Georgians combined evangelical Protestantism, community structure, and political beliefs into a system that favored local white male elite authority over state authority.

Georgia's economy underwent a transformation during this time as the growing of cash crops replaced subsistence agriculture and as such burgeoning cities as Atlanta, Augusta, Savannah, and Macon began to offer increased employment and educational opportunities. The growth of industry was particularly evident in the Upper Piedmont, where even such smaller towns as Rome, Gainesville, and Marietta attracted new businesses: by the 1890s, Rome's four textile mills employed almost five thousand whites, and Dalton's Crown Mill provided jobs for hundreds of white farmers who had lost their land. After the Southern Railway built a line through Harmony Grove en route to Richmond,

Virginia, Harmony Grove Mills began operations in 1893 with sixty looms, and in 1904 the town changed its name to Commerce.[25] A shoe factory and a clothing factory were built in Lawrenceville in Gwinnett County, and the Bona Allen tannery began operations in Buford.

Although Georgia's Upper Piedmont lacked the enormous textile manufacturing sector that transformed the North and South Carolina Piedmont, the industry dominated certain Georgia districts, including the northwest. Most of the area's county seats, including Gainesville and Marietta, became centers of the textile industry as well as of cotton production and shipment. These new market towns featured shops, railroad stations, hotels, and restaurants as well as the professions necessary for modern industrial growth—bankers, lawyers, and physicians. White farmers who fell into debt and lost their land migrated to the towns in search of employment at the mills, creating a new working class. Similarly, African Americans who sought to escape the dependency of sharecropping left the countryside in hopes of finding jobs as domestic workers, laundresses, and day laborers.[26]

Gainesville typified this new Georgia town: its population exploded from 407 whites and 65 blacks in 1870 to more than 4,000 whites and 1,629 blacks in 1910. In 1900 South Carolina's Pacolet Manufacturing Company built a $1 million textile mill at New Holland, outside Gainesville, and employed 1,400 workers, most of them white. By 1902 a hydroelectric plant along the Chestatee River generated electricity for the town. Most of the African American population growth occurred after the turn of the century, as blacks migrated from Georgia's Plantation Belt and the Upper Piedmont. Attempts to establish a mattress factory, a shoe factory, and a match factory failed, and Gainesville's primary importance lay in its development as a regional cotton center: cotton gins came to be located there, and growers from Hall, Jackson, Gwinnett, Forsyth, and Dawson Counties shipped their crops to market via the Gainesville area's railroads and bridges. While whites found employment in the mills, in mercantile and service establishments, and as professionals, blacks worked in less desirable support positions as servants and building railroads and roads. Calling itself the "Queen City to the Mountains," Gainesville promoted its cool climate, railroad facilities, water power, and progressive population in attempts to attract industry.[27]

Green Street, which ran northwest of Gainesville's center, became the town's fashionable residential area for merchants, lawyers, and bankers, who built homes featuring pillars, long front porches, and as many as ten rooms. Streetcars transported whites to their offices and stores and black maids and gardeners to the Green Street homes. As in rural settlements, whites built neighborhood churches. Gainesville's largest church, First Baptist, dedicated a new sanctuary in 1909 on Green Street. A few years later, the First Presbyterian Church moved to Green Street, and the First Methodist Church followed.

Despite these changes in Georgia communities, the state remained predominantly rural, with life grounded in households, churches, and cotton gins. Cotton culture, with its emphasis on evangelical Protestantism, temperance, hard work, and self-sufficiency, persisted into the twentieth century. In 1915, Georgia ranked second in the country in cotton production: better seed, fertilizers, and farming methods led to increased cotton yields. Eighty percent of Hall County's farmers raised cotton, as did more than 90 percent of Gwinnett County's farmers. At the same time, 60 percent of Hall County's farmers were tenants: some were family members who rented land from relatives; others were African American.[28] Not surprisingly, the region retained its hierarchical social system, with the largest white male landholders and town professionals holding the majority of political and economic authority. White mill workers and tenants and sharecroppers had less influence, while black tenants and sharecroppers occupied the bottom rung of the social ladder.

BLACKS, TOO, built communities, eventually claiming a section of southeast Gainesville along Athens Highway and establishing a barbershop, a theater, several restaurants, a boardinghouse, and a grocery store. Churches remained central to African American life: by 1910, Gainesville had three Baptist churches, a holiness church, a Colored Methodist Episcopal church, an African Methodist Episcopal church, and a Methodist Episcopal church. The Reverend Green Hunter, a former slave who had arrived in Gainesville in the 1870s, promoted black education and organized several area churches. By 1877 nine of these churches formed the Northwestern Missionary Baptist Association, which became part of the National Baptist Convention.[29] Rev. Hunter then focused his efforts on black denominational education and formed a building committee, leading to the 1911 completion of Northwestern Normal and Industrial School. For a brief period in the early twentieth century, the community had its own newspaper, the *Gainesville Messenger,* although no copies are extant. A black physician and a dentist opened offices in the black section of Gainesville. Like the newly prosperous white community, Gainesville's blacks organized lodges such as the Good Samaritans, the Independent Benevolent Order, the Knights of Pythias, and the Ladies Court Heroines of Jericho.[30] These fraternal orders offered financial and emotional support to black families and provided strategies for racial pride and uplift.

African American organizational development in Gainesville paralleled that in larger cities such as Augusta, Savannah, and Atlanta and in towns such as Rome and Marietta.[31] In Marietta, black men found jobs with railroads, the Brumby Chair Company, and the McNeel Marble Company.[32] African Americans established businesses, lodges, fraternal orders, funeral homes, bands, and a baseball park along with churches and schools. Decatur's Atlanta Avenue hosted a variety of black businesses—restaurants, a funeral home, a barbershop, and a beauty parlor.[33] Although most black women worked as domestics for white farm owners or middle- and upper-class urban residents and most black men toiled as tenants or sharecroppers on land owned by whites, during the 1870s and 1880s blacks began to make claims to self-sufficiency by owning businesses or working for wage labor in towns, expanding their horizons to include more than the realm of cotton agriculture.

As African Americans worked to expand their economic opportunities, they also continued to push for increased social rights.[34] By 1895, tensions had emerged within the black community as groups took sides on the question of how best to reach these goals. African American reformers William Jefferson White, Henry McNeal Turner, and Lucy Craft Laney advocated black political and economic rights, while Benjamin Davis, the editor of the *Atlanta Independent*, followed Booker T. Washington's beliefs in economic power and accommodation.[35] Despite these fissures within their community, African Americans agreed that education, economic opportunities, and safety from violence were vital for freedom.

Responding to African American achievements, white supremacists' antiblack violence increased. The escalation of violence, choices of landowners, and availability of black communities determined blacks' decisions about where to live if they could leave rural areas in the Plantation Belt. From 1880 to 1930, 38 blacks and 4 whites were lynched in the Upper Piedmont, compared to 196 blacks and 6 whites in the Plantation Belt. In 1899, for example, Georgians lynched 27 African Americans. One of the most infamous was the lynching of Sam Hose in Newnan, a brutal and horrific example of what some whites regarded as a public festival. To William Jefferson White Jr., Hose's lynching represented "anarchy pure and simple." In the wake of Reconstruction, white supremacists instilled fear in blacks to reestablish racist boundaries about labor and rights. Until after World War I, Georgia had the highest lynching rate of any state.[36] Fear and violence became white supremacists' tools for preserving racist boundaries. No less consistently, African Americans answered by moving to black communities or living near whites who knew them, affording a degree of protection.

Yet African Americans wanted more than safety. Since Reconstruction, African Americans had labored ceaselessly to build churches and schools. With the assistance of white missionary societies, blacks had launched their own schools throughout Georgia, most frequently in churches or in deserted barns. From the outset, African American education was identified with religious training.[37] White evangelical Protestant churches also linked education with religion, but their expression of their faith and educational training differed. They favored safeguarding education as a measure of elite status and continued to oppose secular schools. Blacks in Georgia and elsewhere in the South saw education from a different perspective, drawing from religious beliefs to define a broader means to educate all African Americans. In contrast to most white Protestant denominations, black Baptists relied on visions, shouting, clapping, and calling to joyously pronounce their deliverance and experience of God's presence on earth. African Americans saw visions as a potent means by which God could communicate with individuals.[38]

African Americans' blend of evangelical Protestantism relied on personal and collective jubilation in God's presence. Salvation for black Baptists merged the redemption of an individual's soul with the deliverance of a people on earth; their faith coalesced the individual's faith in God with faith in other people. To see "the light," in Beulah Rucker Oliver's words, combined a worshipper's emotional and physical expression of God's forgiveness with acceptance in the congregation of believers. To spread this light in the community merged salvation with educational uplift and social reform. Thus, the individual and the collective proclamation of the divine coexisted, and the tensions between these strands manifested themselves in diverse ways as congregations responded to needs such as education.[39] In contrast to white Baptist congregations, which stressed humanity's sins and damnation, black Baptists identified salvation and redemption with social and spiritual liberation.[40] Moreover, work was seen as a sacred and indispensable means to salvation on earth, which was regarded as tantamount to salvation in the future; thus, sacred and secular realms were united in the efforts to uplift the race. Oliver promoted hard work as the "the great principle that carries our race upward" while borrowing biblical passages, notably John 9:4, to merge an earthly emphasis on labor with Jesus' claims to divine inspiration for work.[41] To Oliver and others like her, the kingdom of God could be obtained on earth by uplifting their race out of ignorance and poverty into education, landownership, and wage labor.[42] Unlike most of Georgia's white Baptists, who preferred church and family control of education, blacks believed in a connection between education and freedom. Along with property ownership and political rights, literacy became a top priority.[43] In the words of William Jefferson White, "the greatest boon of all others [brought by the demise of slavery] was the opening of the school book and the school house to the emancipated people."[44]

During the early years of Reconstruction, African American adults and children flocked to schools established by the Freedmen's Bureau, the AMA, and the American Baptist Home Mission society. In Jackson and Gwinnett Counties, the Freedmen's Bureau established schools at Rakestraw and Sugar Hill.[45] In Augusta, White preserved the school he had begun at Springfield Baptist Church in 1859 and established additional schools in black churches in the late 1860s and 1870s, while Turner did the same in Cobb County.[46] Former slaves in Marietta formed Zion Baptist Church in 1866 and immediately established a school.[47] African American Baptists in Gainesville started the Northwest Normal and Industrial School. Cartersville's African Americans created church schools with black trustees, a system of organization that persisted until the 1960s.[48] In Atlanta, Savannah, and Augusta, former slaves established larger schools such as Atlanta University and Ware High School.

From the outset, African Americans made clear their intention to eventually conduct their own schools, although financial assistance from whites would be needed.[49] Ministers or other literate black men and women served as teachers, with many using as the textbook the Bible, the book to which African Americans had easiest access. The sacred and secular realms thus merged in education, and congregational autonomy became identified with educational autonomy.[50] Receiving little or no financial support from the state, black schools arose in existing facilities with funds from churches or northern missionary organizations. Teachers inculcated in students a blend of inherited rural values such as collective support and hard work and such newer ideas as self-sufficiency, racial uplift, and black Protestantism. Popularized by Booker T. Washington in his famous Atlanta Compromise Address in 1895, self-help had long been touted by some black leaders as the best means of improving the race.[51]

Yet Georgia's elite African Americans—those who taught school, owned businesses or land, or ministered churches—persistently debated notions of self-help and goals for blacks in the late nineteenth century. Educators like White and ministers and politicians like Turner frequently encountered threats and violence. A cadre of the state's African Americans refused to relinquish political rights in spite of the rising tide of racial violence, continuing to focus on equality in all areas. Lucy Craft Laney, an Augusta native and in 1876 one of the first graduates of Atlanta University, eventually founded a school, Haines Normal and Industrial Institute, in her hometown. By the 1890s, as African Americans became targets of white supremacist violence, some white Georgians withheld funds from and burned the proliferating African American schools.[52] By 1892, Tom Watson, Georgia's leading white Populist and an advocate of land reform, who had argued for African American political rights, joined the many Populists who opposed funding black education. Other Populists in Georgia's legislature supported an 1891 measure that required segregated seating on railroad cars, one of the state's first Jim Crow laws.[53]

PRIOR TO THE turn of the century, state leaders debated the extent to which Georgia was obligated to provide an education to anyone as well as what kind of an education should be provided. Georgia's 1877 constitution provided state funding only for first through eighth grades and shifted the responsibility for equitably educating both races from the state to counties. This document was, in the words of historian Numan V. Bartley, "the most profoundly conservative constitution in Georgia history."[54] Limiting public funds for education crippled the development of black public schools for the next seventy years.

White county officials had unlimited discretion in distributing what money the state did provide; predictably, they chose to provide the lion's share of the funds to white schools. The state appropriated money based on a county's total population, including African Americans, a state of affairs that benefited Plantation Belt counties, which had higher black populations and consequently more funds to divert from black students to white students.[55] Because black population figured into the state's funding calculations, rural white schools in counties with small black populations suffered, as their counties received smaller slices of the financial pie.[56]

Although schools—some little more than wood-frame shacks or deserted barns—appeared across the land, most children still lacked access to education beyond the sixth grade, which was limited primarily to residents of the towns that built high schools. Rural Georgia still had only a rudimentary transportation system: roads across the up-country consisted of dirt tracks made by wagon wheels and horses, and winter rains prevented travel. "When it rained," recalled Jimmie Kate Sams Cole, "most people could not get to town."[57] "People just didn't go to high school," explained Ruth Smith Waters. "There was no way to get there."[58] Furthermore, farm families were unwilling to spare older children's labor and considered an education less important than learning how to farm and help the family's financial survival.

As had been the case during Reconstruction, late-nineteenth-century Georgia blacks relied on private schools funded either by black churches or by white northern philanthropic organizations such as the AMA, the largest white denominational education group, which provided hundreds of northern black and white teachers and funded new schools such as Atlanta University and the Knox Institute in Athens, which Beulah Rucker Oliver attended.[59] From 1867 to 1897, black Baptists founded five higher education institutions in Georgia, including Spelman Seminary and Atlanta Baptist College, which later became Morehouse College. Emphasizing a classical curriculum, these schools began training students for teaching in normal programs in the 1870s, creating a professional opportunity for black women.[60] Although most black families agreed with the moral and academic instruction provided by the AMA schools as well as the lessons in manners, speech, and dress they provided, African Americans generally opposed the inculcation of Congregational Church religious practices, which eschewed emotional expressions during worship, in favor of traditional Baptist practices.[61]

The burgeoning black educational system angered and frightened many white Georgians. Throughout the Populist years, wealthier rural whites demanded increased opportunities for schooling, while some white leaders, including Rebecca Latimer Felton, an advocate for white educational reform and temperance, and educators at the University of Georgia and the State Department of Education, expressed outrage at the establishment of schools for blacks while education for whites lagged.[62] In a February 1891 speech called "The Industrial School for Girls," Felton advocated educating poor white girls rather than allowing them to work in the fields while black girls attended school.[63] Ella Gertrude Clanton Thomas, another temperance supporter and former member of the planter class, echoed Felton's fears, writing in her journal, "The boys of our country poor as well as rich must be educated, must have instilled and ever kept before them the idea of social and mental superiority."[64] Other white reformers and some parents advocated increased educational opportunities simply because of the belief that they were necessary for a successful future in a changing world.

The development of public education for whites was hampered by state leaders' lack of attention to the problem and the lack of general popular support for the idea that the state bore responsibility for funding education. Although such prominent whites as Watson and Felton championed public schools for white children, Georgians paid less heed to school reform advocates such as Walter Hill than did North Carolinians or Virginians to leaders in those states. School proponents in Georgia—the most populous southern state, with the largest number of African Americans, a high birthrate, and an extraordinarily high number of counties—faced not only the restrictions imposed by the 1877 constitution and the greatest number of children to educate but also counties' power to limit taxation and the entrenched tradition of church and family authority.[65]

Despite these obstacles, many rural communities built one- and two-room schools at crossroads that also featured cotton gins, gristmills, and general stores. These country schools had fewer materials than city schools and operated in leaky, drafty wooden buildings. Classes had as many as sixty students, and teachers were poorly paid.[66] Nevertheless, there were few complaints. Many Georgia whites were loath to relinquish local church and parental control of education to a state-supported, secular system of public instruction. Robin Clark, for example, contended that states had a responsibility to honor the rights of men, rather than the reverse.[67]

Other white Georgians still clung to the traditional belief that Baptist or Methodist churches could best educate children. By the turn of the century, 92 percent of all Georgians who claimed church membership were either Baptist or Methodist. Almost 600,000 white Georgians were Baptists, while close to 350,000 were Methodists.[68] Unlike African Americans, who sought education from all sources, white residents feared secular education and guarded their schools staffed and funded by evangelical Protestant churches.

As church memberships grew, congregations began to shift their charges against members. Until the 1930s, most Baptist and Methodist churches diligently criticized members who had been dancing, drinking alcohol, lying, or using profanity. To regain membership in the church, individuals had to confess their errors in front of the entire congregation. Commerce's First Baptist Church passed a resolution against the rising influence of Satan in the form of alcohol, the "insidious invasion of modern dance," and the "growing tendency to profane God's name." The congregation's more than four hundred members pledged to help the pastor "save our people from the ever-increasing and subtle schemes of Satan." In 1905, members of Liberty Baptist Church in Gwinnett County, an independent congregation that practiced foot washing and segregated men and women until 1933, voted to join the Georgia Baptist Convention to more completely "allign themselves against the forces of darkness." Two years later, the congregation passed a resolution that stated that members were "opposed to dancing in any form whatever and if any member should be guilty of violating this resolution they shall be dealt with as violations of other rules of the church."[69] In the *Christian Index*, a Georgia Baptist newspaper, minister M. E. Dodd claimed that "a modernist in government is an anarchist and Bolshevik; in science he is an evolutionist; in business he is a communist; in art he is a futurist; in music his name is jazz; and in religion he is an atheist and an infidel."[70] Dodd's "modernists" included liberals, Unitarians, and anyone who denied the inerrancy of the Bible, notably Christ's deity, atonement, resurrection, and Second Coming. To white Georgia Baptists, secularized schools threatened these religious beliefs. In 1915, the Reverend W. H. Faust from Winder, in Jackson County, wrote that the biggest question for Christians was, "In the matter of schools, where does the authority of the church start, and where does that of the state end? . . . Is the church and home to surrender all to the state?"[71] Communities banned alcohol consumption, dancing, cigarette smoking, and profanity as means to enforce order. Condemning these acts had less to do with theology than with the scandalous trends some black and white Georgians feared. What Baptists deemed respectable and dignified excluded intemperance, contact dancing, and gambling because such actions aroused temptation for promiscuity, danger to the family stability, and risks to community harmony.[72]

Like other southerners, most white Georgians viewed an education as a tool for preserving traditional rural values of hard work, evangelical Protestantism, and temperance rather than as a means for change. John Riley Hopkins, a Primitive Baptist who owned more than two hundred acres in Gwinnett County, contended that public education was unchristian. When he ran for state representative in 1888, he stated that "each school community" should be allowed "to choose their own text books" and should defy outside challenges to parental authority.[73] Education was an issue for churches and families to decide, not the state. Although many schools met either in churches or in one-room cabins, attendance was sporadic. Parents believed that they knew best when their children should or should not attend school and insisted that schools include reading the Bible, prayer, and memory work.[74] Some parents considered Sunday school the only instruction necessary for their children outside the household. In this view, with the exception of learning the Bible, a child learned everything suitable for adulthood by helping with household chores. In an early form of vocational education, girls learned from their mothers by helping with their household labor, while boys helped their fathers with farming. Such expectations suited rural lifestyles because most children would grow up to form their own agricultural households.

Many reformers working for state-supported education encountered similar fears of state monopoly and unchristian teachings. In 1903, Annie Mae Horne, who was interviewing Georgians about education, wrote to E. C. Branson, president of the State Normal School in Athens, that Georgians were "all very strict in church matters" and therefore were reluctant to support schools unaffiliated with Baptist or Methodist churches.[75] The University of Georgia sought public support, but state officials balked at interfering in what was perceived as a realm for churches. Throughout the nineteenth century, Georgia allocated less public funds to its state university than did North Carolina, Virginia, or South Carolina.[76] Although many white schools met in buildings not explicitly affiliated with churches, white education, no less than its black counterpart, used Christian principles, intermingling prayer, devotions, hymns, and Bible readings with lessons in reading, writing, and arithmetic. At the turn of the century, parents retained the authority to decide which children to send to school and when to send them. And local communities, including churches, safeguarded the curriculum and the teachers.

Yet these expectations also illustrated a fundamental problem southern states faced with public education. Living in a rural society increasingly governed by a national market, southerners immersed in a cotton economy had little cash with which to buy books, pay teachers, build schools, and support libraries. At the same time, Georgia had one of the highest populations of African Americans in the South, and, like other southern states, maintained a high birthrate until the post–World War II era.[77] Even if white Georgians had wanted to support separate and equal school systems for more than eight hundred thousand black and white children, which the state's citizens did not, funding education demanded more than property taxes, notably because much of such revenues came from small-scale farmers who could ill afford the levies.

In the 1890s, towns and cities began to increase taxes to improve white schools, creating city school systems distinct from those operated by counties. That these towns had separate school boards from the county was scarcely surprising given contemporary economic exigencies. Georgia's constitution severely limited counties' ability to raise taxes for schools, but loopholes allowed separate districts to form within each county and raise taxes. In addition receiving to public funds, these town and city schools often charged parents as much as fifty cents per year to educate each child, particularly for higher grades. New school districts proliferated, especially in communities that wanted to attract industry. Many mills also created their own schools for children of employees. Jackson County, for example, had a segregated county district and four separate segregated town districts in Jefferson, Commerce, Braselton, and Maysville as well as a mill school in Commerce and private religious academies. Town residents had greater access to cash than did rural dwellers, enabling white students in Gainesville, Commerce, Marietta, Augusta, and Atlanta to attend school in brick buildings with smaller classes and better-paid teachers. Despite the better conditions in urban schools, however, residents of those areas voiced complaints similar to those of rural residents: the lack of religious instruction, interference with parents' right to educate their children, and poor moral training.[78] Here cotton culture's tensions between self-sufficiency and interdependence become apparent. Some parents contended that providing public funds for schools would lead some citizens to depend increasingly on public support. Only the earliest grades that provided basic reading and arithmetic skills would receive public funds. Moreover, some residents objected to the tuition charges, claiming that some children could not afford to pay to attend school.[79]

In addition, Baptist, Methodists, and Presbyterians founded schools for white children, often segregated by sex. The Baptists created the Georgia Baptist Seminary for women (later Brenau College) and the Georgia Military Institute (eventually Riverside Military Academy), moved Mercer University to Macon in 1871, and assumed responsibility for Bessie Tift College in Forsyth in 1898. In 1886 the Baptist-affiliated Lawrenceville Female Seminary and Lawrenceville Academy were consolidated into Lawrenceville Seminary. In 1897 Methodists founded Piedmont College and expanded Emory College. By 1900, a variety of school systems, separated by class, race, and sex, dotted the state.[80]

HAND IN HAND with the shift to a modern cash and credit economy, increased political authority of counties, and creation of public education, lines began to separate economic, political, and cultural authority. What families and communities had enforced was now shifting to county and state authority. Even so, the early stages of modernization in Georgia continued to stress the separation of church and state, family and public authority.

African Americans rarely questioned the value of public education and the significance of economic rights. They continued to build and enlarge schools, increasing the threat perceived by many whites. The tensions between increasing numbers of African American schools and stumbling efforts at white public education exploded in 1899, three years after *Plessy v. Ferguson*, in a Georgia court case regarding an African American high school in Richmond County that white trustees planned to close. The publicly funded Ware High

School for blacks had opened in 1880, with Richard R. Wright, valedictorian of Atlanta University, as principal. In 1891, Wright left Ware to become president of Georgia State Industrial College in Savannah, a public African American college. Six years later, the Richmond County School Board voted to close Ware High School, primarily because it offered professional training and a liberal arts curriculum rather than trade and industrial education—Booker T. Washington's racial uplift rhetoric providing a convenient cover for white supremacists' arguments. Board members publicly claimed that closing the high school would enable more funds to be directed to primary education for blacks. Privately, the board undoubtedly saw the school as a threat to white supremacy.[81]

African Americans saw the closing of Ware as an effort to prevent blacks from obtaining a public high school education, and more than fifty community leaders, including William Jefferson White and local businessmen John C. Ladeveze, Joseph W. Cumming, and James S. Harper, formed the Educational Union of Richmond County to defend the school. The union filed a lawsuit against the Richmond County Board of Education under the "separate but equal" doctrine, alleging that the closing of Ware meant that the school board was failing to operate a separate high school for black children. After the Educational Union prevailed at the state level, the county appealed the verdict, and the case wound its way to the U.S. Supreme Court. African American educators across the country, among them Booker T. Washington, understood the significance of the case and sent contributions to the union. On December 18, 1899, Associate Justice John Marshall Harlan read the Court's unanimous decision in *Cumming v. Richmond County Board of Education* that the closing of Ware did not violate the Fourteenth Amendment because the action was intended to provide more funds for primary grades for blacks. Harlan's opinion stated that the case as presented did not challenge the doctrine of separate but equal because the plaintiffs had failed to demonstrate that the board had specifically refused to use funds for a black high school after the plaintiffs had requested such a school. The Supreme Court regarded the allocation of funds as a state rather than a federal issue.[82]

So while *Plessy v. Ferguson*, the increasing frequency of lynchings and other antiblack violence, and efforts to prevent blacks from voting had clearly set the stage for the Jim Crow South, *Cumming* gave strong legal sanction to the color line in education. Not only could schools be separated according to race, but public black education could be restricted to the primary grades. Moreover, limiting education for African Americans also limited their economic opportunities to agriculture and low-level industrial jobs. The case reinforced localism, opening the door for states and counties to determine how to fund African American education without federal intervention. And finally, *Cumming* demonstrated the flimsiness of white paternalism and revealed white racism.

White supremacists in Georgia gradually escalated control over black male voters through the late nineteenth and early twentieth century. The first measure passed was the poll tax, which also excluded poor whites. Then came residency requirements and the white primary. By 1904, only 4 percent of eligible African American voters had registered, a decline from 53 percent in 1876. Still, white supremacists wanted to ensure even that miniscule number could not vote and began discussions about a constitutional amendment to ban black men from voting.[83]

Some African American leaders, including Henry McNeal Turner, began to advocate black immigration to Africa, while others continued to fight for equality in Georgia.[84] White, for example, continued to denounce violence and legalized segregation in the *Georgia Baptist*, actions that eventually cost him his printed voice. On May 31, 1900, he condemned Augusta's efforts to segregate streetcars, asking, "What in the name of high heaven do the white people want the colored people to do?" he asked.[85] He soon had an answer. On June 2, three weeks after an Augusta black man was lynched, a group of whites of all classes gathered to discuss White and his infuriating newspaper. The mob grew to more than three hundred people and marched to White's home. White turned to Augusta's police chief for protection and publicly apologized for his comments on June 7. This incident, along with a riot in Statesboro and continued lynchings, led White to call for an assembly in Macon on February 13, 1906, to establish the Georgia Equal Rights Convention. Among those who attended were John Hope from Atlanta Baptist College, Bishop Henry Turner, W. E. B. Du Bois from Atlanta University, and many Atlanta clergymen.[86]

Du Bois later contended that this convention began the chain of events that led to the 1906 Atlanta Riot. At the convention, Atlanta blacks protested Jim Crow laws and began to boycott streetcars and stores. In September, several Atlanta newspapers ran stories accusing black men of raping white women. White mobs gathered and headed for Atlanta's black neighborhood, killing blacks and destroying property along the way.[87] The riot confirmed elite African Americans' suspicions about the illusions of black and white cooperation. White and his family left Augusta. Du Bois left Atlanta University. Washington's hopes in his famous speech, "The Atlanta Compromise," and subsequent efforts for accommodation between the two races lay in tatters.[88] White Georgians, even those with moderate views, believed that the Atlanta Riot demonstrated the truth of white supremacists' arguments that Georgia was unsafe as long as any black male could vote. Consequently, Georgians ratified a 1907 amendment to the state constitution that required property ownership, literacy, and a testimony about a man's character before he would be permitted to vote.[89] Such measures constituted aspects of Progressivism in the New South.

After the Civil War, elite African Americans—those who were educated and worked in professions—had relied to some extent on the traditional code of paternalism for the creation of the African American order. While some whites practiced portions of the code and a few even favored aspects of separate and equal worlds, more whites increasingly dropped the bonds of reciprocity, duty, obligation, and honor. As blacks and whites moved away from agricultural labor, face-to-face meetings between members of the two races became less frequent, underscoring the two groups' lack of knowledge of each other. Even on large farms where blacks worked as sharecroppers or tenants, relations between landholder and worker rested on cash payments. Landholders no longer had an abstract responsibility for their laborers. Race became defined in terms not only of labor and color but also of legal and social definitions of blood.[90] White Georgians, searching for a means to control blacks' growing demands and institution building, found solutions not in traditional codes but in the law and in the invented tradition of the color line.[91] Distinctions between gradations of color disappeared. As the nation lost interest in black economic, social, and political rights, southern states tightened restrictions on blacks' movements and opportunities through violence and the law.

WITH BLACKS DENIED the vote and thus effectively removed from the political equation, Georgia's elite rural whites turned their attention to preserving their power against the encroachments of white voters from such growing cities as Atlanta, Augusta, Macon, and Savannah. In 1917, the Georgia General Assembly passed the Neill Primary Law establishing the state's county unit system. This law effectively weighted state elections in favor of rural counties, which received votes equal to those of the more populated urban counties. In other words, voters in sparsely populated rural counties had a disproportionate say in state elections. In addition to underscoring localism and retaining the state's tradition of rural power, the county unit system reinforced the dominance of precisely those elite whites who sought to control African Americans and working-class whites, most of whom continued to reside in rural areas.[92]

As white paternalism dwindled and fragmented, a virulent and often ruthless racism appeared that judged African Americans by the content of the blood rather than the darkness of the complexion. Most members of the African American elite turned their gaze toward the black community.[93] Relying on a foundation based on race rather than on interracial cooperation, African Americans and whites worked from separate directions to build separate social institutions. Yet many parallels between black and white efforts remained: both groups relied on women to teach, expanded notions of community to include schools with churches and families, and based education on evangelical Protestantism, a construction of uplift modified to fit industrial and agricultural labor, and values of work and behavior that drew from cotton culture.[94] Drawing on social and economic structures within the black and white communities, Georgians constructed a school system that articulated the state's distinct social strata. For both African Americans and whites, the school joined the household and the church as a location of instruction and socialization, although the two races had different goals. Education became a means for whites to accommodate their beliefs to social and economic change. For blacks, in contrast, education provided a way to challenge the inherited order. In both cases, however, schools reinforced parental and church authority, and teachers were expected to share these values.

The expansion of the educational system of course required increasing numbers of teachers. Women were the logical choice for that role, in part because they outnumbered men and because families were more likely to spare girls than boys from agricultural labor.[95] By 1900, almost 70 percent of southern teachers were female. Teaching became a respectable position for black and white women, offering an escape from the drudgery of rural life and a measure of independence without threatening accepted ideas of appropriate activities for women.[96]

Moreover, by claiming God's authority for founding schools, as Beulah Rucker Oliver did, black women mitigated opposition to black education. Few white people would challenge God's will. Visions from God provided black women with a powerful means to assert their authority in schools, all in the name of God.

When Oliver arrived in Gainesville in 1910, she observed and recognized both the persistence of old ways and changes in the region. While in Athens, she may have learned that Gainesville's African American population was growing. She may have heard her fellow Baptists tell of the denomination's new school for blacks in Gainesville. She probably realized that if the black and white communities were expanding, potential funding sources existed, as did

Beulah Rucker Oliver graduated from Knox Institute in 1909, when this photograph was taken. (Courtesy of Dorothy Oliver Rucker, Carrie Oliver Bailey, and Magic Craft Studio, Gainesville, Ga.)

the need for another school. Combining her religious beliefs, ambition, and awareness of her race's educational needs, Oliver set about redeeming herself and "fallen humanity" by lighting the path to spiritual and social redemption. By 1911, with the assistance of the Reverend Green Hunter's fund-raising efforts, she had established the State Industrial and High School on Old Athens Highway, outside the Gainesville city limits. She combined her household with her school and church by using the Bible and hymns as the bedrock of her pedagogy, replicating the African American community's basic structure. Close enough to Gainesville that students could walk to the campus and could find employment with town-dwelling whites, her school was far enough away to allow twelve acres for farming and raising livestock and to prevent excessive white scrutiny. In keeping with her culture and vision, she re-created a pastoral space for her students.

Her choice of Gainesville was wise. In 1912 she observed exactly how Gainesville whites treated blacks. In the years following Emancipation, racial violence erupted sporadically in the Upper Piedmont. During this era, upcountry racial violence often pitted white tenants against black tenants rather than white landlords against black sharecroppers, a pattern that recurred in Forsyth County on September 8 of that year, when an eighteen-year-old white woman asserted that three black men had raped her.[97] Coming on the heels of two racial clashes in Dahlonega and Cumming, the young woman's claims ignited the countryside. Three black men were immediately arrested, and two were taken to Gainesville's jail for safety. A white Forsyth County crowd removed the third man from a Cumming jail, dragged him through town behind a wagon, and eventually hanged him from the top of a telephone post. The other two men were tried and convicted, and in mid-October a white mob, or whitecaps, rode through Forsyth and Dawson Counties, burning black churches and homes. More than a thousand blacks from both counties fled, leaving behind their property and possessions. By October 25, when the two convicted men were hanged, not one black resident remained in the two counties.[98]

Many of the blacks, including Rev. Byrd Oliver, a widower, and his children, fled to Hall County and Gainesville. The Olivers took shelter on a farm owned by a man named Barry Brown, who hid the refugees under some fodder and took them across the Chattahoochee River into Hall County. Brown then introduced Oliver to a man who let the family live in an old house and work his land. Gainesville and Hall County's whites probably allowed blacks to resettle there because extra hands were needed for domestic and farm labor. In any event, Gainesville's African Americans never forgot the lesson of Forsyth and Dawson Counties, remaining wary of Hall County's whites for decades following the incident.[99]

Oliver subsequently moved with his three children to Gainesville, where he met and married Beulah Rucker in 1914, devoting the remainder of his life to supporting her school and their family. A self-educated minister, Oliver had less schooling than his wife.[100] Living near Gainesville allowed him to earn money at day labor jobs such as road work or by selling wood, thereby providing income sorely needed for Beulah Rucker Oliver's school.

Unlike Gainesville's Northwest Normal and Industrial School, Oliver's State Industrial and High School, as it was officially known, was nondenominational and did not receive direct church support. Oliver lacked even the meager public funds available to Gainesville's Graded and High School for blacks. At first, a few local residents resented her presence: "the general public didn't believe a young woman should head an institution."[101] Black Baptist ministers in particular wanted schools to be run by men, who had few opportunities to earn wages apart from farming or day labor.[102] Many whites, notably school superintendents, also opposed women's service as principals, believing that women could not control older male students.[103]

Nevertheless, Oliver's school prospered and by 1920 had grown into a wood-frame school with three teachers, aided by the Julius Rosenwald Fund, one of the largest northern philanthropic organizations dedicated to black schools.[104] The school, one of four Rosenwald schools built in Georgia's up-country at this time, was the region's largest black educational institution, with three classrooms, an industrial room, and a movable partition between two of the classrooms. During the 1910s, Oliver raised $1,900 from local blacks and $350 from local whites, with an additional $600 from the Rosenwald Fund for building the school.[105] Established in 1917 by Julius Rosenwald, Sears, Roebuck, and Company magnate, the Rosenwald Fund provided matching grants ranging from $500 to $2,000 to community funds and donations for African American education in the South.[106] Students performed day labor and sold rugs they made at the school. While most funding came from the black community and students, moderate whites who supported a measure of education for blacks also contributed to Oliver's school. Oliver received additional Rosenwald monies in 1924–25 and 1926–27 for a teacher's home and an industrial shop.[107] Although in keeping with the guidelines established by the Rosenwald Fund, the school and property now belonged to the Hall County public school system, no public funds were provided for these additions. Thus, by 1928 Oliver had realized her dream of owning a house, although northern philanthropic assistance had been required to help her meet her goal.

Students came to Oliver's school from a broad swath of north Georgia, often with no money for tuition, but Oliver found jobs for the students as domestic help or day laborers. Most students sat on benches in the classrooms and wrote on painted boards that served as chalkboards. They read secondhand books and carefully handled family Bibles.[108]

As Oliver's school became part of the permanent landscape outside of Gainesville, a generation of women grew to maturity in Georgia. Black and white women nonetheless understood their adult experiences in distinct ways. Never permitted protection from violence and harsh labor, black women perceived their public roles in much the same ways as their fathers, brothers, husbands, and sons. They used their position as teachers and reformers to instruct their race on moral uplift and social change.[109] Despite being treated as inferiors, they understood themselves as just as good as anyone at any time and looked for opportunities, covertly and overtly, to demonstrate their equality. For white women, public work was carefully construed within the restrictions of white femininity. Once married, they tended to quit public life to focus on their role within the family. Most of their reform efforts occurred safely within conservative constructions of the social order of white rural and town elites. Becoming a teacher, Leona Clark Williams believed that she would work only until she married. Although she firmly believed in public education and the expanding authority of teachers, she maintained her views on the influence of family and church. Women of both races melded the rural values inherited from their parents with facets of modernity, adapting to a world that was becoming increasingly secular and modern. The ways in which black and white women adapted, however, differed. To black teachers, modernity offered a glimmer of social and economic advancement—the potential for change and equality. To white teachers, modernity constituted a necessary transformation that had to be shaped by traditional beliefs in class and race status.

Notwithstanding these changes, Georgia life remained bound by class and race barriers, and churches preserved their prominence in family and community matters. Streetcars, restaurants, and other public places practiced strict segregation, and white newspapers frequently complained about "loafing negroes," "steaming bucks," and "duskey damsels . . . who help to compose the seething mass of putrefaction."[110] Whatever the success of her school, Beulah Oliver knew her place in Hall County: incessant messages of inferiority from the white community and being denied the vote made sure of that. Surrounded by African Americans who struggled to survive by washing clothes or farming for white people, she understood the patterns of dependency that haunted her people. Oliver saw the limitations of segregation, however, and sought to teach her students and her children how to become more than whites expected yet seem to conform to whites' parameters.

For Williams, the expanding relations to a market economy meant the end of her parents' life of self-sufficiency and opened a door to a profession that allowed her to escape the endless labor that had plagued her mother's life. Yet she preserved the central tenets of her childhood and avoided some of the political potential of her role as a teacher. She supported professionalization while believing that few women with young children should work outside the home. She knew that black schools received less public funds than did white institutions but evaded political challenges to Jim Crow. Sympathetic, compassionate, and often horrified at how her society treated working-class and black people, she also knew that the cost of any confrontation was high. She preferred to wait and hope that gradual change would come.

2 · We Learned from Our Mothers' Knees

Families, Churches, and Communities

THE ONLY SPECIFIC date that Beulah Rucker Oliver mentions in her auto-biography, *The Rugged Pathway*, is the date of her graduation from Knox Institute—May 28, 1909. That day marked a watershed moment in her life. Although she depicts her graduation as the point at which she chose to turn away from her ambition to own property and toward a life of self-sacrifice for her race's improvement, the day also represents the convergence of modern ambitions and traditional values. Highlighting her story of individual success, Rucker details her struggles to support her school. Yet because she became one of the black community's leading residents and eventually owned a house and a buggy, she was unquestionably a woman of the modern world who sought respectability and status in her community. Her possessions, while minimal compared to those of the community's leading whites, acquired cultural value and contributed to her social standing. At the same time, Rucker preserved her culture's beliefs in evangelical Protestantism, hard work, and collective support.[1]

Leona Clark Williams's story of her family and siblings, *We Remember*, combines similar themes of the individual drive for success with those of community values of evangelical Protestantism, hard work, and self-sufficiency. As the Clarks moved from farm to farm, struggling to survive the South's transition from small-scale farming to agribusiness and industrialization, Leona and her siblings did whatever they could to avoid farming. They became members of the modern world through such professions as teaching, nursing, aviation, and business. While the Clark children honored their parents' work and values and remained dedicated to the church, their success embodied a break with the past. Like Rucker, they drew from a collective memory of a region's traditions, or at least the family's construction of those traditions. But the accomplishments of ambitious young women such as Rucker and Williams would have been impossible without substantial transformations in the southern way of life, most notably increased opportunities for women and a growing industrial economy.

Beulah Rucker's and the Clark children's stories demonstrate these transformations and continuities within southern culture in the early decades of the twentieth century. What some historians have called the "darkness at dawning" or the "paradox of progressivism" that occurred within southern attempts at reform from 1900 to 1940 was actually the manifestation of tensions among traditional household relations and market demands, hierarchy and individualism, evangelical Protestantism and secular society. As rural Georgians in the early twentieth century relied on households, churches, and eventually schools to maintain cultural values, residents also recognized needs for reform in education, politics, and social life.

Expanding state and federal governments, along with the national growth of consumer culture, stretched into Georgia's structure of localism. By the 1920s, Progressive era legislation such as the 1914 Smith-Lever Act, which created the federal extension service for farmers, and the 1917 Smith-Hughes Act, which provided for vocational and agricultural education, spread the reach of the federal government into rural communities. Jim Crow laws and customs dominated Georgia's society as southern blacks and whites worked for school reform, social services, health care, Prohibition, and women's suffrage. Consumer culture seeped into rural areas as country stores began to stock canned goods, cloth, shoes, and ready-made clothing. Many country residents eagerly awaited the arrival of the Sears catalog, which offered a glimpse of the wider world of goods. Some families, including the Clarks and the Ruckers, understood that store-bought fabrics, shoes, and household furnishings marked class and race status. Consumer goods also required a dependence on the fickle market for cotton.[2]

Reforms and consumer items engendered mixed reactions in Georgia's foci of localism—the grid of family, community, church, and eventually school. World War I offered sporadic profits to southern cotton farmers, but prices declined precipitously after the war and limited farmers' ability to buy consumer goods. In this and other respects, southerners responded to the 1920s in a wide range of ways. Like some northerners, Georgia white supremacists joined the Ku Klux Klan in the 1920s, vehemently denouncing perceived threats to family and evangelical Protestant traditions. These fears reappeared during the famous John Scopes trial in Tennessee, as most southerners supported the inerrancy of the biblical interpretation of the beginning of the world. Lynchings of black men had begun to decline before 1910 but again began to increase, a fact that pushed many African Americans to the North for better jobs and opportunities in what became known as the Great Migration. The possibilities that had opened to African Americans during the late nineteenth century for voting and property ownership collapsed. Categorizations of African Americans, once understood by gradations of color, were cast aside in favor of an all-encompassing perception of inferiority to whites by 1900. Blacks were now locked into social, economic, political, cultural, and legal codes that created some of the most virulent manifestations of racism in American history.[3]

Equally visible were the changes occurring in definitions of masculinity and femininity. Indeed, one of the most remarkable changes modernity brought to Georgia was public opportunities for women, although African American and white women teachers viewed these opportunities in distinctive ways. For black women, teaching carried family and community duties to uplift the race with hopes for equality, a public evocation of race work and race pride. Most of the black women who became teachers had been specifically selected by their families for that public role. For white women, teaching represented a means to leave the farm and to expand educational opportunities for individual students. But ambition drove both black and white women—the determination to escape farming and particularly their mothers' endless and backbreaking labor. Becoming public women with authority and respect meant that all teachers culturally reappropriated values, taking traditional beliefs and assessing and combining them with modern beliefs in individual betterment, government support of public institutions, and women's paid labor.[4] Rarely as demonstrative or organized as northern women in settlement houses, the National Consumers' League, or the Women's Trade Union League, Georgia's female teachers stretched gendered constructions. As Jimmie Kate Sams Cole claimed, "We learned from our mother's knees that we could get our own way if we were sweet and didn't make an issue out of it."[5]

What some historians have described as the emergence of the "New Woman of the New South" actually represented the tensions between traditional rural beliefs and an emerging modern secular world that opened new opportunities for women and constructions of gender—the push and pull, the stretches and accommodations that appear within cultural transformations as rural worlds adapt to or resist capitalist modifications and expansion within a national market.[6] Women teachers who came of age in the 1920s and 1930s claimed femininity as much as their mothers had but insisted on greater independence and the public ability to announce their beliefs. Black and white teachers' personal narratives reveal the ways in which they acquired their culture's inherited beliefs from their families and communities.

Future teachers came from families that shared a commitment to women's career choices, attended church, appreciated their community's beliefs, valued education, and preserved family unity. Moreover, teachers' stories of their day-to-day lives as children indicate how they came to identify distinctive goals for their futures—ambitions combined with a modicum of luck that set these women apart from their peers. Living in a period of transformation and shifts in constructions of power yet drawing from traditional beliefs learned in childhood, these young women carved authority for themselves and their respective races. In the guise of preserving the past, female teachers created their version of the New Woman. In the name of race work, African American women struggled for equality.

To TURN-OF-THE-CENTURY GEORGIANS, local authority encompassed the church, the family, and the immediate community. All three social units functioned as quasi-regulatory agencies, but the family was the most important. It set goals for children; encouraged or discouraged behaviors; established means of interacting with others, belief systems, values, and expectations; and shielded members from external forces and institutions. How each family interprets experiences among members, interactions with the community, and life-altering events such as marriage, death, and childbirth forms part of each individual's core. By the late nineteenth century, American families, notably in urban areas, redefined many of their relationships. Their understanding of the future, the relationship of the individual to society, and the means to regulate behavior included modern notions of individual worth. Borrowing from sociological and psychological studies of behavior, families came to believe in an individual's ability to improve behavior and desire to control the future. These themes challenged traditional beliefs that focused on subordinating individualism for the good of the community.[7]

Georgia families negotiated traditional and modern notions.[8] Paternalism, the social code born in slavery for the inclusive household of black and white families, began to fragment. As African American and white families literally moved away from each other, even in rural areas, declining personal contact decreased notions of responsibility and obligation between blacks and whites. Constructions of the household that had stretched into slave cabins now stopped at the door of the house, thereby feeding modern values of individualism. Future teachers belonged to the generation that espoused some modern beliefs in the role of the individual, family, and women. Most parents considered children to be potential adults who needed to be controlled. Childhood was rarely deemed a stage prior to adolescence and adulthood but rather was seen as the time to eradicate bad behaviors and set expectations.[9]

Gendered roles varied in African American and white families, although some commonalities existed.[10] All mothers were expected to raise small children, and all women provided such services as canning, making preserves, selling eggs and/or butter, cooking, sewing, and working in the fields, although the specific nature of these services varied with race and class.[11] Yet African American families preserved gendered roles that were distinct from those of white families from slavery through the 1940s. Black women's accomplishments outside the home were honored as an adaptation to social and economic oppression and a definitive cultural value—a contrast to the ways in which other ethnic groups defined gendered work. Most black women worked as teachers, domestic laborers, or sharecroppers. What made some black families' labor decisions unique was that the mothers' work allowed daughters to remain in school, become teachers, and help their race. In other ethnic groups or classes, daughters joined the labor force so that mothers could remain at home. That African American families chose to keep some daughters in school attests to the commitment to education and race work. Teaching provided a rare chance to uplift the race and serve the family and the community.

Black teachers' narratives also emphasize the tremendous cohesion of black families. Contrary to racist stereotypes, black men and women married and stayed married. Between 1910 and 1940, more than 85 percent of black women younger than fifty years old were married. Divorce was rare, and women who lived alone usually did so because of the death of their spouses.[12] Furthermore, the majority of African American families, like the Ruckers, had many children. Family size in the United States as a whole had begun to shrink by the 1880s, with more than half of all women having no more than two children and less than one in two hundred having more than ten children. In the rural South, however, black families remained larger than those in northern rural areas until the 1940s. In 1910, southern rural black women averaged nine children each, compared to five in northern black families.[13] Southern women may have had more children because they lacked knowledge about birth control, because their families needed farm labor, or simply because they followed their parents' patterns of childbirth. Most black teachers interviewed for this project came from families ranging between five and twelve children.

White teachers' family size varied according to class and labor. More than half of rural white families, like the Clarks, had more than seven children in 1910, whereas nonfarm families had begun to reduce family size. White teachers from rural families that could afford to hire some labor had fewer siblings.[14] White women helped in the home and frequently in the fields but were generally expected to marry and subsequently remain at home without engaging in paid labor. Their accomplishments were measured by their roles as producers in rural households, as mothers, and as wives. As towns and cities grew, many white women came to be involved in voluntary organizations such as the Southern Baptists' Women's Missionary League, but wage labor after marriage remained a sign of lower-class status for blacks and whites. White middle-class and elite Georgians saw women who worked at factories and most black women as unladylike. Respectability meant staying at home and performing volunteer work. But teaching opportunities changed these perspectives, creating a level of esteem for wage-earning women of both races that was more socially acceptable than factory work.[15]

At the turn of the century, southern education had evolved into a system that generally replicated northern public schools in their reliance on formal institutions to instruct children on educational essentials such as reading, writing, and arithmetic. In many cases, the federal government and northern philanthropic agencies had imposed these changes on southerners, who were perceived as ignorant, backward, and in need of guidance and advice. Nevertheless, both African American and white southerners retained some of their values in the new schools. Evangelical Protestantism, racism, and class divisions defined Georgia's public education.

By the 1930s, opportunities for black and white teachers began to expand in Georgia.[16] In 1911, women constituted more than 6,000 of the state's almost 9,000 white teachers for grades one through eleven, while more than 3,000 black women and 600 black men taught in black schools.[17] By 1930, more than 12,000 white women were employed as teachers in those grades, nearly six times more than the number of white men who held such positions; almost 5,000 black women and 500 black men taught the same grades.[18] In 1910, Gwinnett County's seventy-seven white schools employed 138 teachers, 88 of them women, while the county's fifteen black schools had 18 female teachers. By 1932, 182 white teachers, 144 of them women, taught in Gwinnett's consolidated schools, while the number of black women remained at 18. During the same period in Hall County and Gainesville, the number of white women teachers increased from 116 to 206, while the number of black female teachers doubled to 17.[19] As in other states, teaching became feminized in Georgia.

Ambition drove black and white women to become teachers. They came from families that encouraged their daughters to stay in school and frequently made economic sacrifices to do so. Notwithstanding the increasing number of black and white women who became teachers, the overwhelming majority of rural children of both races followed their parents' paths and became farmers, tenants, or sharecroppers. Georgia's literacy rates increased by 1930, but not all families shared an interest in educating their daughters. Some girls had few options because of class, race, and gender barriers. Cindy Wright, an African American midwife in Athens, recalled that no school existed near her parents' home in Oglethorpe County.[20] Other black and white children had parents who saw little value in education. By 1900, some African Americans' enthusiasm for schooling had waned because of the poor quality of black schools, their inaccessibility, and the growing belief that education would do little to alleviate poverty and Jim Crow.[21] Other families of both races kept their children out of school to work on farms. The poorer the family, the more it relied on children's labor.[22] Marvin Thompson, the son of white renters, recalled that his family believed that the basic skills of reading, writing one's name, and counting were all that anyone needed to survive.[23]

ONE OF GEORGIA's earliest examples of the combination of luck, determination, family support, and church attendance that led some women to become teachers was African American Lucy Craft Laney. Laney, born in 1854, became one of the first graduates of Atlanta University in 1873. Her father was a slave who had bought his freedom before the Civil War and worked as a carpenter and a Presbyterian minister. Her mother was freed by the war and went to work for the daughter of a college professor, who taught Lucy's mother to read and write. Lucy dusted the professor's library, where she discovered the wonder of books. Like most black families during Reconstruction, Laney's parents encouraged their ten children's education. At age fifteen, Lucy Laney left home to attend Atlanta University, where she became one of the first students to enroll in its teacher training course.[24]

After graduating, Laney returned to Augusta, Georgia, in 1886 and founded Haines Normal and Industrial Institute. Like many southern black colleges and institutes, Haines was named for a white northern benefactor, Mrs. T. E. H. Haines, a Presbyterian. Laney became the first black woman to start a school in Georgia, and her reputation as a dedicated teacher spread across the state. She, like other black women and some men who founded schools, created new professional wage opportunities for other black women as they attended schools and then either taught at established educational institutions or started their own. Laney's story illustrates the pattern that African American families replicated across Georgia. Families who could spare daughters from farm labor or family support sent them to private schools across the state to create better opportunities for their race and find respectable work as black women. Laney relied on black and white churches for support even while she demanded that the black community learn to rely on itself for survival.[25]

Laney believed that black women had a specific task. In an 1899 speech at Virginia's Hampton Institute, she stated that educated black women "of character and culture" should become teachers and uplift the race.[26] Laney contended that black mothers and teachers carried the duty and responsibility not only to educate children but also to instruct them on moral behaviors such as temperance, manners, attire, and Christianity.[27] Laney drew on black women's traditional roles as community mothers and leaders but added contemporary themes of education and Victorian morality. Laney bound black women's position to their community. She renegotiated gendered values for the black middle class, the model of educated and evangelical Protestant women in the late nineteenth century. Notions of motherhood and reform tied race work and empowerment to the ideology of uplift. Even as equality was increasingly denied to African Americans in the Jim Crow South, Laney politicized public spaces such as schools to espouse a discourse of rights and opportunities and worked to strengthen cross-class alliances among blacks. She believed that education could allow an individual to "make most of himself" and "render the greatest and best service to his fellows."[28]

African American teachers such as Laney helped black women who had been born during slavery and had come of age in the early years of Jim Crow's rule to realize that teaching offered a far better opportunity for their futures and more benefits for their race than farming. Black families and friends devised ways to send daughters to high schools and normal schools. Black communities constructed gender roles that enabled them to go beyond class and racial barriers.[29] While critics of racial uplift ideology note its implicit endorsement of dominant white bourgeois values, racial uplift drew African American communities together, creating ties that worked to improve education and skills.[30] More than an effort to prove themselves equal to whites, race uplift constituted the earliest race work and efforts at race pride in the Jim Crow South. Most African Americans realized that racial uplift depended on the public work of black men and women, with the role of minister reserved for men and teaching reserved for women.

This was clearly the case in the Rucker family. Beulah Rucker Oliver was born on April 4, 1888, to former slaves Willis and Caroline Wiley Rucker, who worked from daybreak to late evening as sharecroppers on land owned by Joe Gunnels ten miles north of Commerce, in Banks County. Neither parent was educated, but the Ruckers were devout Baptists. To help support their five boys and three girls, Caroline Rucker also worked as a midwife and did laundry for Mrs. Gunnels, while Willis sold coal in Commerce. The Ruckers' oldest daughter and fifth child, Beulah recalled that she learned about white education from her mother's stories about the Gunnels children's education, which provided "a broader vision of public life."[31] Beulah's mother almost certainly overheard intense debates over the lack of white public schools throughout Georgia in the 1880s and 1890s, especially in comparison to the growing number of black schools funded by northern philanthropy. At the same time, however, Beulah struggled to learn words from newspapers plastered on the Rucker cabin walls to protect the family from harsh weather.[32]

All manner of compromises and extreme effort were required to enable black children to attend school. The extra money the Ruckers earned went for their children's books. In 1893, Beulah Rucker Oliver started attending a school that operated for five months out of the year at a church five miles from her home. At the end of her first day, she announced her intention to become a teacher. After she completed the sixth grade, her parents sent her to Athens's Jeruel High School, run by the American Baptist Missionary Association with the assistance of African American Baptist churches.[33] In a few years, however, crop failure forced her family to ask her to return home. Rucker persisted in her studies, occasionally paying a local black or white teacher to help her through a problem.[34] Oliver's efforts reveal her extraordinary determination to complete her education, in contrast to many of her black and white peers. Most children at that age stayed home to help the family through economic crises. Oliver did that and more. Caroline Rucker remained supportive of her teenage daughter's efforts, accompanying Beulah on her visits to these teachers to protect her from racist violence and to make sure that she avoided getting into trouble with other children along the way. As the family's oldest daughter, Beulah Rucker Oliver carried her parents' hopes, and she returned to Athens approximately two years later and tried to enter Knox Institute, knowing she had no money for tuition. Cleaning the principal's home and nursing in the Athens area provided Oliver with enough money to stay in school, and while there, she followed her parents' advice to avoid ball games, dances, shows, and dates with men.[35]

In 1909, after almost ten years of struggle and poverty, Beulah Rucker Oliver graduated from Knox Institute and began to have visions about establishing a black school in Gainesville. Raised with traditional values that stressed both the individual's calling and collective needs, Oliver merged her desire for success and social advancement with her religious values concerning the redemption of "fallen humanity" in her Gainesville school. She could assuage those who doubted her ability to teach and lead her race by claiming God's inspiration, and she frequently quoted John 9:4 to her students: "I must work the work of him that sent me, while it is day; the night cometh, when no man can work."[36] Rucker's use of the Bible verse underscored the contrast between the dark and the light. During life, work became a sacred means for racial uplift, education, and spiritual salvation. Oliver no doubt saw herself as divinely called to convert and educate her race. But if religious faith was important, so too was the influence of community. The ethic of "socially responsible individualism," derived from kinship networks during slavery, persisted at the turn of the century as a means of racial uplift.[37] From such networks, Rucker learned about her duty to improve her race using the advantages of education she had acquired.

Some African American teachers, including those at the school Oliver founded, came from rural families that owned about fifty acres of cleared land or from town families with parents who worked as day laborers or taught school. For example, Laura May Mosley Whelchel and Annie Ruth Mosley Martin were two of the twelve children born to Jessie Salmon Mosley, the daughter of former slaves who had attended Spelman Seminary in the early twentieth century and taught elementary school at Oak Hill Baptist Church in Summersville, and Charles Mosley, a farmer and carpenter.[38] Dorothy Oliver Rucker, the oldest daughter of Beulah Rucker Oliver and the Reverend Byrd Oliver, grew up during the 1920s outside Gainesville on land that served as her mother's school, family home, and farmland to support the school and family. Rosa Penson Anderson grew up during the 1920s and 1930s in Fayette County, where her family raised cotton and vegetables. Her mother, Rosa, taught school at Willis Grove Baptist Church. Rosa Penson Anderson recalled, "My mother wanted things to be better for us than it was for her, and she knew that we needed an education in order for it to be better for us."[39] Nancy Stephens's father worked as a railroad porter while her mother remained at home.[40] Other teachers, including Susie Weems Wheeler and Jessie Mae Spears Taylor, came from sharecropping families. Wheeler, a teacher in Cartersville, remembered that her mother "encouraged me to do anything that I wanted and to do it well."[41] After Wheeler completed the elementary grades at Cartersville in 1930, her mother decided to send her to Cabin Creek High School in Griffin, a boarding school sponsored by black Baptists in the area.

Most of these women had mothers who earned wages, predominantly from teaching, to supplement their families' income. All the families thus relied on some sort of cash income to supplement household production. Using a family strategy unique among American families, African American mothers worked to ensure the future of their children, notably daughters. Teaching provided extra income—albeit small and sporadic—for the family's survival. Jessie Salmon Mosley was paid about thirty dollars a month by Chattooga County. According to her daughter, Laura, she had to travel seven miles to Summersville to get her salary. Never sure when the white superintendent was in his office, Jessie Mosley sometimes had to return home without her pay.[42] Rosa Penson Anderson's mother earned about twenty-five dollars a month, which at the time "was a lot of money. It was a big help."[43] Male teachers always earned more than female teachers, and white women teachers earned more than black women: for example, in 1932 in Hall County's public schools, white female teachers had an average annual income of $578, while black women averaged $215 per year.[44]

White schools did not permit married women to teach because it was believed that they needed to devote all of their attention to their own children. Black women, in contrast, were allowed to teach not only after marrying but also after bearing children, reflecting a pattern that had begun during the days of slavery, when black mothers had no choice but to work.[45] At the same time, professions such as teaching and nursing offered a measure of respectability in the black community to a much greater extent than becoming a laundress or domestic worker. Becoming a member of the black middle class had as much to do with occupation and social standing as with actual finances. Yet to most whites, even black professionals lacked the status of a professional worker, and black women could never access the standing of the southern lady. A lady was always white, and the only work a southern lady did was voluntary or unpaid work in the home or in one of the emerging Christian women's associations.

Daughters who eventually became teachers recall their families' rules regarding proper behavior. According to Dorothy Oliver Rucker, "Mama only spanked one time a week. That was on Tuesday. And I was in every whipping line. . . . When she'd whip you, she always said, 'I'm whipping you because I love you. And I don't want somebody else to have to do it.'" Dorothy described how Beulah Rucker Oliver placed her hand on a table with her fingers arched. She told her children and students what would happen to them as adults if they continued to behave the way they did, sometimes telling them that their behavior could mean time in jail. "Mama could always visualize some awful things when you got out of line," Dorothy Oliver Rucker explained. "You didn't even draw a loud breath; you'd just be quiet and listen. She'd get you for rocking the boat and doing things that were undesirable."[46]

To Beulah Rucker Oliver, "rocking the boat" included wiggling in class, talking out of turn, failing to complete homework, swearing, drinking alcohol, gambling, and dancing—rules handed down by her parents and the schools she attended. Most African American families of the era followed similar rules. Laura Mosley Whelchel's parents enforced strict rules that included respect for adults, property, and each other.[47] Rosa Penson Anderson recalled, "We did not do any cursing; we did not talk like that. And my mother, she didn't allow us to talk about other people either because she said God made everything. You didn't talk back to your parents. [My mother] would get after you about that. We got spankings."[48]

Some fathers, like the Reverend Byrd Oliver, allowed their wives to serve as primary disciplinarians. Oliver did, however, preach to his children about the Ten Commandments and New Testament lessons about salvation, carrying "his Bible everywhere he went," as his daughter recalled.[49] The preacher at Sanders Chapel, Oliver commanded a measure of respect, and he too enforced the household rules, which, like those of most African American families, reflected community and evangelical Protestant values about how neighbors and parents should be treated and how dignified people acted. In addition to avoiding foul language, alcohol, and gambling, respectable women wore hose and shoes with heels and avoided trends of the 1920s like smoking cigarettes. Such rules taught sons and daughters how future spouses should act and what characteristics they should possess, providing rules for interactions among members of the black community.

Striving to claim the moral high ground for blacks and often borrowing from southern middle-class notions of respectability, the emerging black middle class contended that gambling, drinking, smoking cigarettes, or dancing at dance halls added to whites' perceptions of black inferiority.[50] In a world where achievement and respect reflected not only a family's stature but also the black community's self-sufficiency and responsibility, individual behavior was important for how whites regarded blacks as a group. During the early decades of the twentieth century, African Americans hoped that behavior, educational accomplishments, and economic achievements would convince whites of African Americans' worth and merit even as their political, social, and economic rights were eviscerated. African American leaders from W. E. B. Du Bois to Lucy Craft Laney to Beulah Rucker often saw themselves as custodians and instructors of African American character. Du Bois envisioned a cadre of educated blacks, the "talented tenth," that would lead blacks to equality.[51] Often divisive among black Georgians, this code of respectability, as well as calls for political and economic rights, lay at the core of black educators' teachings, a class privilege that distinguished them from working-class blacks who frequented nightclubs and juke joints in towns and cities.[52] Some African Americans feared that the movements and gyrations of dancing undermined women's virtue. Benjamin Davis, editor of the *Atlanta Independent,* and Lugenia Burns Hope, an activist in the Atlanta Neighborhood Union, insisted that public dancing exposed young black women to moral decay and attacks on their purity.[53]

Furthermore, at a time when a misplaced comment or a misinterpreted glance could cost African Americans their jobs or even their lives, black children had to learn proper behavior for interactions with whites. Beulah Rucker Oliver believed that her children were better off learning the rules of conduct from her than from a white man or woman. The ever-present possibility of lynchings, the potential of white men raping black women, the memories of riots, and all manner of racial insults lingered among Georgia's black communities.[54] The survival of the black community was at stake. As Dorothy Oliver Rucker remembered life in Gainesville in the 1920s and 1930s, "We used to go down the road every day and white people would drive by and hit the side of the car. Bam, bam, bam. Call you two or three ugly names. Scare you to death. We'd get out to sell those rugs we used to make [at Beulah Rucker Oliver's school]. We were trained to go around to the back [of houses]. And sometimes an old dog would jump out. They'd sic the dogs on you." Nancy Stephens agreed: "We were walking back to the school from church services, and some fellow passed in a car. It was a white fellow. Do you know, he swerved and just did miss? I mean, it was so close, [the car] hit the clothes."[55]

Teachers such as Lucy Craft Laney, Beulah Rucker, and Jessie Salmon Mosley, born to former slaves and raised in rural families, knew well the consequences of alcohol and gambling. To purchase property, become educated, or find jobs as wage laborers, blacks had to avoid wasting money on frivolous pleasures. Instead, the money should be used to buy land or help the family raise itself to middle-class status. An extra twenty-five cents allowed Dorothy Oliver Rucker to take piano lessons for one year, permitted Annie Ruth Mosley Martin to attend Beulah Rucker Oliver's school, or bought pencils for Oliver's students. In her autobiography, Oliver mentions an incident in which she paid a bill in postage stamps.[56] Money spent playing cards or buying a pint of liquor could be better used for educational, family, or church support, helping to ensure that "our race builds on a sure foundation."[57] Furthermore, girls who drank alcohol or danced were believed to risk sexual abuse and pregnancy. Dating a man who gambled or drank presented the potential for abuse or neglect in a marriage. The respectability of middle-class status provided a degree of protection for black survival.[58]

Although the rules espoused by black parents and educators seem to emulate

traditional values of obedience and regulation, the cultural context of white supremacy renegotiated these values to accentuate modernity's focus on individual potential. To emphasize what their children could become, black parents
gave clear instructions on what to avoid, how to be adults, and how to survive
in a racist society. Ercelene Adams stated that her parents were the most important people in her life and used "every moment to be a teachable moment."
Awake by five in the morning, the ten Adams children had farm chores to do
before leaving for school; if those chores were not completed, they were wait-
ing when school let out in the afternoon. Adams was also assigned a week when
she would serve as the family cook, a task that required her to plan meals as well
as prepare the food.[59]

Beulah Rucker Oliver's emphasis on moral, upright behavior also included
encouraging her students to learn to manage independently. As her daughter,
Dorothy, remembered, "Mother was strong on being self-sufficient. She was
against handouts because she believed that you had to have a commitment
to education and work. She was always walking around the school and saying,
'Get those hands to work! Hang that nap on a bedpost!'"[60]

Beulah Rucker Oliver's children and students began their daily activities at
five in the morning, washing and dressing before starting their chores. Some
students, usually girls, cooked breakfast, while others fed the chickens, the
cows, and the mule. Water had to be pumped from the well for the school and
livestock. Following devotions, Bible study, and academic instruction, students
had more chores—caring for crops, maintaining the property, doing the laundry, making candles or lye soap, or remaking donated clothing. During the late
1920s and 1930s, the school sold student-made rugs, and many students also
raised money for tuition by traveling into Gainesville and working as maids or
as day laborers on road projects. Rucker's students learned steady work habits
while obtaining education intended to keep them from having to do such menial labor in the future.

On their forays into Gainesville, Beulah Rucker Oliver's students were
clearly identifiable by their well-worn clothing. During her childhood, Dorothy
Oliver Rucker never had a new dress and like her mother washed her dress at
night and wore the same garment again in the morning. This attire was the subject of derisive comments from both whites and better-dressed uptown blacks:
recalled Dorothy, "We had a name. They had a way of saying, 'Here comes Beulah Rucker.'"[61]

While Beulah Rucker Oliver's family relied on a combination of wage labor
from Oliver and her husband and crops grown in the garden, other black fami-

lies planted cotton for the market as well as items needed for family subsistence. "We raised cotton and corn and vegetables like peas, peanuts. We had a lot of foodstuff. We even had a little wheat just for bread. We had cows and hogs. There was very little bought from the store. You know, it was real thrilling to get a little bought fish or something," recalled Rosa Penson Anderson. "When you went in the store, the merchant might wait on all the white people before they waited on you. . . . We knew not to say anything because people could get nasty."[62]

Decisions about which children did farm labor reflected African American strategies for their daughters and race work. Most families relied primarily on their sons' labor for the farm chores. The Pensons and Mosleys had several sons, who were responsible for plowing. Yet when the time came for hoeing and picking cotton, daughters had to help. This labor occasionally prevented Rosa Penson Anderson and the Mosley daughters from returning to school. After Rosa's father died, the family increasingly required the daughters' assistance in the fields, and Anderson did not start school and college until October each year because she had to help her family pick cotton.

Daughters followed a career pattern decided by their mothers or mother figures, yet parents made this decision based on their perceptions of their daughters' ambitions and independence. Dorothy Oliver Rucker claimed that her mother always knew that Dorothy would be a teacher because she excelled in schoolwork and enjoyed working on her own. Most black teachers interviewed for this project stated that their mothers made arrangements for their daughters to attend school away from home. Jessie Salmon Mosley saw an advertisement for Beulah Rucker's school in the *Atlanta Independent* and became determined to send her four daughters there to get more than the six grades of schooling offered locally and thus become teachers. Each girl had to wait her turn; only when one completed her education could the next one go. Oldest daughter Annie Ruth went first, working her way through tenth grade before taking the teaching exams at the Hall County courthouse and clearing the way for her sisters. Laura, the youngest daughter, also completed tenth grade at Oliver's school. As in most African American and many white families, the Mosley sons attended school locally but then went to work on the family farm. Similarly, Rosa Penson Anderson's mother, a teacher at Willis Grove Baptist Church, knew that her daughter would have to leave home to attend high school and found work scholarships to enable the girl to do so, and Susie Weems Wheeler's mother decided to send her daughter to high school in Griffin after she completed elementary school in Cartersville.

Fathers also had a role in determining their daughters' futures. Nancy Stephens's father decided that she should go to school, and parents jointly settled on education strategies. But mothers bore the responsibility for articulating the family's plans to the children. It is also clear that families chose daughters when deciding which children, if any, to keep in school for more than four or five grades. Sons could not be spared from farm labor. Female students always outnumbered male students at Oliver's school as well as across the state, especially in grades seven through ten.[63]

Outside the classroom, women and mothers practiced race work in organizations or community meetings. Women like Beulah Rucker Oliver and Jessie Salmon Mosley lacked the time to join black women's organizations like the National Association of Colored Women, and rural black churches lacked women's missionary unions. Still, women found methods for community involvement. Oliver organized black ministers and their wives in the "Starry Council" that met at her house every Wednesday evening to discuss and debate Bible readings and local race work. At times, she helped ministers write their sermons. Rarely subscribing to a subservient role, Oliver calmly insisted on her vision for the school and community. Dorothy Oliver Rucker recalled that one minister objected to her mother's assertiveness and asked her to assume a more passive role, but Beulah Oliver refused because "Mama wasn't built like that, nohow."[64]

African American female teachers frequently perceived students as family members, blurring the lines between kinship and community and continuing a pattern established during the slavery era. In an extreme example, Dorothy Oliver Rucker remembered "a lady who brought her six children to Mama and then went to Florida to earn some money. We had those kids all the way through school. See, we always had other people staying in our home. [The students] were like a family because we had to share everything with the others."[65] Rosa Penson Anderson and Jessie Salmon Mosley also cared for their students just as they did for their own children.[66]

From schools and families, daughters learned the meaning of self-sufficiency and race work. However, this view of self-sufficiency was broad enough to include U.S. Extension Service assistance, federal funds for vocational programs, neighbors, churches, and northern philanthropy. Because support from the federal government and northern philanthropy always combined work with financial aid, Georgians rarely defined this assistance as a handout. By the early twentieth century, the language of self-sufficiency had been redefined to combine work and economic assistance, individual enterprise and outside support.

At the same time that black families claimed self-sufficiency, they honed and stretched its meaning.

THE WHITE WOMEN who became teachers in the early twentieth century came from rural families that owned at least fifty acres of cleared farmland or from urban families that were part of the emerging middle-class professions such as law, insurance, and small businesses. Despite such similarities, these women's social and economic circumstances differed in several respects. Ruth Smith Waters's paternal grandfather received some land in Jackson County, apparently from local officials, because of his service in the Confederate Army. Waters's father, Charlie Eugene Smith, and his brothers rented the land to tenants, and Smith bought sixty-three acres of land at Chestnut Mountain in Hall County during the 1920s and raised cotton. In addition, however, he worked as a bookkeeper and postmaster at Jackson County's Thompson Mill cotton gin and gristmill.[67] Leona Clark Williams's family worked one hundred acres of land that had been in the Clark family since approximately 1840 at the head of Ellijay Creek in North Carolina. Relying on family labor, the Clarks were self-sufficient, but they never raised cash crops for sale on the national market, probably because Robin Clark adamantly refused to go into debt.[68] Jane Thigpen Alexander's family raised cotton on approximately two hundred acres near Dublin, Georgia, and employed at least two sharecropping families.[69] And Jimmie Kate Sams Cole's family owned approximately eight hundred acres of land in Fayette County and raised cotton, as generations of Samses had done before the Civil War. Martha Breedlove Buice's family owned and operated a Walton County dairy that supplied Monroe with milk.[70] While these families differed in their ability to hire outside labor and the size of their holdings, they shared property ownership regardless of whether they chose to produce market commodities such as cotton or milk.

Many aspects of turn-of-the-century white Georgians' lives resembled those of African Americans. Bunice Waldrip Reed, born to a white farming family in Forsyth County in 1905, recalled that there was "always a church in that community. Of course, you had some families around that wasn't members. But members of your church and your family all belonged there. Just like a family."[71] To Reed, family meant kin and religious ties. When someone was sick or died, community members tended that person's farm. And like black parents, whites taught their children skills that would be needed during adulthood. Hall County resident Velva Tanner Blackstock remembered that she learned to hoe, clean, cook, sew, and crochet from watching her five sisters and her mother.

Girls learned cooking not from recipes but from observing mothers who never used measuring cups or spoons.[72] Stories of rural families' labor in cotton culture abound, but the drudgery and lack of rewards gave some women pause and provided an incentive to find respectable careers. Ruby Smith Byers, one of seven children of a white tenant family from Jackson County, recalled that before daylight, her mother built a fire in the stove and started cooking sweet potatoes for lunch or dinner. Then her mother prepared cornbread, made biscuits, and cooked breakfast. By the time the family finished the meal and the dishes were washed, "the dinner was ready to pack in whatever they carried it to the field in. We'd work all day and come home at night."[73] Mothers joined the family at the noon meal, worked in the fields during the afternoon, and then returned to the house to prepare the evening meal. After the family ate, women washed dishes, mended clothing and bedding, prepared the children for bed, and finally went to sleep. On washing days, water had to be hauled up to the house and a fire built. Clothes were then hand washed and beaten, allowed to dry, and ironed, a process that took more than an entire day.

Ruby Smith Byers was typical of most daughters, who seemed unaware of choices other than marriage and farming. After moving from Jackson County to Forsyth County, where her family found a better sharecropping arrangement, Ruby met Sanford Byers at her new church and school in 1938. Sanford courted her at her parents' home and married Ruby in 1941, when she was fifteen. The marriage took place on a Saturday, and Ruby was at work on her in-laws' farm early the following Monday morning. Ruby and Sanford continued living with his parents for the first seven months of their marriage.[74] Velma Blackstock and Ruby Byers never considered pursuing a profession, although both girls did well in school. Other women recalled that their parents—and particularly their fathers—or family needs prevented children from attending public schools beyond the first six grades. For example, the death of Inez Dennis's mother forced her, the oldest girl in a family of twelve, to quit school to assume her mother's role.[75]

Like African American parents, whites rigidly enforced specific rules for their children's behavior. Fathers headed households and set rules for children's behavior. As the oldest child, one of Leona Clark Williams's duties was to prepare some of her ten siblings for school. One of her brothers, "the twistiest little old thing I ever saw," refused to stand still while she checked behind his ears for dirt. Williams had heard children order each other around by saying, "Damn it! Do so and so!" and on one occasion, she became exasperated and said to her brother, "Damn it, Andrew, stand still till I get your neck washed." As she later recalled, "I hadn't more than said that till my daddy came on me with a broom handle. He'd like to have beat me to death. . . . He said, 'There's three things you don't do in my house. If you're a woman, you don't whore hop. If you're a man, you don't come in drinking. You don't use ugly words.' . . . And we never did." During the Great Depression, Robin Clark told his children, "We'll get out here, and we'll work hard, and we'll have cabbage and potatoes. We may not have good clothes, but there's two things we won't do: we won't go hungry and we won't go on welfare."[76]

When Leona started attending a school located five miles from her home, she took her five-year-old brother, Walter, along with her. He grew tired during the walk, and both children were tardy and were kept after school to make up their lessons. After they returned home late, Leona remembered, "Daddy would paddle my butt and say, 'You've been playing along the road. You got to get home early.'"[77] Only six years old at the time, Williams remembered that she "never felt quite the same about him anymore." Robin Clark made sure that his children knew who was in charge, but his discipline frequently crossed the line into abuse. He beat them with a broom handle for things over which they had little control or before they could explain what had happened. Leona Clark Williams could do little to speed her little brother along the miles from school to home but was nevertheless punished for the situation. She saw this behavior as unreasonably harsh and as intended to harm children both physically and emotionally. Like the values her father had intended to convey to his children, this lesson remained with Leona Clark Williams for the rest of her life.[78]

Ruth Smith Waters tells slightly different stories about her father's household rules, which stressed that his daughters must act like ladies. Like most southern Methodists of his day, he meant "that you would never drink, you would never use any foul language, you would never be guilty of telling jokes. We didn't play Old Maid at home because cards were associated with gambling with daddy. We didn't dance initially, but later we were allowed to square dance. And you dressed properly, and you behaved like a lady when you were out with men. You'd never do anything that would cast a reflection on your character. And go to church and listen." One Christmas, Ruth learned exactly what Charlie Smith meant by listening in Liberty Methodist Church. Wearing new stockings and cap, Ruth hopped into the church aisle when the music started and began to dance down the aisle. "Daddy swept me up, and he pried off a piece of oak hickory. I got switched outside church. That was the one time Daddy switched me."[79]

Martha Breedlove Buice, Jimmie Kate Sams Cole, and Jane Thigpen

Alexander tell similar stories concerning their fathers' rules about swearing, playing cards, dancing, and other social behaviors. In church, children sat still and listened or napped on floor pallets. When their families had visitors, children sat quietly and listened. In most instances, white women ascribe rules of behavior to their fathers and/or recall that they referred to "my house," clearly indicating male parental household authority, challenges to which were swiftly punished. Household rules also paralleled evangelical Protestantism, reflecting the Ten Commandments and the traditional denominational consequences of sins such as drinking and disobedience to parental and particularly paternal authority.

Respectability, increasingly assailed by a consumer culture of the Sears catalog, hairstyles, and fashion, framed the ways future teachers redefined appropriate styles and behaviors. Waters mentioned a classmate at Chestnut Mountain School who had bobbed her hair: "It was just scandalous to be bare-legged and have bobbed hair. She was talked about. . . . No one would have anything to do with her."[80] Such a perception was quite conservative and underscores tensions within southern culture in the 1920s. To some white rural southerners, styles such as bobbed hair, shorter dresses, and bare legs designated the incursions of commercialism and modernity in addition to wanton displays of sexuality. Fears about women's fashions signaled suspicions about the presence of the New Woman and all that it included—looser morals and the popular culture of the city.[81] That some white women cut their hair was apparently less relevant than the style, for the flapper look meant something quite different than shorter hair. To evangelical southern whites, the flapper denoted acquiescence to modern values of disintegrating families, fractured households, and the collapse of the evangelical church's authority. As among the black middle class, white families saw new dances and fashion styles as signs of decadence. In 1910, Atlanta's white residents debated whether women should wear hats to movies. Even as commercial entertainment became acceptable to middle-class patrons, they sought to preserve a respectable atmosphere in the movie house.[82] Atlanta clergymen and then a censorship committee monitored what was shown at movie houses through World War I.

Although each household enforced rules differently and some families were more severe than others, children learned what was considered respectable behavior. Yet rules against dancing, playing cards, and drinking alcohol had less to do with biblical imperatives than with evangelical values and moral beliefs of southern rural regions. For example, jazz dances such as the Charleston let men and women hold each other close and feel each other's bodies through clothing, thereby threatening community and family norms of courtship and challenging the traditional ways that children came to know each other—through church, school, or family introductions. Other forms of music and dance were far more acceptable. As Florrie Still explained, her parents enjoyed square dancing and gospel music. Churches offered singing schools for children, sometimes without their parents. Aubrey Benton and others bought fiddles, guitars, and other instruments from the Sears and Roebuck catalog and played for community square dances after crops were picked or harvested. During the 1920s and 1930s, families that could afford to purchase battery-powered radios from the catalog invited friends and neighbors to listen to gospel music and other broadcasts.

The father's authority regulated respectability within the household as well as decisions such as moving the family to another settlement or changing businesses or determining school attendance. Between 1913 and 1936, Robin Clark moved his household seven times before the family finally settled outside Gainesville, Georgia. The moves reflected the Clark family's desperate struggles to continue farming when agricultural prices had dropped precipitously and self-sufficiency had become a less tenable way of life.[83] In addition to improving his social and economic position, Charlie Smith moved his family to Chestnut Mountain to enable his daughters to attend better schools.[84] In 1924, Baptist minister Jim Still moved his family, including daughters Florrie and Nelle, from a cotton-producing farm in Walton County to Clermont, in Hall County, so that he and Florrie could attend the Baptist Chattahoochee High School and complete their education.[85]

White mothers supported and enforced their husbands' household rules. Sudie Bowman Clark whipped her daughter, Leona, with a hickory switch for taking a pencil from a neighbor even after the neighbor said that Leona could keep it: "If she gets by with this," replied Sudie Clark, "she may take other things." The message got through. Leona Clark Williams recalled, "That's the first thing I stole and that's the last thing." She viewed her mother's authority with respect: unlike Robin Clark, Sudie punished her children only after she saw what they had done.[86]

Ruth Smith Waters recalled that although her father was the unquestioned head of the household, her mother, Nancy, did most of the disciplining: "Mother would send us out to get good peach tree hickories, and we knew better than not to get a good one or we'd be sent back." Nancy Smith believed in the importance of both her daughters' public behavior and the ways in which they acted within the family. Recalled Ruth, "We had to behave, and when we

Ruth Smith Waters (fifth row, fifth child from left) attended Clermont High School in Hall County, where her father, Charles (third window, center), was a trustee, 1920s. (Courtesy of Ruth Smith Waters.)

went visiting with Mother and there were no children, we sat around and very respectfully listened." Ruth and her sister were not allowed to quarrel and never talked back to their parents.[87]

Teaching children these values protected the community's hierarchical structure and demonstrated the extent to which families respected the society's mores. Furthermore, instilling respect for rules provided a means through which parents could order what they perceived as a harsh and often arbitrary world. At an extreme, Robin Clark's rules tolerated no room for excuses or explanations. Sudie Clark's reaction to the seemingly trivial theft of a pencil reflected both the biblical injunction "Thou shalt not steal" and the fact that in rural early-twentieth-century Georgia, personal possessions were costly and difficult to replace: had Leona been allowed to keep the pencil, her mountain neighbors would have had to travel miles to the general store to replace it. If

one household tolerated theft, the survival and interdependence of a settlement could be threatened. Adding this punitive power to the belief in a God
that punished sinners for the slightest bad thought or deed created little room
for children's independence. Children grew up in a world based on fear of disobeying God and their parents.

Disease and natural disasters were other prominent fears for early-twentieth-
century Georgians. Infant and child mortality rates remained higher in the
South than in any other region in the United States until after World War II.
Rural residents lacked decent health care and access to doctors and often had
poor diets. Every family at least knew someone who had had a child die. Common diseases such as colds could turn into fatal pneumonia or the flu, and even
if a doctor practiced in a nearby town, few parents could afford to use him. Both
the Clarks and the Stills lost children, and Ruth Smith Waters recalled that an
aunt underwent surgery for breast cancer on the kitchen table. Ruth's mother,
Nancy, was orphaned as an adolescent and briefly went to work at the Gainesville Mill. In 1903, a terrifying tornado struck and destroyed most of the mill
buildings, leaving Nancy Smith with a lifelong fear of storms. Another tornado
hit the town in 1936, killing more than two hundred people and causing millions of dollars worth of property damage. Thus, weather and disease combined
with fears of parents and God to create a frightening and seemingly capricious
world in which children had to navigate their futures.[88]

Disease and accident could have even worse consequences for African
Americans than for whites. Injuries from farm machinery or disease eliminated
some blacks' ability to work. Injuries to children affected their future as adults
in the labor force. Rural blacks had almost no access to medical care: Nancy
Stephens recalled going to the back door of a white doctor's office for treatment
and even then occasionally being refused. Cobb County, for example, did not
have a black doctor who offered reliable health care for African Americans
until after World War II.[89] Most ailments from tooth decay to broken bones to
illness had to be cared for by laypersons. Beulah Rucker Oliver's mother worked
as a midwife in the Gainesville area and delivered Beulah's children.

Although the degree to which rules were enforced varied among households,
all families used some form of corporal punishment. As an adult, Aubrey Benton, who grew up in Jackson County, joked about his father using "Dr. Green,"
a hickory branch, to tan his children's legs if they were disobedient or refused
to pick cotton.[90] Some women who grew up to become teachers remembered
corporal punishment as frightening and avoided it with their own children and
in their classrooms. Leona Clark Williams came to see corporal punishment as

a loss of personal control and as abuse, thereby indicating her acceptance of modern beliefs in individual choices and autonomy rather than total acquiescence to communal authority.

Along with rules of behavior, children learned the importance of work. Just like the character Joe Christmas in William Faulkner's *Light in August,* children learned "that the two abominations are sloth and idle thinking[;] the two virtues are work and the fear of God."[91] White rural children universally helped their families with farm labor. For girls, including Ruby Smith Byers and Leona Clark Williams, the first jobs frequently involved looking after younger siblings, while boys often began by learning to use a hoe. By the time Florrie Still was eleven, she could pick more cotton than her father—as much as 211 pounds a day—although she had little use for domestic chores. Ruby Smith Byers and her brothers and sisters began to work on their family's farm when they were four or five years old. On Saturdays, while sons continued to do fieldwork, some mothers kept their daughters at home to sweep the yard and clean the house. For example, Velva Tanner Blackstock's mother had her daughters use corn shuck mops, scrub the kitchen, and clean the dirt fireplace.[92]

Like African Americans, future white teachers acquired work habits from observation of their parents. While few of these women's mothers had more than a seventh-grade education, they fulfilled an essential role for their families. "My mama," stated Leona Clark Williams, "didn't have time to do a whole lot because with twelve children . . . she would carry one in her stomach and hold one by the hand and carry one in her arms and take them out there to the farm and put them on a pallet and put a sheet over them." Sudie Bowman Clark hoed, planted, and worked the family garden. She canned and dried fruit and made most of the family's clothing.[93] Similarly, Jane Thigpen Alexander recalled, "We all worked in the fields," but like Sudie Clark, Alexander's mother raised vegetables and canned and preserved vegetables and fruit for winter. Rarely buying anything at the stores, her mother also helped cure hog meat to get the family through the winter.[94]

White farm women's lives consisted of cooking, keeping house, and sewing clothing, since few people bought any clothing aside from overalls from the Sears catalog. Women also crocheted and quilted and made sheets, towels, and table linens. Sewing clothing and household items was limited by the cost of buying fabric, and like Beulah Rucker Oliver and her daughter, many white girls had only one dress. Ruby Smith Byers recalled, however, that "when we got to raising chickens and got feed sacks, our problems were solved."[95] The sacks could be used to make clothing or to make numerous other items for the home.

White youngsters, like all rural children, were expected to help with the household chores, with specific duties allocated according to gender. Ruth Smith Waters and her sister did the dishes, drew water from the spring and carried it home, made their beds, tended the family vegetable garden, and hoed and picked cotton.[96] Jimmie Kate Sams Cole and Jane Thigpen Alexander did similar chores in addition to caring for their younger brothers and sisters. Leona Clark Williams, whose parents did not raise cash crops, had a particularly broad range of household responsibilities—tending her younger siblings and getting them ready for school, taking cows to the pasture, gathering eggs, carding and spinning wool from the family's sheep, and collecting walnuts and berries.[97]

As the twentieth century progressed, white households increasingly required cash for seed, tools, fabric, coffee, sugar, and schoolbooks. Yet although residents of cities and towns enjoyed the economic prosperity during the 1920s, in rural families "there wasn't any money along there from the late twenties on till about the late thirties."[98] In most families, wives and mothers obtained money by selling butter and eggs to peddlers or to local grocers.[99] Mothers found creative ways to acquire school supplies because the state required students to pay for their own books, pencils, and paper. In the Smith household, Ruby Byers recalled, eggs became "a precious commodity because as long as the old hen laid, you could kinda count on falling back on that to get some things."[100] On one occasion, Sudie Bowman Clark took her daughter, Leona, to a mountainside ginseng patch, where in one day they gathered twenty dollars worth of ginseng roots, enough to pay for the Clark children's schoolbooks for the following year.[101] Ruby Smith Byers remembered, "When we were little, you could get pencils, two for a penny, a little brown pencil with the eraser just down in the wood. And Mama took them and cut'em in three pieces so we'd all have a little pencil to write with. Now we were poor. Paper—I learned to write on the back of sale papers. They just printed the sale items on one side at that time, and Mama would take'em and cut'em up in sheets and divide'em out and we'd take'em to school to write on. But, you know, we got an education."[102]

While rural families struggled to raise cash to buy goods, gender roles shifted as some tenants and sharecroppers moved off the farms in the 1920s and 1930s. After the Clarks left their mountain home in favor of town life, household responsibilities diminished, and the children went to work in cotton mills or other growing industries to supplement household resources.[103] The Great Depression proved to be a watershed, as many rural white residents realized that farming was becoming less profitable at the same time that wage-labor and educational opportunities were increasing. Some parents recognized that their daughters required skills other than farming to preserve their self-sufficiency, at least until marriage. And with public education expanding in many up-country areas, parents were able to send their daughters to school. By the early twentieth century, attendance at high school became gendered, a shift from the nineteenth century. From 1900 to 1940, more girls than boys of both races attended school beyond the seventh grade.[104]

As in black families, white children often had to leave home to obtain education beyond the primary grades. Sudie Bowman Clark no doubt missed her daughter while she attended high school in Franklin, North Carolina, but that separation would have been eased by the knowledge that education and a career in teaching or nursing would allow Leona to improve her life by earning wages before marriage. Sudie and other mothers recognized a shift in gendered wage-labor possibilities and hoped to enable their daughters to take advantage of the new opportunities. By the time Florrie Still had completed high school in 1925, when she was sixteen, her mother had become an invalid following a series of strokes. Still's salary helped to pay for a companion to care for her mother. Leona Clark Williams frequently used part of her salary to help her younger brothers and sisters remain in school. Many teachers, including Ruth Smith Waters and Jimmie Kate Sams Cole, found jobs because of their fathers' connections to the school board. Waters was certified to teach at age seventeen but was too young, according to state regulations, to obtain a position; nonetheless, trustees from Monroe knew her father and "took care of me on that," hiring her to teach at Walker Park in 1928.[105] Fayette County School Superintendent Ferrel Sams hired his daughter, Jimmie Kate, in 1939.

Several teachers acknowledged that community support was vital to their ability to remain in school. Leona Clark Williams gratefully recalled her first teacher's persistence in teaching reading. Leona started school when she was eight and twice quit because of injuries. But her teacher worked with her after school to keep her in the proper grade: in her words, "I would have never finished school if it hadn't been for her." Martha Breedlove Buice credited the Georgia Federation of Women's Clubs, which provided a work scholarship that enabled her to attend the State Normal School in Athens. That the federation became involved in scholarships indicates the growth and impact of white women's volunteer associations in Georgia.

Women's Missionary Unions (WMUs) grew in Gainesville, Fayetteville, and Marietta as well as in other towns and in cities, and the extent of the groups' organized assistance grew as well. When their mothers joined the WMU, Ruth Smith Waters, Jimmie Kate Sams Cole, and Charters Smith Embry observed the connection between Christianity and volunteer work. Doing God's work bound these women to help the needy and the poor. Charters's mother, Isabel Smith, and the other members of the Gainesville WMU frequently collected funds for the orphans' home in Atlanta or for Beulah Rucker Oliver's school as a means of giving thanks to Jesus, who was the "giver of every perfect gift."[106] This WMU diligently followed the daily Bible readings and prayer calendars suggested in *Royal Service*, the WMU publication of the Southern Baptist Convention. Smith's Baptist faith and cultural values defined how she understood her social duties as well as her personal salvation. Charters often accompanied her mother on visits to Oliver's school or to poor families. Cole's mother believed that duty included helping tenant families with extra food or old clothing. Waters's mother, Nancy, saw duty as allowing a tenant's wife to sleep on the floor of the Smith family's house, away from her abusive husband, and Ruth and her sister occasionally went with their mother or by themselves to deliver food to neighbors, as did Leona Clark Williams and other daughters.[107]

Concomitant with the religious expression of duties existed a public means for women to demonstrate this duty to others. But white women always understood this assistance in terms of their class and race superiority. What they did could be stopped at any time if the recipients failed to act according to accepted definitions of what was appropriate and what was not. At its worst, this individualized interpretation allowed white men and women to determine who should be helped. Community members who were regarded as lazy, unchristian, or immoral were beyond anyone's support. That church members construed their duties individually reinforced cultural constructions of self-sufficiency and modernity's emphasis on the individual. Black and white recipients tiptoed a precarious line within this nexus of social relations, often manipulating this system for their own ends.[108]

Part of understanding the community's social relations included preserving Jim Crow boundaries. Families, communities, the state, and the church enforced white supremacy. From sheet music on pianos to advertisements in magazines and catalogs, racist caricatures of grinning, wide-lipped black men and women dressed as Aunt Jemima fed stereotypes of black masculinity and femininity.[109] Daughters' lives were bookmarked by the premier of *Birth of a Nation* in Atlanta in 1915 and *Gone with the Wind* in 1939, films that depicted African American stereotypes at their worst. From 1890 to 1940, either a lynching or "whitecapping violence" exploded in almost every Georgia county. As Georgia author Lillian Smith wrote, "The mother who taught me what I know of tenderness and love and compassion taught me also the bleak rituals of keeping

Negroes in their 'place.'" Smith's father taught her compassion for others at the same time he trained her in the decorum she must expect from black men. Smith eloquently detailed the ways in which children learned to be Christians and arrogant white southerners, to believe in freedom and democracy while riding in a Jim Crow railway car.[110]

How living in a racist world with daily reminders of black inferiority affected these women is difficult to determine. The white women interviewed for this project rarely expressed the culture and costs of white supremacy as powerfully as Lillian Smith did. The teachers never described how mental doors closed "until heart and conscience are blocked from each other and from reality."[111] Yet many women understood at some level the wrongness of the economic disparities between black and white schools or of violent acts against blacks. Ruth Smith Waters detested the fact that the bus that took her and other white children to school on rainy days splashed the black children who had to walk to school. Jimmie Kate Sams Cole regarded with disdain the way her grandfather treated some black tenants. Leona Clark Williams abhorred the unequal provisions for blacks and whites yet felt powerless to do anything about the situation.[112] Neither these women nor their parents were activists.

Still, daughters fleshed out their understandings of compassion not only from church and family but also from their experiences as children. While attending the mountain school, Leona Clark Williams asked her mother for a new dress. Sudie Clark purchased outing cloth, a fabric used for undergarments or sleeping clothes, and when Leona wore the dress to school, her classmates ridiculed her. Already accustomed to the students' taunts because she was the oldest student in the first grade, Leona decided, "I can't wear nice clothes like some of them, but I can sure be smarter than any of them. I started reading everything I could get my hands on."[113] Proper speech and education became a means by which she could better her position in the southern social hierarchy. Ruth Smith Waters recalled the divisions between the town and rural people: "Many people in Gainesville had a high-headed feeling about themselves. See, that was when the Green Street, the royal bluebloods ran the town."[114] "Oh, those women at the United Daughters of the Confederacy," remembered Jimmie Kate Sams Cole. "I can still see them with their hats and feathers on talking about who would make it and who would not. So high and mighty."[115] Although white women from lower economic strata could not aspire to elite status, they could pursue teaching, a reputable profession that would further their ambitions.

Nonetheless, daughters absorbed daily lessons on responsibilities to community members from parents who worked for salaries or volunteered. Most daughters noted some relative involved in the school system. Several fathers, including Ferrol Sams, Charlie Smith, and Robin Clark, served as school trustees or Sunday school superintendents. Ruth Smith Waters remembered stories about her paternal grandmother, who taught at St. Martin's Institute in Jackson County. While local trustees searched for a new teacher, Jimmie Kate Sams Cole's mother taught school. Several mothers taught Sunday school.

Family support, women's voluntary associations, increased availability of education and learning the meaning of duties unquestionably merged to motivate daughters to become teachers. Leona Clark Williams's three closest siblings did not finish school despite receiving similar parental encouragement. She and the four Mosley girls who finished high school had a determination and ambition that enabled them to succeed despite the formidable obstacles in their paths. Unlike the majority of black and white women, those who became teachers clearly sought an independent income and a career. These women ultimately drew from aspirations beyond those of most women, believing that they had received a distinct calling for a profession.

RELIGION REMAINED AN important part of community life, providing moral and educational lessons as well as opportunities for rest, socializing, and community building for people whose lives otherwise consisted primarily of farm labor and isolation. Church social occasions included weddings, funerals, baptisms, and building church additions. Many of these events lasted all day and provided food and fellowship. Revivals also provided a major opportunity for social interaction. African American Hattie Gaines Wilson, for example, recalled the annual walk to the revival in Cobb County's Pleasant Grove as fun time when she could talk to friends.[116] Baptist revivals held in August provided both African Americans and whites with a break before crops had to be harvested in the fall. At these gatherings, women gossiped and exchanged recipes, children played, and men discussed crop prices and the latest political developments. Revivals afforded older children such as Velva Tanner and her future husband, Tom Blackstock, opportunities for courting and talking.[117] Because most youths rarely traveled outside their communities, revivals provided one of the few opportunities to meet members of the opposite sex. According to Howard Reed, a sharecropper's son from Hall County, "We didn't have nowhere to go much, only to church. When they had the revival, everybody was there. They filled [Mountain View Baptist Church] up."[118] Similarly, white Methodists held camp meetings on grounds in each county. Meetings lasted for up to two weeks, and families brought everything from tents to livestock to sustain them during that time.[119] Parents could rest assured that their children were supervised by church members and were meeting other children of Christian character.

Beulah Rucker Oliver and her students attended Timber Ridge Baptist Church, arriving at ten in the morning for Sunday school lessons, which she had initiated shortly after arriving in Gainesville. Church services began at eleven o'clock and lasted until one or two in the afternoon, when members adjourned to eat the lunches they had brought. The congregation carried benches out of the church, turned them toward each other, spread out blankets, shared food, and sang spirituals and hymns while children played. Members later returned inside the church for evening services. Oliver's students often performed at Timber Ridge, reciting the books of or passages from the Bible or reading poems.[120] Rucker also sent her students uptown to a holiness church on Sunday evenings, helping to maintain her school's nondenominational orientation as well as to expose her students and children to the members of these churches, many of whom were poor and uneducated. Thus, she enabled her charges to learn about different strands of black life. These excursions had additional benefits for the students that Rucker probably did not anticipate: "Most of us were not exposed to holiness people," recalled Nancy Stephens. "It was a new experience for us to go there and see. And we wanted to go uptown. Our boyfriends would come and walk with us." "I'll never forget one night," added Dorothy Oliver Rucker. "Here comes the 10:10 train. And Mama was walking behind us. The lights were flashing, the bells ringing. And we ran across the tracks so we could kiss our boyfriends, and Mama couldn't see that."[121]

Black educators' work never consisted solely of academic instruction within classrooms. Both the predominantly male ministers and the predominantly female schoolteachers moved within the community, spreading various messages from moral conduct to religious instruction to economic improvement. In addition to providing instruction in reading, writing, and arithmetic, teachers urged students to buy property and to seek wage labor jobs and thereby avoid the abuses of sharecropping. Black Baptist ministers urged parishioners to keep their children in school, and some congregations sent funds to the General Missionary Baptist Association for scholarships to Morehouse and Spelman Colleges as well as to the Northwestern Normal and Industrial School in Gainesville.[122] Both ministers and teachers provided instruction on the Bible as well as on values such as hard work, and the two groups supported and reinforced each other's work.

Again, Beulah Rucker Oliver's school provides an example of how black educational institutions reflected their Reconstruction origins in black churches by using the Bible as their primary textbook. Oliver's students called her "Godmother" and began their days with morning devotions that included prayers and singing. Each student memorized a Bible verse every day, and all learned the Sermon on the Mount, the Ten Commandments, and the books of the Bible. Instruction was provided on biblical stories, using a catechismal manner that paralleled Oliver's instruction at Knox Institute as well as the call-and-response pattern blacks practiced in their churches. As Oliver's daughter, Dorothy Oliver Rucker, recalled, students chanted, "'Who's the first man God made?' 'Adam!' 'Who's the first woman?' 'Eve!' 'What'd they make [Eve] out of?' 'Rib from Adam's side!' And we'd just go on and on."[123]

In most respects, white households and schools, like those of African Americans, reinforced Baptist and Methodist prescriptives concerning appropriate behavior and values. Each Sunday in church and every day at home, sons and daughters learned to obey their parents and other authority figures. All children learned the Ten Commandments, and God's laws framed the ways in which people lived their daily lives. Leona Clark Williams stated that her parents "were very religious people. They read the Bible, and we attended revivals in the summer. Whenever one of us children had a problem, Mama would say, 'Take it to the Lord, take it to the Lord.'"[124] As in black households, white teachers' families attended church for several hours every Sunday. Ruth Smith Waters recalled that she and her siblings "had to get up early on Sunday morning and be prepared with our Sunday school lessons and attend church. We had to study the Bible and memorize our little memory verses each Sunday. I can remember when I was quite young there was a corner in the church that extended off the side door that quilts were carried to church if we got sleepy. [At that time, ministers] preached hour-long sermons . . . and church lasted eight hours. We were allowed to sleep on the pallet. If you didn't go to sleep, you had to behave."[125] At schools, the day opened with prayer or devotion.

Because religion was the cornerstone of community life for both whites and blacks, regular churchgoing was de rigueur for both races: "Mama always had us going to church," recalled Leona Clark Williams. "You just went down there and sat down, and the preacher preached hellfire and damnation."[126] Nevertheless, some differences existed. Whereas black ministers usually had to have some other means of supporting themselves and their families, some white communities had full-time Baptist ministers, as Martha Breedlove Buice and Jimmie Kate Sams Cole recalled. Florrie Still and Nelle Still Murphy's father, Jim, was a professional minister, and a few other women had uncles or grand-

fathers who were ministers. Furthermore, many rural whites did not limit themselves to attendance at a single church, making the rounds among several local
congregations. Ruth Smith Waters's parents raised their daughters according to
Methodist doctrines, although Baptists dominated Chestnut Mountain, and
she remembered attending a variety of churches: "We went to Chestnut Mountain Presbyterian one time and to the Baptist one Sunday and then back to the
New Liberty Methodist Church." According to Waters, "Daddy always said you
must respect other denominations. You always stay a Methodist [but] you don't
say anything about the Baptists. If they say something to you, you go ahead and
tell them that you have been sprinkled, that water does not save you. But you
quit when you say that."[127] Similarly, the Clarks attended both Yellow Springs
Baptist Church and a Pentecostal church in the mountains. In a more unusual
move, when Leona Clark Williams left her family to attend Tennessee Wesleyan for her teacher training, she joined the Methodist Church, and after she
married Bill Williams, a Baptist, and bore a child, her husband's minister asked
her to rejoin the Baptist Church, which she did. Such formal switching of
churches was uncommon, however; most women formally remained within
their childhood denominations.

For rural families, evangelical Protestantism, manifested in God's promise of
salvation, structured their understanding of an uncertain world that featured
unstable crop prices, illness, and arbitrary and often volatile weather. Rural evangelical beliefs explained tornadoes or droughts as evidence of God's wrath,
just as good fortune provided evidence of God's approval. Many people prayed
endlessly for God's intercession on their behalf: when three Clark sons entered
World War II, Sudie Bowman Clark and the rest of her family prayed daily for
their loved ones' safe return. The Clarks' youngest daughter, Hilda, remembered learning that "God's will for our lives always came first. . . . Mother said,
'If God called you, answer his call.'"[128]

God's call was a powerful way of legitimating individual action, of overcom-
ing opposition to public acts that might otherwise have been perceived as un-
orthodox or as threatening to southern conventions. Men such as Jim Still and
women such as Beulah Rucker Oliver used the culture's language of evangelical Protestant duty to escape the binds of an otherwise rigid and authoritarian
society.[129] Teachers saw themselves as answering their callings, spreading God's
word by serving him in their churches and classrooms.

Households and congregations practiced their Baptist or Methodist faiths
in different ways. Ruth Smith Waters's family had daily devotions, prayers, and
Bible readings, as did Martha Breedlove Buice's. Conversely, the Clark and

Sams families prayed and occasionally read the Bible but rarely held family devotions.

Membership in a Baptist or Methodist church provided teachers with legitimacy in many parents' eyes. Many families owned only a single book, the Bible. By emphasizing the links between education and evangelical Protestantism and by hiring teachers whom parents knew had undergone the conversion experience and therefore could be trusted to reflect local values, school officials helped to persuade parents to make the sacrifices necessary to obtain schooling for their children. And although white women teachers lacked the elite status of the southern lady, they had to contend with some of the restrictions imposed by the standard of a lady's respectable conduct. No woman who had a reputation for dancing, failing to attend church, smoking cigarettes, or unsupervised dating would be hired.

Several teachers had close relatives who served on local school boards. Robin Clark was a school trustee, and Charlie Smith served as the only Methodist on the Chestnut Mountain school board for most of his life, hiring teachers who emphasized academics and Christian practices.[130] Martha Breedlove Buice's second husband, Carl Buice, was a principal of a Gwinnett County High School who hired teachers primarily because they were Christians. In many cases, being a Christian was not enough—school boards preferred Baptists and Methodists, who were known to have rejected sin and vices such as drinking or dancing.

Because character and community standing was so important for white teachers, school officials would sometimes seek out women known to be upstanding and ask them to serve as teachers. School board members or trustees visited Ruth Smith Waters, Florrie Still, Nelle Still Murphy, and Leona Clark Williams to ask them to teach or return to teaching. Even if they lacked previous secular teaching experience, many of these women had already proven themselves as good Sunday school teachers. When Ruth Smith Waters was fourteen, her father, Charlie, the Sunday school superintendent at their church, asked his daughter to teach a class. For Florrie Still and Nelle Still Murphy, the connection between evangelical Protestantism and teaching was even clearer. Their father was a Baptist minister, and they watched him return to school for Bible classes at Chattahoochee High School. Because his childhood education had been limited to a few grades, he believed that more schooling would make him a better minister by helping him to understand the Bible better.

By the time these black and white women decided to become teachers, they had absorbed many and discarded some of their culture's values. Following their ambitions and drawing on gendered constructions, they sought professional respectable work outside the home. Yet as the strains of the hymn "Work for the Night Is Coming" drifted across Georgia's hills and farms, many black and white congregants became enmeshed, sometimes unconsciously, in the push and pull between traditional beliefs and modern values. As black and white daughters created their version of the New Woman, learned at their "mothers' knees," they carried family and community beliefs in evangelical Protestantism, self-sufficiency, and interdependence. They became part of and invested in the expanding public school system. While black and white women sought to improve education for their respective races, black women's efforts incorporated more radical notions of race work. They wanted nothing less than an equal education for black children.

3 · *Holding the Torch*

Education and Early School Reform

DURING THE 1920S, two girls who planned to become teachers attended their local schools. Leona Clark Williams, born in 1911, attended a white school in Ellijay, North Carolina, where her father was a trustee. Dorothy Oliver Rucker, born in 1919, attended the State Industrial and High School for African Americans, which her mother, Beulah Rucker Oliver, had founded in 1912 outside Gainesville, Georgia. Both women's schools provided educational fundamentals such as reading, penmanship, history, geography, and arithmetic in addition to nondenominational religious instruction. Rucker's education included some industrial training in farming and rug making, which also supported the school.

In the 1920s and 1930s, Williams and Rucker continued along their path to becoming teachers. When Williams finished sixth grade, she left home to attend high school in Franklin, North Carolina. There, she boarded with a merchant, Joe Asher, in return for English lessons for members of his family, which had immigrated from Syria. After completing high school, she received a work scholarship to attend Tennessee Wesleyan College. Rucker moved to Atlanta to attend Booker T. Washington High School, one of Georgia's few accredited public high schools for blacks. While Williams prepared breakfast and mopped floors to pay for her tuition, Rucker worked and lived with family friends in Atlanta. Fifteen years old, Rucker had never been to a city larger than Gainesville, which had some 8,000 residents. Atlanta, with more than 250,000 people, might have frightened other Georgians, but not Dorothy Oliver Rucker. Displaying characteristic moxie, Rucker marked telephone poles with chalk to find her way to and from the high school. Following graduation, both women took and passed the state teachers' exam. Williams took a position in Lula, Georgia, where her family had recently moved, while Rucker taught at her mother's school. Neither woman received extensive training, yet both became noted as exemplary teachers.[1]

The women's stories illustrate the different routes to becoming a teacher—attendance at a white denominational college and attendance at a black high school. Both patterns included an eleventh-grade education—more than either woman could have obtained at a local rural school—in addition to some form of industrial training in agriculture and home economics. The ways that these women became teachers mark the beginning of changes in southern communities during the Progressive era. Family, churches, and neighbors constituted the bedrock of socialization and apprenticeship for children in the late nineteenth century. By the turn of the century, many parents and their children increasingly used public and private schools to acquire more knowledge and skills beyond their local experiences—expertise in subjects such as mathematics and reading that became necessary for survival in the modern world.[2] Education constituted a path toward individual success and achievement rather than simply a tool for subsistence and continuity.

Yet how parents chose to educate their children varied considerably according to race, class, and location. Indeed, by the 1930s, Georgia, in contrast to more than forty other states, including North Carolina and Virginia, had little more than a patchwork approach to educational policy. How much most children were educated, while increasingly in the hands of school boards or trustees rather than parents and churches, was emphatically bound to class and race. Here was a state whose main claim to Progressive reform consisted of Prohibition and voting restrictions, a state that fought funding a public school system beyond the eighth grade, a state where legislators were far more interested in benefits for their counties than in the public good. In the development of a public school system, local school board members and trustees, almost all of whom were white, controlled fund distribution, teacher selection, and classroom materials.[3]

Black and white teachers, children, and families coped with this system's shortcomings in various ways. White teachers coped with few resources and absenteeism among farm children during the planting and harvest seasons. Rural white children lacked the educational options of children in Georgia's towns and cities, and some parents devised means to send their children to high schools in nearby towns. Paying for schoolbooks and clothing often required improvising family finances. Black teachers and families faced an even more daunting prospect. Georgia, a state with more than 1 million African Americans, failed to fund anything more than the most basic level of education for African American children, an appalling testament to racism in Progressive reform.[4] In an overwhelmingly rural state fraught with violence against blacks, white Georgians rejected the allocation of public monies for African American colleges. No survey of the state in the early twentieth century can avoid confronting the horrific consequences of Jim Crow. Some white landlords refused to allow black parents to send their children to school, insisting that the children stay home to help with planting, hoeing, and harvesting.

From the 1900s until the post–World War II era, black and white women employed several means to take the teachers' exam and could become certified through the Georgia State Board of Education or through a county superintendent's approval.[5] This system permitted local white school superintendents and trustees, elected by white men in county or city school districts, an extraordinary amount of authority in determining who would teach in their schools. School officials used criteria that combined religious beliefs, morality, family connections, regional ties, and schooling to decide which teachers were acceptable. In some cases, notably in white rural schools and black schools, this process allowed people who had received little training to become teachers. Many teachers had only a high school education and relied on their experience rather than on education courses to gauge their methods and curriculum. At the same time, the system allowed dedicated women to return to their local settlements to guide the next generations into the modern industrial era and maintain many of the rural values these women had learned as children. Black and white reformers learned ways to maneuver within the gaps in educational policy to accomplish their goals. Black and white teachers had to balance traditional moral, religious, and community values with gendered notions of professional authority.[6] By the eve of the Great Depression, teachers of both races drew from prevailing cultural standards and a modernizing public education system to elevate the role of the teacher.

Despite the system's numerous flaws, the disparate means of certification presented options to prospective teachers and their families, many of whom could not afford the tuition at Georgia's normal schools and colleges. Yet the shifts in Georgia's teacher certification policies from 1910 to the 1940s illustrate some of the tensions between rural and urban cultures as the state became more industrialized, a process that redirected the focus from traditional households to developing technologies in agriculture and new towns. These tensions arose from an increasing emphasis on teacher training from professional books and manuals as opposed to the previous reliance on practices and values acquired from families, churches, and communities—a shift from practice and tradition to uniformity and rationalization. Moreover, Georgia education reformers, particularly those in the state's Department of Education and colleges and universities, campaigned to centralize teacher certification within the department and to mandate specific education courses for prospective teachers. Reformers thereby intensified the shift to centralized state authority from local authority, a change intended to accentuate individual merit over community ties and networks.

In Georgia, the battle for higher professional standards for teacher certification from 1910 to 1940 articulated the tensions among Georgia's traditional forms of education, which relied almost exclusively on apprenticeship and training in the community from parents and leaders and the reformers' call for a modernized, bureaucratized school system that would require significant social, political, and economic realignments within a rural culture. This tension paralleled Progressive reformers' campaigns across the nation as state and national authority began to supplant local control. Certification was gradually recognized and legitimated in a complex system in which African American and white women shared and were differentiated by issues of taxation, access to higher education, family financial limitations, and preparation for teaching. Centralization of the authority to certify teachers in the Georgia State Department of Education by 1948 effectively neutralized local communities' opposition to internal improvements and taxation as well as their expectations of teachers. As the fight over advanced education moved beyond issues of individual women's financial circumstances and motivations, the cultural and political domains became the places at which localities confronted the state's authority. While black teachers and their students never shared the same public school revenues or derived the same professional expectations from reformers as white schools and teachers did, African Americans' circumstances inevitably drew the attention of northern and some Georgian reformers who began to understand the grim price of preserving hierarchy and power. Even though white reformers initially urged teacher training reforms to educate the expanding white middle class, the reform movement's language and policies also improved some of the most egregious abuses for black and white rural teachers.

Just as the campaign for centralized certification slowly rooted in Georgia, so did the drive for distinct teacher training schools. Prior to the twentieth century, white Georgia teachers were drawn from local schools that offered grades beyond seventh or eighth grade, were sent to Nashville's Peabody College for training, or graduated from Baptist or Methodist colleges such as Georgia Baptist Seminary (later known as Brenau College) in Gainesville or Wesleyan College in Macon. Although Georgia's General Assembly created Georgia Normal and Industrial College in Milledgeville in 1889 as a state-supported institution for white women's higher education, the school was inadequately funded and was able to accommodate only approximately one hundred women, yet the state required more than seven thousand teachers.[7] Moreover, the college intended to focus on teaching white women industrial skills such as dressmaking, bookkeeping, and stenography that reinforced white women's subordinate yet feminine role in southern society.

Part of Georgia's problem in establishing adequate normal colleges lay in the limitations of the Georgia Constitution of 1877, which provided state funding for the "elementary branches of an English education only," the same problem that plagued county schools.[8] In 1891, Dr. J. L. M. Curry, agent of the Peabody Fund, suggested that Georgia create normal colleges within the University of Georgia, thereby circumventing the restrictions since the constitution provided state appropriations for the university. In keeping with Curry's suggestion, Georgia in 1895 established the second normal school, State Normal School, in Athens as a branch of the university system with the sole purpose of training the state's teachers. Still, State Normal faced many of the same problems as Georgia Normal and Industrial College. Neither could house more than 100 to 150 students, and few women could afford the hundred or so dollars required for fees, books, and uniform.[9] While individual Georgians sponsored fifty-dollar scholarships for women who needed financial assistance, students still had to furnish forty dollars and pay thirty-five dollars in advance.[10] According to E. C. Branson, president of the State Normal College, few women in 1903 were able to remain at the school for more than one term.[11] To supply white teachers with a modicum of teacher training, Georgia continued to rely on summer teacher institutes in Macon, Savannah, Atlanta, and other cities financed by the Peabody Fund.[12] In the 1890s, these summer institutes eventually became restructured, with each county offering teacher training in June, July, or August for African American and white teachers with financial aid from the Peabody Fund.[13]

Still, county institutes neither reached all teachers nor satisfied educational reformers' desire to mandate specific training courses for all white teachers in such subjects as child psychology, practice teaching, or principles of education. Georgia education reformers and members of the General Education Board (GEB), formed in 1902 by John D. Rockefeller to fund black and white higher education in the South, proposed several state institutions across Georgia to focus on teacher preparation. Through the beginning of the twentieth century, legislators, the chancellor of the University of Georgia system, and reformers consistently fought about where these schools should be located as well as how they would be funded. For example, university administrators believed that the state's normal school should be part of the Athens complex, but legislators

Contrasting images of schools in the 1920s and 1930s.
Town schools tended to be constructed of brick, had better facilities, and
had high school grades. Black and white rural students fared less well.

Third-grade class at Haynes Street School, made of brick, in Marietta, Georgia,
1922. (Vanishing Georgia Collection, Georgia Division of Archives and History,
Office of the Secretary of State.)

Miss Maddox and students of various grades of Dunehoo School in Floyd
County, Georgia, in the 1930s dealt with broken windows and outhouses.
(Vanishing Georgia Collection, Georgia Division of Archives and
History, Office of the Secretary of State.)

Henderson Grove School, a one-room school for African Americans in
Gwinnett (later Bartow) County, was built in 1911 and used until 1950.
(Vanishing Georgia Collection, Georgia Division of Archives and History,
Office of the Secretary of State.)

wanted to have these schools in their districts.[14] Lack of cooperation among the
colleges in addition to the fight for meager state funds meant that state colleges
and universities could accomplish few of their educational goals.

So, given the cost of attending these schools and the controversies surround-
ing them, most prospective white teachers continued to rely on high schools for
education to pass the teachers' exam. Yet even this path to certification presented hurdles for rural white women as well as working-class white women in
towns and cities. Because the 1877 constitution denied state or county funds
beyond the sixth grade, most rural areas were unable to fund further education.
The only means of increasing local school funds was to obtain recommendations from two successive grand juries in addition to a two-thirds vote of all registered voters, including people whose names remained on voter lists but who
had moved away or not voted in many years.[15] State legislators from growing urban areas such as Fulton County might have longed for increased funding for
schools, but Georgia's use of the county unit system (a constitutional method
of dividing county votes according to unit votes rather than popularity) favored
rural communities and legislators opposed to major educational reforms.[16] Despite the provisions of the 1904 McMichael Bill, which allowed counties to call
elections without grand juries, funds for high school grades were still restricted,
and even funds for elementary grades were limited to a local tax of .5 percent.

The McMichael Bill had greater consequences for white rural districts. County school boards divided the county into even smaller districts, separating wealthier areas from poorer ones. Cities and towns created independent school districts that levied higher local taxes on corporations or taxable businesses. These districts subsequently acquired sufficient funds to build high schools and pay teachers higher salaries at the same time that rural districts lost their taxable base. Many rural families, notably those attracted by the promise of New South industrialization and modern education, moved to towns and villages.[17] The families of Ruth Smith Waters and Leona Clark Williams, like many other rural families, moved to different counties in pursuit of better schooling and economic opportunities. For the Smiths, who lived in Jackson County, the school situation "deteriorated . . . and [Daddy] bought the land in Hall County because Chestnut Mountain had a better school."[18] County school units may have reinforced Georgia's political and social structure, but early educational reforms began to crack localism's authority and cohesiveness.

No Georgia white family exemplifies this effort to change traditions while retaining some parts of the past more than Walter B. and Sallie Barker Hill. Born in Talbotton, Georgia, in 1851, Walter Hill grew up in a slaveholding family outside of Macon, where his father, Barnard, read the law. The Hills, members of the Old South aristocracy, were devout Methodists and were interested in expanding Methodist schools in Georgia. During the Civil War, the Hills split their family for safety but apparently survived financially. Like many sons of the elite, Walter attended the University of Georgia, graduating in 1870. He then received his law degree from Mercer University and formed a law partnership with a friend in Macon in 1873.

In 1879, Walter met and married Sallie Barker, who would help shape his vision for Georgia's future. Barker's father was a liberal Episcopalian businessman from Connecticut who made sure his children were well educated. Why the Barkers moved to Georgia is not known, but Sallie attended Wesleyan Female College in Macon and later did postgraduate work at Fort Edward Institute in New York. She returned to teach at Wesleyan, where she met Walter Hill. The couple eventually had two daughters, Parna and Mary, and two sons, Roger and Walter B. Jr.[19] Young and educated, Sallie and Walter Hill represented the post–Civil War generation that believed some reforms were necessary if Georgia was to become a part of the modern world. Unlike some New South advocates who focused on industrial development, including Hill's prominent classmate, Henry Grady, the editor of the *Atlanta Constitution,* the Hills emphasized education reform as the means to accomplish changes.

Walter B. Hill, ca. 1900. Hill was a staunch
education reformer and eventually became
chancellor of the University of Georgia.
(Courtesy of Hargrett Rare Book and
Manuscript Library, University of
Georgia Libraries.)

In the early decades of their marriage, the Hills worked for temperance and
frequently held temperance meetings at their home in Macon. Walter Hill re-
vised Georgia's legal codes three times from 1873 to 1895 and was eventually
elected president of the Georgia bar. But the Hills' interest in Progressive reforms extended beyond temperance and particularly included education. As
Methodists, the Hills believed in denominational education, yet they also
donated to the law school at the Southern Baptists' Mercer University. The
Hills' stance on Prohibition made them attractive to Baptist and Methodist
advocates of denominational education as well as to reformers who sought to
strengthen a nondenominational public education system. So when Hill decided to seek the chancellorship of Georgia's contentious and belligerent university system, he seemed the perfect candidate for the job. Embodying Progressive beliefs in education reform, centralization, efficiency, and temperance
in addition to advocating moderate reforms for black education, Hill took over
the post in 1899.[20]

Reconstructing a gendered public role for white middle-class women, Sallie
Barker Hill organized the Georgia School Improvement Club, affiliated with
the Association for the Betterment of Schools in Southern States, and served
as head of the Georgia Educational Campaign Fund in the early 1900s. As her
husband spoke publicly about the need to modernize Georgia's university system and teach such utilitarian subjects as education, agriculture, economics,

and sociology, Sallie spoke across the state about the need to improve the appearance of and to invest more money in public schools.[21] She urged white women's clubs and church groups to purchase books and equipment for local schools. Together, the Hills created a gendered framework for advocacy of Progressive education policies in Georgia.

Walter Hill's many accomplishments during his brief tenure as chancellor include increasing funds for the University of Georgia, constructing more academic buildings and a new library, promoting normal schools to train teachers, and defusing the denominational battles between Methodists and Baptists over the university's status. Hill ensured that the University of Georgia would retain its status as a Morrill Land Grant school by creating an education department that admitted men and women.[22] Demonstrating the penchant for efficiency and rationalization that marked many Progressives, Hill sought to coordinate curriculum between black and white colleges and to establish a state system of accredited high schools.

Following Walter Hill's death from exhaustion in 1906, Sallie Hill remained active in the temperance campaign and the School Improvement Club, joined by the indomitable Rebecca Latimer Felton. While Felton worked primarily for white school reform, Hill visited black and white schools across the state in the early 1900s, endlessly encouraging counties to raise taxes to improve their schools. Working with the Georgia Federation of Women's Clubs and the white Georgia Education Association, Hill urged teachers and Georgians to "arouse minds and hearts of our people to the needs and rights of the children."[23] But she recognized, as did some other reformers and philanthropists, that the fundamental problem in southern education was "essentially the problem of reaching the farmers for their children." Rural schools, black and white, represented the most serious obstacle in southern education because white rural men had "an intense, hard-to-be touched individualism [and were] slow to change, wary of new ideas, and not easily converted to any scheme out of [the] usual order of living."[24] Southern lady that she was, Sallie Barker Hill gracefully captured the tenacity and obstinacy of southern paternalism.

Walter and Sallie Hill bequeathed a gendered legacy to their sons and daughters, who also became advocates for Georgia school reform. Parna Hill attended Wesleyan College in Macon and Randolph-Macon College in Virginia. Returning to Georgia, she attended the State Normal School in Athens and later become a home economics teacher there. With her mother, Parna became a suffragist and later joined the Georgia League of Women Voters. Because the league advocated informed citizens, it provided another venue for the Hills' agenda for education reform, with the league pushing compulsory education and more county libraries. Mary Hill taught in Savannah and married a fellow teacher, Brian Brown. Walter B. Hill Jr. worked for the Georgia Department of Education under Dr. Marion Luther Brittain in 1920 and became rural inspector of black schools for the GEB in 1924.

In spite of the Hills' extensive advocacy of black education reform, most Georgia reformers ignored that effort and heeded only the calls on behalf of white rural schools. In a world where blacks were seen as little more than menial laborers, many reformers saw African American education as irrelevant. White rural schools were a different matter. Brittain, who served as state school superintendent from 1910 to 1922 and was a staunch Baptist, like most other Georgia reformers, knew that provisions had to be made on behalf of white rural students primarily to avoid white desertion of farms in favor of areas with better schools, as had occurred in the cases of the Clark and Smith families.[25]

School funding was also hampered by a deeply ingrained opposition to taxes. As State Superintendent Brittain wrote in 1910, "The man living in the country, in this State at least, besides his ancestral antipathy toward taxation has generally been marked by his intense individuality and love of freedom." Brittain explained that the tax system failed to support rural schools adequately, which he believed led to migration to towns and desertion of the countryside. "Injure the country," he wrote, "and, as a great statesman has declared, the grass will grow in the streets of the town. The country has always been the nursery of our great men and it should be fostered, not drained."[26] Five years later, Brittain again excoriated state legislators, stating, "The idea seems to have been that it were better to educate a few of us to rule over and manage the affairs of the many. To this very hour it is practically impossible to change the inborn and inbred feelings of many old leaders on this subject."[27] Brittain's comments echoed remarks from GEB members regarding many rural Georgians' and their legislators' hostility to taxation. Yet he also expressed a concern with the potential migration from rural to urban areas, a move he feared would break Georgia's cherished rural lifestyle. Still, his statements demonstrate the appalling lack of interest in education in many counties. Even by 1930, when most counties had increased their educational appropriations, the collapse of the cotton market meant that few counties could meet their obligations to support public schools.

Although some fathers seemed reluctant to relinquish control of their children to public schools, other parents clearly recognized the need for better education. With the assistance of the GEB and the advocacy of Chancellor Hill, Joseph Stewart, a professor of secondary education at the University of Georgia, was appointed state high school inspector. Stewart's responsibilities included promoting rural high schools and implementing Hill's plan for accrediting high schools. Indeed, because of Hill and Stewart's efforts, Georgia became the first southern state to propose a system of accreditation.[28] Still, Georgia's schools faced numerous obstacles. In 1904, Stewart reported that a scant .5 percent of white students attended a high school. Of that number, 58 percent resided in towns or cities. If local superintendents hired most teachers from local schools, then the teachers obviously lacked even a high school education, much less any normal training.[29]

Yet the problem with teacher training was more than the restrictions of a conservative constitution, more than inadequate funding for high schools or normal schools. At issue were some fundamental values for Georgians who privileged local control over state mandates. While reformers such as Hill, Brittain, Stewart, and Branson used the Progressives' language of efficiency, hierarchical management, and professional training for teachers, local school board members and their constituencies fought to preserve their authority over how and by whom their children were taught.[30] County and independent school boards graded teachers' exams and issued local teaching certificates. These certificates, which were not transferable among counties, allowed neighborhoods to determine the sort of women who should teach their children—primarily local women who echoed their communities' religious and moral standards.[31] Baptists dominated most school boards, although some Methodists were also members, and their religious belief in local autonomy shaped their claims for preserving their authority. To demand centralized state authority over teacher training and hiring quashed traditions of community and religious control. As Joseph Stewart wrote to Dr. Wallace Buttrick of the GEB in 1903, "There had been so much said against the University by preachers in their annual sermons on 'Christian Education' that the people in many sections did not look upon the University as theirs but as an alien institution tending to develop godless men, because [it was] opposed to religion and manned by infidel professors."[32]

All that Chancellor Hill had tried to accomplish for the University of Georgia, Georgia colleges, and high schools seemed to face constant threats from Baptist and Methodist ministers who believed in denominational schools for higher education. In 1913, the Georgia State Department of Education agreed to the GEB's proposal to fund a rural school supervisor, and Brittain appointed George D. Godard, a white educator and large landowner from Moultrie. Godard noted the "peculiar" situation in Georgia "on account of former religious emphasis laid on things in the South."[33] Indeed, such concerns about Georgia's state of educational affairs were noted through the 1920s. Philanthropist George Foster Peabody wrote to Dr. Wickliffe Rose of the GEB in 1925 that Georgia politics were "a dreadful mess" in part because of the "insistent pride in 'old Georgia,'" a factor that Peabody thought it would be necessary to "break down."[34] Peabody echoed many of his friend Walter Hill's concerns by addressing two main issues. First, few white Georgians had any interest in changing the essential hierarchical structure of southern society: not only should blacks be denied educational opportunities, but women also should be carefully screened before they were allowed out of the household and into a classroom. Many Georgians agreed with author and columnist Corra Mae White Harris when she wrote that "mass . . . training can never produce the same effect in character and efficiency" as the family and the church. Harris noted that teachers needed to be chosen for qualities other than their knowledge, including Christian background, moral habits, and proper values, that should be inculcated in their students.[35]

Concerns about the religious background of instructors at universities, colleges, and high schools focused not only on the morals prospective teachers would learn but also on the type of supervision students would have while attending school away from their households, churches, and communities. Several writers in the *Christian Index*, Georgia's white Baptist newspaper, feared that secular education might ignore children's spiritual interests.[36] The Reverend W. H. Faust wrote that local residents must "evangelize then teach. Make disciples and then teach them to observe all things that He commands."[37]

Many Georgia Baptists and Methodists linked Christianity with education because being a Christian meant being a better citizen. Reformers therefore sought to reassure Baptist and Methodist leaders in communities as well as at Mercer University and Emory University that students would be instructed and supervised according to cultural standards of appropriate religious and moral behavior.[38] Stewart modified his rhetoric in speeches at Georgia churches, crafting his crusade for secular high schools in language acceptable to Baptist and Methodist members. "The new school," he declared in a speech at the Conference on Education of the Methodist Church, South in 1911, "is not as godless as some declare. . . . Religion or its opposite is present just as surely as the teacher is present." Stewart maintained that communities could maintain religious life by insisting on teachers' high moral character. Combining schools with churches and households would effectively train the character of both students and teachers. The church, Stewart insisted, must guide people to see that education was part of their Christian duty.[39]

Notwithstanding piecemeal attempts by Georgia Baptist reformers such as Brittain, Stewart, and Mell L. Duggan to centralize and standardize the teaching profession, teacher training and requirements for teacher certification remained securely in the hands of local superintendents and school boards. In 1910 Brittain called for the state board of education to begin granting professional teaching certificates that would be valid in any Georgia county. Brittain claimed that Georgians' "nightmare about centralized power from which we have suffered so long" had hindered efforts to find qualified instructors for the summer teacher institutes.[40] He also noted the lack of education among county school superintendents and local politicians. Without educational reforms, Brittain argued that Georgia children would lag behind other children in the modern age.[41] Brittain, Godard, Stewart, and Duggan reiterated the concerns of many GEB executives, such as Buttrick and Abraham Flexner. All shared an interest in developing an efficient, organized hierarchy in the State Department of Education as a means to implement improved teacher training and schools.[42] These reformers believed that better-trained teachers would result in improved literacy rates for whites as well as more efficient workers for expanding industries.

Godard, for example, traveled throughout rural Georgia and received an annual salary of $3,500 from the GEB between 1913 and 1919. Although his primary duties entailed supervision of African American schools and teacher training, he also observed and reported flaws in white county teacher institutes. "In the South," he wrote to Buttrick in 1914, "the word 'training' and not 'Education' expresses the need of both races."[43] For these men, training entailed vocational instruction that organized skills for the new industrial world defined by such northern philanthropic organizations as the GEB or by state specialists in education. Such skills included greater efficiency in agriculture, diversity in crop production, improved methods for canning and preserving fruits and vegetables, and a minimal educational level of literacy and arithmetic as determined by the State Department of Education.

From 1910 to 1940, these needs led to greater legislative actions by the Georgia General Assembly that resulted in state certification requirements and a centralized university system in which teacher education could be controlled.[44] In 1912 the General Assembly approved the Stovall Amendment, which recognized the state's responsibility to provide a high school education, making Georgia the last state in the nation to approve of public high schools.[45] Other legislation included reorganization of the State Department of Education and designation of the authority to grant teacher certificates to the department. Counties still retained the power to grant local licenses, but the state now issued three types of licenses, all of which could be recognized by any Georgia county. In addition to a primary elementary, general elementary, or high school license, a prospective teacher could obtain a professional normal certificate if he or she had graduated from a state-approved normal school or a professional college certificate if he or she had graduated from an approved college where the curriculum included three education courses.[46] Brittain had initiated the process of locating the authority for certification in the state rather than the county. Moreover, by offering two types of professional certificates, the Department of Education had underscored the benefits of specific state-approved education or normal instruction.

Still, GEB members remained dissatisfied and pushed for greater centralization. Calling Georgia "the most primitive State educationally that I have yet been in," Dr. Frank Bachman, a member of the GEB, noted in 1925 that the state did little to exercise its power of certification and continued to leave this authority to local county school boards. While astounded at the lack of state mandates concerning teacher certification, Bachman also remarked that to "take this power away from the County Superintendents and require certificates of all city teachers is a brave undertaking."[47] Georgia reformers knew that any certification reforms had to come from fellow Georgians, since "Our people seem to resent any outside interference."[48] And slowly yet deliberately, the Georgia State Department of Education began to do just that.

Other reforms, such as the Barrett-Rogers law, passed in 1919, furnished state funds for school districts that consolidated schools and established high schools, thereby providing ninth and tenth grades locally for white women who wanted to teach. In addition to the 1919 Elder-Carswell Bill, which required counties to levy a five mill tax to support schools, and federal legislation such as the 1917 Smith-Hughes Act, which appropriated funds for industrial education, most Georgia counties managed to fund two-year high schools for whites by 1935. By 1937, through the combined efforts of State Superintendent Brittain and Duggan and agents paid by the GEB such as Stewart and Godard, only the State Department of Education issued certification for white teachers, and all teachers were required to take courses on the science of teaching and to study the state manual for teachers. To make these courses accessible to white teachers, the state continued to sponsor summer institutes and evening courses on educational training.

Although these reforms increased the state's authority over teacher certification, white women continued to use a variety of means to acquire their normal training until after World War II. Reflecting a persisting hodgepodge of county requirements, prospective teachers achieved certification by attending county or city high schools, district agricultural and mechanical (A & M) schools, or normal or four-year colleges. How they obtained certification was contingent on their family's economic means. Daughters from families that lacked access to high schools and could not afford to pay board at normal or A & M schools could not become teachers.

Some women, predominantly those from middle-class families in cities and towns, earned four-year degrees with their families' assistance. Charters Smith Embry and Margaret Andreae Collins attended private women's colleges supported by Baptist or Presbyterian churches such as Brenau College in Gainesville and Agnes Scott College in Atlanta. In fact, Georgia white women who wanted four-year degrees had to attend private colleges, since the state university did not admit women until 1918, when the policy was changed to reflect the impact of women's work during World War I as well as the suffrage movement. Private women's colleges offered a traditional or classical education, including academic subjects, foreign languages, religion, and domestic skills.[49] Unlike many rural women, students at these schools avoided work scholarships and uniforms. Yet these opportunities largely resulted from an education at a city high school.

Most white prospective teachers from rural areas managed to attend a summer session or at least one year at a normal school. Ruth Smith Waters, for example, went to the State Normal School in Athens after her first year of teaching in 1929. She took courses in the history and principles of education, reading texts such as John Dewey's works as well as Georgia's teaching manual, written by the University of Georgia's Thomas Jackson Woofter.[50] Similarly, Martha Breedlove Buice attended the State Normal School for two years, with funding provided by a loan from the General Federation of Women's Clubs in Monroe, Georgia. In addition to the courses Waters took, Buice studied child and educational psychology, tests and measurements, and public school curriculum. At the completion of the course, Buice earned a normal certificate that allowed her to obtain a professional teacher's certificate.[51]

Normal schools reinforced the religious, familial, and cultural values with which students had grown up, even as the institutions replaced these values with formal educational structures, including matrons who supervised women's attire and behavior. To attend the State Normal College, renamed Georgia State Teachers College in 1926, women had to bring bedding, towels, and personal items.[52] Board and fees rose from $110 per year in 1913 to $165 in 1930, not including the cost of books.[53] Students also had to pay for their uniforms, which cost approximately $20 and had to be purchased in Athens. Dormitory matrons inspected female students' appearance and attire: "I wore navy blue suits," recalled Martha Breedlove Buice, "and white blouses. . . . They had to be kept clean, and they had the stiff collar, big collar."[54] According to Waters, the matrons "walked around with a yardstick, and if your skirt was not down to the proper length, you would catch it. We wore uniforms of blue dresses with a black scarf and on Sundays we would have a white blouse with a dark suit. [The matron] inquired about the glint in my hair. She thought it was dyed," a clear infraction of the rules.[55] In addition to their courses, students had to attend church on Sunday mornings and vespers services on weekday evenings as well as study the Bible. Visiting hours and curfews were strictly enforced, and students who violated the rules were sent home.

Some women enjoyed their years at the normal schools in Milledgeville and Athens; others did not. Waters objected to the matron's questions about her hair. Mary Hall Swain from Calhoun loathed the rules and found the uniforms "horrible." Swain recalled hiding in a closet or under her bed to avoid having to march in line for a mile from campus to church.[56] In contrast, however, Fanny and Charlotte McClure from Acworth loved the uniforms and church attendance.[57]

Some women who could not afford the fees at the normal school attended one of the district A & M schools created by the Georgia legislature in 1906 to supplement the newly created white normal schools in Athens and Milledgeville and high schools in urban areas. These A & M schools, one located in each congressional district, offered advanced education specifically for white rural youths who lacked access or funds for high schools. Funded by fertilizer inspection fees from the State Department of Agriculture, the twelve A & M schools offered agricultural and domestic courses at the high school level and provided dormitories for some students. Counties within each district eagerly competed to host the schools, which also served as sites for teacher training.[58] Powder Springs in the seventh district and Clarkesville in the ninth qualified as locations for agricultural and mechanical schools in the up-country.

White rural women who desired education beyond ninth or tenth grade grabbed opportunities for advanced education at the A & M schools. Ruth Smith Waters's parents sent her to Monroe A & M for eleventh grade and teacher certification. At the school, each student worked in addition to attending classes. Every morning, Waters "got up and went over and brought Dr. J. Herbert Walker and his wife's breakfast back to the cottage. While they ate breakfast, I made up the feather bed. I had to turn that feather bed over every morning." The school deducted fifteen cents for every hour she worked from her bill, but the work "was required. You had to put your time in when you were there."[59]

White A & M schools taught primarily home economics and agricultural classes. Female students wore uniforms, some made before entering the schools and some made while attending school: as Waters remembered, "We all had to make our Sunday uniform—the winter coat, the suit, and the white blouse—at the school. That was our assignment. We started that in September and had to have that suit ready to wear by November. There was no academic preparation for a teacher, but you had to be good enough academically to pass the test." After she completed eleventh grade, Waters took the teachers' exam and got a perfect score. Although she was only seventeen and teachers were supposed to be eighteen, Walker awarded her a first-grade certificate and gave her a teaching position at Walker Park School. Within two years, Waters's father, still a trustee at the Chestnut Mountain Schools, coaxed her to return home to teach.[60]

Still other women improvised other means to become teachers. Jane Thigpen Alexander, who came from a rural family with ten children, saw a brochure on Rabun Gap Industrial School in Rabun County. Founded by Presbyterian missionaries in 1905 in White County for mountain children, the school offered white students classes, work on the school farm, and worship in chapel services. "We worked in the summer and then we worked two days a week, which paid our way through school," Alexander remembered. "At that time we wore uniforms, which was good, because most of us didn't have many clothes anyway. . . . We went to the Methodist church one Sunday and the Baptist one Sunday. We lined up and walked in twos to church."[61]

As at the state A & M schools, Rabun Gap assigned male and female students different chores. Women worked in the laundry, worked in the kitchen, or cleaned the floors. "My job," recalled Jane Thigpen Alexander, "was to clean the halls, to mop them, the bathrooms."[62] Alexander also cleaned one of the faculty cottages and was startled to discover that one of the instructors had multiple pairs of shoes lined up under the bed. Alexander had only one pair of shoes. School subjects included the Bible, English, history, math, and science. After she finished her studies at Rabun Gap, Alexander found a teaching position at Clarkesville in Habersham County.

For Leona Clark Williams, family and friends furnished the means for her to become a teacher. After Joe Asher, a peddler and department store owner in Franklin, let Williams board in his home and attend the local high school in exchange for housework and English lessons for his relatives, she considered the possibilities for attending college. After completing high school in 1928, an uncle who was a Methodist minister got her a work scholarship at Tennessee Wesleyan College. To earn her board, Williams "had to clean the matron's room and the office. And I had to get up and fix breakfast for eighty-five girls in the dormitory. Then after that first year, a teacher got interested in me, and she taught me to talk different. You know, I had all that mountain brogue. And I won a full scholarship for debating on the debating team." Williams received some teacher training and even had practice teaching, although her large family had already prepared her to handle children. Although she never wore a uniform, Williams, like other future teachers, faced regulations concerning curfews, socializing, drinking alcohol, and dancing. During summers, Williams worked in a woolen mill or did housework for relatives to earn extra money. She graduated in 1933, although she missed the ceremonies. Lacking funds for a cap and gown, she simply packed her belongings and headed to her parents' home, now in northern Hall County.[63] Without the assistance of such friends, family members, and teachers, Williams undoubtedly would not have attended school beyond the sixth grade, since her parents had little to spare for advanced education for their twelve children.

Whatever means Georgia women used to attend school beyond the seventh or eighth grade, becoming a teacher required them to pass the state exam, which covered such topics as agriculture, arithmetic, geography, spelling, school law, grammar, history, physiology, reading, and school management and was administered by county or district superintendents. Future teachers were advised to read standard teaching texts like Woofter's *Teaching in Rural Schools*. Woofter, dean of the University of Georgia's School of Education and a close friend of Walter B. and Sallie Hill, included information on rural schools, organization of the schoolroom, classroom management, and lesson plans for the fundamentals of education like reading, arithmetic, history, penmanship, and sanitation. Woofter maintained that teachers should have "a pleasing personality," "a lively imagination," "an appreciation of rural life," and "good moral character," as well as good health because of the strain of the job.[64]

Some exam questions, notably those in arithmetic or spelling, demanded exact answers, whereas other answers, such as those regarding the "ideal rural school" or how the school should relate to the community, were open to interpretation by the superintendent who graded the exam.[65] These questions allowed superintendents to hire preferred candidates and did little to present an objective standard for employment.

BLACK WOMEN IN the early 1900s faced the same barriers to becoming teachers as rural white women did, with added obstacles posed by the fact that Georgia's certification system was fraught with racism and inadequate funding for African Americans. Georgia education reformers struggled to convince counties to increase taxes to support local schools and teacher training but paid scant attention to teacher training for blacks, especially after the turn of the century. Northern philanthropic organizations such as the GEB and the Julius Rosenwald Fund (JRF) pushed their agendas for industrial training schools and county teacher institutes in the South.[66] Rather than offering the same general education or industrial education white southerners received, these schools accorded teacher training along industrial methods that modeled practice teaching for manual labors such as laundry work, domestic labor, agricultural labor, and sewing.[67] At times, the GEB's and the JRF's priorities supported white Georgians' concerns about education for blacks. Officials of these philanthropic organizations often had their own reasons for enforcing what became known as the Hampton-Tuskegee model. While these leaders wanted to support southern education, they also wanted to create good workers for the nation.

Fort Valley High and Industrial School in Fort Valley, Agricultural and Mechanical School in Forsyth, and Atlanta University, among other African American institutions, periodically received funds from the GEB.[68] Industrial training for African Americans, however, differed considerably from that offered to rural whites in A & M schools. Whereas white schools provided instruction on better farming methods for landowners and training in repair of textile machinery or automobiles in accordance with the state manual for teachers, African American rural schools provided training in janitorial work, dressmaking, cooking, and carpentry.[69] From the outset, education beyond grade school reinforced the hierarchical social system. If few counties funded schools beyond the seventh grade for whites at the turn of the century, far fewer allocated public funds for such schools for African Americans.

Obtaining funds from Baptist, Methodist, Episcopal, and Presbyterian churches outside the state, Spelman College, Morehouse College, Knox Institute, and Paine Institute, among others, offered high school and industrial training for blacks. Of all the denominational organizations, the American Missionary Association (AMA), founded by black and white northern abolitionists, was the most successful in the South. Among the many AMA universities and institutes, Fisk University, Knox Institute, and Talladega College emphasized academic training in addition to industrial work and religious instruction. At the same time, AMA schools sought to undermine black evangelical Protestant practices, deeming them inferior to northern Congregational practices.[70] Southern blacks objected to these criticisms and eagerly reasserted traditional worship traditions. Still, AMA schools provided invaluable assistance to Georgia blacks by offering education similar to that offered to whites and by underscoring the black communities' regard for family and community interdependence.

One of the first AMA schools in the South was Atlanta University, founded in 1865. After five years, the Georgia legislature allocated eight thousand dollars to the school under the provisions of the Morrill Land Grant Act of 1862. Almost immediately, white Georgians attacked this appropriation of public funds on the grounds that the school's curriculum was too advanced for Georgia's black students and that the school practiced social equality. Not only did white teachers work with African American teachers, but white students attended classes with black students. Various legislators tried to cut public funds for Atlanta University, favoring the creation of a separate institute for African Americans that would teach only black students and train them for elementary school teaching and agricultural labor. Finally, in 1887, the state withdrew its appropriation when visitors once again complained about the presence of white students—in this case, some faculty members' children. To ensure that such integrated education would never again occur, the legislature considered mandating that all educational facilities be segregated by race, and in 1889, Georgia legislators passed the Glenn Bill, which did just that.[71] However, the bill also provided for the creation of a normal school for African Americans.

The state initially chose Athens for the site of this new school for training black teachers, but following protests from Athens's white residents, Savannah became the location for the Georgia State Industrial College for Colored Youth (GSIC). Richard Robert Wright, an 1876 graduate of Atlanta University, former president of Ware High School in Augusta, and organizer of the Georgia State Teachers' Association, was chosen as president. Wright established a normal, industrial, and college curriculum. By 1898, the school admitted black women in a domestic science program. Lacking a separate dormitory, these women boarded with members of the black community.[72] In 1899, Wright began a series of conferences that drew black farmers from Georgia, Florida, and South Carolina. By 1906 he and several farmers organized the Annual Colored State Fair in Macon, a weeklong event that drew thousands of African Americans.[73]

Active in the Republican Party, Wright constantly sought ways to organize Georgia blacks as well as educate them. In 1912 he and other blacks established the Negro Civic Improvement League, which met at the college. These efforts alienated northern philanthropists concerned about the collegiate education at the school and antagonized white Georgians, who wanted the school to offer only industrial and basic normal courses. Wright also estranged himself from other black Republicans in Savannah. They believed he monopolized the position of Republican delegate to the national and state political conventions and wanted other African Americans to have the opportunity to serve.[74] Wright tired of the controversies after more than forty years in Georgia education and in 1921 left with his family for Philadelphia, where he began a banking career.

White reformer Walter B. Hill's work complemented Wright's efforts at GSIC. From 1887 until his death in 1906, Hill called for better schools for blacks. As a racial moderate at a time of disfranchisement, establishment of poll taxes, and escalating violence against black men and women, Hill was appalled at Georgia's rising crime rate. As a member of the bar, he advocated legislation that would ban lynchings and hold officers in charge of prisoners responsible for their safety.[75] At the same time, Hill believed that blacks were little more than children who had to be trained and educated. In a famous address, "Uncle Tom without a Cabin," printed in the *Century* in 1887, Hill described the problems blacks faced after slavery. African Americans lacked the "assured peace and plenty of the old regime, unable to reap any benefits of the new."[76] To Hill, blacks needed to be educated in the "responsibilities of citizenship," and states must work to eliminate illiteracy. But this, he argued, was not simply the responsibility of the South but was also the responsibility of the nation, and he called for federal education assistance. He opposed the 1890 Blair Bill, an unsuccessful congressional measure that would have provided national funding for segregated schools but without racial discrimination in the distribution of funds. Yet he argued that new legislation could be passed that would allow manual and agricultural training for blacks.[77]

While serving as the University of Georgia's chancellor, Hill became a member of the Southern Education Board, a coalition of white northern philanthropists and prominent southern educators, and he stated in 1903 that the South had a duty to educate blacks. In the Old South, he continued, slaves had been faithful to their masters; now it was whites' turn to be faithful to blacks by offering education. Paternalist that he was, Hill believed that the Hampton and Tuskegee Institutes provided the best models for educating blacks. To him, black education had to be suited for black life, which meant agriculture and manual training. Still, Hill realized that some blacks needed advanced education to become physicians, teachers, ministers, and lawyers. In believing that blacks deserved better medical care and legal advice, he distinguished himself from other white Progressives. More than any other Georgia white male re-

former, Hill and his family clearly modeled the best of the New South and il-
luminated the problems that black educators faced while advocating higher
education for blacks.

Other African American college presidents met obstacles from Georgia
whites and northern philanthropists. John and Lugenia Burns Hope and Henry
and Florence Hunt worked for black education much more forcefully than the
Hills. In 1898, when John Hope began the formidable task of making Atlanta's
Morehouse College one of the best educational institutions for black southern
men in 1898, his wife, Lugenia, taught at neighboring Spelman College. Ten
years later, she organized the Neighborhood Union, which created a citywide
black women's network for child care, sanitation, educational improvements,
and political discussions.[78] The Hunts, graduates of Atlanta University, left
teaching positions in Alabama with their three children in 1904, when Henry
became principal at Fort Valley High and Industrial, where both he and his wife
also taught.[79] Henry Hunt fought to build the school's reputation as he, like
John Hope, walked a fine line between paternalist white benefactors' restrictions on black education and the African American community's needs and
desires for better education. Like Wright at GSIC, Hunt tolerated periodic ob-
servations and reports from whites, including unannounced visits from Chancellor Hill, who was determined to ensure that Fort Valley follow a strict industrial training curriculum.[80] In addition to her teaching responsibilities,
Florence Hunt organized a temperance legion for the students.[81] The Hunts'
work eventually reached beyond Fort Valley, as the school began to present
agricultural exhibitions for other central Georgia blacks. Furthermore, urged
on by their notion of racial uplift, the Hunts combined the efforts of Fort Valley High and Industrial and local black and white churches to sponsor health
programs and aid to black schools.[82]

In addition to these efforts not explicitly associated with churches, black
evangelical Protestants sought to establish schools with black southern instructors. African American Methodists and Baptists funded Morris Brown
College and Northwest High and Industrial School in Gainesville, among
other such institutions. Jeruel High School in Athens, for example, was
founded by the Jeruel Baptist Association in 1879 for the purpose of education
and salvation.[83] While the school offered competent instruction to blacks, it,
like other schools funded by black Georgia associations, was consistently
plagued by financial problems. Similarly, Northwestern High and Industrial
faced economic problems throughout its fifty years of existence. Part of the
problem was the inability of black Baptist associations to unite and consoli-

date their resources. Not until 1915 did black Georgians form the General Missionary Baptist Convention, and even then, the group's limited funds were stretched among fifty-two schools across the state. Located in towns and cities, black denominational schools lay beyond walking distance of most rural blacks. For any education beyond the sixth or seventh grade, then, blacks had to relocate to different areas and find resources for tuition and board.

Like white women, black women had a variety of routes to teacher certification, although one significant distinction existed. Unlike white women, who had access to higher education supported by public funds, black women sought private institutions funded by religious denominations or northern philanthropy largely because the Georgia legislature allocated minimal funds for black education beyond the elementary level.

Board and fees were beyond the reach of most women of both races. White women who managed to attend a state normal school paid more than one hundred dollars, while black women who attended GSIC paid half that amount. Yet other obstacles black women faced contributed to higher overall costs. First, African Americans frequently had to leave their families to attend high schools in cities or towns, and families sacrificed to keep their daughters in school. Second, black families scraped together the financial means to purchase fabric for clothing and sheets, books, and personal articles necessary for school. During its first thirty years, GSIC awarded only forty bachelor's degrees and 387 normal diplomas. Most students enrolled in the college's industrial programs or its high school.[84] Like Lucy Craft Laney, some black women attended private colleges such as Atlanta University, Spelman College, and even Haines Institute.

From the beginnings of public education in Georgia in the 1870s, all counties had discretion over the distribution of these funds. Even with changes from the 1919 Elder-Carswell Bill, which allowed counties to levy higher taxes, Plantation Belt counties in particular continued to divert public funds from black schools to white schools. Up-country counties objected to higher county taxes because they had lower combined populations of black and white children and less state funds to redirect to white schools (see chap. 1).[85]

Financing black schools faced other obstacles. Georgia, like all southern states, used monies intended for both black and white schools to improve white schools alone. Contending that African Americans contributed little to state revenues, white education reformers zealously guarded tax revenues for white schools. Despite paying county and state property, alcohol, and gasoline taxes (direct and indirect taxes), African Americans received little from this fund. Denied all but a small percentage of the public monies allocated to schools (which also included a portion of corporation and railroad taxes), blacks had to find additional resources. At times, this meant that the black community had to provide maintenance or building materials for schools; at other times, property for a school had to be deeded to the county.

For example, to receive Rosenwald funds to build a school for black children, African Americans had to match the amount requested from the fund, which varied from $500 to $1,500 depending on the size of the school. Community members often contributed equipment and helped build schools to keep costs low. According to a summary published in 1927, the total cost of schools built with Rosenwald Fund assistance totaled more $730,000. One-quarter of the money came from African Americans, with just under half from public funds and .06 percent from local whites' donations.[86] Even this amount fails to reflect the labor, supplies, and property blacks gave for schools. Thus, although blacks paid taxes for schools, the African American community, moderate whites, and northern philanthropy had to provide additional funds to build elementary schools for black children, a method blacks referred to as a double-tax system. Walter B. Hill Jr. warned in 1920 that the argument that blacks paid little tax for schools had no merit, especially when some counties drew "more money from the state than they paid in taxes."[87] Without black community support and Rosenwald funds, few elementary schools for blacks would have existed. In fact, black community traditions of self-help and interdependence were sustained by northern philanthropists. Moreover, because blacks had no choice but to send their children to private denominational schools for higher education, families compounded their financial burden, a compelling indication of their tenacity to educate some of their children.

Beulah Rucker Oliver's education illustrates the difficulties some families faced in obtaining schooling for their children. After she completed the sixth grade at the local school in Banks County, Oliver's parents sent her to Jeruel High School, no doubt because they were Baptists and because it was closer than schools in Atlanta. Yet Oliver remained at the school for only one month. Although jobs such as milking cows and cleaning for the principal's wife paid Oliver's tuition and even allowed her to send some money home to help her parents, crop failure forced her family to ask her to return home. Oliver desperately wanted to return to Athens for teacher training at Knox Institute. To attend Knox, Oliver rose before dawn, milked cows, and then completed chores at the principal's home before classes began at nine. At the school, she learned industrial teacher training and domestic skills such as sewing and cooking in addition to Latin and music. Each night she washed and ironed her only dress.

By the time Oliver graduated from Knox, almost ten years had passed since she left the Rucker home in Banks County.

Not all black women faced economic hardships as dire as Oliver's. Some of the first black educators in Georgia came from families like Lucy Craft Laney's that had marketable skills and could pay board and fees at colleges. Jessie Salmon Mosley, a teacher in Summersville, managed to attend Spelman Seminary in Atlanta for several terms with the assistance of work scholarships.

Godard's appointment as rural school supervisor for blacks indicates exactly how much interest the state had in black education, how far it had drifted since Walter B. Hill's call for black literacy in 1903.[88] Godard, who believed that he was qualified for the position by virtue of his experience as a large landowner supervising black sharecroppers, indicated his enthusiasm for the GEB's program of industrial training for blacks.[89] His enthusiasm no doubt came from the prospect of defusing the idea of black education once and for all by teaching blacks the most menial tasks possible to make them better and more pliant sharecroppers—quite a different standard than the Hills'. By the fall of 1913, Godard was journeying from county to county to stir interest in industrial training for black teachers. To Godard as well as GEB members and other Georgia educators, industrial training meant training teachers to instruct their students in manual labor and hygiene. In fact, the GEB paid for Godard to travel to Hampton Institute in Virginia to observe the "appropriate" method of training black teachers.[90]

Part of Godard's job entailed convincing Georgia whites that this industrial training differed decisively from the training whites received. "I have not found a man," wrote Godard, "who is unalterably opposed to this plan of education when it is properly explained to him." Godard emphasized that he was urging minimal industrial training rather than the more controversial meaning of classical education "as the view which [whites] should take." In one of his first reports to the GEB, Godard complained about African American teachers who taught students "a smattering of reading, writing, arithmetic, theoretic grammar, and a little geography, with no just comprehension of the meaning of any of it. These teachers are the most impractical part of the Negro population, and this is the reason why the white people are so much prejudiced to the education of the Negro: the training that the Negro child should get is omitted while a little theoretic education is poured . . . into his brain, without any means or ability to digest mentally what is poured in." Such academic learning was far less important, in Godard's opinion, than learning "how to sweep a house clean, or to make a bed decently."[91] Godard consequently sought to inform Georgia blacks and whites about the need for industrial teacher training rather than a traditional general education, thereby preparing African Americans for their "proper" position in the southern labor hierarchy.

Industrial training was advocated for most of Georgia's whites as well as the state's blacks.[92] Considerable differences existed, however, between industrial training for rural whites and blacks. Through district A & M schools in addition to home demonstration agents, Georgia reformers sought to improve farm and home production by increasing cotton yields and providing more efficient canning. Directed at rural white landowners, this training was intended to solidify their position in the hierarchy. In a similar manner, industrial training for white mill workers was intended to hone their labor skills by teaching them how to repair textile machinery and learn new textile technologies.[93] These industrial skills at best perpetuated a dependent rural and working class and at worst removed the possibility for many rural whites to enter such New South elite professions as law, medicine, and insurance sales. For blacks, the consequences of industrial training were even more detrimental. To maintain blacks' station as mudsills, reformers touted training in sweeping floors or making baskets, a substantially lower skill level than even that intended for mill hands.[94] From the outset, whites received all mill work except for the dirtiest, heaviest jobs, like janitorial tasks. More important, reformers always devoted more funding for and consideration to industrial training for whites than for blacks.

Brittain and Godard framed their appeal for black teacher training by using religious and cultural values of interdependence, duty, and obligation. Concerned that most whites no longer knew what African Americans were doing in their churches and schools, Brittain wrote that "our negligence about this injures us as much or more than the negro. As a matter of safety, protection, and insurance alone, to say nothing of any higher obligations, we should see that he receives [our attention]."[95] Part of the reformers' appeal was couched in language that bound the destiny of whites to that of blacks. If Georgia intended to improve its educational and literacy standards, it needed to "carry the Negroes along with the whites."[96] Reformers' appeals relied on biblical references that also urged whites to offer greater support to their schools. "No man," quoted Fort Land, supervisor of south Georgia's schools, "liveth unto himself and no man dieth unto himself."[97] In 1920, Brittain stated, "Every white man in Georgia must carry—besides the burden of educating his own family—practically the obligation of educating a negro family as well."[98]

Just as reformers like the Hills had in other educational campaigns evoked paternalism's language to renew white southerners' historical sense of responsibility for their community's education, Brittain and those like him used these terms to remind Georgians of their neglect of black teacher training.

Reformers' assurance that such training would only preserve blacks' status as manual laborers helped mitigate many whites' fears that educated blacks would no longer want to work as sharecroppers or domestic workers.[99] Even Walter Hill had repeatedly insisted that black education would lead to better citizenship. But he went further and suggested that properly educated blacks eventually might run their own farms and industries.[100] Such self-sufficiency, however, raised the specter of blacks existing beyond the reach of white authority and aroused fears of miscegenation. Hill's moderate paternalism in 1887 shifted to an explicit campaign to offer African Americans as little education as possible and to place it in the guise of industrial training. Paternalism, now underscored by virulent racism, could offer only the most limited gestures toward education for millions of people desperate to read.

Yet Brittain and Godard knew that they had to solicit support for black industrial schools on grounds other than white Georgians' Christian and paternalistic duties. Ever mindful of Georgia's poor reputation in the nation for inadequate education and increasingly cognizant of the state's agricultural predicaments of low returns and black migration to the North, these reformers insisted that improved literacy and schools would make African Americans better farm laborers and keep them in Georgia.[101] Godard noted that if black farmers learned better farming methods, "larger returns may be had for all interested parties."[102] "If the Negro," he wrote, "is a resource of the state, and he is, why should he not be made as profitable a resource as he may be?" Moreover, if African Americans continued their migration to the North, cotton production was at risk. And reformers knew that one way to keep blacks in Georgia was to improve education and teacher training. Godard noted the increased white interest in black education in Georgia that had been "brought about by the immigration of the negro."[103] The emphasis speaks volumes about Georgia's attitude toward black education. If expanding education would retain the cheap labor supply, then surely a few more shacks for black children could be built.

Walter B. Hill Jr., who became rural school agent for Negroes after Godard's 1919 resignation, brought a more modern attitude to the position. Just as his father saw southern education as a national problem, Hill regarded African American migration to the North (known as the Great Migration after World War I) as a national problem. Commenting on tensions between blacks and whites in northern labor unions, Hill stressed the need for improved educational facilities in the South as a means to slow blacks' migration.[104] He knew that many African Americans left Georgia because of poor schools and continuing frustrations about the lack of equality for blacks following their service in World War I. Citing North Carolina's success in using schools to keep black agricultural workers, Hill contended that Georgia had to increase school funds for blacks.[105] To preserve their rural agricultural heritage, Georgians had to convince local African Americans to remain.

Hill also mentioned that some blacks were heading north because of that region's better educational facilities.[106] Throughout the 1920s and 1930s, Georgia reformers such as Hill, Brittain, and others preached the need for better teacher training. Hill, scarcely a racial egalitarian though clearly a moderate, observed the Rosenwald schools' impact on many black settlements. He firmly believed, like his parents, that blacks deserved better educational opportunities than were currently available (see chap. 1). He knew that many African American families relocated to communities that had Rosenwald schools.[107] Hill faced a more difficult situation regarding teacher training than did other state rural agents, including Nathan Newbold of North Carolina, because Georgia relied almost exclusively on private funds from northern philanthropic organizations or religious groups to support black high schools and normal schools.

Georgia had the largest black population of any southern state during the early twentieth century, with more than 1.2 million African Americans, 41.7 percent of the state's total population of 3 million. Nevertheless, Georgia appropriated less money for the higher education of blacks than any other state with segregated land-grant schools.[108] In 1920, for example, state-funded white higher education institutions received almost six hundred thousand dollars, with Georgia Normal and Industrial College in Milledgeville alone receiving more than ninety thousand dollars. Yet only two institutions of higher education served the state's African American population—GSIC and Georgia Normal and Agricultural College—and they received ten and fifteen thousand dollars, respectively.[109] Walter Hill Jr. found this situation abominable.

Early in his tenure as rural school agent, Hill expanded two programs begun during Godard's years. Anna T. Jeanes, a Quaker philanthropist from Philadelphia, had become interested in improving education for southern blacks. Acquainted with members of the GEB and Southern Education Board, she donated more than $1 million in 1907 to the GEB for rural black schools. GEB officials used the money to hire black women teachers as district supervisors, enhancing black schools, assisting black teachers with curriculum, and relating schoolwork to black communities. These supervisors became known across the south as Jeanes teachers. Administered through the GEB, salaries were originally paid from the Jeanes Fund but were eventually taken over by counties. Up-country counties, including Hall and Gwinnett, had fewer than thirty black teachers and consequently failed to qualify for Jeanes teachers, although Jackson and Cobb Counties did. But even eligible counties had often refused to fund Jeanes supervisors. By 1924, Hill expanded the Jeanes Program into twenty-six counties. Hill also enlarged the teacher training institute program, insisting that each county build a training institute for black teachers and spend more money for black schools.[110] Notwithstanding Hill's efforts, however, no county training institute was ever located in northeast Georgia, which meant that Beulah Rucker Oliver and educators like her continued to train teachers without the interference and mandates of the GEB but also without financial assistance.

Hill wanted better black teacher training accomplished at GSIC because it received public funds and federal funds from the Smith-Hughes Act and the Morrill Land Grant. Of the more than four hundred students enrolled at GSIC in 1922, only sixteen took college courses; the rest attended the elementary and high schools. Moreover, at eight hundred dollars, the average faculty salary was more than three hundred dollars per year lower than the average salaries at the nation's other black land-grant schools. But Hill's actions for the Jeanes Program and determination to improve black teacher training in Georgia came at a time when most of Georgia's politicians were more concerned with membership in the Ku Klux Klan. In 1923 Hill reported GSIC to the federal government for abuse of funds and gross neglect. Following an investigation of the school, the federal government withdrew more than ten thousand dollars in Morrill funds in 1924, at which point State School Superintendent Nathaniel Ballard fired Hill.[111] Ballard, who the JRF and the GEB believed had connections to the Ku Klux Klan, was outraged that Hill had notified the federal government about the conditions at GSIC without notifying the Georgia State Department of Education. One of Hill's sisters, Mary Hill Brown, wrote to the other, Parna Hill, on June 1, 1924, "It makes my blood boil that Walter has to encounter all this rash injustice." Brown suspected rank political cronyism.[112]

Hill and federal government investigators were clearly appalled by the school's white trustees, who forbade the college president to leave the campus without their permission, and the abysmal educational courses, which advertised agricultural training while lacking any land or equipment to use. Pressured by the federal government to offer more academic courses, replace the current trustees, build a library, complete a women's dormitory, and provide toilet facilities for the men's dormitory, Ballard and the General Assembly assured the U.S. Department of Interior that the state would improve the school.[113] The federal government also demanded that the Georgia legislature increase the college's appropriation to at least thirty thousand dollars per year.

Many African American educators, including John Hope and H. A. Hunt, expressed to the GEB their shock at Hill's dismissal. They believed that Hill had made sincere efforts to improve education for blacks. Hill was reappointed to his position after Fort Land was elected state school superintendent in 1925 and kept that position when M. L. Duggan was elected in 1927.[114] To improve the conditions and curriculum at GSIC and ensure that the state would receive federal land-grant funds, Land, Hill, and the General Assembly created a board of trustees for the college. The trustees then appointed a new president, Benjamin F. Hubert, a graduate of Morehouse College who had completed a master's degree in agriculture at the University of Minnesota. He and the trustees started to implement changes recommended by the U.S. Bureau of Education evaluator. Hubert served at the college for more than twenty years.

Hill's firing demonstrated some white Georgians' continued reluctance to improve teacher training for blacks even when that training included only menial tasks such as domestic labor and farming. The incident indicated many Georgians' hostility to interference from the federal government, specifically when that interference had been instigated by a Georgian. Yet Hill's reinstatement also shows the extent to which organizations like the GEB and the federal government could affect southern education. By threatening to withdraw needed funds, the GEB ensured that reformers like Walter Hill Jr. remained in Georgia's Department of Education. Although the federal government refused to act on behalf of African American voting rights, the Department of Interior's actions showed that it could force states to improve education for blacks.

In the midst of the plethora of controversies and debates over teacher training for African Americans, some black women—like white women, with the assistance of their parents and communities—purposefully identified the best means to obtain certification. Some of Beulah Rucker Oliver's students, including two of her daughters, followed a career pattern decided by their mothers or mother figures.

African American teachers did not argue with their parents plans' for the future. Most of the daughters somehow knew they wanted to teach. Laura Mosley Whelchel and Dorothy Oliver Rucker, students at Beulah Rucker Oliver's State High and Industrial School in Hall County, never doubted that they would eventually become teachers. Dorothy, whose mother directed the school, felt herself almost preordained to become a teacher. At age fourteen, Dorothy had completed her education at the school. Because she was too young for college or normal school, her parents sent her to Atlanta in 1933 to attend Booker T. Washington High School. It never occurred to Rucker to question her parents' decision. "Your parents thought for you," she recalled, "and Mama decided I would be a teacher." In Atlanta, Dorothy boarded with the Burnses, longtime friends of her parents. Although Dorothy Rucker was the youngest student in the twelfth grade, she claims her biggest problem was finding the school each day. Still too young to attend college at Savannah or Atlanta, Rucker took the teacher's exam in Hall County, passed with a third-grade certificate, and was hired to teach at a school at Pleasant Hill with eighty-one students for fifteen dollars a month. She was sixteen years old. In 1937 she moved to her mother's school, where she taught grades one and two for the next fifteen years.[115]

Annie Mosley Martin, the oldest daughter in the Mosley family, took the teacher's exam in Hall County and began teaching at Beulah Rucker Oliver's school in the 1930s. Laura Mosley Whelchel taught in Greene County and then returned to the up-country to teach in Banks County. Like Dorothy Oliver Rucker, the Mosley sisters always wanted to be teachers, following in the footsteps of their mother and godmother, Beulah Rucker Oliver.

Other black women received advanced education at private schools. Rosa Penson Anderson attended Fort Valley State College for tenth and eleventh grade in 1938. By this time funded by the Episcopal Church, Fort Valley was one of the main teacher training schools for blacks in Georgia. Like other black women, Anderson funded her education by working at the school laundry and later in the office. Fort Valley structured the school day much the same way as Oliver's school did—scheduled study hours, Sunday services and vespers, and curfews. Anderson took specific teacher education courses such as methods of teaching in addition to general education courses in algebra, history, and English.[116] After Susie Weems Wheeler completed the elementary grades at Cartersville in 1930, her mother decided to send her to Griffin's Cabin Creek High School, a boarding school sponsored by the area's black Baptists.

Like the white schools with their enforcement of behavior codes, black schools upheld the moral standards expected by most African Americans. Before the 1930s, African American colleges and private high schools followed behavior and dress codes similar to those at white schools. Dress codes for black students never included uniforms but instead specified colors and fabrics. Students worked on campus, attended church services, and lived in sex-segregated dorms. With the exception of Spelman and Morehouse Colleges, black students, in contrast to the majority of white students, attended mixed-sex classes and church services. Students at GSIC began their day with morning prayers and attended church services and Sunday school. Students were forbidden to smoke, play cards, or dance. They followed curfews each evening and performed chores on campus. For violating the rules, students worked one hundred hours on the campus farm or were expelled.[117] At private colleges and universities such as Atlanta University, students wore simple white and navy blue clothing intended to promote democracy and habits of economy. Elaborate fabrics like silk and chiffon were banned for women. Students were expected to attend church and pledged to avoid using alcohol and tobacco.[118] By 1930, most schools began to ease these restrictions, reflecting the changes occurring in families across the nation as families modernized and recognized members' individual needs.

If white reformers continued to demand that blacks teachers train students to sweep floors or make hammer handles, black educators were equally deliberate in their pursuit of academics and racial uplift.[119] From the beginning, educators like Lucy Craft Laney and Richard R. Wright combined a classical curriculum with industrial training. They insisted that students receive a solid academic background with courses in Latin, music, philosophy, mathematics, science, history, and English.[120] Beulah Rucker Oliver included black history, oral recitations, Spenserian handwriting, and other general education subjects along with rug making and farming.[121] Using memorization work, spirituals, plays, and oral drills, Oliver's students sustained theological distinctions between black and white religions by learning a gospel of hard work and salvation. Salvation included work on earth—race work for their communities. Indeed, educators such as Oliver, Wright, and Laney raised money for their schools using industrial skills (for example, farming and rug making) that whites had intended as means of keeping black students in subordinate positions.

Oliver avoided using textbooks or manuals to train her students for teaching and prepare them for certification. Rather, she gave them practical experience in the classroom before they took the exam. "One time [Oliver] went off and left and didn't tell us where she was going," recalled Laura Mosley Whelchel. "Reverend Oliver said 'Well, you know Godmother wanted you to go ahead and open up the school. . . . You go on and do what she told you.'"[122]

To be sure, lowered expectations for black teachers affected their schools' resources. Teachers made do with secondhand books, benches instead of desks, painted boards for blackboards, and poor salaries. Yet because white reformers expected so little of black teachers and wanted even less from their students, Oliver and other educators were able to choose their own curriculum, away from the interference of white demands. Moreover, rural supervisors such as Godard and Hill rarely traveled as far as the up-country counties.[123] Focusing on the old Plantation Belt, which had the lion's share of the state's black population, supervisors repeatedly visited county training institutes funded by the GEB to insure that the appropriate teacher training was offered.[124] From 1915 through the 1930s, reformers expended little effort to oversee the curriculum in up-country counties. While black schools could have used GEB funding for teacher training institutes, Rucker and her fellow educators profited in a distinct way by avoiding white scrutiny. Believing blacks to be at a slower "stage of development," reformers apparently assured themselves that teachers would focus on making brooms and baskets rather than instructing students on arithmetic and history.[125] In any event, reformers were much too preoccupied with elevating white teachers' standards to be overly concerned with what was deemed an inferior people.

Although northern philanthropists and evangelical Protestants insisted on specific forms of education, the existence of African American education in Georgia nonetheless depended on such groups' help.[126] Even whites' best efforts resulted in little more than paternalistic banalities. Following a 1919 wave of violence against blacks, educated blacks and moderate southern whites formed the Commission on Interracial Cooperation (CIC) in Atlanta. For the next twenty years, black and white professionals debated how to improve blacks' lives, necessarily focusing on education. Yet the CIC rarely did more than discuss issues. It did little to promote antilynching legislation or to change public attitudes about funding education for African Americans.[127] At the core of moderate white thoughts about the potential of African Americans lay notions of dependence or mental defects. Agendas for meetings underscored the broader perception that black people had problems to be managed. White sympathies notwithstanding, race relations—referred to as the "Negro problem"—were little more than a cover for racist language drawing from white supremacy or white Progressives' pity.[128]

REFORMERS FOCUSED ON greater centralization and professionalization of teacher certification, especially for white women. Closely observing GEB fund allotments and the proliferation of Rosenwald schools across the Georgia clay, white reformers urged counties to increase their taxes to build better high schools and support improved teacher certification. To M. L. Duggan, a former rural supervisor and state school superintendent from 1927 to 1932, the "Rosenwald schools in Georgia have provoked much dissatisfaction on the part of white citizens with their own white schools in various communities. In many instances, the white citizens have used the Rosenwald plans for improving their white schools."[129] Other Georgia reformers, including Philip Weltner, who

served as chancellor of the state university system from 1933 to 1935, claimed more state authority over teacher certification by increasing the educational requirements for normal diplomas and certification.

After the State Normal School became Georgia State Teachers College in 1928, prospective white female teachers could earn bachelor's degrees.[130] Included in this change were more professional requirements in education, such as child psychology, educational psychology, the history of education, principles of education, and tests and measurements. The state was slowly redefining teaching, at least for white women. Women who had relied on practice and experience for teaching skills were now required to learn professional standards espoused by such national educational experts as Stanley Hall, Edward Thorndike, and John Dewey. The requirement of sixty hours of course work for a normal certificate was increased to seventy-two hours for a bachelor's.[131] Furthermore, in 1933 all state colleges were reorganized and placed under the authority of a central University Board of Regents. The president of the University of Georgia served as chancellor of the board of regents, which bore responsibility for coordinating degree programs for all higher education, although the board initially focused on white colleges. The reorganizing legislation also abolished the district A & M schools and terminated the separate boards of trustees that had governed each college. Consequently, competition between schools in various locations was eliminated in favor of improving a statewide system and circumventing Georgia's "deeply ingrained individualism."[132]

By 1934, certification authority began to rest in the State Department of Education. No longer "hampered by the extreme reactionary movement in a system of certification of teachers," Georgia now legislated uniform requirements, with most certificates to be issued by the department's Division of Certification.[133] White women with county licenses had several years to fulfill the new educational requirements for three types of certificates. Three years after the passage of this legislation, under the leadership of Governor E. D. Rivers, the General Assembly fixed a teachers' salary scale and mandated a seven-month school year. Two-year teacher-certification programs at colleges resulted in lower salaries than four-year degrees, and local superintendents could no longer issue as many provisional certificates—except, of course, to black women.

Yet the same legislation, intended primarily for the benefit of white education, also improved the circumstances of black colleges and teachers. In the early 1930s, the GEB began to push Georgia to assume financial responsibility for black colleges.[134] Because the JRF was bankrupt for the early part of the decade, the State Department of Education started to deal with the inevitable.

The pressure to fund black schools was more than a simple change of heart, however. J. C. Dixon, head of Georgia's Division of Negro Education since 1929, and other reformers continued to point out that Georgia lagged behind other states in higher education for blacks.[135] Dixon noted that county superintendents continued to issue county certificates to African American teachers. As a result of the continual low pay and lack of attention to black education, some black teachers moved to other southern states, including North Carolina, that paid better wages.[136] Once again, African American migration for improved conditions provided a catalyst for reform. In 1937, black teachers received 75 percent of the salary given to white teachers, an increase of 15 percent in a decade.[137]

In the end, white Georgians still relied on northern philanthropy to improve African American education. Yet by 1940 Georgia was also on an irreversible track to improve and professionalize teacher training for both blacks and whites. Since Reconstruction, black and white female teachers had shared the frustrations caused by low local taxation for support of education, changing requirements for teacher preparation, and difficulties in financing education and traveling to teacher training facilities. Without question, African American women encountered the greatest obstacles, yet they were not always insurmountable. Confronted by low expectations, no public funds from taxation, and ceaseless efforts to restrict or even prohibit black higher education, these women nonetheless discovered the means to become teachers. Although many of these women possessed only a high school education, they promulgated black community values of racial uplift and self-sufficiency. Buttressed by their families and communities, they sustained the drive for literacy and education that had begun during the promises of Reconstruction. As the nation geared up for World War II, African American educators began to witness the fulfillment of some of their goals.

So did many white rural women. Facing similar obstacles caused by lack of funds and nearby schools, white rural women refused to allow class limitations to confine their options. They found work scholarships, attended summer institutes, and managed to blunt the limitations of their society. Often ridiculed by middle-class city students who attended school with family financial assistance, many rural women ignored the fact that they lacked the funds to buy caps and gowns for graduation or new shoes. Leona Clark Williams recalled that when she graduated from high school and from Tennessee Wesleyan College, she stood in the last row of students for the graduation photograph. Embarrassed because she could not afford a cap and gown, she nonetheless posed in the photo to mark her graduation. She wanted to teach.[138]

In the end, the battles for teacher certification—between the State Department of Education and local districts, between public institutions and churches, between blacks and whites, between towns and rural settlements—resulted in a centralized system that left the power of certification in the hands of the state. Merit displaced kinship and community ties; professional training outranked practical experience. Yet many of the tensions, notably those between blacks and whites and between county and state authority, had yet to be resolved completely. Not until World War II would Georgia wrestle with equitable treatment of black teachers or gain total authority over teacher certification. North Carolina led the South with 675 Rosenwald schools in 1928, while Georgia had just 218 two years later, a disparity exacerbated by Georgia's larger black population.[139] And Georgia continued to trail other southern states in school funding until after World War II.

At the same time, female teachers, black and white, considered seriously their roles as educators and cultural mediators. Frequently battling tremendous obstacles, including family economics and lack of neighborhood schools, black and white teachers were remarkable. If schools became a pivotal site for confrontations between change and continuity, rural localism and modern bureaucratization, hierarchy and racial uplift, teachers also occupied a central position in the debates about school reform. Teachers' role shifted from preserving social distinctions to teaching increasing numbers of children new skills to survive in the modern world. Seeing themselves as those who carried the light of education and redemption to their communities, these women supported many reforms—in particular, those that would enhance teachers' position as professionals.

4 · Carrying the Torch

Teachers and Professional Culture

AFTER COMPLETING the eleventh grade at Booker T. Washington High School in Atlanta in 1936, Dorothy Oliver Rucker returned to Hall County to find a teaching position near her family. Rucker's first school was called Pleasant Hill and was located near Gillsville, at the southern end of Hall County. Unlike the Gainesville black community, Gillsville's blacks were predominantly sharecroppers and tenants. Rucker earned fifteen dollars a month, and she remembered, "The school was held in the Baptist church. I had eighty-one students from primary through the seventh grade. We just had the church benches and very few books."[1] The next year, when Rucker taught at her mother's school in Gainesville, she earned twenty dollars a month and followed Beulah Rucker Oliver's teaching methods, which Dorothy had observed since childhood.

In 1934 Leona Clark Williams, who had just completed her bachelor's degree at Tennessee Wesleyan College, also wanted to teach near her family's new home in Alto, Georgia. She found a job teaching seventh grade at Lula, in northern Hall County, for fifty dollars a month. During the Great Depression, the state often issued vouchers that could be redeemed at a later date instead of paychecks. The previous teacher had left the trustees with an automobile, and they told Williams that she had to buy the car to have the job. Determined to find a teaching position and fearing unemployment, Williams agreed, even though she had never learned how to drive. A Lula banker agreed to sign a note for the car and cash the voucher with the provision that if the state failed to live up to its financial obligations, Williams would have to reimburse him. Fortunately for Williams, three months later, Georgia paid its teachers. And Williams learned how to drive, apparently teaching herself. "I got [the car] down to the boardinghouse. I didn't know how to back it up, and I didn't know how to stop it. I ran right in front of a train that was coming. There was a fruit stand up there, and I took that car and ran it all around the fruit stand and turned it back down the road. That's how I learned to drive a car."[2]

Rucker's and Williams's stories represent shared yet distinctive characteristics of African American and white female teachers during the Great Depression. While both women were certified teachers, they faced difficult circumstances of uncertain pay and large classes. Each woman confronted her circumstances with characteristic pluck. To them, teaching meant more than the salary, although their wages were important. Teaching meant helping students and the community as the state modernized, a combination of duty and self-sufficiency that defined the profession. Teaching also meant a respectable job outside of agricultural work, textile jobs, or domestic labor—a tribute to these women's determination to improve their lives socially and economically. Neither woman questioned the small salaries, lack of teaching materials, or trustees' expectations. Neither woman necessarily viewed herself as a "New Woman," part of the contingent of professional women who sought careers and freedom apart from their families in their new working positions. Rather, Williams and Rucker measured their worth—their practice of professional labor—by their ability to perform a unique service for their students and communities. Both deliberately searched for teaching positions near their families to assist them financially during the Great Depression. Through teaching and work in their respective professional organizations, they influenced public policy, often unconsciously, and boosted public recognition of teachers' work.

At the same time, Williams's and Rucker's stories illustrate the distinctions between the African American and white worlds. Rucker initially earned thirty-five dollars less per month than Williams. Even if Rucker had attended Atlanta University and received a bachelor's degree, she still would have earned only half of Williams's salary. Trustees would never have "offered" Rucker a car because of her race. Rucker taught in a one-room school that lacked materials and transportation to school, whereas Williams taught in a consolidated, graded white school where most students had books and rode buses. By the Great Depression, many white schools resembled modern institutions, unlike the segregated black rural schools that were of less concern to the counties and to the Georgia General Assembly. Although Rucker and Williams answered to white male trustees and their expectations for teachers, Rucker's position was more tenuous. She faced racist assumptions of what she should teach in her classroom. She discussed African American equality only with selected black friends. Rucker nonetheless used her position to achieve her goals of racial uplift. Her efforts mark African Americans' growing agency as they confronted modernity. Blocked from voting, using most public facilities, and establishing an equitable school system, blacks persistently negotiated means to empower their race.

From their experiences as children and students, black and white teachers like Rucker and Williams constructed notions of professionalization and autonomy, of what it meant to be a teacher and a woman, from interlocking grids of household, religious, and community beliefs and changing ideas about women's identities. As part of Georgia's rapidly expanding early-twentieth-century public education system, black and white teachers' definitions of the modern teacher and perceptions of their duties occasionally merged and frequently clashed with the views of churches, communities, and the state, notably in the case of African American educators. To ease students in an evolving modern industrial system, teachers became agents of change to modernity. For black teachers, this phenomenon unquestionably included funding schools equally but not necessarily integrating them with white schools. For white women, this phenomenon meant expanded public and wage opportunities for rural whites. For teachers of both races, agency constituted merging inherited and modern ideas of duty, self-sufficiency, and respect to create a professional identity that would garner authority. Out of a confluence of distinctive cultural notions of duties, respectability, religion, and autonomy, African American and white women constructed a professional culture circumscribed by restrictions and possibilities governed by a white masculine hierarchy. Gaining support from the Extension Service of the U.S. Department of Agriculture (USDA), Georgia reformers, the General Education Board (GEB), and the Julius Rosenwald Fund (JRF), black and white teachers trod a careful but unmistakable path toward increasing their expertise.[3] This achievement was extraordinary. It was also subversive. By rejecting racist limitations, black women insisted on equality by claiming professional status. By rejecting the absolutism of the ideal of the southern lady, white women called for a renegotiation of womanhood that allowed for marriage and a career.

IN SOME RESPECTS, culture and society defined what it meant to be a black or white teacher. For African American women, teaching included a broad commitment to race work and community uplift. Drawing from gendered traditions of authority and given families' and communities' specific goal of educating certain daughters as teachers, black women experienced few gendered limitations on combining a career with a family.[4] Still, they faced racist stereotypes ranging from the mammy-like Aunt Jemima to the seductive temptress that limited their professional authority in the public realm dominated by white male elites.[5] Yet because black teachers were accorded respect within their communities as a consequence of their education and their work, teachers were known as professors. Denied the title of Mr. or Mrs. from most whites, African Americans consistently used these titles among themselves. So to black educators, the professors and mothers of their communities, teaching entailed a commitment to their race, spreading evangelical Protestantism, and fulfilling personal ambitions.

White women coming of age in the early twentieth century discovered new professional opportunities for women, including teaching and nursing. Still, ambitious women faced other obstacles from their culture and society. White Georgians perceived teaching as women's work to supplement their families' income or support themselves until marriage. The widowed Amelia Akehurst Lines, a teacher in the 1880s, consistently struggled to pay her bills because of her low salary and poor health.[6] To Lines and other nineteenth-century women, teaching was scarcely a stride to independent living, as Catherine Beecher, a nineteenth-century proponent of women teachers, proclaimed. Moreover, white women teachers confronted the cultural expectations from the feminine code of the southern lady—social taboos that clearly limited what a woman could do before and after marriage. Trustees and school boards refused to hire married white women, believing that their vocation consisted of sustaining ideals of home and family. Southern white women also contended with feminine conventions for attire, speech, mannerisms, and church attendance. Few white teachers, including Leona Clark Williams, could afford to wear stylish dresses, hats, and gloves every day. Yet Williams made sure she dressed appropriately, practiced her speech to erase her Appalachian accent, and attended church.

Even as African American and white women grappled with constructions of femininity, they stretched the nuances of self-sufficiency and women's work to fulfill their ambitions. Few teachers in the 1920s understood that cotton agriculture would no longer dominate the state by the end of the 1940s. Yet even the most basic aspects of their training gave teachers recognition of what it meant to succeed in a changing world. As some of the only community members who had gained a wider knowledge of the world, they grasped that this specialized knowledge they received from agricultural and mechanical (A & M) schools, colleges, or training schools could provide advantages for children's future. More than fulfilling aspirations, teaching provided black and white women with a mission to their regions.

Black women knew that children needed to understand advances in agricultural and domestic science in addition to national consumption patterns and models of hygiene to improve their lives. To educate their race, black women uncovered tensions within their culture that encouraged self-reliance even as it reinforced duty and the dominance of a white elite. Black teachers modified what local trustees and educational reformers desired to achieve limited control over the African American school system. In so doing, these teachers created space within which to resist racism and preserve African Americans' struggle for freedom with their examples of race pride and modified curriculum.[7] Forming networks in black communities, teachers often created civic leagues that sustained black activism. Teachers not only educated black Georgians but also taught them how to work together and preserve respect in an era that repeatedly sought to deny their humanity, a version of social protest.[8]

Borrowing from similar cultural values of self-sufficiency, interdependence, and evangelical Protestantism, white women expanded notions of femininity by insisting on respect for their profession and their work. Because rural households blurred distinctions between private and public realms, gendered roles became increasingly difficult to define as white teachers' aspirations defined a respectable career for women. They worked to improve teacher training, raise salaries, and expand education for white children. In the name of educating children and enlightening their communities, teachers reappropriated these beliefs to define their profession and autonomy, thereby reshaping preconceptions of white women's respectable labor.

By the turn of the century, as college degrees became accessible to women across the nation, women's occupations in teaching, social work, and nursing moved toward professional standing. Social reformers such as Jane Addams, Florence Kelley, and Edith Abbott drew their beliefs from their class and gendered roles, claiming specific feminine knowledge of women's roles as mothers, caregivers, and nurturers.[9] Moreover, reformers argued that specialized academic training set them apart from other workers because they alone understood what was necessary to investigate working conditions and child labor. These women expanded professional work, a bastion of middle-class male success, to include women's occupations that increasingly required unique studies, including social work, educational psychology, and curriculum.[10]

Some historians argue that women faced barriers to professional status, largely in nursing and teaching, because women lacked the autonomy required for such status.[11] Given the rapid changes in the South after the Civil War, including industrialization, the expansion of the middle class, the entrenched codes of Jim Crow, and the creation of a public education system, the issue of professionalization overshadows those of gendered autonomy. Rather than using what occurred in the North as a model for defining professionals, historians can examine unique regional adaptations to modernity.[12]

Southerners constructed notions of professionalization based on cultural definitions of identity and agency. As previously noted, African American teachers held an elevated position within their towns and settlements because of their advanced education, their consistent wages, the limited career choices for black women in the early twentieth century, and black communities' specific goal of educating certain daughters as teachers.[13] Yet white supremacists' efforts to limit black educators' authority contested teachers' position within the entire community.[14]

Restricted by customs, late-nineteenth-century white women—notably those in urban areas such as Savannah, Macon, Augusta, and Atlanta— became involved in reform through church organizations. This volunteerism informed public discourses about reform.[15] Sallie Hill and Rebecca Latimer Felton, among others, demonstrated that white women could carve gendered authority in the late nineteenth century. But most southern white women agreed with writer Corra Harris and educator and author Mildred Rutherford that women's power could best be used within the home.[16] White women's professional work drew from these strands. Respectable white women could teach and nurse, but marriage and family trumped public work during the early twentieth century.

At issue is the degree to which teachers created and participated in a definitive professional identity structured by specific training and standards. Some African American and white teachers described themselves as public servants and as naturally suited for teaching.[17] School reformers began to hire women because they worked for lower salaries and were believed natural caregivers and educators for children. Yet black and white female teachers emphatically saw themselves as professionals who knew better than the untrained how to educate children. By the turn of the century in the South, as in the Northeast and Midwest during the nineteenth century, mill work and domestic labor had become far less desirable for women of both races than were clerical fields, teaching, and nursing.[18] So women sought to distinguish occupations such as teaching from less respectable ones even as teaching became feminized.[19] Not only teachers but other southerners began to perceive teaching as dignified, middle-class labor.

At the same time, many African American and white teachers, particularly in the South, stressed their calling to teach, an emphasis that evoked the region's predominant evangelical Protestant values.[20] This link between southern educators and evangelical Protestantism underscores the distinct ways southern culture construed autonomy as a product of duties, respectability, and self-sufficiency.[21] Evangelical Protestantism thus became a means for black and white women to emphasize their identity and agency, their individual conversion experiences, and their fellowship with other believers. Drawing from these strands of autonomy and solidarity, women, who had always seen one of their duties as the salvation of their household members, redefined witnessing for their faith, extending its meanings beyond their households to include witnessing in classrooms.[22] Southern black and white teachers thus created a profession that redefined women's sense of autonomy and dignity away from inherited beliefs in an evangelical Protestant calling and duty to their households and toward modern notions of individual ambition and greater public roles for women.[23]

As black and white women borrowed from gendered values of labor, religion, respectability, and self-sufficiency in their move to teaching, the values of classroom and household often merged to create a perception of professional labor grounded in traditional rural values yet reemerging in cultural constructions of teaching.[24] While these women rarely saw themselves as separate from their God, households, or settlements, they presented themselves as respectable, middle-class, educated women who knew better than parents what students required in the modern industrial world. In a congruence of distinct cultural beliefs, African American and white female teachers in the 1920s and 1930s merged racial and class solidarity and autonomy in their female identities, presenting a distinct grasp of what it meant to be a professional woman. In fact, personal narratives indicate that most teachers had as children begun to construct their perceptions of what being a teacher meant and did not mean.

During the Progressive era, most of Georgia's white male officials fought standardization, consolidation, and social welfare programs, among other educational reforms. Yet black women such as Lugenia Burns Hope and white women such as Rhoda Kaufman boldly formed the Neighborhood Union and the Georgia Training School, respectively.[25] Hope, Kaufman, and hundreds of Georgia teachers demonstrated what women could accomplish within the restricted understanding of reform. Along with their male allies, these women discovered gaps within which they could create and advance their agenda for change. White elite men continued to hold power, but black and white teachers used New South beliefs in harmony and progress to promote plans for education. Lynching retained its gruesome hold; tenants and sharecroppers faced often unimaginable poverty and poor health; black soldiers returned from World War I to find a society as ordered as ever by race, class, and gender; conservative evangelicals railed against Charles Darwin's theories of evolution. Black teachers never gained equal funding for schools and failed to increase voting rights. At the same time, black women's work demonstrates the problem of viewing racism as a static construction.[26] Health campaigns, cleanup programs, and education improved lives—at least to some extent—for thousands of Georgia's African Americans. White teachers, while neglecting to publicly oppose the neglect of education for blacks, made significant gains for public education through improved instruction, increased funding, and better facilities. Yet female teachers, occasionally with their husbands' or other men's assistance, wound a narrow path to modernity. They recognized, as many Americans eventually would, that education was a key to individual accomplishment and fulfillment. By becoming teachers, women could benefit the public good as well as their own. By the 1930s, Georgia's teachers of both races sifted through traditional beliefs and covertly and overtly elaborated new cultural views on feminine agency and identity by claiming a specific cultural and professional realm in their classrooms. To do so was a bold accomplishment.

MOST AFRICAN AMERICAN teachers report that their mothers or other female teachers provided role models from which to borrow and to which to add while pursuing the profession. Dorothy Oliver Rucker, Susie Weems Wheeler, Laura Mosley Whelchel, and Rosa Penson Anderson decided that they would become teachers at an early age and then absorbed and rejected the various teaching styles and practices they encountered during their own schooling. Whelchel recalled that she "always wanted to be a teacher." As a Sunday school teacher, Whelchel encouraged children to "be the best you can be because if you don't, the world's going to go on without you."[27] Narvie Jordan Harris, a Jeanes teacher in De Kalb County, also stated that she had always wanted to be a teacher and took the role of teacher when she and her friends played school. She and many other black teachers from Reconstruction to the 1940s saw teaching as a "special gift to work with others."[28] Whelchel; her sister, Annie Mosley Martin; Dorothy Oliver Rucker; and Rosa Penson Anderson attended elementary schools at which their mothers taught, watching them discipline students, maintain classroom order, and teach educational fundamentals such as reading, writing, spelling, history, math, and religion. "Everybody had to obey," remembered Whelchel. "You didn't disturb anybody."[29] Young women may have observed the respect their mothers received in their households and settlements and may consequently have learned the profession's importance to the community. Deciding that she wanted to become a teacher gave a girl a specific goal toward which she could work, observing, studying, and choosing among pedagogical styles.

Lucy Craft Laney, ca. 1910. One of the first graduates
of Atlanta University, Laney opened the Haines
Institute for black children in Augusta. (Courtesy of
the Lucy Craft Laney Museum of Black History.)

To African American women coming of age in the 1920s and 1930s, Lucy Craft Laney's example resounded across Georgia and provided a professional foundation for black teachers. Laney, whose Haines Normal and Industrial School was accredited by the state of Georgia in 1886, embodied black women's social and political roles. Always advocating political and civil rights, Laney's speeches and articles combined black women's professional roles as teachers and reformers with their household work as mothers and wives. African American women had consistently worked in public roles since the end of slavery.[30] Laney did more than open her own school, however; she also defined black women's vital contributions at a time when some black men chose to limit women's positions. Although John Hope applauded female reformers' work in neighborhoods, he scolded some women in 1898 for acting like men. Other men admonished black women for disloyalty to black men. The harshest criticism came from William Hannibal Thomas in 1901. He castigated the members of the National Association of Colored Women who had stated that "a race could rise no higher than its women." If that were true, wrote Thomas, then African American problems, which had become mountainous by the turn of the century, must be black women's fault.[31]

In a climate that featured weakened opportunities and deteriorating rights, competition for wage labor positions fostered Hope's and Thomas's statements. Hope supported his wife Lugenia's Neighborhood Union as a notable effort to improve Atlanta for blacks but was concerned about the growing number of black women teachers and white trustees' overwhelming willingness to hire female instructors. What, then, could black men do other than becoming ministers or doing agricultural work?[32] To Hope, professional opportunities comprised a vital part of masculinity, precisely the idea that white southerners consistently challenged by the 1890s. Black men, perceived as lustful, rapacious brutes or grinning Sambos, had to prove their mettle by supporting their families.

In fact, few black men ever became sole providers for their families, and trustees of black schools never relied solely on female teachers. That more black women became teachers resulted from family and community strategies as well as deliberate tactics by ambitious women who ignored misogynist statements from men such as Thomas. Hope's anxiety resulted more from white perceptions of black masculinity than from black women's dominance. Encouraging his wife's work, he continued to view Lugenia as a helpmate rather than an equal. Like his friend, W. E. B. Du Bois, Hope was committed to "femininity rather than feminism."[33] So as a pioneer in education and the director of a school, Lucy Craft Laney carefully negotiated tensions among African Americans and between blacks and whites. She did so by combining motherhood with professional work.

In 1897, Atlanta University sponsored a conference on the "Social and Physical Conditions of Negroes." Laney chaired the women's session, during which several female graduates of Atlanta University discussed issues of womanhood. In her address, Laney contended that motherhood was the solution to problems blacks experienced. By motherhood, Laney conceptualized a gendered construction that included black women's work in the home and the community. Black women had a specific task. In a speech delivered two years later at Hampton Institute, Laney stated that educated black women, "the women of character and culture," should become teachers. These women, Laney argued, "can do the successful lifting, for she who would mold character must herself possess it."[34] She contended that black teachers and mothers carried the duty and responsibility not only to educate children but also to instruct them on moral behaviors such as temperance, manners, attire, and Christianity.[35] Laney drew on black women's past roles as community mothers but added contemporary themes of public education and reform.

By drawing on resonant meanings of motherhood, Laney tried to ease tensions about professional black women's work. Mothers, she insisted, carried responsibility and power. Since slavery, their work had stretched beyond the home into the community. With professional training and the commitment to uplifting their communities, black women could provide indispensable aid, particularly in the area of education. Focusing on work that drew on gendered terrain, Laney and Lugenia Burns Hope used their education and training to improve neighborhoods and teach children.[36] With tensions eased, men and women worked together to support antilynching legislation, voting rights, and better education.

In Cartersville, Susie Weems Wheeler and her classmates experienced different circumstances. Black trustees had operated black schools in the town since Reconstruction. Wheeler's first-grade teacher, Myra Williams, inspired Wheeler to become a teacher. Williams and her husband, C. W. Williams, founded a school in the early twentieth century. Learning about the JRF, the Williamses convinced the black trustees of the need for a new building. Parents and neighbors, including Wheeler's grandfather, contributed labor and supplies for the new Rosenwald school at Noble Hill. Wheeler and her peers transferred to Noble Hill when it was completed in 1923. Myra Williams encouraged her young students and "went all out for them."[37] From her, Wheeler learned how to conduct an open and tolerant classroom. C. W. Williams, who taught grades five through seven, was sterner. He instilled fear in students by using his belt or a switch to preserve order.

Wheeler, Whelchel, and other women moved to areas that had schools beyond grade seven to find further training. Laura Mosley Whelchel and Annie Mosley Martin eventually joined Nancy Stephens, Dorothy Oliver Rucker, and approximately one hundred other students at Beulah Rucker Oliver's school in Gainesville, whereas Rosa Penson Anderson moved to Fort Valley to complete her education, taking specific teacher training courses such as the history of education. Oliver's school was the only institution in northeast Georgia that permitted young women to work their way through school while they took teacher training. At Beulah Rucker Oliver's school and at Noble Hill School, students continued their religious and academic learning, and those who eventually became teachers absorbed what their teachers practiced, drawing on those lessons as they fashioned their own careers.

Long before anyone thought about black history month, black women incorporated their history into the curriculum. Oliver, Williams, and Laney's teaching comprised a combination of Protestant evangelical instruction, educational fundamentals, and moral values. Students started the day with devotions and sang what became known as the black national anthem, James Weldon Johnson's "Lift Every Voice and Sing." They recited poetry by Johnson and Langston Hughes and learned about Frederick Douglass, slavery, Nat Turner's rebellion, Booker T. Washington, and W. E. B. Du Bois. Oliver often wrote plays that her students performed for black and white audiences that emphasized aspects of her beliefs. One such play, "The Garden of Education," demonstrated her association of work, education, and redemption. In the play, Oliver's students tried to reach the "Spring of Knowledge" in the "Garden of Education." Along the way, they met various temptations or "people trying to get you not to pursue your education." For example, one character was dressed to go fishing and kept asking the travelers to stop and go with him, which they refused to do.[38] While the play reinforced the importance of an education, the biblical imagery suggests a link between education and salvation, between idleness and damnation. Yet the play also underscored the need for racial cooperation and interdependence, as the students traveled together to the Garden of Education just as they farmed or made rugs collectively for the school's preservation.

As Laura Mosley Whelchel recalled, "Even now, I know the books of the Bible from Genesis to Revelations from memory. We learned scriptures and memorized them and would go to different churches for programs. Godmother [Beulah Rucker Oliver] would write poems and I had to recite some."[39] Like the plays Oliver's students performed, poems and songs composed by Oliver reinforced the link she perceived between the black church and the black school. This tie inextricably both bound African American institutions and designated them as the cornerstones of the race's survival. The poems encouraged church boosterism and support as well as active witnessing within the community for the church and school.

Thus, one of Oliver's pedagogical principles, the interplay of Protestant beliefs with academic knowledge that Laney had used at Haines, upheld the two key institutions Oliver deemed essential for racial uplift. She believed that uplift constituted a dual emphasis on educational fundamentals and evangelical Protestantism. At Noble Hill School, the Williamses followed similar practices. Students began their day with devotions and a reading from the Bible, sang spiritual or gospel songs, and then put their coats away. They prayed every day, and their academic work included the basics.[40] Just as each believer received the authority to determine his or her own conversion experience, so black educators identified their formulation of racial salvation within their culture's values. For Oliver, receiving visions from God and believing herself called to do his work legitimated her work. Telling the story of her visions to the black and white communities increased her authority and ability to teach black children reading, writing, arithmetic, music, and all the other subjects she had learned in Athens. Because her vision followed traditional rural black beliefs in God's call to individuals, its familiarity appealed to African Americans, who also identified education as a primary means of uplift for their children. Expanding African American women's family and community roles, Oliver solidified her racial community by leading her students to collective salvation through belief in God and the necessity of an education. Moreover, these students identified the means to self-sufficiency as they proclaimed their educational achievements and dignity.

Other black schools taught similar lessons. After finishing at Noble Hill, Susie Weems Wheeler attended Summerhill School in Cartersville, eight miles away, boarding with an aunt. One of her eighth- and ninth-grade teachers, Mrs. Morgan, strongly influenced Wheeler's career as a teacher. Wheeler initially thought Morgan was mean, strict, and intolerant of poor grammar and speech patterns. Morgan insisted that her students "be the best person you can be with an eye towards the world."[41] Morgan's students read Hughes's poetry, Du Bois's essays, and other Harlem Renaissance writers. By the time Wheeler left Summerhill, Morgan's refusal to accept poor work had become one of the most important lessons Wheeler learned. Similarly, Narvie Jordan Harris, like every teacher interviewed, remembered a combination of moral training, Protestantism, and solid educational standards at school in Wrightsville and Atlanta. Her teachers "inspired each child to become somebody."[42]

Northwest Normal and Industrial School, also located in Gainesville and supported by the district's African American Baptists, provided a classical education, teaching its students no industrial skills. Most black students learned about Frederick Douglass, Mary McLeod Bethune, Booker T. Washington, and W. E. B. Du Bois, a distinct historical curriculum that separated them from county and state expectations for black education. These pedagogical strategies figured prominently in efforts to emphasize uplift and self-sufficiency in the black schools.

As black students learned lessons of respectability such as how to set a table, how to speak clearly in complete sentences, and how to walk proudly, their actions served several purposes. It taught them ways to present themselves to black and white communities that increasingly counted decency and respect by manners, dress, and speech.[43] All black leaders, even those like Du Bois who demanded political equality, insisted that blacks should act, dress, and behave according to prevailing middle-class standards. Although black teachers earned little money, they donned dresses or suits every day, in keeping with the professional dress code. Dorothy Oliver Rucker remembered that as part of her claim to respect, her mother wore stockings, even though they had "nothing left but the seams. There were runs everywhere."[44] As part of the racial uplift ideology, some blacks still believed that moderate whites, despite the reign of scientific racism and the thrall of *Birth of a Nation*, would eventually recognize that blacks deserved more than they received in social, economic, and political rights. By assuming these respectable characteristics, teachers like Beulah Rucker Oliver, the Williamses, Laney, and Morgan accomplished some of their goals of racial uplift within their communities. To demonstrate these qualities meant potential access to public and private funds, which could ensure literacy and possibly wage-earning jobs for students.

But even when blacks assumed proper deference to whites and followed middle-class codes, the world persistently designated African Americans as inferiors.[45] John and Lugenia Hope, C. W. and Myra Williams, Lucy Craft Laney, and Beulah Rucker Oliver often worked as double agents in a precarious world that, as one historian writes, "required them to be forever careful, tense, and calculating."[46] They knew they could lose their positions at any time. Their efforts cost them their health and created anxiety. At times, working-class blacks misinterpreted moral standards for uplift as highfalutin rebukes to their culture, which included expressive religious practices, slang, and clothing such as head wraps. Oliver believed that her darker skin and shouting at church services caused tensions between Gainesville's black middle class and her authority.[47] Still, teachers made an unmistakable mark.

Black teachers' agency and leadership stretched into communities and nourished blacks' beliefs in empowerment. From Oliver, Morgan, and Laney, who taught about African American leaders, students learned precepts of religious salvation and educational uplift. Like Wheeler, Harris, and Whelchel, students commonly recall public recitation exercises. To learn proper speech, Oliver's students recited Bible passages or stories from books donated by the Moody Bible Institute. Most of these tales conveyed moral lessons about individuals who had strayed from God's path by succumbing to alcohol or gambling and eventually returned to God's community and families after learning the need for forgiveness and salvation. A redeemed student meant as much to Beulah Oliver as one who could spell correctly and recite a speech by Frederick Douglass. But redemption never meant submitting to abuse. "She taught us," remembered the Reverend L. C. Teasley Sr., "the fear of God and the fear of white boys."[48] Oliver was reiterating the theme of racial survival. She recognized the realities of the southern black experience, the potential for unpredictable explosions of racial tensions and violence. Living in the world required more than reading the Bible. Blacks had to learn to recognize danger and avoid inflammatory situations whenever possible.

Replicated throughout the South by other African American teachers, the emphasis on evangelical Protestantism, respectability, duty to the community, and academic work served as preparation for racial self-sufficiency.[49] Schooling constituted a multifaceted effort to prepare students for racial autonomy. Articulating a professional role for herself, Oliver re-created this cultural agency for the future teachers and ministers who attended the school. Intent on enhancing black respectability and dignity, teachers merged sacred and secular labor to preserve settlement independence and interdependence. While Oliver gladly accepted funds from the JRF in the 1920s and the National Youth Administration (NYA), which sought to keep students in school during the 1930s, any assistance she received required some form of work. "Whatever program it was," recalled Nancy Stephens, "these kids would be given their responsibilities to do. Godmother had them work to help pay their school fees." Stephens also remembered that the jobs Oliver found included picking cotton, domestic work, work on the school farm, and work in the lunchroom.[50] At Griffin High School, run by another African American husband and wife, Susie Weems Wheeler prepared meals in the kitchen. Students at Georgia State Industrial College (GSIC) worked on the school's farm or in other parts of the school. Their labor underscored the practice of supporting school and community.[51]

JRF and GEB agents generally approved of black teachers' efforts to improve the race's living standards, but Rosenwald schools and GEB county training schools promoted basic educational foundations and directed students toward gendered industrial work: making baskets, increasing sharecropper efficiency, or improving domestic skills for work as maids. Most of this work was designed to keep black students in the southern labor supply, a principle compatible with white supremacy. In some respects, teachers such as Oliver and Laney appear to have followed these guidelines, because female students performed domestic labor (including scrubbing floors with a mud paste and corn shuck mops, canning peaches with their sides symmetrical in jars, and ironing and sewing clothing), raised corn and peas, and eventually made rugs. Male students learned to plow even rows of cotton, to raise cows and chickens, and to grow vegetables.[52] Dorothy Oliver Rucker recounted that when whites such as the First Baptist Church Women's Missionary Union or the Hall County school superintendent visited her mother's school, "we put a program together in two or three minutes. We would have something like reciting the books of the Bible or recite the Sermon on the Mount. We sang spirituals and school songs we made up."[53] Thus, observers perceived Oliver's school as an innocuous place where blacks learned the Bible, sang, and performed industrial tasks. Oliver must have been prepared for these visits because programs were performed almost effortlessly with only a few minutes' notice and conspicuously eschewed demonstrations of excessive scholastic excellence.

Like Laney, Oliver initially faced some hostility from black men in her efforts to start a school, but by 1920 she had convinced them of her mettle. In fact, she became one of the leaders of Gainesville's black community. Counseling blacks to buy property, encouraging students to reach for salaried positions, and urging the community to build more churches, Oliver facilitated the consolidation of the African American section of Gainesville. More to the point, Oliver's vision reached beyond the realms of education and incorporated a view of an African American settlement that would include distinctly black churches, schools, and businesses, a means by which Hall County rural blacks could live separately albeit unequally near Gainesville, with its expanding labor market and growing industrial economy.[54]

Above all, African American teachers helped to prepare students for a polarized world. As Rev. Teasley stated, "Mrs. Rucker gave you the assurance that you could be somebody. . . . She wanted to equip you for life so that you could take care of yourself."[55] Other students agreed. "I believe that I could talk to anybody, do anything I want to," recalled Christine Rucker.[56] This is precisely the same lesson that Susie Weems Wheeler, Narvie Jordan Harris, and Rosa Penson Anderson learned from their teachers and taught to their students. So while most white professional educators counseled blacks to be content with their lot and acquire limited industrial education, black teachers countered by challenging students to be self-sufficient and to work for the benefit of the race. Teachers prepared other teachers, ministers, and small business owners for the future, beginning modernity's process of separating those with expertise from those who relied on oral traditions for instruction.

Measured against standard definitions of professionalism that required college or university education, Beulah Rucker Oliver and other black educators fell short. Many had little more than a ninth- or tenth-grade education, although even that represented far more than was the norm in their communities. Few had college or university degrees. In some counties, blacks complained that their teachers had little more than a fourth-grade education and were incompetent. These teachers knew little math beyond basic arithmetic and frequently read at approximately a fourth- or fifth-grade level. Double sessions during the day, leaky buildings, poor attendance, lack of materials, and occasional abuse from white superintendents often overwhelmed teachers.[57] Yet few reformers, apart from those such as Walter B. Hill Jr., cared whether black teachers received adequate training.

With the exception of Cartersville and possibly a handful of other towns,

African American teachers in most areas depended on white trustees or super-intendents for their jobs. Nonetheless, the black community as a whole saw teachers as professionals to be supported. Teachers knew the broader world be-yond their communities; had learned to achieve what they wanted from whites; were more educated than most blacks; and could shrewdly define, communi-cate, and articulate a vision of what blacks could accomplish in the Jim Crow South.[58]

For example, when African Americans visited her school, Oliver presented a slightly different version of education. During her tenure as director of the NYA, Mary McLeod Bethune and other black educators traveled to Gainesville to visit, witnessing students in classrooms reading, giving speeches, and solving arithmetic problems on the blackboard. Bethune spoke to the students, urging them to stay in school and improve the race.[59] Black educators saw in the school the potential for racial improvement, the chance for blacks to shape their com-munity and to gain respectability by preparing students to become part of the black middle class.

Of course, black teachers' political efforts varied. While Beulah Rucker Oliver's efforts to establish a self-sufficient black community outside Gaines-ville were unquestionably political, her daughters and other students offer little evidence that she ever voted or worked for voting rights. In contrast, when William Jefferson White called the 1906 Georgia Equal Rights Convention in Macon, Lucy Craft Laney attended. She then joined the National Association for the Advancement of Colored People (NAACP). For the rest of her life, Laney worked for political and civil rights for black men and women.[60] By 1919, Lugenia Burns Hope joined Laney in calling for black women's suffrage, and other Georgians in the National Association of Colored Women agreed. Yet how many black teachers publicly acted on behalf of suffrage is difficult to de-termine. Black teachers, dependent on conservative white men for their jobs, were understandably leery about discussing the right to vote. They could—and later did—lose their jobs for mentioning the subject or discussing the NAACP. Consequently, their political activities were centered on the Georgia Teachers and Education Association (GTEA).

As early as 1879, two thousand black teachers, led by Richard Robert Wright, gathered in Atlanta to organize the Georgia Teachers Association. Over its first two decades, the organization drew thousands of teachers to its meetings and repeatedly called for the Georgia legislature to equalize state funding for black schools.[61] By the turn of the century, when Jim Crow was flourishing, the organization's membership declined to approximately three hundred. In 1913, the president of the association declared that Georgia "is probably the most backward state in the whole South with respect to its teachers' associations."[62] H. A. Hunt, president of Fort Valley High and Industrial, organized the Georgia Association for the Advancement of Education among Negroes in 1917. Recognizing teachers' vulnerability to reprisal, Hunt believed that any black education association needed to include black businessmen, members of fraternal orders, and other individuals in nonteaching professions. Meeting in Macon, the group called for better teacher salaries, better schoolhouses and facilities, normal training schools, district agricultural schools, and funds for summer schools.[63] While the platform and attendance went beyond what the teachers' organization had called for in the 1910s, Hunt and his colleagues realized that they needed teachers in the organization.

In May 1921, the organizations met jointly in Atlanta, with speakers including Hunt, Laney, and Professor C. L. Harper, a future principal of Atlanta's Booker T. Washington High School. In 1923, the organizations officially merged to form the GTEA. From its origins, the organization understood two central ideas. The GTEA had to be a professional association that worked for educational equality, but it also needed to include nonteaching professionals who could push for equality and change without the fear of retaliation from white school boards. Thus, the GTEA drew from precursor education associations such as White's Education Union in Augusta and Wright's Negro Civic League in Savannah. Black teachers used GTEA meetings to discuss pedagogical methods, how to improve schools, and how to gain funds for teacher and agricultural training. More importantly, GTEA meetings provided a forum in which black professionals could discuss race work and potential activism.

The GTEA was the only African American organization that maintained any momentum for challenging unequal funding for education. While sixteen NAACP chapters existed in Georgia after World War I, membership dropped and branches closed during the 1920s.[64] More than thirty branches of the United Negro Improvement Association formed in the 1920s, but they folded after Marcus Garvey's deportation in 1925.[65] White Georgians and Klansmen terrorized members of those groups, with members losing their jobs or being forced at gunpoint to leave the state. In contrast, however, most whites viewed the GTEA members as innocuous teachers without an explicit political agenda. These whites were wrong. The GTEA, even in its lean years in the 1930s, maintained its political agenda for equal education. During the 1920s, GTEA leaders John Hope, Hunt, Benjamin Hubert, Laney, and J. W. Holley saw membership explode from just under a thousand in 1925 to more than twenty-five hundred four years later.[66] The group's annual meetings featured such speakers as Mary McLeod Bethune, Benjamin Davis from the *Atlanta Independent,* and individuals from the GEB and the JRF. Because the GTEA was determined to improve education for blacks and teaching conditions and training for teachers, the organization connected with the USDA Extension Service.

The USDA began its Extension Service in 1909 with a network of county agents and home demonstration agents that grew to sixty-five white agents spread across seventy-five counties by 1914. In 1914, white state agent Phil Campbell recommended that Georgia hire a black agricultural specialist to work with black farmers. Eugene Williams was hired and began working out of GSIC, the black land-grant school. Williams faced the nearly impossible task of meeting with black farmers throughout the state. He held institutes at night and on Sundays, refused to take a day off, and tried to tell his listeners that the white farmer was their "friend and desired to see [them] improve." But how convincing could Williams be when, as he noted in the same report, his life was threatened several times?[67]

Hundreds of blacks attended Williams' meetings. In fact, white agents frequently noted that blacks' desire to improve their farming methods exceeded that of whites. With the addition of the federal Smith-Lever Act in 1914 and the Smith-Hughes Act in 1917, the Extension Service began to work directly with schools. Black and white agents along with the USDA recognized that the "part of the trained teacher in community organization is invaluable; and can be brought about only by making the school house the community center for meetings of the various clubs."[68] Teachers, recognized as professional community leaders, could play a central role in standardizing agricultural and household production. As boys' and girls' clubs learned how to use USDA-approved methods of raising cotton and livestock, planting vegetable gardens, and standardizing butter molds, teachers and schools became part of the national plan to regularize and modernize country life and production. For the USDA, standardization of most aspects of agricultural life meant better crops and lifestyles for farmers. Furthermore, improved living standards meant that rural families could participate in the early twentieth century's expanding consumer culture, surely a benefit to the nation. By 1919, Georgia, which trailed only Texas in amount of cotton produced, had been battling the boll weevil for four years. The Extension Service's agents knew that survival required that Georgia farmers diversify their crops and raise livestock. At the same time, the agents needed to assure bankers that other crops or livestock production could raise as much cash as King Cotton.

Beginning in 1921, Williams and his successors held an annual statewide meeting of black farmers, usually at GSIC, outside Savannah, picking up on a practice started by Wright, the school's former president, who had held the first such conference in 1893.[69] Black farmers, Jeanes teachers, other teachers, faculty from black colleges, and white editors and businessmen attended. At the meetings, speakers encouraged blacks to remain on farms and avoid the temptations of cities and towns. Presentations also touted improved methods of raising cotton, called attention to hygiene and home improvements, and spoke about blacks' significant contributions to Georgia. GSIC President Benjamin F. Hubert, a frequent speaker, reminded blacks to "Know Georgia, Believe in Georgia and Build a Better Georgia."[70] Telling black farmers that they were vital to Georgia's improvement both encouraged blacks and reminded whites that the state could never improve without African American help. Establishing a home economics program in 1926, GSIC eventually incorporated this program into the home economics degree that trained teachers for the state and drew on the USDA Extension Service.

Although the USDA focused on helping white rural families more than blacks and always hired far more white Extension Service agents than blacks, African American teachers and agents used whatever materials they could to improve their race's living conditions. GTEA field representatives worked with Extension Service agents, teachers, and the state Department of Education to coordinate curriculum and community assistance. The core of black support and improvement came from within the community, but the USDA's services were welcomed, like those provided by the JRF or the American Missionary Association. Any economic aid would help.

In 1919, ten years after the Extension Service began its work in Georgia, 119 of 155 counties had white male county agents who worked with male farmers, whereas only 13 black agents covered 79 counties. In contrast, 98 counties employed white female home demonstration agents who worked with women, while 47 counties hired black women.[71] Some counties employed both black and white home demonstration agents and male county agents, while other counties chose to hire only white agents. Other counties had no agents because of a lack of funds or interest. Officials based their decisions on the number of African Americans in the county as well as the level of commitment to assisting black rural families. Because many more men than women served in World War I, women's work was emphasized and increased. Women hired as Jeanes supervisors usually did Extension Service work as well, although Walter B. Hill Jr. pressured state leaders to hire both more Jeanes teachers and more black home demonstration agents.[72] From supervising teachers to designing curriculum to building water wells, Jeanes teachers became forces for change and reform at black schools and communities.

Black teachers quickly learned about the Jeanes program. Jeanes teachers traveled to approximately thirty schools in their assigned areas, organizing canning clubs for girls and corn clubs for boys. They demonstrated improved sanitation methods for families, held summer training schools for teachers, and campaigned for better schools and salaries for their work. They pushed for improved academic training for teachers. As in the past, Hill supported black teachers' requests for better county training schools and state contributions to Jeanes teachers' salaries.[73] Jeanes teachers, Extension Service agents, and other teachers shared racial uplift goals, with some individuals holding all three positions simultaneously.

Beulah Rucker Oliver, like other black teachers, learned about the Extension Service's work and incorporated it into her school. Erma Ellis, Hall County's white home demonstration agent, noted in 1921 that Oliver's school was doing some of the county's best work. Girls learned to can and preserve vegetables and fruit according to USDA guidelines. They made tablecloths from feed sacks and practiced setting a proper table. Boys made chairs and birdhouses. Rucker also taught landscaping at the school and had it repainted each spring. At the Northeast Georgia Fair, held during the summer, Oliver's students exhibited their products, winning notice from Ellis for their work.[74] Like much of the Extension Service's work, the intent was to standardize not only agricultural practices but home production. While Oliver followed the guidelines to improve conditions for her race, she, like other teachers, shifted the emphasis on instruction for rural livelihood from the family to experts like herself. Telling students how to set a proper table was far removed from helping them to obtain jobs that would finance the purchase of dining table sets, but it was a step in that direction.

A measure of the popularity of Extension Service work in Georgia was the number of African Americans who participated in county fairs and organized annual fairs for blacks. Agents and presidents of black colleges like Hubert and Fort Valley Normal and Industrial School's H. A. Hunt encouraged teachers and agents to continue to emphasize proper diet, health, food preparation, hygiene, and improved morals. Whereas 131 black communities had participated in Extension Service work in 1928, the number nearly doubled to 251 three years later. Under the leadership of P. H. Stone, who was appointed black state agent after Williams's death, and Camilla Weems, the black state home demonstration agent, adult and child participation in USDA programs grew rapidly. More than 3,600 boys participated in 4-H programs in 1931, compared to about 2,100 in 1929.[75] After decades of dealing with poor soil and dilapidated homes, in addition to the infestation of the boll weevil, blacks continued to push for improvements.

Black county and home demonstration agents and teachers also began to request additional financial support from the federal government through state agents Stone and Weems. At the 1928 annual meeting of black farmers at GSIC, participants called for more federal funds, given the lack of financial support from the state and counties. Weems requested that the University of Georgia's College of Agriculture directly pay black agents because county offi-cials frequently failed to do so.[76]

Again, agencies outside state control, like the USDA, enhanced black teachers' professional position. Black farmers may initially have been suspi-cious of what black employees of the white power structure could accomplish.[77] But combining their efforts with those of the GTEA and the Jeanes teachers, black Extension Service workers incorporated the traditional structure of the black community. Practicing an ethic of "social responsibility," Jeanes teachers used their position as diplomats to relay specialized knowledge of new farming methods or nutrition to students and the broader community.[78] Jeanes teachers were community leaders who could teach others how to live in a changing world and improve their lives.

Unlike the USDA's work in white schools, African American girls and boys competed for prizes in livestock and agricultural production and household skills. Black children of both sexes raised cows, pigs, and chickens and farmed. Boys learned basic carpentry skills and how to repair farm equipment; girls sewed and prepared food. But the gender boundaries between black girls and boys were less rigid than those between white girls and boys, partly as a result of blurred gender divisions within the black community and partly as a result of racist expectations of what black boys and girls could accomplish. Some USDA projects, including installing indoor plumbing and modernizing kitchens, seem absurd for black families, given their poverty and lack of resources. Moreover, how many white landholders would have permitted such modifications to ten-ants' homes? That Jeanes teachers, USDA representatives, and teachers suc-ceeded in any improvements underscores their aspirations for change.

Oliver, Laney, and other teachers guided students on their career paths. All of Oliver's former students interviewed assert that her vision inspired them whether they later became ministers, teachers, or skilled laborers. Like many other African American teachers in Georgia, Oliver's belief in education was palpable to blacks. One former student who later became a principal, Cleophus Allgood, recalled that "to Mrs. Rucker, learning was as good as a meal. She encouraged us to do our best, to improve the race and get out of sharecropping."[79] By combining and expanding on traditional rural work habits and her Baptist faith, Oliver's school helped students adapt to a changing world.

While some historians have cogently described the restrictions white philanthropic foundations and towns and settlements placed on African American teachers, black teachers' work reveals a broader definition of African American education that combined community uplift with social services and education. Such women's insistence on professional goals cautions against facile assumptions concerning the failures of black schools or black teachers' autonomy.[80] African American teachers unquestionably faced barriers in curriculum, pedagogy, resources, and teacher training. Yet many black teachers circumvented these restrictions by presenting one aspect of their classrooms to white visitors and another to the black community.[81] Such strategies necessitated resourcefulness and the cooperation of many teachers.[82] Throughout Georgia and the rest of the South, pedagogical similarities far too common to be considered coincidental demonstrate that these women must have communicated orally or via correspondence. Antebellum ties within the slave quarters reappeared in postbellum black churches and settlements, and African American women reappropriated these links for their schools. Living in a hierarchically segregated world that denied them authority and autonomy, early-twentieth-century black teachers nonetheless devised a pedagogy to suit their race. Borrowing beliefs in autonomy from their culture, teachers elaborated these beliefs to fit their professions.[83] Yet as the 1930s began, teachers such as Susie Weems Wheeler, Narvie Jordan Harris, and Laura Mosley Whelchel knew that their communities needed something more. Such women became part of a reorganized GTEA in 1941 that began to challenge inequalities in their profession.

AT THE SAME TIME that African American teachers slowly earned some whites' professional respect, white female teachers had to prove they could be both women and professional workers. Few African American women considered staying at home after marriage and having children. For example, Lugenia Burns Hope, who was among the Georgia black elite, made her mark in her community and national organizations. Like black educators, white female teachers drew on cultural values of duty, respectability, and self-sufficiency to frame the ways they understood their positions as teachers. Yet white teachers, often with less collective economic support from their communities, cautiously and distinctly circumscribed their ambitions for women's professional work. Their race gave them benefits such as access to public facilities and, after 1920, voting. Still, working for wages tended to be a path for working-class white women or a temporary stage for other white women until marriage. Few elite white women became teachers.

Conventions about southern womanhood nonetheless generally applied to teachers. As the examples of clothing and behavior regulations at normal or industrial schools indicate, male trustees and school board members ensured that white teachers understood codes of white femininity. At Georgia State College for Women in Milledgeville, the college bulletin recognized that women had "interests and ambitions and spheres of usefulness of their own." The publication then reminded women that their education should serve "the home, the school, the farm, the child, and . . . society in general."[84] Individual ambition and duty to family and community were combined in terms of "usefulness."

These views rang familiar to the rural and middle-class white women who became teachers in the early twentieth century. Never seeing themselves as the elite, they believed they had a calling and duty to help their communities. They sought an alternative to marriage, although they rarely completely rejected it. They also wanted an escape from agricultural work. So they combined notions of white femininity, duty, respectability, ambition, and self-sufficiency to create the professional teacher. To their traditional beliefs in evangelical Protestantism and hard work, these women added modern values of individual ambition and respect, creating a model for professional white women. Less tied to community needs and obligations than black teachers, white educators fashioned a model of the feminine scholar and citizen that satisfied white male authorities and, like black teachers, relied less on college and university training than on what education was available and the teachers they observed.

Like Lucy Craft Laney, Beulah Rucker Oliver, and Lugenia Burns Hope, white teachers such as Mildred Rutherford, Moina Michael, and Katherine Dozier claimed a public discourse that drew from cultural beliefs in duty, self-sufficiency, and evangelical Protestantism to renegotiate feminine identity. Some white women, including Martha Berry and Dozier, borrowed from modern notions of feminism. Through their cultural agency in the 1890s and early twentieth century, the women teachers who followed expanded what it meant to be a professional woman safely ensconced within southern womanhood.

By the turn of the century, white women teachers began to shape the professional role of the teacher by drawing on existing cultural notions of evangelical Protestantism, women's duties, and self-sufficiency to create respectable women's wage labor outside the home and the church. Amelia Akehurst Lines, who taught before Georgia's push for public education for whites, consistently struggled for respect and better wages. By the 1890s white women teachers increasingly demanded respect for their vocation. Moina Belle Michael, born in Walton County in 1869, attended Martin Institute but left in 1885 without graduating because of family financial problems. At age fifteen, she began teaching in a one-room school in her neighborhood. Receiving eight cents per day for sixteen children for five months, she kept twenty dollars for herself and gave ten dollars to her father. For the next three decades, Michael taught in one-room schools, some in Baptist churches and some in larger town buildings, at Bessie Tift College, and at State Normal College. Proud of her accomplishments in the classroom, Michael nonetheless framed her work in terms of helping her family and her community—her duty as an evangelical Protestant woman. In 1917, she became housemother at Winnie Davis Memorial Hall, a women's dormitory at the University of Georgia. After World War I, she established a chapter of the Red Cross at Georgia State Teachers College in Athens. She also started the practice of placing a poppy on veterans' graves each Memorial Day. For her work, she was recognized by the United States, England, and Columbia University. With all the acclaim, Michael referred to herself as "a little wren, just a simple little common place person."[85] Using the metaphor of a wren minimized Michael's achievements as an educator in a manner acceptable to cultural standards of what a respectable white woman should be and do. For all of Michael's work as a teacher and housemother to future teachers, she wanted to be remembered for distributing flowers to World War I veterans, for honoring white soldiers rather than for educating future generations of teachers and children. Duty overshadowed any reference to self-sufficiency or her thirty-year career.

If Michael underscored her volunteerism for veterans rather than her remarkable self-sufficiency, other teachers began to announce claims to an independent career while circumscribing it in the name of duty and evangelical Protestantism. Eight years after Michael was born, Katherine Dozier entered the world in La Grange, although her father, a successful lawyer and insurance agent, subsequently moved the family to Gainesville. Dozier graduated from Brenau College in 1893, when she was sixteen, and moved to Thomasville for her first teaching assignment. She was later assigned to teach at Rabun Gap Industrial School, where she began her lifelong passion for educating working-class white children. By the turn of the century, she returned to Gainesville to teach at Gainesville High School, a prestigious assignment given the marginal conditions in mountain schools. Yet Dozier believed her calling lay in helping working-class families and children, and when the Pacolet Mill Company asked her to become the superintendent of the school for mill workers' children, she quickly accepted. Dozier's career path illustrated conscious choices to combine an independent living with the vocation to work with poor children. As Dozier wrote to Wickliffe Rose, a GEB member, she saw herself as a "mission school teacher" and loved working with and for working-class children. Being able to watch "such marvelous development" in mill children combined duty and respectability. She clearly intended to teach as long as possible and never seemed interested in marriage. During the 1920s, New Holland Mill School became her mission and model for educating members of the working class. The school had a swimming pool, physical education programs, and home economics laboratories. Dozier insisted that the school have an eleven-year program, and although many children no doubt left school without completing all the available grades, she demanded that the children have access to every advantage accorded the children at Gainesville High School. She hired each teacher and required church attendance and involvement in such extracurricular activities as pageants and the May Day festival. Teachers also had to dress appropriately, which, during the 1920s, meant dresses and skirts reaching to the lower calf as well as hose. At church, teachers wore gloves and hats. Most of the mill school's teachers lived in a "teacherage," similar to a dormitory, which outdid boarding conditions for public school teachers in the 1920s. Each teacher had twenty-five students, fewer than white teachers in rural schools. Dozier convinced the mill owners to pay teachers more than Gainesville or other school districts did, thereby attracting teachers, like Florrie Still, who had other offers. Still respected Dozier's methods and professional attitude, which shaped Still's teaching style. Dozier expected teachers to teach Sunday school and visit every student's home. By seeing mill families in their homes and at church, Dozier hoped that teachers would understand the issues mill workers faced and help them—part of her construction of public feminine duty that drew from traditional beliefs in women's private roles with regard to child care and education.[86]

Dozier's combination of duty, style, ambition, professionalism, and traditional women's family roles opened paths for teachers following her. Choosing a career rather than marriage, using a chauffeur to drive her around Hall County, challenging mill owners to create a reputable school, Dozier redefined the representation of the southern lady. A devout Baptist and a member of a Women's Missionary Union, a woman who seemed married to her school and children, a professional who followed conservative clothing styles and refused to learn to drive, Dozier deftly navigated the boundaries between the respectable woman volunteering in charities and the public woman who fashioned dignified wage labor. Outspoken and an activist, Dozier believed that "when you think [someone has] a good idea, go to that person and tell them that the idea they had was a good one. Then they'll do it."[87] By drawing from expectations of southern femininity, Dozier created a position of authority without antagonizing mill or school superintendents. Before her retirement in 1938, she contributed frequent articles to the monthly publication of the Georgia Education Association (GEA), the *Georgia Education Journal*. In one article, "Curriculum Making in Elementary Grades," Dozier subtly rejected modern educational expertise from John Dewey and Stanley Hall in favor of a conservative emphasis on traditional subjects needed, a curriculum based on the activities of an adult rather than the experiences of children.[88] She claimed professional expertise while insisting on preserving some traditional pedagogies. A highlight of her career was her 1921 election as GEA president, the first woman to hold this position.

Born in 1866 to wealthy Episcopal parents, Martha Berry started several day schools in 1901 for children from families who lived in the mountains. In 1902 she opened a boarding school for boys, and over the next decade the facility, located near Rome, Georgia, expanded to include a girls' high school. The school provided industrial and vocational training in addition to an academic curriculum. Combining her Christian beliefs with education, Berry enforced mandatory chapel and worship services for students as well as rules against drinking alcohol and smoking tobacco. Students had to remain in the dormitories during the term—home visits were not permitted. To Berry, mountain children had to learn how to live as well as become educated. By keeping them away from their home environments, she could instruct them on hygiene, work habits, and attire. The emphasis on work at what eventually became known as Berry College drew the attention of northern industrialist Henry Ford and former President Theodore Roosevelt.[89] Like Dozier, Berry used Christian beliefs to claim a professional status as a woman.

Mildred Rutherford, born in 1851 to a wealthy planter family, attended the Lucy Cobb Institute, a school founded by her uncle, Thomas Cobb, in 1859. After completing her education, Rutherford taught in Atlanta for several years before returning to the institute in 1876 to teach history, the Bible, and literature. She taught at Lucy Cobb for almost fifty years and served as the school's director for more than two decades of that time. She focused the curriculum on educating southern ladies, and female students followed strict behavior codes in addition to dress codes. Unlike most teachers, Rutherford wrote her own textbooks, including one on southern history and literature for which she is famous. A member of the United Daughters of the Confederacy, Rutherford instructed her students on the glorious southern past and provided an idealized version of the southern plantation. She grilled students on secession and its legitimacy. At the same time, she refused to allow women to entertain males guests outside their families, to wear expensive fabrics like silk or satin, and to walk to farther than a magnolia tree in the front of the main building. Appalled at some women's brazen behavior, such as allowing men to address them by their first names or failing to discourage men from smoking in women's presence, Rutherford contended that this behavior endangered a southern lady's claim to deference and protection. At Lucy Cobb, students wore no makeup and did not wear skirts above their ankles. One of the most recognized women in Georgia, Rutherford opposed suffrage for women because she feared that it would allow black women to vote and because she believed it violated states' rights. As a staunch Baptist, Rutherford believed God had ordained social differences and to resist a position in God's order defied God's will. Moreover, she believed that suffrage was unnecessary because women's true influence lay within the home. Never married and always a professional, Rutherford idealized women's position in the hierarchy at the same time she demonstrated women's ability to influence education and politics without the vote.[90]

Borrowing various degrees of a religious calling, of ambition for a professional career, and of a desire for respectability and duty, white teachers redefined women's identities while maintaining traditional objectives of evangelical Protestant white womanhood. Like African American women, white women frequently claim to have always known that they would become teachers. In many cases, family members who were teachers told their stories, prompting these girls to pretend to teach their dolls. Ruth Smith Waters's paternal grandmother, Delia Brooks Smith, taught at Martin's Academy in Jackson County for seven years before she married, and Waters stated, "I was born to teach school." Family members, including fathers, apparently encouraged their daughters to teach school because communities defined it as respectable feminine labor, in contrast to work in the expanding textile industry. Martha Breedlove Buice's oldest sister repeatedly told her to become a teacher, and Jimmie Kate Sams Cole's father, the local school superintendent, offered her a teaching position until she decided whether she wanted to teach permanently. Florrie Still and Nelle Still Murphy's father left farming for teaching after God called him to preach. Moving from Walton County to Hall County, James Still found a teaching position in Chattahoochee High School, a Baptist school in Clermont. When he moved to Corinth to teach, both daughters attended the school. Sixteen-year-old Florrie graduated on a Saturday in October 1925 and began teaching with her father the next Monday. Cobb County's Fanny Mc-Clure and Mary Hall Swain wanted to follow their mothers in becoming teachers. "In those days," recalled Swain, "there wasn't much a girl could look forward to doing. You could be a nurse or a teacher, but you didn't think of much of anything else."[91]

As Swain noted, there were limits on white women's professional work. Leona Clark Williams waited until she graduated from Tennessee Wesleyan before deciding to teach. Her debating coach had suggested that she become an attorney, and she remembered, "I would have liked to have done that. I'd been working at . . . mopping floors or anything I could to pay my way through school. I went up to my room and thought, 'There's only two things that women do now. They're either a nurse or they're a teacher.' I didn't have money to buy law books. I'd have starved to death. So that's how I ended up being a teacher."[92]

Considerations of respectability and self-sufficiency thus motivated white women to enter the teaching profession. As ambitious as many teachers were, they had few options for professional work. Teaching was an esteemed activity, even though it lacked the status of other professions such as law or medicine. At no time did any of the white women interviewed for this project consider working in the mills or returning to farming after school. Raised to be self-sufficient and hardworking, they viewed teaching as a means to support themselves and often their families until they married and had children.

Most women tried to find teaching positions close to their families. In 1934, Leona Clark Williams taught at Baldwin and Lula, Georgia, where her parents were living. Florrie Still taught with her father for two years. Ruth Smith Waters took a teaching position in 1928 as principal at Walker Park Grammar School, near Monroe A & M, where she had attended eleventh grade. Then her father and other trustees convinced her to come teach at Chestnut Mountain. A few years later, she took a position at Brazelton in Jackson County and boarded at the local hotel until she married. Jimmie Kate Sams Cole returned to Fayette County from Bessie Tift College and taught at the local high school in 1937. Family ties obviously played a significant role in these women's decisions concerning where they wanted to teach, especially if both parents were still alive. And some fathers, notably those who were school trustees or superintendents, wanted their daughters to teach in local schools, as in the cases of Waters and Cole.

Part of the decision probably represented the fathers' desires to secure teachers of good upbringing and training. Fathers and mothers also seemed to want their single daughters to remain close to home so that their characters would remain impeccable. And most teachers came from close families that sought to preserve family relationships. Yet few daughters expressed any desire to move out of the region, even when other school positions offered more money. Many of these women perceived Atlanta or other large cities as an entirely different world and stated that because roads were so bad, they had never even been to Atlanta. Like many rural residents, some teachers feared city life and its reputation for crime. Other women took trains to Savannah, Macon, or Atlanta but had little desire to stay. Economic circumstances no doubt played a role in their decisions, as did prospects for marriage. Some families needed the extra income provided by working daughters, while others hoped that friends or relatives would provide introductions to future spouses. Indeed, Cole, Williams, and Waters remained in the up-country after their parents' deaths, near the same communities where the women were raised.[93] Yet the lack of mobility meant that teachers remained bound to some of their communities' standards and values and must have limited the extent to which these women dared to challenge hierarchical racist beliefs: doing so would have required confronting family members and lifelong friends.

During the 1920s and 1930s, school trustees and superintendents continued to require certain moral standards of the women they hired. Leona Clark Williams remembered going dancing with her Uncle Vic while she was teaching at Lula: "He picked me up and carried me up to Demorest to the dance. There was a lady over there, and she said, 'They'll fire her. They'll fire her if they know she went to a dance.' So I went and told Uncle Vic to carry me home." According to Ruth Smith Waters, "When you taught under the trustees, you knew your trustees and they knew you. They knew your background. They knew your grandpa and your grandma. They knew if you went to church, but they wouldn't tell you you had to go."[94]

Trustees such as those at Chestnut Mountain and Lula expected certain moral standards of their teachers, notably church attendance and proper attire. Until World War II, white women had to quit teaching when they married. Women were to embody respectable community values such as temperance, hard work, and evangelical Protestantism. Such requirements may appear restrictive, but it is also open to question whether many of these women would have acted differently if they had been allowed to do so. By hiring women who attended local Baptist or Methodist churches, trustees knew they were getting teachers who avoided playing cards or drinking alcohol, who had been raised to work long hours, and who had little tolerance for classroom behavior perceived as lazy or foolish. Such women had little in common with the somewhat frightening image of the modern "New Woman" of urban industrial areas. Film stars who smoked cigarettes, flirted, and danced to jazz music seemed alien to most rural women. To their parents and churches, urban and movie culture represented secularization, decline of authority, and decadent modernity. Not all rural women agreed, of course, and some heeded the cities' beckoning lights and opportunities for entertainment.[95] But the women who became teachers were not enticed. As Waters stated, the trustees hired only women who regularly attended church, so there was little need to require them to do so. None of the teachers recall any rules concerning attire, possibly because the women who were hired were unlikely to adopt the flapper attire of shorter hemlines and hairstyles. Parents, church, and community had taught these women that bobbed hair was scandalous, as was premarital sex. And none of the women demonstrated any inclination to disagree with these norms.

In fact, while future white teachers such as Williams and Waters attended either high school grades or college in preparation for teaching, they complied with the rules of their schools. After Williams was appointed chaperone for a group of students one weekend, she turned in two classmates for drinking beer. She was reluctant to do so but took seriously her responsibilities as chaperone. Waters was relieved when two fellow students at Monroe A & M were reprimanded for putting shoe polish in another girl's hair. Conversely, singing after lights out, dating, going to the movies, and learning how to drive were memorable and enjoyable times. For example, when Williams was dating her future husband, Bill Williams, she claimed, "we probably could have bought the . . . theater in Gainesville because we went there every night."[96]

There were, of course, teachers who transgressed the commonly accepted mores. Waters knew an unmarried teacher who became pregnant, and Williams met students at college who drank alcohol and smoked cigarettes. Moonshine in the up-country was prevalent, as was sexual activity during evening rides in wagons or cars. Yet by and large, the women who became teachers regarded such pastimes as outside the boundaries of respectable behavior. Even if they had never taught school or been expected to uphold community morals by school trustees, these women would have undoubtedly followed similar values. Cole, Florrie Still, Waters, Williams and those like them also differentiated themselves from the town elite. To Waters, the Green Street residents in Gainesville "had a high-headed feeling about themselves. Most of them belonged to the First Baptist Church. Real uptown people, very prissy."[97]

As with African American teachers, many white teachers claim to have known how to teach well before taking training courses or teaching in the public schools. Leona Clark Williams learned throughout her education the difference between good and bad teachers, at least from her perspective. To her, a dedicated teacher was a person who worked after school with students who needed additional help. The teacher at the mountain school who worked with Williams on her reading and the college English teacher who taught Williams about double negatives and put her on the debating team modeled the kind of devotion to students she always valued. Florrie Still's model of a good teacher drew from her experiences with Katherine Dozier. Still taught in Corinth for two years before being hired at New Holland Mill School by Dozier. For the rest of Still's career, she insisted on home visits and a combination of religious instruction with academics. Fanny McClure's influences included science and history teachers.[98]

Teachers also learned how they wanted to teach from negative experiences in their own schooling. For example, Williams recalled that her English teacher at the Franklin high school "was as mean as the devil. She told us that if you said a word incorrectly when you came in the class, it was five points off your report card. . . . I'd get my paper back and it would look like it had been bled all over with all of this red pencil." Williams was so afraid of her teacher that she never asked questions in class.[99] Williams's school experiences taught her the value of teacher assistance, the need for teachers to be approachable and accessible to students.

In addition to learning such "people skills" and possessing an appropriate moral, Protestant background, future teachers obviously needed academic training, an aspect that Cole's and Waters's fathers particularly stressed. Unlike black teachers, white teachers had teaching manuals, although they tended to add and subtract from the curriculum. Teachers taught penmanship, reading, arithmetic, and other academic core courses. Williams assigned writing themes, spelling lists, and sentences. Williams, like all elementary school teachers, divided her class into groups (the red birds and the blue birds) according to students' reading level. Williams and other teachers extensively used memorization—excerpts from Shakespeare, Lincoln's Gettysburg Address, poetry, and so on. Book reports were also common. Many white women taught history according to southern texts that never mentioned slavery, glorified the myths of the plantation, and referred to the Civil War as a fight for states' rights.[100] Teachers' manuals suggested programs for certain holidays, including Robert E. Lee's birthday on January 12 and Confederate Memorial Day on April 26. These teachers were also expected to teach physical education, music, and art.[101]

As professionals, teachers devised their own methods for instruction. Ruth Smith Waters taught her students Georgia history from the state bird to Rebecca Latimer Felton. Mary Hall Swain and other teachers used readings from magazines such as *National Geographic* or *John Martin*. Although debates about Darwinism raged across the South, Jimmie Kate Sams Cole was the only teacher interviewed who included Darwin's theories in her classes. All teachers included religious instruction, and the day opened with prayer and devotional readings, usually from books provided by their Baptist and Methodist churches. To Fanny McClure, prayer and Bible readings were the most important part of the day. Whatever they taught and however they taught it, teachers built on their reputation as professionals. Only they knew what students should know and how they should know it. The formula for success continued to separate the teacher and the school from community traditions. By supplanting oral wisdom with knowledge from books, teachers subverted traditional forms of learning—parents, the community, and the church—thereby fashioning gendered clout.

Most white teachers, like their African American counterparts, had experience in handling children. Some women were the oldest children in their families and had to take responsibility for younger siblings: as Leona Clark Williams put it, "I had to get them to school. . . . That way I learned to work with children. Then when I took teacher training at Tennessee Wesleyan, I didn't have any trouble making an A on my training because I'd already been trained."[102] Williams always had at least one sibling with her wherever she went until she left for high school, and this arrangement was common.

Other women gained early experience in teaching by teaching Sunday school classes at age thirteen or fourteen.[103] Ruth Smith Waters's father was the Sunday school superintendent at their Methodist church and had his oldest daughter teach third- and fourth-grade children. "Daddy would go over the Sunday school lesson as we walked to church. We had cards with a religious picture on them, and there would be a memory verse. We called them card classes."[104] All teachers of both races interviewed for this project taught Sunday school at some point, and many continued to do so through adulthood and even into retirement from secular teaching. Teachers unquestionably connected public and sacred education, combining their religious responsibilities for saving and redeeming young children with their duties as teachers. Devotions and prayer were as important to their lesson plans as reading and arithmetic.

Although white teachers drew from traditional values, their ambitions pushed them off their parents' farms and in so doing redefined what it meant to be a reputable white woman.[105] They witnessed the constant chores of child care, housework, cooking, and sewing. "I have never been attracted to housework," stated Jimmie Kate Sams Cole. "I find it excruciatingly dull." "I never did stay at home and knit and crochet and darn," agreed Leona Clark Williams. "I never did that sort of thing." Mary Hall Swain stopped teaching after marrying and bearing children: "I was going to be the sweet little wife and stay at home," she recalled, but "I got bored to distraction" and returned to the classroom. Other teachers, including Ruth Smith Waters, enjoyed quilting and sewing. Yet none of the white women interviewed had more than three children, a striking contrast to most of their mothers, who had at least four and as many as eleven. Whatever method of birth control was used—and the interviewees scrupulously avoided the subject—these women clearly limited their families in ways their mothers had not. Following national patterns of smaller families, white teachers adopted modern trends and had fewer children. When the state began to hire married women to teach in the late 1930s, white women saw a means to combine a respectable career with marriage and motherhood. "I felt that I was a better mother because I taught," claimed Cole. "When I stay at home all day, I get cross."[106]

In most instances, white teachers, like black teachers, used any available resources to improve classroom instruction and enhance the profession. As the USDA increased its role in the state, white teachers drew from the Extension Service to clarify their domain of expertise. Predictably, Georgia counties approved more funds for white Extension Service agents than for black agents. In 1910, Georgia's Extension Service allowed local county officials to appoint former Confederate soldiers or county school superintendents to promote programs. By the 1920s, county agents received some funds from University of Georgia's College of Agriculture and obtained training in objectives of service work.[107] Demonstrations of better farming methods, home gardening, cooking, and sanitation were held at rural schools. Some home demonstration clubs sponsored school fund-raising programs such as quilting parties. Connecting the USDA's extension work with white teachers added to reformers' calls for standardization in curriculum because schools offered courses in domestic science and manual training. White colleges, agricultural and training schools, and the University of Georgia, the home of the state's Extension Service, created departments of domestic science and expanded agricultural programs. Recognizing schools as "community centers for meetings of various clubs," Extension Service agents noted that "the part of the trained teacher in community organization is invaluable."[108]

Some historians have noted the consequences of Extension Service work in communities, as hundreds of rural men and women attended meetings to learn ways of improving life in a state that continued to obtain most of its poultry and grain from other states. Black and white farmers acquired similar training in agricultural methods, crop rotation, and prevention of the boll weevil, while women learned about canning, nutrition, and home gardens. Nevertheless, differences remained. White women in home demonstration clubs used standardized butter molds and USDA recipes for relish and preserves and donned caps and aprons that marked them as club members. These meetings provided men and women with opportunities not only to discuss the USDA's agenda but also to share the latest events in their lives. Some farm families increased their cash income by participating in livestock and egg production programs, and the Extension Service unquestionably contributed to the rise in poultry and egg production in northeast Georgia, later known as the capital of the poultry industry.[109]

At the same time, the Extension Service weakened community structures by emphasizing advice from experts rather than inherited oral instructions. Furthermore, the tomato clubs and beautification programs for women attracted those who had the time and the means to attend meetings rather than tenants and sharecroppers. Enrollments in white southern women's clubs remained at less than 5 percent of all farm women.[110] Similar to African American families, few white farmers could afford to upgrade their kitchens in rented homes. According to the agents, farmers ignored advice about crop rotation, and many remained ineligible for loans from local bankers because they had little collateral. Moreover, bankers persisted in demanding cotton yields for loan agreements. Many Georgians continued to question the value of standardization, professional advice, and modernity: although white Georgians had become accustomed to federal aid since Reconstruction, they preferred to control the national government's reach and power.

To overcome this reluctance, white Extension Service agents continued to work with adults but focused their efforts on the next generation. Lurline Collier, a home demonstration agent in Jackson County, reported in 1919 that schools accomplished more with girls because they "realize more the value of Domestic Science being taught."[111] "Showing the Way," a play written by Laura Blackshear for the Farmers' Conference at the University of Georgia in 1924, conveyed the significance of clubs for girls and boys. In the play, John and Laura Neidlinger are the son and daughter of poor farmers. The father wears patched clothes and overalls, a cultural indicator to professionals of the "ignorant, superstitious, and pessimistic" traditional farmer. His wife bears the stereotypical demeanor of the "old fashioned . . . cheerful and hopeful" farm wife. John and Laura's attire and personalities change during the play. John's clothes "gradually change from neat, patched overalls to correct suit for conservative college student," while Laura changes from a barefoot girl with braids and "a ridiculous broad brimmed hat trimmed with flowers" to a girl with shorter hair and "plain, neat, and modern" clothes.[112]

The children then carry the message of agricultural science and consumerism to their parents. John and Laura join local clubs and complete projects that earn them cash and scholarships. While attending the University of Georgia, John learns about electricity, telephones, and indoor plumbing as well as better farming methods. Laura attends a girls' club camp in Athens where she cuts her hair and shortens the hems of her dresses.[113] With their new knowledge, John and Laura help their parents make a profit on their farm by raising tobacco in addition to cotton and improving the family home with curtains, flowers, and better furniture. John decides to return to his county as an Extension Service worker and run a model farm to serve his community.[114] The play works at several levels. John and Laura embody the future hopes for Georgia agriculture, willing to learn about new methods. Moreover, John and Laura change. They lose their distinctive, absurdly replicated southern drawl; they adopt attire more attuned to national, middle-class norms; they continue their education; and they desire modern conveniences. They represent modern farmers who can participate in national culture. More importantly, local schools and the university play the vital role in this transformation. Without teachers and professors to spread word of scientific methods, standardization, and efficiency, John and Laura would remain caught in debt, ignorance, and poverty. Teachers represent a break with a past that counts for little more than silly folk tales and superstitions.

White county and home demonstration agents consistently emphasized work in the schools. Club membership earned boys and girls promotions or rewards for school attendance. To the Extension Service's and teachers' credit, some children earned scholarships to attend high school or even college. Agents in Hall County helped students open bank accounts and secure loans to go to college.[115] Teachers taught sanitation and hygiene by discussing how to dress and bathe. They sponsored cleanup days at schools, with grounds swept, outhouses scrubbed, and flowers planted. Students learned about improved diet and nutrition as well as disease prevention. Screens appeared on windows and doors to keep insects out of homes and schools. Teachers began to have students bring drinking cups from home to avoid using the common gourd at the well.

Even teachers' attire distinguished them to some extent from many children's parents, who wore overalls and patched dresses and shoes with cracks or holes.

Teachers began to help students adapt to modern culture, to teach what they needed to succeed in a less parochial world. To do so often required their understanding of classroom management, language taken from Progressives concerned about efficiency and organization.[116] Preserving order in the classroom meant relying on different techniques for discipline. While some teachers' manuals approved of corporal punishment, educators such as T. J. Woofter recommended other methods, including individual talks and conversations with parents.[117] Some teachers never used corporal punishment. Recalling confrontations with her father, Leona Clark Williams never spanked children but preferred to talk to them and their parents. Ruth Smith Waters, among others, agreed. Fanny McClure, Jimmie Kate Sams Cole, and Florrie Still believed corporal punishment was necessary at times but always did it themselves rather than sending students to the principal. Most white teachers, like black teachers, knew that if students were punished at school, they would also be punished at home. How they disciplined students came from cultural expectations and individual experiences.

Beyond classroom and community, white teachers renegotiated their goals for public policy and education in their professional organization, the GEA. Because of a lack of state-supported education, teacher organizations repeatedly collapsed until 1867. In 1867 the Georgia Teachers Association met in Atlanta with twenty-five teachers—all men—attending. The organization held its first annual meeting in 1869, with forty-five teachers, including some blacks, present. The organization called for public funds for education, boards of education in each county, and teacher training programs. In 1900, the organization changed its name to the Georgia Education Association and excluded black teachers. For the next two decades, the GEA lobbied the state legislature for compulsory attendance laws, better teacher training, local taxation measures, and efforts to equalize education for rural and urban white children. The group also called for higher standards for teacher certification, including two years of education beyond high school and special courses in education. Because of the GEA's lobbying, women were finally admitted to the University of Georgia in 1918. The GEA's membership began to expand significantly in the 1920s, nearly doubling in size from just over six hundred members in 1920 to almost eleven hundred members. Local branches ran campaigns to encourage teachers to join. Some teachers looked forward to the annual conventions, held in Atlanta, Savannah, Macon, and Augusta, that provided an opportunity to meet other teachers and to shop at city stores. The GEA paid little attention to the state of education for African Americans, however; from the organization's perspective, education for whites was their priority.[118]

Even as teachers redefined professionalism, they occasionally limited its connotations. Cotton culture's values of duty and obligation—the shards of paternalism that still existed in Georgia—undermined teachers' claim to professional status when they worked for free or discounted wages. During the Great Depression, when Georgia lacked the funds to pay teachers for months in 1937–39, Jimmie Kate Sams Cole and others worked for free, deeming the students' need for an education to be greater than the teachers' need for a paycheck. Waters and Williams often used personal funds to purchase school supplies. Superintendents occasionally rewarded these contributions by offering teachers their choice of school positions or newly painted classrooms. If teachers wanted communities and school boards to regard them as experts, however, these labors seldom enhanced their goals. Rather, teachers tried to negotiate constructions of the public servant with professional authority.

AT THE SAME TIME African American and white women struggled to define themselves as professionals, leading Georgia education reformers and northern philanthropic foundations such as the GEB and the JRF sought to improve teachers' salaries and credentials. From the beginning of Georgia's efforts to create a public school system, teacher training presented a central concern of state reformers such as M. L. Brittain, Joseph Stewart, Walter Hill, and T. J. Woofter (see chap. 3). One of Brittain's primary concerns during his tenure as state school superintendent was the lack of sufficient salaries for white teachers. Male teachers, black and white, received more money than women teachers; urban teachers, black and white, were better paid than rural teachers. Brittain believed that students, "the future citizens of the State," suffered because of teachers' low salaries.[119] In some instances, teachers received less pay than female mill workers, although few middle-class daughters chose mill work because of its less respectable reputation. Brittain argued that the state needed to pay more "to retain the competent, to say nothing of making the profession attractive to the best."[120] But Brittain's suggestion that married white women be permitted to teach was not implemented until twenty-five years later.

Yet another chronic problem all teachers confronted from the early twentieth century through the Great Depression was the failure of the state and counties to pay teachers on time. More often than not, Georgia was unable to pay the sums appropriated for educational expenditures.[121] Thus, many schools closed early unless their districts could manage to allocate emergency funds to supplement state monies. The only districts that usually could obtain additional funds were town or city school systems, which had greater tax bases than poorer rural systems. Again, rural teachers, black and white, male and female, bore the brunt of Georgia's poor financial status, with black women occupying the lowest rung of the salary ladder. In an effort to keep white schools open for seven months and black schools open for six months, many districts discounted teachers' salaries by issuing warrants or paper scrip that could be redeemed at local banks or stores. As mentioned earlier, Leona Clark Williams was paid with a car and a warrant rather than cash. In such cases, warrants were always exchanged at lower prices than the promised salaries. But Georgia educators as well as GEB representatives constantly reprimanded counties and the state for low teacher salaries, which deprived the state of good teachers.[122]

Teachers' salaries sometimes remained unpaid until the fall, when crop taxes were collected. For single women who lacked nearby family or friends, such a predicament was fearsome indeed. To live from March or April until October without remuneration required some fancy budgeting. As State School Supervisor I. S. Smith commented in 1933, the teachers were making "great sacrifices" for the students by working at times without pay.[123] Teachers such as Leona Clark Williams, Ruth Smith Waters, and Dorothy Oliver Rucker wondered whether they would receive vouchers for their work and if so, whether banks or department stores such as Rich's would honor the vouchers. Yet the system underscored the favoritism trustees and superintendents demonstrated for local women, who were apt to have family or friends to assist them through such dry spells. Because many African American female teachers were married, they could, at least theoretically, rely on their husbands' income, although that income was often also precarious. H. A. Hunt from Fort Valley Normal and Industrial School and other African American educators repeatedly warned the GEB about Georgia's failure to adequately pay black teachers.[124]

Part of Brittain's and other reformers attempts to improve salaries entailed improving teacher training, or professionalizing the training required for teaching, notably for white women. Greater emphasis was placed on specific education courses at the State Normal School in Athens or Georgia Normal and Industrial School in Milledgeville. Consequently, from 1915 to 1940, Georgia's Department of Education repeatedly modified and upgraded teacher certification requirements, offering lifetime professional certificates to women who had completed teacher training at one of the state normal schools or the University of Georgia's School of Education.

The GEB and the JRF encouraged and financially supported these state efforts to improve teacher training. As late as 1925, most women still received their certificates by means of exams administered by city or county superintendents. Some white women attended summer training institutes in their districts or traveled to Athens or Milledgeville to take specific courses such as child psychology, history of education, or educational theory. African American women attended summer institutes offered at Fort Valley, Albany, Forsyth, and Atlanta, while white women attended Athens, Milledgeville, or one of the county institutes. Beginning in 1921, teachers could obtain professional normal certificates, which meant that they had graduated from an approved Georgia normal school and had taken two years of courses beyond high school, including practice teaching and the history of education. Teachers could also acquire professional college certificates, which required a bachelor's degree, educational courses, and practice teaching. These certificates secured the highest wages for teachers.

From the beginning of their involvement in southern education, the GEB, the John Slater Fund, the Anna T. Jeanes Fund, and eventually the JRF were concerned about Georgia's inability to organize teacher training, at least according to GEB standards. In 1924, the GEB's Frank Bachman complained to fellow board member Abraham Flexner about Georgia's poor libraries and lack of practice teaching for prospective teachers. By this time, the northern and midwestern states had established teacher training programs in normal schools and colleges that included practice teaching. Most twentieth-century educators believed that practice teaching was essential because it provided students with actual teaching experience under the supervision of experienced educators. Bachman also objected to what he perceived as a lack of organization in Georgia's State Department of Education and believed that Georgia lagged far behind even other southern states such as North Carolina and Virginia. In December 1924, Bachman recommended that teacher training be reorganized and that certification be removed from local officials and that practice teaching be required.[125]

To assist Georgia and other southern states in preparing suitable teacher education programs, the GEB held conferences and urged improved certification requirements. Bachman and Woofter, chair of the Education Department at the University of Georgia, corresponded about ways of improving white teachers' professional training at the university. Woofter sought an expanded curriculum for all prospective teachers, notably white teachers, including those who taught elementary school, that would entail courses in the history of education, educational psychology, and methods of teaching certain subjects. His beliefs in teacher training emphasized a broader approach rather than specific courses according to content and grade level.

Another Georgia reformer, E. A. Pound, who served as the director of the Division of Certification for the Department of Education, complained to Bachman that as of 1925, Georgia spent less per capita on education than any other southern state. Educators in the Georgia Department of Education agreed that teachers needed additional course requirements and increased course work at the State Normal School in 1926. Congruent with this plan, educators insisted on better salaries for all teachers, although salaries for white and black teachers remained unequal. As noted in chapter 3, educators Walter Hill and J. C. Dixon realized that many blacks left Georgia after graduating from school to take better-paying teaching positions in North Carolina and elsewhere. And Hill consistently reminded the General Assembly, the GEB, and the Georgia Department of Education that African American teachers needed better salaries and appropriate training institutes from which they could also obtain professional certification.[126]

Whereas Woofter and Bachman were concerned primarily with certification of white teachers, the GEB and later the JRF also examined African American teacher training. In 1921, Jackson Davis, the general field agent for the GEB, reported that in the South, there was little interest in teacher training for blacks because "any attempts for public support and control were branded as an unwarranted invasion of individual liberty, socialism, and at best, as an expedient for the education of the poor."[127] For most southern states, agricultural schools, largely funded through the Smith-Hughes Act, provided teacher training for blacks. Yet as Davis noted and as Walter Hill Jr. reported to the federal government in 1925, Georgia in particular failed to provide adequate state facilities for black teachers' certification, which meant teacher certification for industrial teaching.

Confusion regarding black and white teacher certification requirements continued throughout the early 1920s. In 1926, eight white public colleges and universities and three African American colleges were technically part of the University of Georgia system, but each branch was controlled by its own board of regents, which competed with other boards for funds in the General Assembly and rarely agreed on statewide professional standards.[128] Because of this arrangement, not only did some schools like the University of Georgia become favorites of the General Assembly, but black colleges, already operating under racist pedagogical and economic restrictions, lacked the political clout necessary to obtain needed funds.

In 1917, Georgia had added the Georgia Normal and Agricultural School in Albany and the Forsyth A & M State School to the GSIC to provide state-supported black education. Still, none of the schools had the libraries, classroom space, dormitories, and other facilities needed to provide proper teacher training. And for Davis, teacher training meant only training black teachers at the industrial or low-skilled level. As many educators observed, beginning in 1918, the black migration northward encouraged Georgia legislators to appropriate more funds for black education. Nevertheless, just as white schools and teachers rarely received their full appropriations from the General Assembly, black schools and teachers continued to receive far less than was promised. As late as 1927, the GEB continued to note that Georgia required financial assistance for teacher training, unlike North Carolina and Virginia.[129]

The GEB was scarcely alone in its condemnation of Georgia's professional education facilities. The JRF had its own anxieties concerning teacher training during the 1920s heyday of its school campaign in the rural South. Throughout this decade, the fund sponsored conferences for state agents of Negro schools. Georgia's state agent, Walter Hill Jr., repeatedly mentioned the deplorable lack of funding for black schools. At the 1929 conference, Hill reported that only two Georgia counties provided transportation for black students to black high schools and that more than a third of Georgia's counties failed to offer high school courses for blacks. Leo Favrot and Fred McCuistion, agents for the GEB and JRF, respectively, noted that Georgia paid its teachers less than any other southern state, spent the least per student, and received approximately 85 percent of its higher education endowment from private sources such as the GEB and JRF.[130]

Notwithstanding the JRF's preference for industrial training for black teachers, fund agents agreed that African American instructors needed better training in the educational fundamentals. At the 1928 conference, Bachman presented a plan for a two-year teacher training program that included English, history, geography, math, and practice teaching. Conference participants maintained that such a definitive program was required for professional work. Because few teachers were able to attend such a program and few states were willing to fund it, Jeanes supervisors observed and commented on as many black teachers as they could, although up-country counties such as Hall and Gwinnett with few black residents remained on their own. Still, Hill continued to protest the lack of a state-funded professional teacher training program for African Americans.[131]

During the 1930s, under the direction of Edwin Embree, the JRF and the GEB increased the pressure on Georgia to improve black teacher training.

Dixon continued to complain about the large number of teachers who "still teach under the authority of county licenses issued as a result of examination by the County School Superintendent."[132] Part of Dixon's and Hill's concern unquestionably stemmed from the Progressives' penchant for efficiency and organization. They saw the Georgia Department of Education as a morass of standards and requirements, an unmanageable agency that lacked any resemblance to a proper bureaucratic mechanism. Still, Hill and Dixon deplored the state's failure to provide public funds for black teacher training and schools. And given many white Georgians' fears concerning professional as opposed to industrial training for African American teachers, any reforms in teacher training had to proceed slowly and, at times, clandestinely.

Embree, regarded as a liberal by many blacks and whites, soberly noted the predicament of black teacher training in Georgia. Convinced that part of the South's need included an emphasis on rural education, Embree instigated a rural teacher training program in Georgia that would use Fort Valley State College and West Georgia College at Carrollton as rural teacher training colleges. JRF funds would pay for instructional salaries, building repairs, and other operational expenses. In 1936, GEB and JRF agents recommended that Georgia purchase Fort Valley State College from the American Church Institute, thereby resulting in a state-funded college for African Americans that offered both agricultural and educational programs.[133]

These plans ceased during the late years of the Great Depression, which dried up state public school funds and silenced much criticism from both inside and outside the state. Whatever chances Georgia's reformers or teachers might have had to enact improvements were squashed by the collapse of cotton prices from 1928 through the 1930s. Like other southern states, Georgia's inability to collect taxes practically crippled public funds. Between 1928 and 1940 Georgia rarely paid its full school appropriations. For example, in 1933, the state owed almost three million dollars to the Department of Education.[134]

To the members of the State Department of Education and other educators, such a position was at best untenable. By this time, teachers had supplanted parents in educating children and needed public recognition for their professional labor in the classrooms. As the JRF's S. L. Smith remarked, "Most of our teachers are employed because they have the professional training to teach and have demonstrated that ability in previous work. Surely they are in a better position to do the teaching than the parent or the older brother or sister who has not had the professional training and the experience or who does not have the time to teach the child at home."[135] To buttress their argument for raising teachers' salaries, Georgia educators emphasized the professional skills and expert knowledge teachers acquired before practicing their craft. The public schools had evolved from an educational system that relied on households to teach children for a rural world into a system that demanded expert training as well as removal from the household to teach survival skills in a modern industrial world.

To improve the university system and attempt to standardize teaching requirements, Governor Richard Russell reorganized the Georgia university system in 1932 and appointed a board of regents that would set policies for all colleges. Following the election of Governor Eugene Talmadge, however, centralization and standardization slowed considerably. Talmadge had been elected with the support of Georgians who opposed the shift from local authority to centralized state authority.[136] Still, reformers had attempted to solve some of the Georgia school system's flaws before the Great Depression and had finally begun to recognize the need for better schools and teacher training in a changing world. No longer could parents count on teaching their children how to plant cotton and farm for a practicable living. At the same time, Georgia had, perhaps unintentionally, improved standards for African American schools and teachers. If, as Georgia reformers insisted, white teachers required professional training, how could industrial training suffice for black teachers?

Surrounded by change and continuity in their schools and settlements, African American and white female teachers maintained professional standards, perhaps regardless of what state authorities and professors deemed necessary for proper teaching. African American teachers defied efforts to restrict their cultural work in the classroom by claiming it as a cultural domain for race work. White teachers challenged notions of southern womanhood by carving a professional space outside the family. Together, the two groups subverted expectations of subordination for women. Raised in a culture that emphasized individual conversion, duty to God, and traditional values, these women defined their classrooms as extensions of these beliefs at the same time that they began to distinguish their profession from past constructions of womanhood. The classroom became the domain in which teachers promoted new national norms they believed could be successfully combined with the best of their inherited values. That modernity with its promotion of secularization, individual accomplishment, and consumer culture might conflict with evangelical Protestantism and community and family ties rarely, if ever, occurred to them. They preserved their beliefs in uplift and insisted on receiving professional respect.

5 · Passing the Torch

Teachers, Jim Crow, and New Deal Politics

THE GREAT DEPRESSION, which struck southern agriculture as early as 1926, forced many students to leave school to work and pushed families off farms in search of wage labor in cities or towns. For the first time since Beulah Rucker Oliver's school opened, she faced a chronic shortage of students. The trickle of blacks leaving for cities or jobs in the North swelled, while other black families needed their children's labor in the fields. Oliver refused to migrate north because of her overriding commitment to her school and racial uplift; instead, she, her teachers, and her daughters began walking around Hall County looking for students. Black parents who worked as janitors or maids in New Holland, in Hall County, where Pacolet Manufacturing operated a textile mill, agreed to let their children attend as long as Oliver or one of the other teachers accompanied them to school. While the increase in students allowed the school to remain open, Oliver and her staff exhausted themselves because they had to get up earlier in the mornings, walk to New Holland, bring the students to school, teach all day, and then return the children home. At the end of the 1930s, Oliver purchased a Model T bus with which, for about three years, she transported children from outside the Gainesville area to and from the school.[1]

For Leona Clark Williams, the Great Depression and the New Deal changed her and her family's lives. Although Williams had planned to teach French and Latin in the public schools, Georgia's education system was bankrupt by the 1930s. A school at Baldwin offered Williams a job sponsored by New Deal funds. Williams "took fifteen children that were malnourished and making poor grades." In a pilot program for school lunchrooms, the children ate lunches prepared by the school principal's wife, and a local dairy provided milk. Williams tested the students every three months. The lunchroom program studied the correlation between better-nourished children and academic performance. At the same time, Williams's parents refused to take food or clothing from relief officials but moved to Lula, Georgia, where a tuberculosis sanitarium was located, to grow vegetables for the state and the sanitarium. Robin and Sudie Bowman Clark deemed "welfare," or aid without work, shameful and embarrassing but, like other Americans, accepted state or federal help tied to work. After reading about beekeeping and honey, Robin Clark, with the support of county agricultural extension agent John Arendale, placed hives throughout Macon County. For the next thirty years, Clark sold white honey to Carter's Wholesale in Gainesville. Beekeeping and raising vegetables for the sanitarium, forms of government work aid, helped the Clark family survive the Great Depression.[2]

Oliver's and Williams's stories of bankrupt schools and poor facilities, of families searching for better jobs and new means of survival, and of the failure of localism represent the common threads that led to upheavals sweeping across Georgia and other states during the Great Depression. By the late 1920s, Georgia still faced the dilemma of funding four different school systems—black and white, rural and urban. As Extension Service agents, home demonstration agents, Jeanes teachers, and black and white teachers sought to improve educational standards and inculcate modern values, northern philanthropists and women's missionary groups provided economic props for an inadequately funded educational system founded on a racist and class-based hierarchy. To some Georgians, the system as it existed adequately prepared future adults for agricultural employment, particularly in cotton. For others, black and white, education rapidly became the capital they could use to define themselves as individuals or practitioners of a new way of life that measured their worth by their income, jobs, attire, level of consumption, and avoidance of backbreaking rural labor. The tension between these two attitudes toward education set the stage for the cultural and political clashes in Georgia from the 1930s through the 1940s.

As economic hardship brought Georgia's meager efforts at social services to their knees, the New Deal and World War II compressed Georgia's modernization into a remarkable fifteen-year period of change. Historians have depicted the challenges to traditions that resulted from heated political battles, efforts to organize workers, New Deal programs that forced farmers off the land, and cultural renegotiation.[3] While state residents had always tolerated federal government assistance from the Extension Service or funds for vocational schools and northern philanthropic aid for African American schools, the growing reach of the federal government and its programs' regulations altered the contours of Georgians' lives from the Great Depression through World War II.[4] By expanding the federal government's role in Georgia and creating a modern bureaucratic state, the New Deal and war-related industrial development changed Georgians through government programs such as the National Youth Administration (NYA), Agricultural Adjustment Act, and the Social Security

Act.[5] As a result, former tenants and sharecroppers began to move to towns and cities looking for new employment, and large landholders switched to agribusiness and mechanized methods. World War II intensified the migration off the land into industry, as military bases and war industries came to Savannah, Marietta, Brunswick, Warner Robbins, and Macon.

From 1930 to 1945, Georgia voters vacillated between Governor Eugene Talmadge's efforts to preserve traditions and reject New Deal reforms and Governors Eurith D. Rivers's and Ellis Arnall's moderate reforms. Families and churches lost control of institutions such as schools, with state and federal governments taking over. Black and white women tossed aside their aprons and hoes and redefined feminine authority in new professional careers as education supervisors and state government administrators. At the same time, African Americans organized and intensified the attack on Jim Crow's denial of access to political and social rights.[6]

Yet of all these changes that swept across the South and Georgia during the 1930s, Georgia's development of public education represented the prime motivator of the contentious transition to modernity. Education became the arena in which traditional beliefs in class, race, gender, localism, and evangelical Protestantism clashed with individualism, separation from family and community identity, secular and consumer culture, and social and economic progress. Through an often convoluted process of action and reaction, accommodation and opposition, Georgia finally assembled a modern public school system by 1946. At times unintentionally, educational reform cut through the quagmire of conflicting cultural and social values, as political leaders, reformers, and parents debated what should be taught, who should teach, and how the material should be taught. At the end of World War II, a new generation of Georgians defined an education as an integral means of improving their lives. They could make better salaries and buy consumer goods; they could gain status with high school diplomas rather than the family name; they could escape what they now perceived as a tawdry and exhausting rural lifestyle.

The more education came to define an individual's worth, the more it fractured class, race, and gender boundaries. Improved schools for all Georgians promised equalization among individuals, an escape from poverty and dependency, an end to the appalling disparities between black and white and rural and urban schools. Since Reconstruction, African Americans had seen education as a means to resist racist assumptions about inferiority and flee the cycle of dependency on whites. By the 1930s, Charles Houston, legal strategist for the National Association for the Advancement of Colored People (NAACP), regarded education as "central to advancement and fulfillment within American culture," echoing the claims of African Americans Booker T. Washington, W. E. B. Du Bois, Lucy Craft Laney, Charlotte Hawkins Brown, and Beulah Rucker Oliver; white reformers such as Walter B. Hill Jr.; and teachers through the century.[7] However unrealistic these hopes may have been, the fact that education became a key issue in elections, legislation, and reform attests to the power most Georgians attributed to the schools by 1930. A centralized educational system cracked the framework of localism that had, along with Georgia's conservative constitution, allowed white county officials to have an extraordinary amount of authority over political appointments, school policies, and most social policies. Losing this authority, some parents and communities raged against the changes, just as in Virginia and North Carolina.[8] Public education, now cut from local control, released the deepest fears of modernity—industrialization, secularization, women's increasing public authority, possible equality between the races, impersonal bureaucracies, and self-serving consumption. Political, social, and cultural tensions raged across Georgia's farms, rivers, hills, and cities.

THE COMBINED EFFORTS of northern philanthropists, reformers, the U.S. Department of Agriculture (USDA), and teachers improved education for many Georgia youths. Yet much more was needed. The demographics of Georgia shifted before 1930 and would dramatically change during the New Deal. In 1910 almost 80 percent of the population was rural; by 1930, that number had dropped to about 70 percent. This trend in Georgia paralleled events in the rest of the South, although Florida and North Carolina witnessed greater increases in urban growth. From 1910 to 1930, rural blacks declined from 46 percent of Georgia's African American population to just over 37 percent. Spurred by labor shortages during World War I, approximately one hundred thousand African Americans left the state for better working conditions, education opportunities, and voting rights in the North, while other blacks as well as whites sought similar advantages in Georgia's towns and cities. Blacks dropped from 45 percent of Georgia's total population in 1910 to slightly more than 36 percent in 1930, still one of the nation's largest concentrations of black people.[9]

As school reformers and teachers fought to improve facilities, curricula, and professional standards, Georgia, like other rural states, faced a crisis in public education during the 1930s. According to the 1930 census, most of Georgia's urban children between ages seven and twelve attended public schools—92 percent of white children and more than 85 percent of black children. The numbers declined among older children, with 77 percent of whites and 67 percent of blacks aged fourteen and fifteen in school and those figures dropping by about 25 percent among children older than fifteen. The numbers for rural children compared favorably, with 78 percent of white fourteen- and fifteen-year-olds and almost 64 percent of black children of those ages in school. For blacks, this figure represented an almost 10 percent jump since 1920. In rural areas as in urban ones, only half of white children and just over 30 percent of blacks continued school after age fifteen.[10]

These data are deceptively optimistic. Few rural schools, black or white, remained open more than six or seven months during each year. Agricultural labor defined the school calendar. Most rural schools opened in July or August, closed in September, and reopened from November to April. Some counties held classes for white schools for as few as 120 days, while others, generally those in cities and towns, had school terms of more than 175 days. Children met in leaky buildings with outhouses and had to buy their textbooks. Many rural schools were still heated by stoves. The state's illiteracy rate stood at 9.4 percent. Only 14.7 percent of black students who attended first grade reached seventh grade, and most members of this group were female. Only half of the white students who enrolled in first grade completed fourth grade. Slightly more than a third of rural white children and 44 percent of their urban counterparts received schooling past seventh grade. Urban whites completed a median ten years of schooling, while urban blacks completed just over five years. The median number of years of school for rural whites was seven but was half that for rural blacks.[11]

Growing up in Forsyth County, Sanford Byers, a white farmer, remembered, "we had to walk two miles to catch the bus, and sometimes it was rainy, or sleet, or snowy—we couldn't get there. And in those days—in '28, '29, and the '30s, things got so bad 'til they closed the schools out in Forsyth County. They didn't have no state or government support for the schools. And I went to school 'til I was twenty years old before I got my high school diploma." Raised outside of Commerce, white farmer Aubrey Benton finished only seventh grade because he would have had to pay tuition to attend the town's high school. Although some of his friends commuted on horses or mules, his family had to spend its spare funds to pay doctors to care for his mother, who was in poor health. Lacking buses, African American children walked to school along muddy clay paths in the winter—when they could. In Decatur County, African American D. G. Ebster and other students attended a one-room school that was so dilapidated that they could see through the roof, walls, and floor while sitting at

Substantial disparities existed between the conditions in Georgia's black schools
and its white schools during the 1930s and 1940s.

Spaulding County High School, Griffin, 1933. (Vanishing Georgia Collection,
Georgia Division of Archives and History, Office of the Secretary of State.)

A one-teacher Negro school in Veazy, Greene County, 1941.
(Courtesy of Library of Congress, Prints and Photographs Division,
FSA-OWI Collection, LC-USF34-046268-D.)

their "seats"—benches or wood boxes. The building was heated by a stove for which the students had to gather wood.[12]

Despite the continuing poor conditions, the contours of teaching were changing for both black and white women. Women increasingly came to dominate the profession, with white females jumping from 73 percent of all white teachers in 1910 to 85 percent in 1930 and black women growing from 82 percent of all black teachers to 90 percent over those years. In the same period, the total number of teachers in the state increased 16 percent. Although the Georgia Teachers and Education Association (GTEA) and the Georgia Education Association (GEA) pushed for better funding, salaries, and teacher training, numerous problems remained. Facilities remained poor, and the average class size was thirty-five students in white elementary schools and almost forty-eight students for black primary schools. Moreover, Georgia paid its teachers less than most states, spent the least amount per student, and received approximately 85 percent of its higher education endowment from private sources like the General Education Board (GEB) and the Julius Rosenwald Fund (JRF). In 1930, Georgia's black teachers received 47 percent of white teachers' salaries, and that ratio declined in the next few years: the NAACP's comparative study of salaries for southern teachers in 1933–34 discovered that Georgia paid white teachers $793.29 annually, while black teachers received $269.53. Alabama, Arkansas, Mississippi, and South Carolina paid white teachers less, while only South Carolina paid black teachers less.[13]

Part of the problem arose from the fact that even though Georgia gave teacher certification authority to the state Department of Education in 1934, counties continued to issue local certificates until after World War II because of the lack of trained teachers and the tenacious grasp of localism. Teachers with professional certification from colleges and normal schools—teachers who had bachelor's degrees—made more money than those who had two years or less of advanced education. Counties often intentionally hired less-trained teachers to pay them low salaries. Elementary school teachers made at least three hundred dollars less per year than high school teachers. White teachers' salaries ranged from $1,810 annually in Atlanta to less than $450 in rural counties such as Forsyth, Grady, Heard, Henry, and Jackson. Some black elementary school teachers made less than two hundred dollars a year for one hundred days of classes.[14] Even so, the state and counties performed mind-boggling feats of accounting. Some Georgia counties, notably in middle Georgia or the old Plantation Belt, diverted more than $1.15 million designated for black schools to white schools or other projects. Georgia's white children were allocated approximately 252 percent more money than black children, although white children in towns and cities clearly received more than rural whites. All graduate programs for black students were offered by southern black private schools or by northern universities and colleges. And from the late 1920s through the 1930s, the state never paid its full appropriation for schools or teacher salaries.[15]

Funding schools became an increasing problem for Georgia because residents continued to rely on cotton as a cash crop, and it was besieged by the boll weevil, cheaper competition from California and the British empire, periodic droughts, and depleted soil. USDA agents encouraged livestock and different crop production but could do little to change national market demands for a cash crop that Georgians saw as their sole source of income in the late nineteenth and early twentieth centuries. Macon, Gainesville, Atlanta, Augusta, Savannah, and other cities encouraged industries such as textiles, yet by 1930 this policy caused problems as well. To compensate for lower prices, farmers planted more cotton, but the more cotton they planted, the lower prices fell. The price of cotton finally collapsed to five cents a pound in 1932, half of what farmers required to break even. Furthermore, the state government began to focus on funding paved roads and increasingly to rely on local sources to finance schools. Not only were Georgia's social and cultural foundations teetering, but its economic base toppled.

From January 9 to 23, 1934, Lorena Hickok, a former Associated Press reporter and a friend of Eleanor Roosevelt, drove across Georgia as part of a nationwide tour. The Federal Emergency Relief Administration (FERA) hired Hickok to report to Harry Hopkins, the agency's head, about conditions in various regions and what Americans said regarding Franklin Delano Roosevelt's New Deal. Because of Georgia Governor Eugene Talmadge's hostility to federal relief programs, Hopkins asked Hickok not only to detail the status of agriculture and industry and the unemployed but also to discover who Talmadge's allies were.[16]

What really struck Hickok during her travels across Georgia's pine barrens, foothills, mountains, and Piedmont regions was something more than who Talmadge's allies were. "Oh, this IS the damnedest state!" she wrote. "I just itch to bring all the unemployed teachers and doctors and nurses and social workers in the North down here and put them to work!"[17] By the end of World War II, however, remarkable changes had occurred. White women had finally been allowed to continue to teach after marriage and motherhood. As the World War II draft and the burgeoning defense industries took the few male teachers in the system and offered better wages than teaching, Georgia education superintendents and administrators faced a labor shortage and had no choice but to permit skilled women to continue to teach.

Across Georgia, families, churches, and towns erratically battled challenges to traditional values and in particular to the racist hierarchy based on white fathers' family authority and a white God's punitive rule. Driven by the New Deal, the USDA, northern philanthropic organizations, and black and white teachers' organizations, some Georgians recognized the necessity for changes in public policy, including an improved educational system with reforms generated by New Deal programs such as the NYA and the Works Progress Administration (WPA). How communities conceptualized these changes and sought to control them can be discerned through the lives of the women who taught the students, witnessed these transitions, raised their children, attended churches, and articulated the needs of their communities. Black and white teachers in the 1930s allowed Georgia to absorb change by maintaining and reappropriating traditional rural cultural beliefs. Teachers redefined women's public and political authority by claiming that interest in children and the family sustained them as mothers and professionals, using classrooms to preserve evangelical Protestantism, and endlessly advocating education as the fundamental means for individual and state improvement. When Georgia's public funds failed, teachers nevertheless kept schools open. Black teachers included the implicit and often explicit message that education cut the path to black empowerment and opportunities.[18]

EVIDENCE OF THE impending crisis in southern agriculture and Georgia's weaknesses in social policy resounded in reports in the late 1920s from USDA Extension Service agents, the NAACP, teachers, state education reformers, and agents of northern philanthropic organizations. Many agents, black and white, continued to sound optimistic hopes for the next year at the same time they repeatedly detailed problems in agricultural methods, poor living conditions, inadequate schools, and battles with local officials. Agents called for diversification, more livestock production, and better state and county support. P. H. Stone, Georgia's Negro Extension Service agent, and Camilla Weems, the state Negro home demonstration agent, asked the federal government to demand payment for black county officials directly from the University of Georgia's College of Agriculture because counties and the state failed to fund projects or pay agents' salaries. Stone and Weems organized annual meetings for black farmers at Georgia State Industrial College, where blacks were taught home improvement, livestock production, and nutrition. Still, Stone and

Weems repeated calls for opportunities for black farmers. Black farmers needed access to wider markets for their goods, not simply sales to other black families. Lacking cash income, families could ill afford better diets, medical care, or even feed for livestock.[19]

White agents' complaints echoed this analysis. J. G. Oliver, state supervisor of county agents, noted constant opposition to Extension Service work from many counties. Gaining local support consumed "one third or more of the time and efforts of Supervisors. It seems we will never get away from adverse court decisions regarding county cooperation." Oliver believed that the most successful means to counter local opposition would be a state constitutional amendment that allowed county taxes for Extension Service work and public school support. Throughout the 1920s, Georgians repeatedly sued county commissioners for levying taxes to support agents and schools. In 1923, the Georgia Supreme Court ruled in *Hanks, Commissioners et al. v. D'Arcy* that imposing county taxes for these purposes violated the state constitution. Of course, other Georgians, like Robin and Sudie Clark, Sanford and Ruby Byers, and Tom and Velva Blackstock, welcomed Extension Service efforts, as agents offered opportunities for cash income through cultivating bees or encouraging egg and poultry production in northeast Georgia. In fact, by 1939, northeast Georgia, with the assistance of local banks and USDA agents, had become the center of a burgeoning poultry industry that would fuel economic growth and social change in this section for the next few decades.[20]

As rural conditions worsened, black and white farmers headed for cities and towns to work in textile mills or as day laborers. In Jackson County, Mrs. Moore, the white daughter of an invalid father, returned to her family's farm after her marriage collapsed as a result of her husband's alcoholism. When her only brother married and took over the farm, Moore moved to Athens, where she worked in dry goods or dress shops. When the price of cotton dropped, Ann Waldrop and her family, white farmers from Cherokee County, headed for Athens, where her husband found work in a textile mill. Other farmers could not find financing for their crops even when they had tools, livestock, and no debt. African American women who had helped support their families as laundresses and domestic workers lost clients. Molly Kensey left Sparta for the promise of better work in Atlanta. She initially earned seventeen to eighteen dollars a week washing clothes for workers at the Chevrolet Company. By the 1930s, when she was more than eighty years old and unable to do much work, she was reduced to relying on neighbors for food scraps and some laundry work. Mary Willingham, a former nurse who earned fourteen dollars a week, washed clothes for mill workers at seventy-five cents per load. Willingham also noted that she had lost more than ten pounds and that she knew African Americans who had died of hunger. When a frustrated Willingham asked a white woman why blacks were having such a difficult time finding work, the woman replied that blacks had brought the situation on themselves with their "sassy ways." Willingham knew better. She realized that because of white supremacy and the Great Depression, fewer jobs existed. Fewer white families could afford to hire blacks to clean clothes or homes.[21]

Class tensions that had always existed grew, accompanied by increasing friction. Some white mill workers resented teachers who forced them to speak differently or write with their right hands. Several African Americans grew tired of black teachers' insistence on education as a means for race improvement. M. J. Woods, black principal at Lemon Street High School in Marietta, recalled that some neighbors believed that higher education served no purpose. Given few options after acquiring a diploma, what could blacks accomplish? A few teachers admitted to their class-based standards in interactions with students and parents. Mary Wright Hill, principal of a grammar school for blacks in Athens, deplored the call-and-shout services at some black Baptist churches.[22] Pearlie Dove, a teacher and worker for the Young Women's Christian Association, was stunned at the living conditions of working-class black children in Atlanta. When Narvie Jordan Harris, raised in the city, taught at a Rosenwald school outside Bainbridge, she thought that white piglets were puppies. Yet many black teachers worked to improve connections with working-class blacks. Harris quickly learned about crushing sugarcane, raising peanuts, and her students' academic needs. She taught ways to improve agricultural production and home economics and started an evening literacy school for adults in Decatur County in 1939. Other black teachers, including Susie Weems Wheeler, Beulah Rucker Oliver, and Dorothy Oliver Rucker, came from rural areas and had an understanding of working-class issues. Oliver, for example, always attended a black Baptist church where she shouted and clapped. White teachers Leona Clark Williams, Florrie Still, and Ruth Smith Waters also came from farms. While the gap between teachers' education and standards for speech and dress and working-class behaviors occasionally served as a barrier, it also provided opportunities.[23] Black teachers, as some of the few professionals of their race, created networks that allowed them to build resistance strategies. White teachers devised tactics to improve opportunities for women and their students.

USDA agents often eased class tensions by helping farmers' children learn new techniques. The department sponsored boys' and girls' clubs that eventually became 4-H clubs and offered cash prizes or scholarships to many Georgia youths. Jefferson's Spurgeon "Spud" Wellborn met the Habersham County agent when his family left Jackson County in the 1920s because of the fall in cotton prices. After joining the Corn Club and entering livestock competitions, Wellborn won a trip to the Southeastern Fair in Atlanta. He finished high school and through the county agent found a job in fertilizer sales that helped him attend the University of Georgia, where he majored in forestry. Home demonstration agents such as Blanche Whelchell in Hall County provided girls with demonstrations and club work that resulted in tuition money for the first year of college. She also secured loans from local banks that enabled girls to continue their educations.[24]

But home demonstration and county agents surely exposed class and gender partiality in selecting these projects as well as choosing certain students over others. This bias is aptly conveyed by a 1927 "better bedroom" contest that claimed "the bedroom expresses you," constituting "an environment for the moulding of your character and those about you."[25] The project instructed girls on how to make closets, dressing tables, and desks and how to choose wall hangings. In a state where few families could allow children individual rooms—let alone closets, study desks, or wall hangings—this project reeked of class bias while reinforcing women's duty to beautify the home. The effort also demonstrates the increasing emphasis on women's role as consumers by underscoring how they could adorn their rooms and later their homes with frills, ruffles, and pictures for the walls. Not surprisingly, this project involved only white girls; black girls learned to remake used clothing.

In 1930, when the gross income of Georgia farmers fell to less than 20 percent of the previous year's income, home demonstration agents persisted in their efforts to modernize rural girls by specifying ways of storing clothing in closets with different hangers for dresses and coats, encouraging girls to buy different shoes for different occasions, and commenting that dirty and worn clothing were clear indicators of a girl's personality. No agent seemed to consider how few rural girls could possibly remake tattered dresses or purchase new shoes. Even Whelchell, who organized one of the most successful women's markets in the state with the assistance of the Gainesville Chamber of Commerce, was attacked by her successor, Grace Adams, in the 1940s. Whelchell apparently selected specific women to operate and supply the market, and they rejected other women's crafts and products. In the 1930s, while white girls learned that sheets, pillowcases, ruffled curtains, and painted desks made them better women, Weems implored the USDA for help as black agents bought their own supplies, children dropped out of school to work, and women and girls worked on farms and other homes as domestic workers. Black farmers had little time or cash to whitewash homes or build outhouses. As the USDA and Georgia responded with typical indifference to static gender roles for black girls, Weems reported that some black girls successfully raised cows and pigs—projects forbidden to white girls.[26]

Class, race, and gender partiality in the USDA combined to encourage the gaps between parents and children and between community authority and advanced education. Children were now learning how to live and succeed from individuals outside of households and churches, a decisive shift from their parents' expectations for the future. Here lay precisely the dangers of education that some Georgians had for decades feared. The political possibilities of education spread from classrooms to communities and households, challenging traditions of respectability, identity, and power. Children who could only dream of a separate bedroom or of new clothing learned how modern, respectable families lived. Aware of the world of consumption, many children began to consider possibilities for life outside of their rural communities, which certainly seemed more exciting than attending square dances or revivals.

Teachers underscored USDA agents' lessons. For example, Beulah Rucker Oliver taught her black students how to set a proper dinner table with dishes and silverware, settings that many of them had never seen. At night, her students listened to a battery-operated radio playing a range of programs from gospel music to jazz to comedy. Mary Wright Hill went to homes where parents worked all day and taught black children about hygiene, nutrition, and standards of cleanliness. For all of its community accomplishments, the Jeanes program served as a means to assert teachers' authority over that of parents and communities. Ruth Smith Waters, Leona Clark Williams, and Florrie Still taught their white students speech patterns, sanitation, and nutrition. Black and white teachers such as Oliver and Williams modeled professional respectable attire and were ogled by many barefoot children clad in feed sacks.[27] Teachers and USDA agents often unintentionally represented the world of consumption, the self-serving aspect of modernity that began to shatter traditional patterns of interdependence and rural living. Moreover, black and white teachers' public authority increased as their acclaim of new standards for apparel and living became increasingly accepted.

The generation of 1920s and 1930s teachers who shaped their craft and framed its contours witnessed the emergence of Georgia's public school system and professional requirements for teachers during the Great Depression. Even though Georgia failed to meet its financial obligations to teachers, schools, and students because of the drop in state revenues, the state moved toward a modern, bureaucratized education system. In 1933 Mauney Douglas Collins, another former teacher and staunch Baptist, became state school superintendent. Born in 1888, Collins came from the same generation of educators as Walter Hill Jr., Beulah Rucker Oliver, and Lucy Craft Laney. Collins remained in the post for the next twenty-four years and supported and promoted reforms long advocated by Progressives. He continued to consolidate rural schools, provided transportation for white students to consolidated schools, pushed for compulsory attendance laws, tried to equalize black and white teacher salaries, increased centralized state authority over curriculum and teacher certification, and fought for more and better-equipped high schools for whites.[28]

As the state educational bureaucracy began to take shape, social and cultural change continued to ripple across the state. Membership in black and white Baptist churches grew, reaching half of all church members in Georgia. Rural churches gradually lost members, while town and city congregations grew as black and white rural residents fled the countryside for jobs in textile mills, tanneries, and eventually war industries. Improved roads and automobiles eased church attendance. More than half a million African Americans attended black Baptist churches, while almost as many whites attended Southern Baptist churches. Approximately 85 percent of Georgia's white population attended either a Methodist or Baptist church, as did almost 95 percent of African Americans. Indeed, Georgia ranked third in the United States in the number of churches per capita. While urbanization and such intellectual movements as rationalism and Darwinism may have ushered in an era of secularization in other states, they had considerably less impact in Georgia. In the 1930s, Georgia remained one of the few states that required daily Bible readings in public schools, and led by Baptist and Methodist officials, the state opposed teaching the theory of evolution.[29]

By 1938, in response to cultural changes, white Baptist churches had officially discontinued disciplinary action against members who became intoxicated or danced. Many small-town and village churches that had only had ministers one Sunday each month now held services each Sabbath, and men and women sat together.[30] While churches still served as sites of worship, they segmented worship into Bible classes, mission societies, Sunday schools, and regular Sunday services. Although members no longer faced discipline for activities outside the church, congregations sought to maintain their influence by offering increased services and activities for members, such as child care and teen groups.[31] This shift in the role of churches, which seemed to occur without members noticing, meant that families and communities now began to look to local and state government for rules and structure.

Still other white evangelical Protestants expanded their benevolent work but did not do so primarily as a result of the Social Gospel ideas that impelled many northerners in the late nineteenth and early twentieth centuries. The Social Gospel ideology reflected the belief that the church could change society, and most white southern evangelical Protestants of both races instead focused on winning souls to Christ. But Georgia's various Baptist Women's Missionary Unions (WMUs) now stated that being Christians meant paying attention to needy persons in their state. At Gainesville's First Baptist Church, Isabelle Smith, mother of Charters Smith Embry and president of the WMU, reminded members of their Christian duties for community service. Still distancing itself from the northern Social Gospel movement, the WMU contributed to Beulah Rucker Oliver's school and to missions in Georgia from the perspective of doing the Lord's work for the glory of the Lord rather than for establishing God's kingdom on earth. As the title of the WMU publication, *Royal Service*, suggests, such acts derived from a sense of the duty to serve God rather than to aid neighbors in need. Moreover, this assistance followed certain patterns. Rather than allocating a specific allotment to Oliver's school every year, the WMU waited for Oliver to write a letter specifying what she needed and how the money would be used. During the 1930s, Oliver asked for tuition assistance for students and funds for a new dormitory. After receiving Oliver's letter, the WMU then decided on the amount of the donation, which ranged from three dollars in 1937 to five dollars in 1941. At a time when dresses sold for a dollar, a quart of milk cost fifteen cents, a loaf of bread cost ten cents, and schoolbooks cost fifty cents, even a few dollars would enable Oliver to buy numerous supplies.[32]

A pattern emerges from these arrangements. As a social inferior, Beulah Rucker Oliver had to appeal to white women in a particular manner and allow them to decide how much to give. WMU members never referred to her as Mrs. Oliver, the courtesy title they used for each other. Black women's status remained beneath that of white women. Any donation was always meted out from the perspective of the biblical injunction from Matthew 26:11: "the poor ye shall always have with thee and ye may do them good when ye will." WMU members viewed themselves as laborers for God, not society, in a mission of proclaiming Christ as their king and promoting his work among all people.[33] These white women used paternalism's language of duties and obligations to remind

Oliver of their power over her and how she should address them. Whatever aid was offered was always offered within hierarchical cultural and racial assumptions. The First Baptist Church's WMU gave Oliver less money than the women collected for a wedding gift or for missions in Latin American, Asia, or Africa. The WMU decided who merited assistance and who did not. Recipients needed to demonstrate gratitude, attend church, eschew drinking alcohol, and demonstrate that they acknowledged their inferior status.

Beulah Rucker Oliver accepted the WMU's conditions of assistance, at least from their perspective. She wrote letters graciously requesting funds. And although she knew the WMU viewed her as a social inferior and gave more money to other causes and although she was never allowed to attend WMU meetings, she consistently wrote thank you letters to the group. On some occasions, however, Oliver was less circumspect. Charters Smith Embry recalled joining her mother for a visit to Oliver's school to deliver some used clothing. Oliver embraced Isabelle Smith, who flinched at Oliver's signal that she was Smith's social equal.[34] Despite her shock at what she saw as a breach of social mores, Smith continued to back the WMU's traditional support of the school, in line with her perception of her duties.

In smaller towns, churches established small women's missionary associations that focused on helping the local poor, raising funds for schools, and collecting clothing and shoes for rural residents. While city churches began these efforts in the early twentieth century, most rural churches in Georgia lacked the membership to undertake larger social reform measures. Methodists such as Will Alexander and Walter B. Hill Jr. joined the Commission on Interracial Cooperation (CIC), while others worked along with Baptist women in the Association of Southern Women for the Prevention of Lynching. In 1931, Isa-Beall Neel became the first woman to serve as vice president of the Southern Baptist Convention. She had long been dedicated to such social reform projects as the Georgia Baptist Hospital, the Orphans Home, and the antilynching league.[35]

Church associations and philanthropic organizations nonetheless lacked the funds and support for the fundamental changes Georgia needed as the national economic crisis worsened. The GTEA, headed by H. A. Hunt of Fort Valley State College from 1930 to 1934, almost collapsed. In addition to membership dues, the organization relied on financial assistance from the CIC and the JRF. By 1932 the JRF was floundering because of the collapse of the stock market and could no longer help. For some unknown reason, the CIC also discontinued its support. John C. Dixon, white supervisor of the Division of Negro

Education, which had been established in 1930, asked the GEA for aid.[36] The GEA contributed more than two hundred dollars, and the GTEA survived. Dixon's assistance established a precedent for the GTEA to work with white moderates in the Division of Negro Education and the GEA.

As the GTEA fought to stay alive through the early years of the Great Depression, other organizations challenged racism. Atlanta's communist organization established an unemployment council in 1932, attracting both black and white workers, nearly a thousand of whom marched to protest the Fulton County commissioners' refusal to provide relief to the poor. This demonstration resulted in a six thousand dollar appropriation from the county for food relief. The city's Communist Party membership briefly increased, but the march provoked white supremacists' fears about interracial solidarity. Eleven days after the march took place, Angelo Herndon, a party member and march organizer, was arrested and sentenced to a chain gang for his role in the protest.[37] Black professionals, including teachers, however, remained involved in the NAACP, with Atlanta hosting the state's largest branch. Well aware of the reprisals against radical threats to white supremacy and class power, black teachers chose to protest racism through the more mainstream GTEA or NAACP.[38] Even membership in the NAACP provided grounds for termination, but dues were mailed to the NAACP's main office in New York, officers closely guarded local branch membership lists, and blacks rarely discussed the organization even with each other and especially with whites, helping teachers avoid reprisals. Still, some people were suspected of joining the group, and their names were provided to white school boards or police. In such an atmosphere, joining the Communist Party did not represent a viable alternative for most teachers, who not only needed their salaries and positions but also believed that they could best meet the needs of their students and communities by continuing to teach.[39] What the state and other Georgians tolerated affected what teachers could do, even as their work influenced some state policies.

When the president of the NAACP's Atlanta branch, A. T. Walden, led a 1932 membership drive, almost nine hundred blacks joined, among them numerous educators, including eight teachers and principal Charles Lincoln Harper from Booker T. Washington High School and black college and university faculty. The response to the NAACP's membership drive marked a resurgence of black activism in the South. Also in 1932, Walden and Lugenia Burns Hope started citizenship schools in Atlanta to prepare blacks to register to vote. Black Republican Atlantans formed other organizations, including John Wesley Dobbs's Atlanta Civic and Political League, founded in 1934.

Combined pressure from these varied organizations challenged facets of Georgia's racist power structure from lynching to unemployment relief to unequal funding for education.[40]

As the social and cultural structures of Georgia's cotton culture began to crack, the state's economic foundations crumbled. Facing economic disaster, closing schools, unpaid teachers, and increasing relief lines, most Georgians voted for Franklin Delano Roosevelt's promise of a New Deal at the same time they elected former state agricultural commissioner Eugene Talmadge as governor. While the two men seemed to be strange bedfellows, the political decision reflected Georgians' uneasiness about their circumstances. Roosevelt's programs might help the nation, but in Georgia, one of their own would guide them.[41]

Talmadge appealed to farmers by reassuring them that cotton culture—its values, profitability, and racist hierarchical structure—remained viable. At other times, his policies belied his rhetoric. His supporters included the Georgia Power Company, textile companies, and other industries as well as large white landholders—economic powers that relied on his hands-off policies toward big business and landowners. Other Georgians applauded the governor's insistence on state control of federal and northern philanthropic funds. Farmers saw Talmadge as thumbing his galluses at city people and modernity as he insisted that Georgians knew how to take care of themselves. He heartened Georgia's white men and rural residents by recalling traditional white masculinity as he caroused with his cronies—the men who still wore the pants in the family and ran the show.[42]

Never oblivious to many Georgians' plight during the Great Depression, Talmadge established the Georgia Relief Administration in January 1933 to distribute state relief. Headed by Talmadge supporter Herman De La Perriere, the relief administration used political patronage as a main criterion for county and state appointments and made little effort to investigate how state funds were distributed within counties. Not surprisingly, De La Perriere used the same county leaders who controlled local county politics, funds for the USDA, and allocations for schools. From the outset, federal supervisors from the Reconstruction Finance Corporation objected to the Georgia agency's apparent cronyism and urged Talmadge to appoint trained workers from Georgia's Department of Welfare, headed by Gay Bolling Shepperson.[43]

Born in Charlotte County, Virginia, in 1887, Gay Shepperson devoted her life to social work after she attended the New York School of Social Work in 1923. Working for the American Red Cross as a field worker in Alabama and

Louisiana, she switched to welfare work in St. Louis until 1928, when she became director of the Children's Bureau in Georgia's Department of Public Welfare.[44] Like Georgia's teachers and home demonstration agents of both races, Shepperson represented the professional woman—the woman who circumscribed her public career and ambitions with gendered definitions of community service, social welfare, and education. As a professional social worker, Shepperson demanded detailed investigative reports of requests for relief and fought to distribute funds equitably. She also knew how to maneuver around the land mines in white male political culture.

Shepperson gained a powerful ally when President Roosevelt appointed Harry Hopkins as head of the FERA in May 1933. Hopkins, a former social worker from Iowa, knew Shepperson from the American Red Cross and trusted her opinions. By the end of the summer of 1933, Talmadge's attacks on the New Deal escalated: he opined that the National Recovery Act and the Tennessee Valley Authority were "all in the Russian primer and the President has made the statement that he has read it twelve times." A staunch supporter of Roosevelt and his wife, Eleanor, Hopkins tolerated few attacks. When Shepperson suggested that Georgia's relief efforts be administered by the Department of Public Welfare to escape the taint of political cronyism, Hopkins agreed. In September 1933, FERA representative Alan Johnstone and Talmadge signed a proposal to establish the Georgia Emergency Relief Administration (GERA), directed by Shepperson with De La Perriere as adviser.[45] Shepperson immediately appointed social workers, most of them white women, as county administrators to investigate applications for relief. Talmadge countered by insisting on signing every paycheck and verbally assailing GERA personnel. In radio addresses and speeches, Talmadge attacked the Civil Works Administration's wage rate and demanded that officials cut wages in the middle of the winter.

Talmadge's opposition to Roosevelt's New Deal programs only intensified as time progressed. A woman was now directing relief funds and projects in his state, and he could do little to stop her. Moreover, she had had the temerity to appoint more women—and social workers at that—as county administrators. But Talmadge's conflicts with Roosevelt, Hopkins, and Shepperson had more to do with preserving localism and traditions. Talmadge valued appointees allied with his political positions. Consequently, out-of-state funds, whether from northern philanthropists or the federal government, were welcomed only as long as the state and counties controlled their distribution.

Yet the FERA attacked localism in four ways. It promoted modern constructions of gendered public authority by allowing women rather than men to answer to the federal government rather than to state and local officials. The federal agency threatened to upset Jim Crow's separate and unequal principles by paying blacks $3.20 per day on public works projects, more than they ever made picking cotton and close to what white men were paid. The FERA usurped county officials' power by granting federal funds to black and white schools. Moreover, it supported urban residents whom Talmadge viewed as nothing more than bums and loafers. In his eyes, farmers needed more relief than city folks, and Talmadge had a point. Georgia's small farmers, tenants, and share-croppers of both races bore the brunt of cotton's collapse. As federal and state governments encouraged crop reduction, the first land taken out of production often was that farmed by tenants. By 1930, many of these farmers had migrated to towns and cities, adding to the thousands already in need of food and em-ployment. Shepperson estimated that at least 45,000 to 50,000 people who still farmed were on relief, half of them white. Talmadge was annoyed that any blacks received relief and insisted that relief denied large landowners tradi-tional sources of labor because the Civil Works Administration paid higher wages than landowners could afford. Talmadge had little use for tenants and sharecroppers and sought relief funds for white large landholders who could vote.[46]

Relief consequently began to tear the fabric of relations between large land-holders and dependent farmers, upper-class whites and working-class blacks and whites, white men and all women—the complex webs of paternalism's dominance and dependency relations in rural cotton culture. Talmadge's dia-tribes thus pointed to the New Deal's potential to overturn class, race, and gen-der roles. Worse still, Talmadge and his supporters believed that these demands came from "outsiders"—non-Georgians. He repeatedly objected to the "men and women from out of the State, utterly unfamiliar with the people and con-ditions of this State," who were largely "responsible for the condition in Geor-gia and constantly increasing complaints" from his constituents.[47] Relief, Tal-madge inveighed, created only a class of people permanently dependent on government assistance. Talmadge's solution was to "get back to fundamental principles. . . . Go back to your Bible. . . . [G]et back out in the country; do not let the old schoolhouse and church rot."[48] At the heart of the confrontation be-tween Talmadge and Roosevelt lay the contested terrain between traditions and modernity.

Talmadge's belief that most Georgians supported his attacks on federal relief reflected a misjudgment about their plight. Beginning with the boll weevil and subsequent decline in the global market for cotton from the U.S. South, farm-ers had lost significant income from crops since the late 1920s. The drop in per-sonal income meant lower tax revenues, which cut public school funds. Despair

and determination fed teachers, many of whom taught without pay or at reduced salaries, and swept through schools and into homes, where many parents
and children struggled to keep schools open for at least six months. The white
GEA and the black GTEA repeatedly asked for state funds that the legislature
had magnanimously appropriated but amazingly misplaced.[49] At the same time
Hopkins federalized the GERA, Walter B. Hill Jr., now working for the GEB,
called on the federal government to stop public works programs for schools because black schools received only 4 percent of the total money allotted to the
state. But Talmadge was more concerned with cutting taxes and claimed that
education "ain't never taught a man to plant cotton."[50] Too much education
threatened to destroy traditional beliefs and constructions of identity.

Many Georgians disagreed. Hundreds of black and white Georgia teachers,
like their counterparts across the nation, wrote to Franklin and Eleanor Roosevelt asking for clothing, books, and teaching materials. Some teachers described the difficulty of living on fifty dollars a month and worried that their
declining salaries would make it impossible for them to survive, let alone help
their families. Black teachers wrote of salaries as low as thirty-five dollars a
month while teaching as many as forty to fifty students in dilapidated buildings.
Some teachers lamented that they looked unprofessional because their clothes
and shoes had holes.[51] How could they teach when few students had books or
supplies and many attended school only sporadically because their families
needed extra income? Educators had no choice but to demand help.

Mothers agreed that schools needed rapid assistance and believed that education and religious training were essential for the next generation of citizens.
One woman wrote to the First Lady, "Our boys and girls of today must be educated to bring our state up to a high standard." Several women noted that higher
education, including high school, was inaccessible to rural Georgia children.
Others described vanishing school funds. Children asked for food and clothing
so that they could attend school. From Conley, a girl wrote that she had "made
a grade every year, but on account of having to walk three miles, I'm afraid I
won't make the tenth. I was sixteen years old in March 17, 1934." A girl from
Climax wrote that she had completed junior high in her area but lived "ten
miles from any place, that I might acquire the remaining two years of my sen-
ior high school. . . . I do not have sufficient clothes to wear . . . through the
long, cold winter I had only a cotton sweater, but I never missed a day." Many
women also wrote that their husbands had left them or were unable to work,
leaving these women as their families' sole support.[52] Women who still believed
that accepting fatherly authority included financial support must have been
devastated to realize that the bargain no longer existed.

The letters also mark shifting gender constructions across the nation as well as in Georgia. Eleanor Roosevelt's radio addresses and columns, in which she asked Americans to write to her about their problems, fostered a public perception of the First Lady as understanding the plight of women, children, and young adults because she was a mother, a wife, and a public advocate of social reform and education. One writer noted, "we have been reading the papers where you were helping the people who are in need," and the more that Roosevelt talked about the need for an education, the more Georgians and other American women wrote to her "because I believe you will understand my problems and because I know you can help me solve it."[53] Women from every state viewed the First Lady as representing feminine ambition, social policy reforms, and the possibility of higher education goals for children and women—public policies with which women increasingly identified. Teachers laid the foundation for women's public work, which women such as Shepperson and Roosevelt reinforced. But even Eleanor Roosevelt could do little about the turmoil at the GERA.

After signing the September 1933 agreement, Shepperson, Johnstone, Hopkins, and Talmadge battled again over one of Shepperson's appointments, Jane Van De Vrede, a nurse and Red Cross worker who became director of women's work. Exasperated by Shepperson's appointments of women, Talmadge fired Van De Vrede in December 1933 as a warning to Hopkins and Shepperson that the governor must approve state appointments. Outraged at Talmadge's actions, Johnstone demanded that Van De Vrede, who knew Hopkins from New Orleans, be reinstated and recommended that Hopkins federalize the GERA because "joint administration of these [federal] funds seems impracticable." Hopkins agreed and did so on January 5, 1933. Now one of the most powerful people in Georgia, Shepperson's position as head of the GERA gave her control of the distribution of federal funds in the state. One of the few women FERA administrators and the only female WPA administrator Roosevelt and Hopkins selected, Shepperson carried women's political clout to the highest level yet in Georgia.[54] Insisting on professional training for women teachers and social workers and then placing them in administrative positions where they could act without answering to local officials, Shepperson struck at the core of Talmadge's ideology and power base.

Shepperson immediately set to work on Georgia's schools and illiteracy. She used $1.6 million in FERA funds to pay teachers in 1934, and she hired unemployed teachers as literacy and vocational education instructors at FERA centers across the state. In March 1935, however, fifteen thousand teachers again faced a spring without pay. Talmadge and Georgia State School Superinten-

Gay Bolling Shepperson, New Deal administrator, and Eleanor Roosevelt, in the center, observe the construction of a Works Progress Administration project, ca. 1935. (Courtesy of the Atlanta History Center.)

dent M. D. Collins asked Shepperson for another $1.8 million FERA grant to keep the schools open. Shepperson and Hopkins sympathized with the teachers but knew that Talmadge had other options: he could borrow money for teachers' salaries from the State Highway Department, which always had a surplus of funds, or he could obtain a loan against the following year's tax revenues. Shepperson and Hopkins also had evidence that Talmadge, Collins, and some county officials had misused the 1934 FERA grant for purposes other than teachers' salaries—repairing school buildings. Shepperson and Hopkins refused Talmadge's request. Hopkins wanted the governor to take the blame for the situation and repeatedly told Shepperson to make sure the press understood what Talmadge was doing. "We certainly told them we wouldn't do it," Hopkins said to Shepperson on April 22, "so if the teachers take it up tell them to go see Governor Talmadge. That is the real thing and I think that somebody is going to have to say it."[55] In the end, teachers and students were pawns in political posturing between New Dealers and Talmadge. Each side refused to budge, blaming the other for the lack of money for teacher salaries. Worse still, the JRF, which had funded black elementary schools, had gone bankrupt with the

1929 stock market crash, so funds were no longer available from that source. Nevertheless, believing in their duty to teach the children, many teachers taught with only sporadic pay until the 1940s. Several counties closed schools. Some past priorities remained unchanged—education was dispensable when political stakes were high.

When pay failed to materialize, teachers relied on their families and friends for support. In some counties, school officials met with teachers to ask them to stay until funds could be found. When some women left for better salaries in other states, a few counties temporarily hired married women. In Fayette County, Florene Huddleston Adams agreed to teach until the county could find more money. "We were dedicated to what we were doing," she stated. "We didn't want the schools to close." Parents tried to help teachers by sending food. One Christmas, Lema Peebles recalled, a boy "came in with a box that had a hole in it and gave it to me. It was a hen. And that was my Christmas present."[56]

Joining Talmadge's stance against the New Deal in the spring of 1935 were some Georgia legislators, including future governors E. D. Rivers and Ellis Arnall, who publicly denounced Shepperson as a danger to local traditions and state authority. Arnall accused Shepperson of hiring "non-resident persons, for the most part of the Republican and progressive party affiliation, notwithstanding the fact that capable Georgians . . . are available for this work."[57] According to Arnall, Shepperson was an outsider and condoned teachings of racial equality and Yankee carpetbag rule. That Arnall referred to the progressive wing of the Republican Party smacked of race and gender issues as well. Although Jane Addams, Florence Kelley, Robert and Mary Church Terrell, Robert La Follette and other reformers failed to make many significant changes in African American lives, these Progressives wrote, spoke, and campaigned for better, equitable social and economic conditions for women, workers, and African Americans. As a social worker, Shepperson resembled these meddling reformers whom conservative Georgians had long fought to block.

Shepperson countered by releasing facts about her staff, noting that Georgia lacked enough professional social workers to fill all the positions in the GERA's Division of Social Service. She could hire black social workers from the Atlanta School of Social Work, which had been established in 1920, but no white Georgia public college or university had a school of social welfare until 1934 because social workers were seen as meddling, intrusive busybodies in men's private households. White teacher Florrie Still recalled that social workers were "dirty words. Goodness, the Talmadges would have blown their tops. . . . Being a social worker meant you believed in people—if they were black, you know? Even one of the state board members told me one day, 'You and your crowd are getting people in school that ought to be in the cotton patch.'" Some Georgians saw social workers, overwhelmingly women, as having authority to intervene in family rules or racist practices that pulled children from school or sent them to textile mills or cotton fields. Even so, Shepperson had hired out-of-state workers only after hiring all available qualified Georgians. Of the 3,900 relief workers in Georgia, 94.2 percent had been on Georgia relief rolls; only fifty-two employees came from different southern states.[58]

These attacks on Shepperson used the old refrain that outsiders or "carpet-baggers" were interfering in local affairs. The charge cloaked fear of shifting values—fears of what educated women or African Americans might do, fears of what a centralized state bureaucracy might mean. Here were black and white women running FERA programs across the state, answering to no one but federal authorities. After Shepperson released the FERA employee data, John-stone met with Georgia legislators in Washington, D.C. When Shepperson proved that her employees were predominantly Georgians, Johnstone then de-scribed what FERA could do for Georgia. Now realizing how much money Georgia could get from the New Deal, several legislators, including Arnall and Rivers, left Talmadge's camp. Rivers then learned how legislation could cir-cumvent Georgia's constitutional restrictions on raising taxes.[59] Because FERA provided funds in proportion to a state's ability to pay tax revenues to the fed-eral government, of eighteen eligible rural states, only Georgia failed to receive federal education aid.

Rivers's legislative proposals, rejected by Talmadge and his supporters, be-came the challenger's platform for the 1936 governor's race. Rivers's "Little New Deal" for Georgia included free textbooks, a seven-month school year, and better pay for teachers. Of course, the reforms targeted white schools, but black schools would benefit to some extent from free but used textbooks and longer school terms. That Rivers chose educational reform as the cornerstone of his platform indicated the issue's importance for many Georgians. Rivers trounced Talmadge's ally, Charles Redwine, in the race, but failed to solve Georgia's constitutional deterrents against borrowing money.[60] For the first two years of Rivers's term, the state returned to the business of consolidating schools and standardizing teacher training and salaries. In 1937, Rivers's school reform package passed, adding a statewide salary schedule for teachers and minimum professional standards, including courses on teaching methods, curriculum, and the history of education. Black teachers now received 75 percent of white teachers' salaries. At the University of Georgia in 1938, the GEB and reorganized JRF recommended and partially funded a position for education professor Walter Cocking, a 1929 graduate of Columbia University. Cocking's responsibilities included the development of a graduate program in education at the university in addition to publishing studies of African American education in Georgia funded by the GEB and the JRF. At the same time, educational reform campaigns funded by the GEA and the Georgia Citizens Fact-Finding Committee directed more attention to Georgia's public school problems. Among the many facts included in the committee's pamphlet was the average Georgia teacher's salary, $587, less than half the national average of $1,283.[61]

The bill soon came due, and Georgia was as broke as it had ever been. As well intended as Rivers's reforms may have been, a state that could barely pay its teachers some of the lowest salaries in the nation could ill afford to supply textbooks and support black and white schools for seven months. By 1940, the state was bankrupt, schools were again closed, and teachers worked without pay or hoped that vouchers would be honored at local banks. Hall, Fulton, and other counties with better tax bases never closed schools; some counties, like Fayette, persuaded teachers to work for three months with the promise of one month's pay in return. Jimmie Kate Sams Cole, whose father, Ferrol Sams, was county school superintendent, recalled a time in January when Governor Rivers announced that there was no money to pay teachers. A teacher from Fayetteville High School moved to the Columbus City system, leaving a vacancy. Cole had just graduated from Bessie Tift College and knew she wanted to teach, so she decided to "go down there and finish out the year to get [those] kids through high school." Rivers's programs, while clearly an effort to modernize Georgia's social policies, cost him Georgians' support and paved the way for Talmadge's reelection in 1940. Talmadge predicted that this victory would secure county unit rule and state's rights against the invasion of New Dealers.[62]

Shepperson and other federal employees failed to revolutionize Georgia's hierarchical structure, but doing so was not the New Deal's intention. Most working-class people, black and white, continued to labor at low-wage jobs in domestic work or the textile industry. Sewing rooms for women of both races neglected to teach women new industrial skills for independent living. Black domestic workers received little or no assistance. But the New Deal began to change Georgia in significant ways. African American professionals—teachers, social workers, physicians, and nurses—gained recognition that they lacked before 1935, including some notice from white social workers who met the professionals through New Deal projects. NYA programs enabled African American Andrew Johnson, an Athens insurance salesman, to complete college in

South Carolina after his father's death. Eugenia Wright, an African American widow in Atlanta, had no income until she found a WPA job studying black women workers.[63]

Section 7 of the 1933 National Recovery Act guaranteed labor's right to organize unions. The following year, working-class southerners in textile mills responded with what became known as the General Textile Strike. Workers in the northwestern part of the state objected to the possibility of black workers' wages being equalized with those of whites. Other white workers struck in New-nan and Columbus and were promptly arrested by National Guardsmen called out by Talmadge. Yet black and white workers learned organizational tactics from the experience, and those who struck indicated their support of New Deal policies. At the same time, other white workers' refusal to strike illustrated their allegiance to New Deal policies only when they reinforced regional and white supremacist conditions.[64]

New Deal benefits began to change African Americans' long-held dedi-cation to the Republican Party into votes for Roosevelt. New Deal programs like the WPA, Civilian Conservation Corps, and the NYA raised expectations among blacks and whites about standards of living, education, and jobs.[65]

One of the most popular New Deal programs, the NYA, established during Rivers's tenure as governor, changed the way many Georgians defined the role of education as well as who should be educated. Prompted by Eleanor Roo-sevelt, Hopkins, and Aubrey Williams, a white social worker from Alabama, Roosevelt created the NYA by executive order in 1935 as a branch of the WPA. Aware that thousands of students across the nation had quit school to support families during the Great Depression, the NYA offered financial aid to enable young people to attend college or high school. Roosevelt appointed Mary McLeod Bethune to head the NYA's Negro division. The fact that the NYA had been created by executive order and that Roosevelt appointed an African American keenly committed to equal opportunities for blacks and whites led to one of the few New Deal programs that would give equal pay to blacks and whites, boys and girls, in its work for education assistance. All students receiv-ing NYA funds had to work fifteen to twenty hours a week.[66] Administered at the national level, the NYA avoided some of the local- and state-level conflicts that had led to inequitable funding for public works projects for black and white schools.

In the NYA's first year, 9,900 Georgia high school and college students re-ceived financial aid. Twelve percent of students enrolled at forty white colleges and thirteen black colleges earned fifteen dollars per month. In northeast

Georgia from 1935 to 1938, more than three hundred thousand dollars was distributed among 4,831 black and white students, of whom 758 attended college. At least twenty students from Beulah Oliver's school received NYA funds, an indication of her consistent attention to the funding possibilities available to her students, although her friendship with Bethune may also have helped. In addition, the NYA sponsored building programs at Georgia State College for blacks in Savannah, Fort Valley Normal and Industrial College for blacks, and Georgia State College for Women at Milledgeville. Blacks never received aid in proportion to their percentage of Georgia's population, however, and as with the USDA's Extension Service work and northern philanthropic guidelines, gender conventions determined NYA jobs for girls and boys: girls did sewing, clerical, or library work while boys did masonry, carpentry, or road repair. Nonetheless, at high schools, aid to Georgia black students compared favorably to whites. For example, in October 1937, 1,897 whites received financial aid, as did 1,082 black students. The difference between funding for black and white students surfaced at the college level: in the same month, 1,551 white youths received aid, compared to only 168 black students.[67] The problem here was the lack of public high schools, colleges, and universities for black students in Georgia.

High school education became something that all young people should have, necessary to become a member of the middle class.[68] Watching families toil for a fickle crop that barely fed and clothed them, Georgia's next generation wanted to become part of the modern world where different job opportunities and consumer goods were available. In addition to providing financial aid to high school and college students, the NYA sponsored resident training camps that taught gendered skills to students who had left school after eighth grade. Georgia boys learned auto or aviation mechanics, carpentry, construction trades, and better farming methods. Girls attended courses on sewing, planning menus and diet, hairstyling, or clerical skills.

But learning a skill or attending school was only part of the NYA's program. The NYA also included camps at which youths could learn social skills and prepare for job interviews. At these camps, participants worked, ate, and slept with residents their own age. Case after case describes how social skills and personality improved during training, giving boys and girls additional means of succeeding in the modern world. John Henry, a white "reticent type of boy" from Fulton County, learned metal crafts, but "the most interesting part of this boy's story . . . is the complete change" in his personality. After working in the NYA craft shop, he "now mingles with the rest of the class, dresses in a clean, neat manner, and feels himself a part of society, where before, he was a backward, nondescript type of boy." After Roy Bane, a black student from Liberty County, attended a course on shop work, he "brushed up on his table manners . . . learned to live and work with people, and to be a jolly good fellow." Nancy Howard, a white girl from Bibb County, changed from "a very timid, shrinking girl into a good office worker." Coming from a family that opposed education, May Hall from Rabun County had "unkempt hair and slovenly dress." After learning to read and write, Hall took courses on homemaking, cooking, and how to serve attractive meals and was hired by a hotel. At nineteen Alice Main "was a headstrong Negro girl with a disagreeable disposition" and two children. Learning modern cooking and domestic skills, Alice found a job as a cook and a maid. She had become "a different girl": she was "neater in her appearance, worked more pleasantly with other girls on the project, really put forth an effort to win the praise of her supervisor."[69]

So the NYA taught more than skills and education. Just like black and white teachers and home demonstration agents, NYA instructors taught students what the modern world required for jobs and success. Who would hire a surly maid or a disagreeable mechanic? How to dress and interact with others was part of learning to live in a changing world. Girls learned how to use makeup and wear fashionable hairstyles and clothing. Becoming a consumer was part of the NYA curriculum, particularly for rural students who either had never bought makeup or had been forbidden to use it. All students were trained to manage personal finances and practice new work habits for urban industries, including filling out payroll forms or using a time clock. Attaining a high school, vocational, or college education redirected Georgia boys' and girls' career and material expectations beyond their parents' rural lives. For white Georgians, education included knowledge about how to negotiate a world of new skills, better education, and individualism within a shifting social hierarchy. For African Americans, the NYA promised equal educational opportunities after decades of racist practices. Headed by Williams and Bethune, a staunch advocate of better education and equal rights for blacks, the NYA encouraged children of both races and both sexes to stay in school, learn any skill that would get them off farms, and use consumer goods for their career goals. Education and personal style created the path to modern success.

NYA programs boosted the NAACP's equalization campaign for all southern schools.[70] While the NYA began, the NAACP, the JRF, and the GEB studied each state's tax system and what percentage of public taxes public schools received. The findings were telling. Part of the problem with southern schools, in addition to racism and localism, was the South's low tax base. Even if white southerners wanted to fund black and white schools equally, which obviously they did not, the South collected low tax revenues on property, even though it contributed as large a proportion of this tax to schools as other states did. If the NAACP, supported by the JRF and the GEB, decided to push for the implementation of separate and equal as established in *Plessy v. Ferguson*, federal funds would be needed to equalize financial support for schools.[71]

The NAACP targeted black teachers' salaries for improvement as a means of keeping professionally trained teachers in the South and thereby improving education for black children. While this goal may seem modest and to overlook black workers' economic needs, black professionals continued to see education as a key aspect of equality and a sound target for the testing of "separate but equal" standards.[72] Like North Carolina, Georgia paid all teachers according to their training and experience. But in the 1930s, Georgia paid some black teachers as little as $175 for seven months because they held county rather than state licenses. Some white Georgia teachers were paid less than North Carolina black teachers. Black and white reformers presumed that better teachers and more educated students would lead to a more prosperous South.

After reading these reports and listening to educators' testimony, members of the U.S. Congress acted in 1936. Once again, as in the 1890 Blair Bill, the federal government tried to enter localism's sacred territory of public school funding. Senator Pat Harrison of Mississippi, Representative Thomas Fletcher of Ohio, and Senator Hugo Black of Alabama introduced what became known as the Harrison-Fletcher Bill, which would have appropriated $300 million in federal aid to all public schools that were in session for 160 days. In states where separate schools for blacks or other groups existed, funds must be equally distributed, but states had the right to allocate funds as they deemed fit.

Debates followed to "insure that Negro schools (in those states where Negroes are forced by law to attend separate schools) would get their equitable share of such appropriations." Amendments insured that the distribution of federal funds would be supervised by the U.S. commissioner of education, who would then report any problems to Congress and the secretary of the interior. On behalf of the NAACP, Charles Houston announced his support of the bill, noting that it was not foolproof but offered a minimum guarantee. The GTEA disagreed: its representative, W. E. B. Du Bois, insisted that "the control of these funds be transferred from the legislature of Georgia, none of whose members my people elect, to the Congress of the United States, many of whom my people elect." No longer a member of the NAACP and breaking with its policy of integration, Du Bois now maintained that because segregation was a fact of life, blacks needed "to make a virtue out of a necessity."[73] Although the bill was never enacted, some members of Congress had sincerely wanted to equalize funding for the nation's public schools. And support from many southern congressmen, including Georgia Senators Richard Russell and Walter George, demonstrated the growing belief that education would enable the next generation, especially of white students, to increase their income and purchasing power and become better citizens.

The NAACP's pending court efforts in Virginia and Maryland to equalize teachers' salaries unquestionably prodded many white Georgians to look for federal aid. The GEA insisted that equalization funds had to come from the federal government, yet another reason for supporting the Harrison-Fletcher Bill. Rarely carrying banners for black educational reform, the GEA consistently adhered to Jim Crow principles. The state could barely afford to pay white teachers' meager salaries, so how could it possibly increase black teachers' pay? Federal money would be required. White women agreed that salaries needed to improve, and they used their expanding political clout to publicize all schools' needs for federal funds. Yet again, Georgians, like other southerners, indicated their willingness to accept federal funds under certain conditions.[74]

Georgia's white educators heard further rumblings of change following the U.S. Supreme Court's 1938 ruling in *Missouri ex rel. Gaines v. Canada*. Sponsored by the NAACP's Campaign for Educational Equality, Lloyd Gaines opposed Missouri's effort to send him out of the state to attend law school because the University of Missouri was segregated. The Court ruled that Missouri had a duty to furnish an equal education to all state residents and violated the U.S. Constitution by providing a state law school for whites but not for blacks.[75]

The decision shocked white southerners. Long accustomed to providing an inferior educational system for African Americans, southern states failed to offer graduate programs for blacks at state-supported colleges and universities. In Georgia, the only higher education facility that provided graduate work was the private Atlanta University. As Horace Mann Bond, president of Fort Valley State College beginning in 1939, wrote to Karl Bigelow, a member of the Commission on Teacher Education in Washington, D.C., *Gaines* created a controversy concerning southern black graduate education. Bond explained in a letter to Fred McCuistion of the GEB that Steadman Sanford, chancellor of the Georgia University System's Board of Regents, had already received two applications from African Americans to attend the University of Georgia. Moreover, Atlanta's blacks united to defeat a 1938 school bond issue that contained few provisions for black schools.[76]

During the latter years of the Great Depression, Georgia had, with the prodding of the GEB and the JRF, begun an effort to expand higher education for

Georgia blacks by using New Deal programs such as the Public Works Administration and the WPA to improve the black colleges at Savannah, Forsyth, and Albany.[77] The GEB and the JRF had provided additional funds for teacher training at Fort Valley College. In 1936, possibly with the ramifications of impending NAACP challenges to segregation in mind, the GEB and the JRF encouraged Georgia to purchase Fort Valley State College from the American Church Institute, with the JRF providing funds for the transfer. Like other southerners, Georgia educators knew they had to upgrade black higher education, and they desperately needed funds from any source for better black schools. In 1939, the Georgia State Board of Education, in the wake of a mandate from the U.S. Supreme Court, finally negotiated the purchase of Fort Valley State College, with the transaction made possible only because the JRF added $50,000 to Georgia's $34,000. Combining the Fort Valley campus with Forsyth's campus, the state at last had a viable public black college that offered bachelor's degrees in education and agriculture.

Fort Valley began hiring faculty members with master's degrees, and Bond, Edwin Embree of the JRF, and J. C. Dixon of the Georgia Division of Negro Education started outlining changes in black teacher education. Equally important, the improved salaries for Georgia black teachers had stanched the flow of Atlanta college graduates to other states.[78] Still, the state was reluctant to increase public support of black colleges not only because of its financial woes but also because of its continued opposition to equal education.

Georgia nonetheless continued efforts to improve its educational system with the GEB, JRF, and University of Georgia's Department of Education guiding the state's Department of Education. After 1941, more teachers of both races with at least two years of college were certified, while fewer instructors with one year or less of higher education were certified. Whereas 14 percent of teachers had just one year of college in 1937, only 5 percent did so in 1941, and the number of white teachers with four years of college increased from 39 percent to 46 percent over the same period. For black teachers, the most significant change involved the decline of county certification. While 48 percent of black teachers held county certificates in 1937, only 18 percent did so in 1941, and the number of black teachers with two years of college and state certificates more than doubled from 14 percent to 30 percent during that time.[79] Georgia planned to eliminate the county certificate by 1946 and to require all teachers to have four years of college education. Although many reformers remained skeptical that the goal would be realized, Georgia had at least made an effort to improve teacher requirements.

Moreover, counties began to consolidate local schools to create larger build-

ings and to bus students, predominantly white, to the new schools. School consolidation, long a goal of education reformers, represented some of the fundamental goals of efficiency and centralized control of education. M. L. Duggan,
state superintendent of schools from 1926 to 1934, listed white school consolidation as one of his greatest accomplishments. Approximately thirty-five hundred rural white schools were consolidated into fewer than nine hundred
schools during Duggan's tenure. Whereas 49 percent of white schools had one
or two teachers in 1937, only 32 percent did so in 1941; the number of schools
having between five and nineteen teachers increased from 30 percent to 47 percent. Change occurred more slowly for black teachers and students because
counties allocated transportation funds only for white students. Nonetheless,
the number of black one- or two-teacher schools declined from 91 percent in
1937 to 84 percent in 1941.[80]

Educational policy clearly moved to the forefront of political and cultural
debates. Education now meant access and opportunities in the modern world
for African Americans and whites, men and women. Merit displaced kinship
and community ties in many school appointments. Teachers' public authority
grew as some parents and children looked to teachers as experts on what children needed to succeed.[81] State and federal educational bureaucracies increasingly determined what children should know and who should teach them.
Faced with the breakdown of localism, some Georgians turned to the man who
had always assured them their traditions were noble—Eugene Talmadge.

In the wake of Governor Rivers's financial disasters, Talmadge easily won the
1940 governor's election by denouncing the New Deal as an assault on Georgia's traditions of femininity, Jim Crow, and the poll tax. His first target, to
him a cesspool of modernity, was the University of Georgia's Department of Education. From 1938 until early 1941, the department's dean, Walter Cocking,
sponsored conferences on black education in Athens and published reports
on the condition of black education and rural education that were in part
funded by the JRF and the GEB. Although Cocking was scarcely the first to
sponsor conferences on education for blacks, his reports came at the time when
Talmadge and many Georgians were debating the extent of the changes they
wanted in their public schools. On May 30, 1941, at a Board of Regents meeting in Athens, Talmadge, an ex officio member of the board, fired Cocking
and Dr. Marvin S. Pittman, president of the Georgia State Teachers College at
Statesboro.

A few hours after the meeting, Harmon W. Caldwell, president of the University of Georgia, threatened to resign if Cocking were refused a hearing be-

Eugene Talmadge's 1940 gubernatorial campaign drew vast, cheering crowds.
(Courtesy of Hargrett Rare Book and Manuscript Library, University of Georgia Libraries.)

fore the state Board of Regents. The board agreed with Caldwell and decided to hold off its decision on Cocking until after a June 16 hearing. That closed meeting featured the testimony of only one witness, Sylla Hamilton, who taught at the practice teaching school for whites at the University of Georgia. Hamilton, a distant relative of the Talmadges, testified that at a faculty meeting in the spring of 1939, Cocking "wished to build a training school within 30 minutes' drive of Athens where graduates of the school could do their practice teaching. . . . This school, he said, was to be for both blacks and whites—in order to uplift the state of Georgia." Following Hamilton's testimony, Sandy Beaver, chairman of the Board of Regents and president of Riverside Military Academy in Gainesville, called for another vote. The board voted to reappoint Cocking beginning in September 1941. Talmadge promptly asked three members of the board who had supported Cocking to resign and replaced them with Talmadge backers. Talmadge then called for a new hearing on Cocking to be held on July 14. During this hearing, witnesses inveighed against Cocking for his connections to the JRF or "Jewish money," and the board refused to rehire Cocking and Pittman.[82]

Chaos reigned in Georgia during the fall. Talmadge supporters scoured local and school libraries for books that advocated liberal racial attitudes; the *Atlanta Constitution*, the *Atlanta Daily World*, and the *Atlanta Journal* blasted Talmadge for his arbitrary and autocratic actions. Students at the University of Georgia, who had come of age during the New Deal and understood that education definitely taught them more than how to pick cotton, marched against Talmadge. In August 1941, the GEB and the JRF ceased all funding to Georgia, and the Southern Association of Colleges and Secondary Schools subsequently yanked Georgia's accreditation. The JRF alone had provided almost $1.5 million for a variety of projects, including the school building program and rural education programs, over the preceding twenty years.[83] White colleges and universities had received almost $400,000 of that amount, funds that had built libraries, contributed to medical and dental schools, and had paid for illiteracy programs. Many middle-class Georgians knew about these contributions and welcomed the financial aid. Moreover, by denouncing Franklin D. Roosevelt and the New Deal, Talmadge had alienated many Georgians who benefited from New Deal programs. Like E. D. Rivers in 1935, Ellis Arnall supported the president, an expedient policy in a time of war. Talmadge unwittingly handed Arnall the issue that would win the 1942 governor's race.[84]

On the surface, the issue motivating Talmadge and his supporters appeared to be fears of integrated schools. But it was more than that. As historians have contended, Arnall's campaign and subsequent defeat of Talmadge represented the beginnings of Georgia's emergence as a modern state and the twilight of the old social, political, and economic order.[85] Traditional rural values of localism and family and church authority collided with secular, individualistic values in the centralizing state. Some Georgians from Gwinnett, Jackson, Floyd, and Watson Counties vehemently opposed school consolidations because of the loss of community and parental authority over attendance, curriculum, and instructors.[86] Part of Talmadge's attack on Cocking included references to the fact that Cocking was from Iowa and an outsider to Georgia's affairs. Talmadge noted that Cocking represented "foreign ideas . . . being taught in our universities."[87] Mrs. Leonard Morey wrote to Chancellor Sanford that Cocking "as an educator who comes in contact with only the higher type of Negro[,] cannot understand the problem of the South as a whole." Other Georgia women stated their case more vehemently. Mrs. E. Stewart wanted to rid the schools of "subverters, they are responsible for these foreign, modernist professors in our schools. While you are at it, go to it, do a thorough job of house cleaning." Talmadge and his supporters directly attacked the JRF for advocating racial

Ellis Arnall campaigned for educational reform in the 1942 gubernatorial primary.
(Courtesy of the Atlanta History Center, KGR Collection.)

integration—"Jew money for niggers." One Talmadge reelection pamphlet repeatedly denounced Cocking as a "paymaster in Georgia for the Rosenwald Foundation," which promoted racial integration in the public schools.[88] Most of Talmadge's supporters identified themselves as traditional southerners opposed to increasing funds for African American education, interference in Georgia by outside agencies such as the JRF, centralization, and, more important, any shifts in southern traditions.

Talmadge also gained allegiance from Joseph W. Holley, the African American president of Georgia Normal College in Albany. Holley had enjoyed a measure of authority by conducting the college's business with a local board of trustees, and he opposed his own subordination to the authority of the reorganized Board of Regents and Chancellor Sanford. During Talmadge's 1942 reelection campaign, Holley appeared at several Talmadge speeches in support of the governor's positions. Following weeks of attacks by black leaders and white moderates, Holley explained in the *Atlanta Daily World* that he advocated separate boards of regents for black and white colleges and universities because the state's appropriation for black public education had been slashed in half since the Georgia Board of Regents was reorganized in 1933. Holley argued that in 1932, the original board had allocated $106,500 for black higher education, but the reorganized board had dropped black funds to $50,000 and increased white funding to $6 million. Holley proposed that a special committee on Negro education be appointed and that $2 million be appropriated immediately to the black public colleges at Savannah, Fort Valley, and Forsyth.[89]

Other Georgians found Talmadge's actions embarrassing. William Fowlkes, an editorial writer for the *Atlanta Daily World*, explained that for white Georgians, the issue was not "the race equality issue, but . . . the democracy issue." Countless black and white Georgians compared Talmadge's attacks on Georgia's blacks to Hitler's attacks on Jews. U.S. involvement in World War II following the December 6, 1941, Japanese attack at Pearl Harbor reinforced attacks on Talmadge. Borrowing the cultural rhetoric of the war, reformers such as Edwin Embree and Fred Wale of the JRF, Fred McCuistion and A. R. Mann of the GEB, and Walter Cocking and the University of Georgia administration depicted Talmadge as a dictator whose arbitrary actions belied the foundations of democracy. In his correspondence to the GEB and the JRF, Cocking referred to the "Georgia Gestapo" whose "gangster methods . . . have a familiar counterpoint in the little countries of Europe which Hitler and his gang have so effectively destroyed." And Ralph McGill, editor of the *Atlanta Constitution* and a segregationist, wrote to Embree that Talmadge's "inflammatory statements against the negro" resembled Hitler's rhetoric.[90]

During the white Democratic primary campaign in the summer of 1942, Arnall supported separate schools and Jim Crow but insisted that democracy required better-educated students. In an ad in the *Georgia Education Journal* before the primary, Arnall promised teachers "a public school system and a university system freed from the slimy hands of dictatorial policies."[91] Arnall envisioned a better-educated populace that could then develop a modern, autonomous, industrialized state. Scrupulously avoiding the issue of race during the campaign, Arnall consistently promoted better education for Georgians. And any educational improvements he advocated would benefit black schools and teachers as well.

Arnall's plan for Georgia's future paralleled that of the federal government and the GEB and JRF. Most New Deal programs accentuated the state's transition from a rural to a more industrialized, bureaucratic state, pushing blacks and poor whites off the land and encouraging training for industrial jobs. Corresponding with Sanford in 1939, Embree noted his belief that rural life was essentially over for African Americans and many whites. With the addition of the *Gaines* decision in 1939, many blacks and the NAACP pushed for more advanced educational opportunities. To the GEB and JRF as well as some members of the Georgia Department of Education, "education of the Negro child is a business proposition and not something to be tied up with the emotional reactions of individuals or groups." Stated differently, many Georgia educators realized by World War II that substandard educational facilities for blacks had to be improved if the state wanted to attract industry and enter the modern world. Education reformers now looked to schools as agencies that could provide a central and efficient means of disseminating information about all facets of life. As the regents of Georgia's university system explained, Georgia, like most other southern states, recast its educational goals from a belief in education as an individual goal or personal capital to "the proposition that higher education is capital for society."[92] In a striking parallel to the Social Gospel movement, Baptist and Methodist reformers and politicians, including Arnall, remade the individualized goal of salvation as an individualized goal of education to save the state and improve its economy.

An individual's identity and training, in short, became increasingly defined by his or her educational status and less by church and family affiliations. And as the GEB, the JRF, the University System of Georgia, and the Georgia Department of Education pressed for even more centralization, efficiency, and bureaucratization, as they acquired authority from local counties and school boards, as they offered funds as incentives for reforms in a time of statewide social and economic collapse, education emerged as the leading and certainly most visible manifestation of the modern industrial world. Time after time, beginning in 1939, the GEB and the JRF, with the cooperation of the University System of Georgia, proposed reorganizations of schools, professional teacher training, and local school units. It seems no accident, therefore, that most rural whites perceived Cocking as a "foreigner" with dangerous ideas. Coming on the heels of the *Gaines* decision and the heightened national attention to parochial southern values, Talmadge's fight against the JRF and Cocking became a cause Georgians willingly espoused.

To teachers, urban residents, students, and reformers, Talmadge represented the abrogation of everything that had been accomplished in the past twenty years. The GEA and GTEA condemned Talmadge, and thousands of white teachers resigned in the summer of 1941. Ruth Smith Waters and other teachers saw Talmadge as opposing education: "He was popular because he was a farmer, but he did not support education. . . . I never voted for him."[93] Beulah Rucker Oliver, Dorothy Oliver Rucker, and other black teachers paid less attention to the turmoil because of restrictions on black voting. To them, Talmadge was simply another one of the many governors who refused to rock the boat. Conversely, reigniting racial invectives scarcely endeared him to them.

The *Atlanta Daily World* urged Georgia blacks to pay the poll tax, register, and vote to support Arnall. The members of the CIC, the editors of most newspapers, and the segregated education associations resoundingly ridiculed Talmadge for his opposition to education and progress. Ninety-seven of the state's newspapers endorsed Arnall, including the *Atlanta Journal*, the *Atlanta Constitution*, and the *Gainesville Times*. Students from the Georgia Institute of Technology and the University of Georgia roused neighborhoods with door-to-door campaigns against Talmadge. Talmadge had nonetheless maintained his support from white, small farmers in addition to vital financial contributions from Georgia Power Company, highway contractors, and several textile and railroad officials. Arnall's support drew from banking and insurance companies, the university systems, oil companies, the Coca-Cola Company, and urban residents. Coca-Cola and most other Georgia companies had previously supported Talmadge, but industry's concerns shifted and his actions came into question. How could Georgia attract modern industries, including World War II defense contracts, that required new skills without better schools? The end result was the collapse of Talmadge's colorful yet autocratic rule and racist invectives and homilies that had earned him the lifelong devotion of many farmers and businesses. Arnall won in 1942, sweeping the urban counties, almost all the middle populated counties, and at least half of the small counties, giving him the majority of the county unit vote. His victory demonstrated to the nation that Georgia could be a more considerate and progressive state than many Americans thought.[94]

Arnall's victory capped a decade of new hopes for change and early political expression by black and white teachers. As Americans entered World War II, expectations for reforms and civil rights organizations grew. Without New Deal initiatives and the early efforts from the NAACP, the GTEA, and the GEA, the foundation for these changes would have been considerably weaker. Black teachers and communities learned means of organization. Although few African Americans voted for Arnall, they knew that his administration promised moderation as opposed to more years of Eugene Talmadge. By 1938, longtime black leaders Lucy Craft Laney and H. A. Hunt had died, and leaders such as C. L. Harper emerged. Harper and the GTEA drew on black women's organizational efforts in communities. As Jeanes supervisors, Narvie Jordan Harris and Susie Weems Wheeler had worked with black communities in addition to schools. They not only taught academic subjects but also informed residents of changes occurring around them. Political expressions that ranged from statements black teachers made to actions they took on behalf of their communities provided the bedrock for the next decade.

White teachers also encountered new expectations for themselves and their students. Elected on the promise of better education, white teachers believed that Arnall would improve educational standards and funding for schools. Organizing more than had previously been the case through the GEA, white teachers increased their political presence by focusing on education as a central issue in the 1942 election. While they had little to do with the GTEA, they had nonetheless made a powerful statement about what Georgia needed for the future. This work added to their authority and their awareness of what they could do in the future.

6 · A Brighter Light

Teachers and the Modern State

DURING WORLD WAR II, Dorothy Oliver Rucker took advantage of the opportunity to increase her pay and earn a college degree. She and her mother,
Beulah Rucker Oliver, attended Georgia State College (as Georgia State In-
dustrial College was renamed in 1932) in Savannah during the summers. In
1944 both women received their bachelor's degrees. After World War II,
Oliver's school offered educational training for black veterans using the G.I.
Bill.[1] Well aware of the difficulties many black war veterans faced as they sought
to combine work and education, Oliver decided to start an evening school, the
Veteran Timber Ridge Industrial School. Most black soldiers from northeast
Georgia had only five to seven years of schooling, depending on the availability of local education and the demands of their family economy. Oliver knew
that most men had been raised on farms and would require training for new
jobs in an industrial world. At the school, Al Roper, for example, learned educational fundamentals as well as how to become a plasterer, a trade he practiced
for the rest of his life. Not only did Oliver succeed in advancing his education,
but she also taught him a trade that severed his families' ties to sharecropping
and provided him with wage labor for the remainder of his working years.[2]
Adding to her political agenda of education for blacks, Oliver adapted her
model to teaching trades to black veterans.

Leona Clark Williams's life also changed during and after World War II. Her
husband, Bill, worked for Southern Railway, and the family settled in Sewanee
in Gwinnett County. When her son turned five in 1942, Sewanee school
trustees approached Williams one Sunday as she came out of church. Facing an
acute wartime teaching shortage, white school boards and trustees turned to
married women who had previously taught school to fill the classrooms. The
war forced the state to eradicate the ban on hiring married women. When
Williams was certain that her husband had a draft deferment, she agreed to return to teaching at the Sewanee elementary school.[3] White married women
could now claim professional status. As white women accumulated experience
in classrooms, they began to insist on better pay, professional training, a retirement program, and better conditions in schools.

Transformations came to the forefront in Williams's and Oliver's lives as well as those of other Georgians during the 1940s. While the New Deal expanded fissures in Georgia's hierarchical structure through programs such as the Works Project Administration and the National Youth Administration, World War II led to greater social, political, and economic changes. Ellis Arnall's efforts to promote economic growth and improve public education flashed across the state and pushed some Georgians to advocate moderate reforms and others to return to traditional sanctuaries in churches, homes, and communities. As a racial moderate, Arnall appealed to a coalition of blacks, white moderates, and some business leaders. Never challenging Jim Crow laws, Arnall believed economic development benefited both races and all Georgians. Arnall embodied hope of southern moderation, the "days of hope" that liberals sought. Emboldened by his administration, efforts by the Georgia Education Association (GEA) and the Georgia Teachers and Education Association (GTEA) to improve schools by state and federal funding began during the 1930s and grew during the 1940s. As Arnall moved his state cautiously, the National Association for the Advancement of Colored People (NAACP), supported by the GTEA, continued to win federal and state court victories equalizing teachers' salaries and school facilities and eliminating the sacred white primary.[4]

World War II and the Arnall administration shattered traditional social and economic systems. Defense industries fed urbanization in Marietta, Brunswick, and Savannah. Military bases in Columbus and Warner Robbins provided job opportunities to former agricultural workers. New industries, including the poultry industry in northeast Georgia, expanded, and the textile industries grew. World War II industrial growth ended cotton agricultural labor by offering better salaries and opportunities for former sharecroppers.

African Americans registered to vote in record numbers by 1946. The NAACP and the GTEA combined resources to launch a civil rights crusade for equal education and voter registration in Georgia. In 1946, the Congress of Industrial Organizations (CIO) launched Operation Dixie, an attempt to unionize black and white workers to increase their pay and benefits. The GTEA reorganized under the distinguished leadership of C. L. Harper and became a force for social, political, and economic change. Underscoring the Double V campaign announced during World War II in black newspapers, Horace Mann Bond, president of Fort Valley College and a member of the GTEA, reminded students of inferior conditions for U.S. blacks as they enlisted to fight for democracy. Indications of the origins of the civil rights movement may seem faint during the New Deal, but during the 1940s, African Americans began to come together in greater numbers, partly through NAACP branches in Savannah and Atlanta. Black teachers in the GTEA also laid much of the groundwork for the civil rights victories that were to follow.[5]

Although few African American teachers voted in 1942, Arnall's election carried a different meaning for blacks than for whites. Denied admission to the University of Georgia, blacks had less of a stake in its loss of accreditation. Talmadge's rhetoric during his reelection campaign nonetheless conveyed ominous meanings. Although Arnall offered no "revolutionary forms" of "economic opportunity," as the *Atlanta Daily World* put it, blacks feared Talmadge because he "deliberately and cruelly bulldozed and plagued Negroes for no reason other than it was his surest escape from reality." African American education had much to lose if Talmadge won. When the NAACP announced its national campaign to equalize black teachers' salaries, white education officials promptly gathered GTEA officers to convince them to avoid legal action. Blacks found Arnall's 1942 victory over Talmadge heartening because it held the hope that an administration would "embrace the interests and welfare of Negroes, as well as other citizens of Georgia." Some hopes were fulfilled. During Arnall's administration, the huge gaps narrowed between the two segregated school systems.[6]

For the next four years, Arnall's administration followed moderate policies while preserving aspects of the old order. Key policy changes included fundamental educational reform. The University of Georgia System's accreditation was restored, the board of regents was reorganized, the Georgia Constitution was rewritten, the poll tax was removed, teachers won a retirement plan in 1945, black and white teachers' salaries became more equitable, and all teachers were required to hold bachelor's degrees.[7] The seven-month school year, free textbooks, and a compulsory school attendance law became realities. Many teachers of both races had to return to college to obtain bachelor's degrees, yet they also gained from improved salaries. And the fact that black teachers could even attend a state-supported college for professional teacher training represented a notable accomplishment.

Yet the gains African Americans accomplished by cracking Jim Crow's reign, and the improvements black and white educators achieved in public education, seemed imperiled by an abrupt shift. After 1946, most white Georgians turned to Eugene Talmadge to restore traditional values they understood. Northern philanthropic assistance and aid from the U.S. Department of Agriculture's Extension Service, the New Deal, and World War II's push for central and efficient administrations, trained workers, and educated youths forged a modern public education system. Tempers again flared over the subject of education, the fundamental social policy that threatened traditional hierarchy and values. Successful GTEA and NAACP lawsuits, the elimination of the white primary, women's professional gains, and the determinations of African Americans to destroy Jim Crow after World War II converged in a conflagration of interest and beliefs. Turmoil, violence, and murder followed. The growing civil rights movement seemingly collapsed after 1946 as NAACP chapters closed across the state. In reality, the GTEA, long a fundamental source of support for the NAACP, assumed the NAACP's role of organizing communities and challenging segregated public facilities. At the same time, the GEA and the GTEA pushed state educational reform in the Minimum Foundation Program for Education and sought federal funds to help equalize segregated schools. By 1950, the result was far from an equalized society or school system. Yet because of black and white teachers and reformers, Georgia became a modern society with a better school system staffed by professional educators that was better equipped to meet the challenge of growing industries and expanding urban centers. Individuals became accustomed to consumer culture and enhanced their lives economically, socially, and politically. More to the point, black teachers managed to uphold a degree of momentum for equality, momentum that would feed the civil rights movement in the 1960s.

IN SAVANNAH AND Atlanta, the two largest sites of black organization, the NAACP remained a small force for change. Smaller groups and some individuals—for example, John Wesley Dobbs's Atlanta Civic and Political League, founded in 1934—led campaigns against white supremacy in both cities. Individuals argued with bus drivers about segregated seating, but no organized action was taken. More than two hundred thousand Georgia blacks had a simple response to racism: they left Georgia for defense industry jobs in the Midwest and on the West Coast. Black leaders such as Benjamin Mays, president of Morehouse College; his wife, Annie; and the Reverend Martin Luther King Sr. avoided segregated facilities, including buses. In 1938 black Atlantans in the NAACP, the Atlanta Civic and Political League, and the Atlanta Urban League (AUL) joined to defeat a bond issue that would have distributed most of the funds to white schools. Atlanta's NAACP branch director, Forrester Washington, resigned one year later to devote more time to fund-raising for Atlanta's School of Social Work. During his tenure, he had for the first time unified Atlanta's black community factions—the NAACP, AUL, and the Atlanta Civic and Political League. Dobbs and C. A. Scott, editor of the *Atlanta Daily World*, now worked on the executive committee of the NAACP, along with

King; Agnes Jones, president of the GTEA; and A. T. Walden, former president of the NAACP's Atlanta branch.[8] While few blacks registered to vote to defeat the bond issue, black leaders saw the election as a victory because they united, organized, and ran a vigorous campaign against the measure.

The NAACP continued its legal challenges to segregated schools and white primaries in the South. To some historians, undertaking a challenge to inequitable pay between black and white teachers was a notable effort that nonetheless favored African American professionals. There is some truth to the charge that little attention was paid to mass movements to desegregate public facilities or work for better employment opportunities for working-class blacks. Few black and white moderates noted the CIO's Operation Dixie, and it met even less consideration from working-class whites. While the AUL and NAACP chapters pushed President Franklin Delano Roosevelt's Fair Employment Practice Commission to train and hire more black workers for Marietta's Bell Bomber factory, the campaign succeeded only in obtaining assembly line jobs for educated blacks, not skilled positions for the black working class that needed vocational training.[9]

Although emphasis on equalizing teachers' pay favored middle-class blacks, the NAACP and black professionals deemed this the best strategy at the time for several reasons. Black professionals were the vanguard. Since Reconstruction, they had believed that they represented black interests and intentionally demonstrated black values and potential at their best, a combination of racial uplift and race work. Unequal pay for professionals was more likely to garner support from southern moderates and northern liberals. Here were college graduates with bachelor's degrees making half of what less-educated white teachers made. The head of the NAACP, Walter White, and Thurgood Marshall, in charge of the NAACP's Legal Defense and Educational Fund, recognized the need for equal salaries for all black workers. Marshall insisted that the campaign for equal teachers' salaries was fought against the "age-old custom in the South of paying Negroes less money for equal services" and that victories in this arena would affect pay for all black workers.[10]

Education framed most NAACP members' and other blacks' strategies for achieving equality. If black children were to gain equal educational opportunities, black teachers had to be paid equitably and adequately. Furthermore, black professionals had resources with which to fund legal challenges and organizations to support such efforts. Before the 1942 election, White considered focusing on defeating Talmadge rather than continuing the fight for equal teacher salaries in Georgia. Yet Eugene Martin, an executive with Atlanta Life

Charles Lincoln Harper, 1940s.
Harper, as president of the GTEA, reorganized it
to become one of the state's leading civil rights
organizations. (Courtesy of Narvie Jordan Harris.)

Insurance, assured White that "equalization of salaries and educational opportunities will represent something concrete and definite" that the NAACP had
accomplished. Benefits from legal actions on behalf of teachers were indeed restricted to black professionals. Still, teachers comprised the largest professional
African American group and had the most contact with black communities.[11]

The NAACP's focus on education benefited from changes in the GTEA.
Agnes Jones, president of the GTEA from 1936 to 1938, joined the NAACP
and remained a member. Her successor, Benjamin Hubert from Georgia State
College, was less willing to commit the GTEA to NAACP issues.[12] Yet teachers clearly wanted action. After the deaths of many members of the previous
generation of black leaders, the GTEA became a more activist organization.
Dorothy Oliver Rucker, Narvie Jordan Harris, and Susie Weems Wheeler were
among the many teachers who knew substantive change in education for blacks
had to come. These voices included the new GTEA president, Charles Lincoln
Harper, former principal of Booker T. Washington High School in Atlanta.

As principal of Atlanta's only black high school, Harper would appear to be
a member of the city's black elite. Yet his early life tells more than a story about
life in the middle class. Harper was born in 1877 to sharecroppers living outside
Sparta, Georgia. He completed eighth grade in Hancock County and subsequently finished his high school and college work at Morris Brown College in
Atlanta. He married Carrie Bell Nichols, with whom he had three children.
The family resided on Atlanta's renowned Auburn Avenue, home to many
members of the city's black middle class. The Harpers worshipped and taught
Sunday school at Big Bethel African Methodist Episcopal Church. Harper
worked at various jobs including the post office and insurance sales before

becoming principal of Morris Brown's high school in the early twentieth century. In 1915 he became principal of Yonge Street Night School. Nine years later, Atlanta's first black public high school was completed, and the city's board of education chose Harper as the first principal. Always understaffed and overcrowded, the high school attracted students from across the state. During assemblies, Harper told his students that while law and custom might dictate that they had to sit at the back of the bus, they never had to accept inferior treatment. He designed elections at the high school that replicated local and national contests so that students learned about the voting process. In the 1930s, Harper joined the NAACP, as did several of the school's teachers. During Jones's term as president of the GTEA, Harper served on the executive committee. When he pushed the Atlanta School Board for better salaries and conditions at Atlanta's schools for blacks, he was fired.[13]

But if white Atlantans thought they were removing an agitator, they were wrong. Elected president of the GTEA in 1941, Harper realized that the organization needed fundamental changes. If black teachers joined the fight for pay equality, some members had to have paid positions to protect them from retaliation, losing their jobs, and violence. Early work by William Jefferson White, Richard Wright, the Hopes, and the Hunts had shown black Georgia reformers that an alliance between black business leaders and educators was necessary. Only with black business's support could teachers risk challenging white school boards and racism. Teachers who were too forceful in the drive for change faced the loss of their jobs and at times were compelled to leave the state. They needed economic resources or local black business leaders to lead the fight for equalization. Because of Jim Crow, black businesses drew clients from within the black community, placing such businesses in a somewhat more secure position than black teachers, who relied on white school boards for jobs.

To position the GTEA for future equalization battles, Harper reorganized the group, making the position of executive secretary into a full-time, salaried post and thereby protecting the officeholder from white reprisals. Harper selected a board of directors from among the members and organized district meetings for teachers and local professionals.[14] Unlike most NAACP branches, which were located in larger cities, GTEA members came from both rural and urban school districts. Teachers who were afraid to join the NAACP belonged to the GTEA and used it as the base for their activism.

Through these changes, Harper stretched the GTEA's reach across the state. District leaders held meetings, sought members, and promoted NAACP campaigns and other legal challenges to Jim Crow. The GTEA's membership climbed to more than seven thousand. A portion of each member's dues went to a standing fund that would contribute to battles for voting rights, campaigns for educational equality, and challenges to segregated public facilities. In contrast to Atlanta's often fractious NAACP and AUL, the GTEA was the only organization that combined black urban and rural professionals from across the state in the early 1940s. Harper also asked Horace Mann Bond, the president of Fort Valley State College, to become editor of the GTEA's journal, the *Herald*, which became more political, printing articles about school conditions in each county and discussions about the G.I. Bill.[15]

Like Harper, Bond was a race man, determined to change Georgia's racist hierarchy. During the early years of World War II, when blacks were encouraged to enlist, Bond addressed the Fort Valley student body, telling them that while they should support their country, they needed to remember that they were fighting a war for freedoms they lacked. Germans in the United States had more opportunities than blacks did. If the United States won the war, Bond told the students to take advantage of the victory when they returned. Here he reworded the "Double V" campaign espoused by African Americans across the country for victory at home and abroad for democracy. His slogan during his stay at Fort Valley was "Help one million Georgians help Georgia."[16] Students recognized the covert meaning of his slogan: Georgia had one million blacks at the time. Had Bond reversed the slogan to ask white Georgians to help blacks, the outcome might have been quite different. But few whites objected to hearing that blacks would help the state. Speakers including W. E. B. Du Bois and Mary McLeod Bethune came to Fort Valley and addressed students about their rights and future challenges.

Bond left Fort Valley in 1945 for the presidency of Lincoln College, his alma mater. Yet his work at Fort Valley inspired numerous students, many of whom became teachers. Like most educators, Bond knew that their battles needed support from black businesses. Bond and Harper apparently believed that NAACP branches, notably in Atlanta, lacked the desire to contest educational equality in other geographic areas. Bond certainly recognized teachers' vulnerability to attacks from white supremacists. By the 1940s, some white conservatives had begun to link the NAACP to communism and anti-Americanism. Like Harper and earlier black reformers, Bond advocated an alliance between black businesses and educators, so in 1943 Bond began to organize Civicle, a national organization that drew from civic leagues in towns and cities. Bond envisioned a broader agenda for the new group than that of the NAACP, including organizing blacks in towns in rural areas, where the NAACP had little success, and mobilizing blacks to fight for voting rights and equal employment and educational opportunities. Moreover, he hoped to avoid linking Civicle with the NAACP, which was acquiring an undeserved reputation from white supremacists for harboring communists. By 1944 civic leagues formed in Fort Valley, Moultrie, Athens, Gainesville, Macon, Dublin, Brunswick, and other Georgia cities, some of which lacked NAACP branches. Leagues in Gainesville and Athens had members who also joined the GTEA and/or the NAACP. Some Gainesville teachers' husbands joined the Men's Progressive Club, a forerunner of the local NAACP chapter.[17] Withal, blacks began to express their opposition to racial inequality.

African American teachers had always viewed their role as extending from the classroom to the community. Not only did most black teachers work with their communities, but Jeanes teachers traveled to at least fifteen schools in their districts to work with black communities and teachers. In 1937 Robert L. Cousins, a Baptist from Luthersville who graduated from Mercer University and did graduate work at Columbia University, became Georgia's director of Negro education. Cousins, unlike some of his predecessors, taught children, served as a principal in Carrollton, and taught at the summer school held at Georgia Teachers College in Statesboro. Cousins favored segregated schools, yet his advocacy of improved education for blacks certainly made him a moderate among white Georgians. As he consolidated black schools during the late 1930s, he also worked to strengthen the Jeanes program. Funding for Jeanes teachers was increased, training workshops were held, and duties were specified. Georgia Jeanes consultant Maenelle Dempsey worked with Cousins to develop leadership and supervisory skills for Jeanes teachers. By the early 1940s, Jeanes teachers not only supervised teachers in the classroom and promoted school attendance but also organized parents in the parent-teacher associations. In effect, female Jeanes teachers were working as black school superintendents.[18]

Viewing themselves as promoting Harper's vision of an equal society, Dempsey and other Jeanes teachers used their positions to talk to teachers about NAACP strategies for educational equality. Meetings with parents also provided the Jeanes teachers with opportunities to discuss court cases, the possibilities for local action, and community needs. In some instances, Jeanes teachers assert that they were the main source through which black communities learned about state and federal agencies as well as about recent events affecting African Americans.[19]

As director of Negro education, Cousins, like his predecessors, Walter B. Hill

Jr. and J. C. Dixon, sought promising teachers to become Jeanes supervisors. After completing high school education in Griffin, Susie Weems Wheeler taught at Adairsville School in 1937 for twenty-five dollars a month. She realized that the more college work she completed, the more money she would earn. She began taking summer classes at Fort Valley State College and in Bartow County. She joined the GTEA. In 1941 she married Dan Wheeler, who enlisted in the military in 1942. During World War II, Susie Weems Wheeler registered to vote and completed her college work at Fort Valley. Her education there was telling for two reasons: first, Bond inspired her to work harder for racial improvement; second, she met Cousins, who asked her take the Jeanes supervisor course at Atlanta University in 1945. She agreed as long as she could return to Bartow County. Cousins arranged for Bartow County to obtain a Jeanes supervisor, and Wheeler remained in Cartersville.[20]

Unique among many Georgia communities, Cartersville always had a black board of trustees for its schools as well as a group of activists. Cartersville's branch of the NAACP, which Wheeler and her husband joined, drew from this group. Wheeler knew that she could be fired for joining the NAACP, but she also recognized that Cartersville's history of black activism would protect her. As a Jeanes supervisor and a GTEA and NAACP member, Wheeler used her position to inform the black communities in her district about campaigns and efforts for educational improvement. By attending GTEA meetings, she learned from Harper what the NAACP was doing and how the GTEA supported it. Harper reported on each lawsuit and requested financial support from GTEA members for the NAACP's legal challenges. Wheeler returned to Cartersville and informed her community about these actions throughout the 1940s. As a Jeanes supervisor of fourteen schools, she helped standardize teaching procedures, provided materials and services, got sources and materials teachers needed, and checked student attendance. She went to homes and walked into cotton fields to find parents and persuade them to send their children to school. At the same time, she talked to community members about what the GTEA and NAACP planned for educational equality and voting rights. In effect, she organized her community politically.[21]

Other Jeanes teachers' stories reveal similar patterns. After teaching for two years in Bainbridge, Narvie Jordan Harris took a position teaching sixth grade at Locust Grove in Henry County in 1941. Her students sat on tree stumps covered with oilcloth and used a stove "from the Spanish-American War." She had majored in home economics at Clark University, so she prepared lunches for community members with government-issued food. The local women taught

Narvie Jordan Harris, 1960s.
Harris, a Jeanes supervisor and community
organizer, worked to equalize schools for
blacks in De Kalb County. (Courtesy of
Narvie Jordan Harris.)

her how to make corn meal mush. At night, Harris taught adult education, including literacy classes. But Harris could not tolerate the blatant racism of her
white superintendent. She resigned after one year and spoke to Cousins about
a position as a Jeanes teacher. After teaching home economics at a high school
for two years, Harris was offered a scholarship for Jeanes instruction at Gram-
bling College. She then received her master's degree from Atlanta University.
In 1944 Harris became the Jeanes supervisor for De Kalb County, a position she
held until 1969.[22]

Like Wheeler, Harris joined the GTEA and the NAACP, and Harper inspired her to do more to fulfill blacks' educational needs. Harris was responsible
for supervising seventeen schools, thirty-six teachers, and fifteen hundred students. Similar to other Jeanes supervisors, she saw her work as that of a black
school superintendent. Both conditions at black schools and low teachers'
salaries angered her: teachers in her district had little money for the commute
from Atlanta to their schools in De Kalb County, a situation exacerbated by
wartime rationing of gasoline and tires. With a single exception, De Kalb
schools had outhouses for students and teachers, and the books provided were
"unfit for use," with the name of the previous school printed inside, which Harris perceived as a clear indicator to black students that they were inferior. As
she fought for running water and better conditions, as she worked with teach-

ers and improved school attendance, Harris, like Wheeler, informed the community about GTEA and NAACP goals and campaigns. She also knew that she had to be careful about what she said or risk losing her job.[23]

The NAACP's agenda for equalization within a segregated school system seems tame in comparison with later civil rights activism, yet even southern moderates believed that the NAACP's refusal to endorse the preservation of segregation made it an extreme and radical organization. Other whites saw the NAACP's actions as nothing less than rampant communism invading the South.[24]

During World War II, Harper guided the GTEA in its new direction and used district meetings to support the NAACP campaigns. After Harper restructured the GTEA, he became president of the Atlanta NAACP branch and later served as vice president of the Georgia's NAACP conference. While no evidence directly links Harper to the NAACP's first test case for equal teacher salaries, Harper certainly knew about the NAACP strategy and may have recommended William H. Reeves as a candidate to challenge unequal salaries. As the former principal at Booker T. Washington High School, Harper must have met Reeves at GTEA meetings. Given the likelihood that Reeves would be fired by the white Atlanta school board, the Reverend Martin Luther King Sr. obtained financial support for Reeves from the Atlanta Life Insurance Company.[25]

In 1941, as Georgians debated Talmadge's actions against the university system, Reeves and his attorney, A. T. Walden, former president of the NAACP's Atlanta branch, filed a suit against the city's school board for a teacher's salary equal to that of similarly trained white teachers. Reeves, a graduate of Fisk University, had taught at David T. Howard Junior High in Atlanta for seven years yet earned more than six hundred dollars less per year than white teachers with the same degree and experience. In the suit, Walden requested that the school board discontinue its policy of determining salaries on the basis of race. The Atlanta school board promptly fired Reeves and then argued successfully in court that the case should be dismissed because he was no longer a teacher. In 1943 another Atlanta teacher, Samuel Davis, filed a similar suit against the Atlanta school board and was also fired; again, the district court ruled that because Davis was no longer a teacher, no grounds existed for a lawsuit. The board thus established a tidy way of legally deflecting protest.[26]

ALTHOUGH THE GEA remained silent about these particular cases, it continued its battle for better teachers' pay, benefits, and support for federal legislation that proposed funding for schools. To GEA members, these issues would improve black schools as well. When the GEA held its 1941 annual meeting in Savannah, the group drafted a resolution that called for higher teacher salaries to submit to Governor Talmadge. But because he had previously rejected their request for a 25 percent increase, they sought federal aid to assist Georgia schools. By 1942 the teacher shortage had worsened as the men who had constituted 19 percent of the white teaching force and 15 percent of the black teachers were called for active duty. Nevertheless, Talmadge rejected federal aid because he believed it would lead to integrated schools. After Reeves and the NAACP had initiated their suit, Talmadge insisted that equal pay would lead to blacks demanding admission to the University of Georgia.[27]

Arnall inherited the problem of low teacher salaries. Moreover, wartime shortages prevented many teachers who lived in rural areas from driving to city schools. Jimmie Kate Sams Cole recalled that "during World War II, [the school board] had a problem filling positions. They filled teaching positions with any breathing body."[28] Caring for children's education outside the home suddenly trumped minding children at home, and married white women were permitted to teach. World War II stretched the definition and limitations of white women's work and the family.

During World War II, the GEA's political agenda focused on placing "our educational system on a sound financial basis" in order "to solve the economic, social, and cultural problems of the people of the state." As the U.S. Congress continued to debate federal funding for public schools and teachers' salaries in the early 1940s, the GEA and the National Education Association called for teachers and Georgians to write their congressmen to pass the bill. Well aware that white supremacists and staunch advocates of localism feared federal intervention in state affairs because of fears of integrated schools or other potential federal mandates, the GEA framed its support of the bills in wartime patriotism. Federal funding would ensure that public schools preserved "the first lines of defense in a democracy." More importantly, the GEA noted that the South needed federal assistance for education because of the rate of illiteracy, the higher number of children southern states needed to educate compared to the North, and the region's lower per capita income with which to fund schools and teachers' salaries. "Education," the GEA argued, "raises the standards of culture, . . . increases the wealth and income of the people, and is indispensable to the national defense." Answering fears about federal intervention in segregated schools, the GEA noted that the legislation specifically provided funding for separate schools in order to equalize them. Schools in the District of Columbia that relied on federal aid preserved a segregated school system. GEA members reminded readers that "no good citizen will object to a just and equitable apportionment" of federal funds to black and white schools.[29]

Black and white teachers' salaries were indeed a paramount issue during World War II. As defense industries moved to Georgia, military bases expanded, textile and carpet industries enlarged, and other new industries grew, the economic expansion brought higher salaries to workers outside the public schools. While some teachers left the state for higher pay, others, like Leona Clark Williams, took jobs in wartime industries. Williams's principal at Sewanee Elementary School, Troy Thompson, told Williams she could earn more money at Bell Aircraft Corporation, also known as Bell Bomber, in Marietta. Thompson and Williams found jobs at the plant, with Williams keeping files on changes to the aircraft. Williams earned higher pay but sensed that some women gained promotions by dating married men, so she obtained a note from a doctor that excused her from working at the plant because driving from Sewanee to Marietta caused her to have headaches, and she promptly returned to teaching.[30]

For white teachers, World War II meant the expansion of opportunities and benefits because of the availability of better-paying jobs. School boards had always refused to allow white women to teach after marriage out of a desire to preserve the ideal of white womanhood. According to trustees and most whites, raising proper white children required a mother at home who would guide and educate them according to southern values and traditions.

But World War II presented a dilemma to Georgia school boards. The draft and the labor demands of war industries left school boards with a severe labor shortage. As men flocked to the armed services and others went to higher-paying defense industries, schools lacked teachers. Even before the United States declared war against Japan in 1941, state officials noted the teacher shortage. Almost fifteen hundred white teachers resigned before September 1941, and State School Superintendent M. D. Collins claimed that the main problem was poor teacher salaries.[31] For decades, teachers had complained about their pay. Now they acted.

When white women returned to teaching during and after World War II, they, through the GEA, demanded higher salaries, better benefits, better school conditions, and professional certification. Their success resulted in part from the labor shortage that existed during the war as well as from their persistence in asserting these demands at the GEA's yearly conventions. Teachers attended conferences in Atlanta, Macon, and Savannah that featured workshops on methods and materials. As Williams, a lifelong member of the

GEA and National Education Association, recalled, "I used to go to all the conventions. Workshop, workshop, workshop. Part of it's not worth a toodle. But we'd talk about how to improve our wages and how to get . . . a teacher's retirement plan."[32]

Some counties claimed that 100 percent of their white teachers belonged to the GEA. Teachers needed the organization to communicate their concerns and to influence state legislation. Professional issues including health insurance, retirement, sick leave, and tenure became key issues for the GEA through the 1950s. With Governor Arnall's support in 1943, the GEA and the GTEA successfully lobbied for the passage of the first legislation for the teachers' retirement program. In 1946, Arnall announced a 50 percent pay increase for all teachers, helping to raise white teachers' salaries from an average of just over eight hundred dollars per year when Arnall was elected to more than fifteen hundred dollars per year in 1947. Black teachers' pay also increased, but they still earned an average of seven hundred dollars less per year than whites did.[33]

With white women back in the pool of potential teachers, trustees rehired many former district instructors. In 1943 trustees of the Oakwood schools in Hall County paid Ruth Smith Waters a visit. As in other school districts, the trustees searched for women who had teaching experience even though they were now married. According to Waters, the trustees visited her home several times and asked her to teach. Now that her youngest son was five and her husband was working evenings and could watch the boy during the day, Waters realized that she could return to teaching. The following year, the principal told Waters she was being transferred to the high school, but Waters refused to go because she disliked the principal there. The trustees again visited her at home. This time Waters explained that she knew the principal was a poor disciplinarian and declined to move to the high school. Because the principal refused to support the teachers, teachers either quit or endured students' antics. The next day, the superintendent and trustees asked Waters to lunch. They offered her fifty dollars more a month "to go into that high school and straighten the crowd out. Fifty dollars a month then was something else," she recalled.[34] Her professional code as a teacher began to outweigh traditional definitions of feminine duty.

Similarly, Cole returned to teaching when she arranged for a woman who had worked on her parents' farm to watch her children. Williams, Waters, and Cole all had children who were at least four or five years old, and these mothers made sure that their children would be well cared for. The women were eager to resume their careers after assuring themselves that trusted individuals could assume care of the women's children, which remained understood as one of a woman's primary duties. Using the GEA and their individual means of negotiating with trustees, teachers demanded and achieved respect as professional married women. They became increasingly aware of what they could accomplish politically.

This issue underscores white teachers' efforts to combine traditional roles with a professional career. While women sought to preserve their roles as wives and mothers, they also insisted on becoming professional women. Once again, they re-created the meaning of the professional woman by using opportunities such as the labor shortage, their continuing ambitions, and goals for family stability. These women devised a new feminine agenda for the post–World War II era. While trustees, husbands, superintendents, and politicians touted children's interests as part of women's roles, it was clearly the women who guarded their children's welfare. Cole, Waters, and Williams all stated that they returned to teaching in part because their families needed the money. Similarly, after World War II ended, white female married teachers could remain in the classroom because their children were in school, and the additional income purchased such consumer goods as washing machines and better cars. Combining their ambitions with family responsibilities, the ability to keep the same schedule as their children was one of the fundamental attractions of teaching for black and white women. As Cole put it, she and her children "had the same hours, the same vacations. I wasn't away from [our children] that much. I was glad to get to teach because I was not a homemaker. You get to feeling narrow-minded and dull. And teaching was a very respectable career."[35] Thus, most women who became teachers were committed to marriage and children and sought ways to combine families with careers.

As Governor Arnall, the GEA, and the GTEA supported proposals for federal funding to equalize schools, they recognized the need for a compulsory attendance law, passed in 1945, that would add to equalizing education for all students. The measure was enforced by "visiting teachers," all of them white, who checked school attendance in each county. Some African American teachers, including Jeanes supervisors, have contended that both the compulsory attendance law and the visiting teacher program were based on the Jeanes program. The visiting teachers were "really social workers," stated Georgia's first visiting teacher, Florrie Still, from Hall County. Visiting teachers went to all county schools and noted which students failed to attend. If a child missed too many days, the teacher made a home visit. Because school funding was based on the average daily attendance, schools wanted to keep their attendance as high as possible. According to Still, using the term "visiting teacher" allowed the women to be included in the teacher allotment from the state and enabled visiting teachers to keep retirement years earned as classroom teachers. The first forty visiting teachers attended a six-week workshop at the University of Georgia in 1946. Still and the other participants believed that "the lack of education was feeding into the problems of unemployment, crime, and increased welfare."[36] They believed education was the key to children's futures.

After Still's appointment in Hall County, the superintendent told her to find all of the county's black schools, since no records appear to have indicated exactly how many such institutions existed. Still rambled across the county in her pickup truck, bouncing along on dirt roads looking for black schools. "I went to this one down at Chestnut Mountain, away back in the field, across some pastures, way back in the woods. There were about ten or twelve children there and a teacher. They were sitting on benches with no desk in front of them, just sitting on benches, writing on their legs. Over in the corner was an old wood heater that had been discarded and sitting on that was a bucket of water and a dipper. They had been bringing the water from the spring." After Still reported the conditions to the superintendent, the county arranged for a bus to pick up the children and send them to Gainesville's Fair Street School, where the teacher was also hired.[37]

Still and other visiting teachers saw their position as resembling missionary work: "We helped a lot of families. We referred them to agencies that they needed to be referred to that they didn't even know about. In our training, we were brought up to date on whatever was available to help people with whatever problem they had—services for crippled children, welfare support, and legal assistance for abused and neglected children." On other occasions, visiting teachers organized local programs for children. During one home visit, a mother told Still that she wanted to send her children to school but they lacked shoes. Time after time, the mother had patched shoes with cardboard or any material she could find, but patches were inadequate for Georgia's cold, wet winters. So Still asked the Gainesville Pilot Club, a white women's organization, to buy shoes for the county's children, and the following year, the club started an annual fund-raising dinner.[38]

This story reveals the persistence of class distinctions but also demonstrates emerging family tensions. According to Still and other visiting teachers, most mothers tried every means to keep their children in school, but when fathers gave education little support, children tended to have poor attendance records. During one home visit, a mother told Still she wanted her children to attend school but their father did not. When Still talked to the father, he replied, "I'm not going to send them as long as I've got cotton in the field. I didn't go to school, and I've worked hard all my life. They're no better than I am. They're my kids and I can do what I want." Even though Still reported the case to the local courts and the judge ordered the father to send the children to school, he refused. Still stated that after several visits to the family, she never saw the children working outside, let alone the father. Not long thereafter, the father was killed, and the mother promptly sent the children to school. Jimmie Kate Sams Cole, who worked as a visiting teacher in Fayette County, related a similar incident in which a father stormed into the superintendent's office and "let me know he was not in violation of anything. Those were his children and he could do what he pleased. He didn't like some *woman* telling him what he had to do."[39] The visiting teacher program detracted from parental authority, notably the father's, and delegated more authority to women outside the family. As with fights about school consolidation, battles over compulsory attendance raged across the South.

Cole and Still agree that some families needed children's labor. Educators and reformers perceived compulsory attendance laws as means of assisting children in a world that demanded an education and better skills, but the measures did little to help black or white working-class families that needed children's labor on the farm or income from low-wage jobs in the textile or other industries. And to have a woman as a representative of state authority challenge the father's rule was simply inconceivable.

Another consequence of Georgia's compulsory attendance laws was overcrowded white classrooms and book shortages. Ruth Smith Waters recalled being moved to Lyman Hall High School because the county superintendent "liked my teaching." Waters recalled book shortages, with several children sharing the same textbook. Teachers continued to instruct their charges regarding hygiene. Waters remembered three distinct odors from children as they gathered around the classroom stove: garlic, Vicks, and lard and sulfur. Some children attended school with garlic bulbs wrapped in cloth around their necks, a measure some rural mothers believed warded off germs. Mothers also used lard and sulfur to stop itches and Vick's salve in stitched seercloth to cure colds. Waters's school lacked indoor toilets, so students used outhouses.[40]

The GEA and the GTEA repeatedly called attention to crowded school conditions and the need for salary increases. In the *Georgia Education Journal*, the GEA's publication, teachers wrote poems identifying their and their students' needs. In 1946, Mrs. R. O. DeLoach of Tattnall Schools wrote,

> I've gone to college and hold a degree,
> For which good money I've spent;
> Five days each week as a teacher I draw
> Four dollars and thirty-three cents.
> My unskilled friend on Elm Street
> At no school learned any trade,
> Yet he proudly proclaims whenever we meet:
> "Seven dollars a day I'm paid!"
> . . . .
> Compulsory Law says, "Go to School"
> But where will Jimmie sit?
> Not enough desks, not enough books,
> My! What's the use of it?
> One teacher I know has fifty-nine
> Sweet cherubs—or are they brats!
> Try teaching that number in one small room,
> You'll wonder where you are at.[41]

Teachers' poems accentuated their escalating political awareness of their ability to call for better conditions, school facilities, and professional training. That white educators wrote poetry to request better conditions suggests that some teachers believed that they could address their predicament only in indirect, nonthreatening means—rhyming ditties that amused at the same time they instructed. Most teachers used the GEA to articulate their agenda for Georgia's school system.

The intensified push for professionalization from black and white women added to the call for federal funds for equalization of schools, salaries, and facilities as well as the African American effort to enforce equal rights and opportunities. These challenges led to school reforms that increasingly shifted authority from parents and churches to teachers and the educational bureaucracy. Georgia's 1945 constitution provided for state-supported education through twelve grades, eliminated more than a thousand local-tax school districts, and established educational and certification requirements for county superintendents. The days of the local favorite who became county school superintendent with little or no background in education began to wane. In 1948, Georgia required teachers to have a bachelor's degree for state certification. At that time, less than 50 percent of the state's teachers held bachelor's degrees, so thousands of black and white teachers returned to school while continuing to teach and raise families.⁴² Professionalization became tied to a bachelor's degree that in-cluded education courses, the specialization that set teachers apart from those who taught with less than one or two years of college courses.

In the early 1940s, even before the state requirement went into effect, blacks and whites had begun to attend classes for bachelor's degrees because attaining a degree both increased pay and enhanced the job's professionalism. Narvie Jordan Harris, Susie Weems Wheeler, Beulah Rucker Oliver, Dorothy Oliver Rucker, Laura Mosley Whelchel, and Nancy Stephens all grabbed the oppor-tunity to improve their positions. In 1940, Oliver and her daughter made plans to attend Georgia State College in Savannah during the summers to earn their bachelor's degrees. At the time, Whelchel was working at Jewell's poultry pro-cessing plant in Gainesville and was going to try to save money to go to school for her bachelor's degree. Whelchel had only forty dollars for college but "did just what Godmother said." As she rode the bus to Savannah, Whelchel en-countered racism that remained with her throughout her life and fed her de-termination to teach and work for her race. The bus driver refused to let black passengers off the bus to buy anything to eat. Some blacks, including Whelchel, gave money to white people who came to the bus windows and offered to get sandwiches for passengers. These actions, ostensibly ones of kindness, exposed the ongoing assault on African Americans' claim to dignity, for the white people took the money and never returned.⁴³

After Beulah Rucker Oliver, Dorothy Oliver Rucker, and Whelchel arrived in Savannah, Rucker took Whelchel to the college president's office. Accord-ing to Whelchel, President Benjamin Hubert repeatedly told her that she had to register, which was impossible because she lacked the funds. After her third visit to Hubert, Whelchel returned to Oliver in tears. Oliver spoke to Hubert about Whelchel's financial situation, and Hubert offered Whelchel a work scholarship cleaning his home. Then Hubert sent Whelchel to the cooperative dining room, where she delighted the supervisor with her knowledge of how to cut chicken. Whelchel remained there for the next four years while she com-pleted her college education.⁴⁴

Oliver and her daughter graduated in 1944 from Georgia State College by taking summer classes and correspondence courses. They still earned less than white teachers but had narrowed the gap. Rucker, Oliver, and Whelchel joined the GTEA, and Rucker and Whelchel served as district presidents. While no direct evidence exists to show that Oliver ever registered to vote, she must have known about the NAACP's registration campaigns because of her membership in the GTEA. Oliver chose to express her politics in different ways—through

Beulah Rucker Oliver, ca. 1950.
(Courtesy of Dorothy Oliver Rucker
and Carrie Oliver Bailey.)

her students. She preserved her community role of motivating students to continue their education. For example, Nancy Stephens attended Oliver's school in the 1940s. When she was eighteen, she eloped after her fiancé promised to support her efforts to obtain a bachelor's degree. Oliver somehow learned about the elopement through rumors and asked Stephens about her marriage: when Stephens admitted the truth, Oliver simply encouraged the girl to continue with her education. Stephens also attended Georgia State College and worked in the lunchroom after her husband joined the army in World War II, viewing work as "just a thing we thought was part of life."[45] After she graduated from Georgia State, Stephens took a teaching job in Ashburn and Ellijay and then moved to Lula, where she remained for the next few years.

To these African American women and many more like them, marriage, teaching, and family were part of becoming an adult woman. Just as their mothers had worked while raising their families, so did these women. Black women saw little conflict between their private and public roles; rather, they understood that higher achievement meant combining the roles of wife, mother, teacher, and church worker.[46] Seeing Beulah Rucker Oliver and Susie Weems Wheeler as successful African American women who provided endless support for their communities and raised families, students followed their teachers' advice without question. Their model for uplift formed part of their students' creed as they matured and became local leaders in their own right.

Like Oliver and the teachers at her school, African American female teachers at city schools continued to participate actively in racial, religious, and educational communities. Mattie Moon and Charity Honeycutt Ector taught at Gainesville's Fair Street School in the 1940s, benefiting from small salary increases and transportation for students. Members of the GTEA, Moon and Ector also joined the NAACP, with Moon serving as the group's youth director during the 1940s.[47] In 1937 the Gainesville City School System had rebuilt the school, with a new brick building that contained a gymnasium, a home economics room, a library, indoor restrooms, an industrial arts room, and a science laboratory. By 1949, compulsory school attendance laws and the availability of busing had increased the number of black students in grades one through eight at Fair Street. Still, other black teachers coped with poor conditions, as at Narvie Jordan Harris's Locust Grove school. Rosa Penson Anderson taught first grade in a school with outhouses, a wood-burning stove, and no running water.

Just as most black women earned diplomas through extraordinary efforts, so did some white women who sought to confirm professional status. Calls for increases in teachers' salaries and guaranteed pay appear repeatedly in the *Georgia Education Journal,* primarily because of the state's failure to consistently pay even low teacher salaries until 1942. Still, the GEA began to emphasize the need for additional college training for teachers. Throughout World War II, the GEA condemned issuing emergency certificates to white teachers and called on the State Board of Education to add education courses to requirement for a teachers' certificate.[48] The state insisted that the last year of the bachelor's degree had to be part of a residence program at a university. White teachers like Leona Clark Williams and Florrie Still attended Oglethorpe University. For the first time in her life, Williams donned a cap and gown for her graduation from Oglethorpe, having finally earned enough money to rent them. For Waters, Cole, Ector, and Anderson, the new requirements meant that their degrees were finally recognized as a professional necessity. Still, the fact that black teachers did as much work for a degree and earned at least six hundred dollars less per year remained a potent issue for many African Americans. If a black professional could earn less money, even with a degree, what was the point of advanced education?

In Atlanta, African Americans decided to act. Moderate white organizations had done little to help them. Black and white supporters of the Commission on Interracial Cooperation clashed in 1942 when blacks demanded a statement that opposed compulsory segregation. White members wanted to continue to rely on white southerners' goodwill for changes. Unable to agree, some black and white members left the commission in 1944 and formed the

Leona Clark Williams finally could afford to
rent a graduation gown when she graduated
from Oglethorpe University in 1948.
(Courtesy of Leona Clark Williams.)

Southern Regional Council, an organization dedicated to guaranteeing equality for blacks, although it failed to make a definitive statement about Jim Crow.
The Southern Conference for Human Welfare, formed in 1938, focused on
abolishing the poll tax.[49]

In the wake of the U.S. Supreme Court's 1944 ruling in *Smith v. Allwright* that
the white primary was unconstitutional, many Georgians panicked about the
possibility that blacks were registering to vote. Arnall stalled on implementing
the decision and even threatened to refuse to give black war veterans the right
to vote in Georgia, but a Columbus activist forced the governor's hand. An
African American Baptist minister and barber, the Reverend Primus King, led
a delegation of blacks to vote in the July 1944 Democratic primary, but the local registrar turned them away. King took the case to court, and on October 12,
1945, the federal district court ruled in *King v. Chapman* that black Georgians
had the right to vote in Georgia primaries. Stunning many white Georgians,

the U.S. Supreme Court in 1946 refused to hear the case. Arnall briefly toyed with the idea of finding a way to circumvent the ruling, and in the spring of 1946, several members of Georgia's General Assembly called for a special legislative session that would deal exclusively with maintaining the white primary. Ultimately, however, Arnall refused to call the special session and announced his intention to abide by the decision. Although Arnall and the Georgia legislature eliminated the poll tax in 1945, they did so to enfranchise more whites as well as soldiers, not specifically to help African Americans.[50] With black schools still far from equal to whites and in a political climate that seemed amenable to change, Atlanta's black organizations campaigned to equalize black schools.

The AUL, now headed by Grace Towns Hamilton, funded a study that compared black and white schools. The consultants who worked on the study, published in 1944, included C. L. Harper; Ira Reid, a sociologist from Atlanta University; and Grace Hamilton's husband, Henry Cooke Hamilton, a professor of education at Atlanta University. The study presented some stark truths about Atlanta's schools: all black students attended half-day sessions; the Atlanta School Board spent $37.80 per black child and $108.70 per white child; the value of school property for white children was more than twice the amount invested in school property for black children; black teachers earned less than whites but worked double sessions with twice the number of students; not one black school had a gymnasium.[51]

The Atlanta Board of Education initially paid little attention to the AUL's publicity campaign, and few changes occurred in the city's black public schools over the next two years. But 1946 was an election year, with gubernatorial and congressional contests and votes on bond issues. Led by indomitable NAACP activist Ruby Blackburn and a coalition of Atlanta civil rights groups, efforts to register black voters had increased the African American voting rolls to twenty-one thousand of the city's seventy thousand registered voters. In May 1946, Atlanta's blacks now had the power of the bloc vote.[52] Their opportunity to use it came before the 1946 Democratic primary.

In Georgia's Fifth Congressional District, Representative Robert Ramspeck stepped down from his seat. A special election was called before the July primary. The NAACP called for a voter registration campaign, and by the time of the February election, almost seven thousand blacks had registered. The African American coalition endorsed Helen Mankin, the only one of the nineteen candidates who had even bothered to meet with the black group. Mankin won the election largely because of the black bloc vote, signaling what black voters could accomplish.[53] The results caught the attention of Atlanta's board of education and in August, after the Democratic primary, the city's voters approved an almost $10 million bond issue, with one-third of the funds reserved for black schools, transportation, and salaries. Here was tangible proof of what African Americans could do.

On the heels of the NAACP's court victories, the escalating attacks on unequal education for blacks, and the evidence of black voting bloc power in Atlanta, some Georgians became determined to strike back. White supremacists feared the return of Reconstruction, when allegedly incompetent blacks ran the state. Black voters in Atlanta had demonstrated that they could affect school bond issues. By the end of 1946, approximately 150,000 blacks had registered to vote in Georgia. Although this number constituted only 18 percent of the state's total black population, these voters nonetheless represented a substantive threat to white supremacy. Only Texas had more registered black voters.[54]

Many white southerners, notably white supremacists, saw efforts to equalize education as codes for integration and social mixing. In 1942 Arnall had emphasized that he did not want African Americans attending schools with whites: he wanted accreditation for schools. Indeed, several studies of black and white Georgians' attitudes about white supremacy found that whites repeatedly stated that Jim Crow provided them with "protection from intermarriage, social mixing, and equal representation in court." Blacks, conversely, were far more concerned about employment and social justice than social contact. The most likely arena for social mixing and eventual intermarriage was the school, where children played and studied with each other five days a week for at least seven months over a period of eleven years. While in school, children made friends and began dating. They took gym classes and showered together. Although the NAACP had yet explicitly to attack Jim Crow, the group refused to support the preservation of segregation.[55]

White supremacists needed to give black voters a clear message. As Eugene Talmadge stated during the campaign, Arnall had "opened the breach in the dike that has protected Southern manhood, Southern womanhood, and Southern childhood for three quarters of a century," a clear reference to white masculinity and femininity, which had come under assault as a result of shifts in the color line. Some white children now stood to lose ground as blacks challenged segregated schools. Talmadge had always insisted that one of his greatest goals was ensuring that all white children "would be able to attend Georgia schools and be able to sit down without finding a nigger beside them."[56]

Consequently, in 1946, after some Georgians had written Eugene Talmadge's obituary, Talmadge ran again for governor as the savior of white supremacy and a bulwark against communism and outsiders. Implicit in this rhetoric were Georgians' fears that too much had changed too quickly. Arnall declared his support for James Carmichael, a Marietta businessman, and attempted to forge an alliance of Georgia's blacks, laborers, and growing middle class. As black and white servicemen returned to the South, racist violence reignited. On May 9, 1946, the Ku Klux Klan gathered at Stone Mountain to initiate hundreds of new members. Although Carmichael won the popular vote in the July 17 Democratic primary, Talmadge won the county unit votes, which continued to favor rural counties over urban areas, and the election. His strongest support came from rural areas and business leaders. After learning that he had won the race, Talmadge promptly announced that "no Negro will vote in Georgia for the next four years."[57]

Until someone challenged the county unit system, rural white Georgians would preserve their dominance. As one historian has noted, most black Georgians congregated and organized in two main cities, where they had minimal impact on state elections. The county unit system stood as the final battleground in the war against white supremacy. Until the county unit system was abolished, white rural voters and county officials would dominate state politics and urban reformers would remain a minority.[58]

For example, a subsequent investigation of the election contended that some county officials had purged blacks from voting rolls, including three thousand black voters in Fulton County. Although most registered black voters lived in Savannah and Atlanta, those in rural areas were often prevented from voting. Schley County disqualified more than half of its registered blacks, reducing them to a minority in the county. Just in case any blacks attempted to vote, the local state representative stood outside the voting booth with a shotgun. It was estimated that more than twenty thousand voters were challenged in thirty-one counties. In Savannah, where state NAACP President Mark Gilbert had succeeded in registering twenty thousand blacks in a massive registration drive, Talmadge cronies minimized the number of voting booths, with the locations known only to whites. In Telfair County, Talmadge's home, an astonishing number of dead voters miraculously marked ballots. The Klan's night rides intimidated some black voters into staying away from the polls, and a Klan member in Columbus sent death threats to blacks who had joined Primus King's campaign. White supremacists in Meriwether, Grady, and Taylor Counties fired guns and burned crosses. Nevertheless, almost one hundred thousand blacks voted in the primary.[59]

The 1946 election was a reprise of the 1941 election, with localism and tradition pitted against modernity. The aftermath of Talmadge's victory seemed to release pent-up rage and racism. Klan violence surged even though Arnall had attempted to revoke the Klan's charter in 1946, a court case that was undecided until after the 1946 election.[60]

Within a week after Talmadge's election, attacks on blacks increased. Five days after Maceo Snipes, a black World War II veteran from Taylor County, voted, four white men shot him. The most sobering event occurred in Monroe on July 25, when a group of white men seized two married couples, George and Mae Dorsey and Roger and Dorothy Malcolm, and summarily shot them: the bodies had "bullet wounds too numerous to count." George Dorsey had served in the army during the war and had been awarded a bronze star for service in the Pacific theater. Area blacks were so terrified that few came to the funerals of the victims. The local sheriff insisted that no evidence had been discovered and no trial would be held. He told members of the national press, "They hadn't ought to killed the two women." Writing for the *Atlanta Daily World*, George Andrews seethed that "Hitler at his worst could not have done a more mutilating job than was done here in Walton County Georgia USA."[61]

The national press, including the *New York Times* and the *Nation*, ran editorials excoriating Georgians. Arnall, now a lame duck governor, called for an investigation by the Federal Bureau of Investigation, thereby endearing himself to few white Georgians. Predictably, a Walton County grand jury stated that it could not find anyone responsible for the lynchings, and the murderers went free.[62]

Talmadge's reelection as governor inflamed the concerns and fears of racial moderates and liberals alike. Hoping to prevent a repetition of the 1941 turbulence, the Julius Rosenwald Fund (JRF) sponsored a conference on Georgia on August 6, 1946. JRF leaders such as Edwin Embree and Commission for Interracial Cooperation leaders such as Will Alexander discussed Georgia's racial violence and the potential for its increase since Talmadge's election. Conference attendees clearly were worried about the African Americans' safety and racial progress. Although the participants applauded the changes in race relations, such as the abolition of the poll tax and the white primary, they recognized that "some are determined to resist this new trend."[63] Conference participants proposed to focus on antilynching legislation in Georgia in addition to exposing Talmadge's relations with industry, supporting the NAACP, and watching for violations of federal laws.

More important, the conference discussed what members perceived as the key issue in the 1946 election—economics. Attendees believed that Talmadge had won because of his support from Georgia Light and Power, mill owners, and Bibb Manufacturing as well as some assistance from the Coca-Cola Company. In 1946, the CIO began an extensive campaign to boost union membership in the South, primarily in the textile industry. But with the nation focused on communism's threat and Congress's passage of the 1947 Taft-Hartley law, which banned the requirement for union membership at many jobs, the CIO campaign met with little success. Nevertheless, it aroused southern industrialists' concerns about labor unions. For some Georgia business leaders, a Talmadge administration meant lower taxes, antilabor policies, and opposition to the Tennessee Valley Authority.[64]

Some businesses had supported Carmichael, the general manager of Marietta's Bell Aircraft Corporation. Well aware that Georgia was attracting more industry and would need workers of both races, some business leaders encouraged racial moderation. They backed Arnall's efforts to expand industry to make the state one of the leaders in industrial growth. Yet because Talmadge allowed cronies such as the head of Georgia Light and Power to do what they wanted, he continued to receive their support.

These concerns became moot when Talmadge died on December 21, 1946, before taking office. Yet another chaotic chapter in Georgia politics followed. Talmadge forces wanted Eugene's son, Herman, to take office, while Arnall insisted that the lieutenant-governor-elect, Melvin Thompson, should take office. In the battle that followed, the legislature elected Herman Talmadge, while Thompson opened another office as governor in exile. The state supreme court finally declared Thompson governor, with a special gubernatorial election to be held in 1948. Thompson never solidified his position, and in 1948, Herman Talmadge was elected governor.[65] Most historians focus on three issues during the 1947 debacle: racism, the county unit system, and the power of corporations. While all three themes resound, there is another aspect to the story.

As Calvin Kytle and James Mackay stated in their 1947 investigation of the crisis funded by the JRF, education remained a fundamental issue to Georgians. Lillian Smith, a white Georgia author, told the researchers that education was the most important right all Georgians should expect from the state. Frank Smith, her brother, added that "the government cannot be far ahead of the culture. What we really need is a revolution in our educational process. People must be brought to understand from the ground up what democracy and self-government require of the individual."[66] This meant not only that blacks and working-class whites would have access to better education and would then demand equal opportunities but also that women, particularly classroom and visiting teachers, had more authority. The call for better schools could topple Georgia's entire social system by educating students about the meaning of democracy.

Moreover, to focus on Eugene Talmadge's 1946 election and Herman Talmadge's subsequent 1948 victory as a sudden reemergence of white supremacists also misses the underlying strains of white conservatism since the New Deal. Although many Georgians supported the New Deal, others rejected its liberalism and even considered it close to communism. For example, some white women blamed the "Eleanor Clubs," alleged groups of black women, for problems with black domestic workers. The rumors about these suspected clubs intensified during World War II as blacks increasingly left domestic work for jobs in cities, other regions, or the defense industry. As African American women asserted their determination to find work outside of domestic labor, their independence exacerbated fears among many whites about the preservation of white supremacy. Some southerners feared that "Negroes will marry white girls and run the country." While African Americans wanted economic independence and autonomy, many whites fretted about racial mixing and intermarriage. As evidence of the possible collapse of white supremacy and potential for miscegenation, many whites referred to a 1935 photo in the *Georgia Woman's World* that showed Eleanor Roosevelt talking to a six-year-old black child in Detroit and consequently "proved" that the Roosevelts disavowed segregation.[67] Georgia Senators Richard Russell and Walter George consistently blocked federal antilynching laws. Few southern congressmen mourned the demise of most New Deal programs during World War II.

Southern Democrats cheered President Harry Truman's neglect of the Fair Employment Practices Commission. But in 1946, Truman took a different stance. When Walter White, head of the NAACP, met with Truman and discussed the violence occurring in the South, Truman decided to act. By executive order, Truman created a special committee to investigate civil rights and propose solutions. In 1947, the committee published its report, *To Secure These Rights*, divulging the realities of Jim Crow: inequalities in education, voting rights, and employment. Most southern Democrats became concerned about Truman's intentions concerning the status of African Americans in the South.[68]

From the late summer of 1946 to 1949, some white Georgians sent a distinct message to black Georgians. That message was violence and intimidation at the voting booths. The violence coincided with Herman Talmadge's gubernatorial campaign that began in 1947. Near Americus, a black woman, Rosa Lee

Ingram, and two of her sons, aged fifteen and thirteen, were charged with murdering a white sharecropper after he attacked her with a gun and a knife. After one hour of deliberation, an all-white jury sentenced the three to death, although the sentence was later commuted to life in prison. The president of the Montgomery County NAACP was beaten after he took several blacks to the polls, while other blacks, including Isaiah Nixon, a black Montgomery County sharecropper, were beaten or shot for voting. Before the Democratic primary, three hundred Klansmen paraded in Wrightsville threatening violence if blacks voted; none of the four hundred registered African Americans came out. After Herman Talmadge won the 1948 election, white supremacists drove three black students from Columbus over the Alabama state line as punishment for participating in NAACP activities.[69] Some Klan members tried to drive all blacks out of their counties, a move reminiscent of the early twentieth century.

Talmadge's response to the violence was a "Four Point White Supremacy Program" that strengthened the county unit system, reinstated the poll tax, and demanded that potential voters explain sections of the federal or state constitution before being allowed to cast ballots, with local registrars determining which thirty questions each voter would have to answer.[70] As a result of these measures, the number of black voters declined rapidly. In Atlanta, where the school bond issue had passed, the school board reneged on its building plan.

The number of NAACP chapters in the state fell from fifty-five in 1946 to fewer than twenty by the early 1950s. NAACP membership, which peaked between 1946 and 1948 at more than eleven thousand, fell to approximately four thousand by 1951. The Reverend Mark Gilbert and C. L. Harper wrote to the NAACP's national office, begging for assistance after the Talmadge election: "The efforts of the present state administration to reduce us to political and economic slavery must be resisted. The people of Georgia are looking to us to lead this fight." In 1949, worn out, Gilbert resigned when the New York offices offered no assistance in the fight against Talmadge. By the late 1940s, Georgia's civil rights leadership and organization seemed decimated.[71]

Even in Atlanta, with the success of the AUL and the NAACP's 1946 voter registration drive, the organizations failed to preserve the masses needed for a bloc vote. Some observers have contended that the black elite from Auburn Avenue made few efforts to reach out to the city's working masses.[72] Other blacks saw the AUL as working only for blacks in the city rather than those across the state. Among those who sought a broader state agenda rather than an emphasis on cities for the NAACP were members of the GTEA. C. L.

Harper agreed and in 1946 developed a strategy of organizing small groups in school districts statewide to challenge school inequalities.

From the time Harper became president of the Atlanta branch of the NAACP, he shared office space and resources with the GTEA, although he eventually asked the NAACP's New York office for personnel assistance because of the drain on GTEA resources. Throughout the 1940s, Harper had effectively combined the resources of the largest Atlanta churches and the GTEA to raise membership in the NAACP, and by the late 1940s, Harper was funneling GTEA funds to the NAACP. Following the 1946 election, most whites attacked the NAACP, the CIO, and the Southern Conference for Human Welfare as communist organizations. Not only did blacks leave the NAACP, but teachers had increasing difficulty in associating with the group. Even suspicions of membership could lead to termination. Most teachers had families to consider and had long-standing commitments to education for blacks. Harper devised a new strategy by forming a committee to investigate the worst examples of educational inequality in transportation, salaries, and length of school term. He suggested that the NAACP file legal challenges against school districts to force them to change.[73]

The GTEA had more than seven thousand members in 1948 and was the largest black organization in Georgia by 1950. Harper realized the problems the NAACP faced and that it could not file the many needed legal challenges, so he suggested that black teachers, principals, and professionals form civic leagues to challenge educational inequality and promote voter registration. Harper offered the tactic to Thurgood Marshall but also stated that the GTEA was prepared to take measures on its own.[74]

One of the first teachers to challenge educational inequality was Horace E. Tate, principal of Greene County High School in Greensboro. Tate and other African American men, including Ulysses Byas, who completed his education using the G.I. Bill, had joined the ranks of teachers and principals following World War II, motivated by a number of factors. Some men were attracted by the increased pay, small as it was, while others believed that men as well as women needed to teach and thereby provide leadership role models for the black community, a view shared by Susie Weems Wheeler and other women. Expanding roles for black men in education were scarcely revolutionary. Throughout African American history, black men and women had shared leadership roles. But changing economic circumstances enabled more black men to become teachers.

Tate was born in Elberton in 1922. His father, Henry Lawrence Tate, was a

Horace Tate, principal of
Greene County High School, ca. 1960.
(Courtesy of Horace Tate.)

Greensboro High School for blacks, as photographed, was torn down in 1948
and replaced with a one-story modern school in 1949. (Vanishing Georgia Collection,
Georgia Division of Archives and History, Office of the Secretary of State.)

race man, standing up for his family and his rights. Some of the town's whites and even its blacks saw Henry Tate as being crazy to take risks to defend his rights. Henry and his wife, Mattie Beatrice Harper Tate, had fourteen children, of whom Horace was the tenth. Henry Tate operated a taxi and a billiard parlor and worked as a janitor at the white school. His success enabled his family to live in the middle-class section of town and permitted Mattie not to work outside the home. The Tates encouraged their children to attend school, and Henry said that as long as they lived at home, they had to complete high school. They did. Yet only three of the Tate children received any college education, and Horace was the first to earn a bachelor's degree.[75]

In the early 1940s, Horace Tate attended Fort Valley State College, where he met Horace Mann Bond, who would influence the rest of Tate's life. Tate worked his way through Fort Valley, occasionally serving as Bond's chauffeur, and took every opportunity to listen to Bond. When Tate graduated in 1943, he became principal of Union Point High School, replacing a man who had left for military service. When the former principal returned in 1945, Tate became principal of the Greensboro School in Greensboro, overseeing eighteen teachers in a building that had been condemned. The school had four rooms with a hall down the center, an auditorium, a stage, and a room off the auditorium. Between four and five hundred students attempted to learn in these improvised classrooms. When the superintendent took Tate to a warehouse to choose schoolbooks, many of them were unusable—torn, moldy, and illegible. Tate knew it was time for action.[76]

As soon as Tate began teaching at Union Point, he joined the GTEA, where he encountered another man who would change his life, C. L. Harper. Although Harper was small in stature, his courage and tenacity impressed Tate. Tate watched Harper reorganize the GTEA and closely followed the NAACP campaigns. By 1947, no NAACP campaign had helped black students at Greensboro. Worse, the state government was in turmoil and the NAACP was in retreat. So Tate, following Harper's strategy, organized a civic league in Greensboro to improve black schools. Tate called together area black professionals and church leaders, attracting eighty men to the group's first meeting. By the last meeting approximately six months later, there were eighteen men left. Most had abandoned the effort out of fear for their families or jobs. But this core group persisted in the school drive until the end.[77]

The men planned to force the Greensboro City Council to float a bond issue to build a school for black children. Calling themselves the Greene County Civic League, the men initially wrote to the city council and requested a new school. Realizing the danger to Tate if his involvement became public, the men told Tate to work behind the scenes, telling them how he thought they should proceed. The men went to every city council and school board meeting, while Tate waited in his car. In 1948, the city council finally agreed to call a bond issue, which passed, providing $84,000 in school funds, with $65,000 earmarked for black schools. A cement block building was built with four rooms across the front, the auditorium in the center, and four rooms down the side.[78]

With that success, Tate began another campaign, which eventually cost him his job. A family named Ward lived sixteen miles outside of Greensboro, and like most rural blacks, the Ward children had no bus transportation to the Greensboro school. Each school day, their father had to spend two hours away from his farm work transporting his children to school by wagon. He wanted his children to have bus transportation, just like white children. Tate initially hesitated to become involved, fearing that people were trying to find out about his involvement in the school bond issue. But Ward returned and asked again for help, so Tate called on the civic league to work for bus transportation.[79]

The group met in Greshamville. As rumors began to circulate in Greensboro that Tate was behind education reform for blacks, Tate refused to quit the campaign. For this campaign, however, Tate wanted Harper's advice, so once a week, Tate drove to Atlanta to pick up Harper, who did not drive, and dropped him off at a church on the road to Greshamville, where Cecil Jackson, a local black mortician, picked Harper up and took him to the group's meeting place. After the meeting, Jackson drove Harper back to Tate, who then drove Harper to Atlanta before returning home at four in the morning. "This was considered subversive activity," stated Tate. "We were going to ask white folks to spend tax money for black kids, to educate black kids." Caution was mandatory.[80]

At one point, the superintendent went to Tate with a proposal to give Ward a station wagon for his children. Ward refused. "I want my children to go to school," he said, "but I'm not doing this just for my children. I'm doing this for all the children." After threatening the school board with a lawsuit, Greene County's blacks received school buses in 1951, but the county had enough of Tate. He initiated a voter registration campaign that resulted in death threats, and the school board finally fired him in 1951. He found another job in Griffin, where he remained until 1959.[81]

As the NAACP declined, the GTEA, one of the organizations that had begun the civil rights campaign in Georgia during the 1940s, continued the movement for education equalization and voter registration. While the AUL focused on Atlanta, the GTEA stretched across the state, using district and state meetings to inform members of possible actions and current campaigns for equalization. The 1949 Georgia State Conference of NAACP branches, held in Gainesville, commended the civic leagues organized by black educators and business leaders in "Irwin, Greene, Baldwin, Bullock, and Walton Counties and Atlanta, Statesboro, and Monroe . . . for their courage in filing petitions and instituting suits in the interest of securing the equalization of school facilities." William Boyd, president of the Georgia conference, noted that Georgia branches of the NAACP had raised more than eighteen hundred dollars, while the GTEA had contributed more than two thousand dollars to the group.[82] Civil rights activities still existed in Georgia but were simply undertaken more covertly under the auspices of the GTEA.

With the backing of the GTEA, a group of parents persuaded NAACP legal counsel A. T. Walden to file a lawsuit against the Irwin County School board in August 1949, contending that the school board refused to provide equal education facilities for black children. The inequities cited included seventeen dilapidated black schools, eleven of which had a single teacher, compared to seven modern schools for whites. White schools had auditoriums and cafeterias as well as better libraries. Only one-fifth of black children had bus transportation, which was offered to all white children. Black children attended school thirty fewer days per year than whites. Moreover, teacher salary differentials still existed. The *Atlanta Constitution* supported the case, saying that school boards needed to plan to start equalizing facilities.[83]

Governor Herman Talmadge fired back on his radio talk show. First, he repeated the charge that the NAACP was a communist organization allied with the Soviet government. The real purpose of the case, argued Talmadge, was not equalization; instead, the lawsuit intended "to abolish segregation in our schools," to move "Negro children into the nearest and most convenient white school." Talmadge also pointed out some fundamental problems that southern schools had faced since the 1880s. To equalize schools would cost the state more than $3 million. Despite the postwar prosperity, Georgia could not raise that much money for schools. Furthermore, as Talmadge correctly argued, the state still had many poor white schools that needed support.[84] A means to finance school construction and raise teacher salaries was needed.

As the GTEA helped organize black communities in civic leagues to push for education equalization and the NAACP increased its legal attacks on unequal schools across the South, the GEA joined the 1946 movement for what became known as the Minimum Foundation Program for Education (MFPE). While the GEA insisted that funds for equal schools and salaries needed support from the federal government, the organization began a campaign for equalization in the state. Director of Negro Education, Robert Cousins, called on the GEA to work for the educational rights of all children. "Every child," he wrote in the *Georgia Education Journal,* "is entitled to attend school in a satisfactory building. This building should meet the minimum requirements of safety, health, and sanitation, and be provided with essential equipment. Every child is entitled to a satisfactory secondary school education."[85] Cousins sought to ameliorate the worse abuses of Georgia's schools for blacks by arguing for better facilities and schools and higher teachers' salaries. His position represented a substantive shift in some white educators' attitudes. In the aftermath of World War II, a costly fight against fascism and totalitarian rule, many white educators looked around American society and saw similar problems. If democracy was to be preserved, schools needed to improve.

In 1947 a committee appointed by Arnall submitted *A Survey of Public Education of Less Than College Grade in Georgia: A Report to the General Assembly of Georgia by Its Special Committee on Education.* The report examined every aspect of public education: all teachers' salaries, buildings, supplies, libraries, lunches, length of school terms, transportation, and revenue spent. Committee members declared that "the school system now faces the worst crisis in its history and is unable to provide the educational facilities due our children even in the face of the tremendous increase in state appropriation." The committee's recommendations included better professional training for teachers, a comprehensive secondary school program for black and white children from thirteen to eighteen years of age, consolidated schools within communities, and improved bus transportation for black and white students. More importantly, the committee urged the General Assembly to pass a new far-reaching school law to replace the patchwork of existing legislation and provide for a more equitable school system with professionally trained teachers.[86] The GEA endorsed the report that year and by 1948 gained the support of the State Chamber of Commerce, the Parent-Teacher Association, the State Federation of Women's Clubs, and the Georgia Farm Bureau.

Passing the MFPE became the rallying cry for the GEA and the GTEA, although the GTEA continued its agenda for organizing civic leagues for social justice and equality. GEA district chapters held rallies to support the MFPE, most radio stations and newspapers backed it, and World War II veterans called for better education for their children. To African Americans, the MFPE consisted of a response to NAACP and GTEA campaigns for educational equality,

a legitimate argument to be sure.[87] Yet the GEA also supported better education for white rural children and used World War II and postwar language about
preserving democracy to support the MFPE. What converged in 1947 were African Americans', white educators', and business leaders' demands for an education system consistent with national standards.

Herman Talmadge and the General Assembly agreed with the principles of
the MFPE and passed the program in February 1949. What remained undecided
was how to fund the MFPE. Once again, the GEA, GTEA, newspapers, radio
stations, and the Parent-Teacher Association pushed for financial support. At
the end of 1951, Talmadge called for a three-cent sales tax to finance the MFPE,
arguably one of the most significant legislative acts passed for public education
for all students, teachers, and parents.[88]

State action regarding education transformed the lives of numerous black
and white teachers. Following statewide trends for white schools, school superintendents began to consolidate black schools. In Hall County, Oliver's school
was converted to an elementary school only. In 1951, the Gainesville City and
Hall County School Systems consolidated grades seven through eleven for
blacks at Fair Street School, with buses provided to transport increasing numbers of rural black students into Gainesville.[89] Yet despite the relatively new
brick building, the better-paid teachers, and the state-provided (although used)
textbooks and transportation, few black youths managed to remain in high
school. Most had to find jobs to support their families.

As ALWAYS, HOWEVER, black and white teachers fought to improve their position as part of their ambitions, duty to God, and duty to their communities.
As Leona Clark Williams emphasized, "You don't become a teacher to get rich.
You do it for the children. Teachers find out your problems and try to help solve
them. It's not about reading and writing and arithmetic all the time." Nelle Still
Murphy agreed: "A teacher needs to be interested in the child and help that
child strive to be the best that they can be and let them believe they can do
something."[90]

The insistence on helping children and communities had driven African
American teachers' work since the 1870s. M. J. Woods, a former black principal in Marietta, stated that to know a child, the teacher needed to know the
child's family and home. If, as he argued, the basis of the school is to allow children to be what they want to be, families and communities must be part of the
effort. "Teachers," he stated, "should play a part in community life."[91] Consequently, teachers, including Jeanes teachers Susie Weems Wheeler and Narvie
Jordan Harris, visited homes to see if families ate properly.

In interviews, teachers of both races frequently mentioned their duties to their students and how they were cared for. Leona Clark Williams recalled a little boy from Sewanee Elementary School in the 1940s whose mother was dead and who often came to school with such a bad odor that other students refused to sit by him. Williams realized that the boy was good at math. She bought him a new set of clothes, took him to the lunchroom, and showed him how to bathe and change his clothes every day. Then she had him add and subtract on the blackboard, and the other children began to applaud his work.[92]

One day the boy's brother had seizures in his classroom. Williams and the brother's teacher took the brother to the hospital and attempted to find the father, believed to be a bootlegger. When the two teachers went to the children's house, they found more than twenty-five gallons of whiskey inside and filth all over the porch. The teachers found the father and took him to the hospital, where the attending physician determined that the boy was suffering from alcohol poisoning. Williams decided to try to have the children removed from their father's custody, but before the state agency could intervene, the father moved.[93]

Williams's story reveals the tensions that permeated teachers' lives in the 1940s. Dedicated to traditional beliefs in family, church, and community authority, they nonetheless saw themselves as professionals who knew what was best for children more often than their parents did. For Williams, being a teacher meant assuming the role of parent as she understood it when necessary—showing the boy how to prepare for school just as she had prepared her brothers and sisters for school earlier in her life. Yet her actions displaced some of the father's authority by trying to remove the boy from the home. And by seeking assistance from the child welfare agency, she sought the state's control over that of the family and community. In the past, a church or community member might have remedied this situation. For example, the Clarks permitted Leona to stay with the Asher family while she attended high school. Decades later, Williams unintentionally undermined the sites of influence that had shaped her beliefs, which, in turn, had formed her actions. Still, her efforts to help the boy demonstrate the ways in which duties to others continued to inform teachers' constructions of professionalism.

Williams was not alone among Georgia teachers in assuming parental responsibilities for students. At times, such care was obviously necessary. Beulah Rucker Oliver occasionally had students whose parents left them at the school and rarely saw them again. That her students referred to her as "Godmother" indicates her intricate relationships with her students. Florrie Still intervened on behalf of a girl whose stepfather repeatedly whipped her. After the girl told

Still about her stepfather's physical abuse, Still talked to the girl's mother, who said there was nothing she could do. So Still found a foster family that bought the girl her first doll and encouraged her to finish school.[94] At times, the actions indicate the extent to which teachers appropriated traditional forms of authority as their own. Framing and contextualizing their classrooms with beliefs in interdependence, evangelical Protestantism, and self-sufficiency, teachers slowly secured authority reserved for families or churches. Seeing themselves as representatives of their culture, they acquired a measure of respect that enabled them to enforce their culture's values.

Teachers, black and white, objected to their low salaries, crowded classrooms, and poor buildings. Yet such issues rarely overshadowed their responsibilities to their students, God, and community. "The best teachers," commented Cole, "were the ones who had a stake in the community. If something needed doing, you did it. We never thought about supplemental pay for doing things. We did it because it needed to be done. We taught generations of families in our careers and gained a sense of the families in the community."[95] Often seeing themselves as public servants, teachers created complex labor patterns and hiring practices hidden from male trustees and superintendents.

Many white teachers nonetheless extracted reciprocal items from superintendents. When Waters told the trustees she was reluctant to teach at the high school because she disliked the principal, the trustees offered her an additional fifty dollars a month. Williams refused to follow curriculum guidelines established by a new principal, and the principal finally relented. Yet while teachers believed they had succeeded by securing some reciprocal recognition from a principal or superintendent, they had, at times, reinforced their image as public servants. Their understanding of what it meant to be a professional woman included public service.

African American teachers articulated a similar sense of duty that was also defined in terms of their race. Bound to follow mandates of white superintendents or risk losing their positions, black teachers placated local white school superintendents by presenting an image of conciliation at the same time they pushed for racial uplift. While some observers believed Beulah Rucker Oliver was teaching only rug making and sewing, the black community knew she also taught students academic fundamentals. And while few people could question the innumerable ways in which she had improved her students' lives, the unassailable fact remained that black schools were underfunded and poorly equipped and that few whites ultimately saw her credentials in the same way they saw those of white teachers.

Oliver also confronted the dilemma of self-sufficiency and the realities of the market. She taught her students jobs that eliminated their dependence on sharecropping, and indeed, most of her students became wage earners or professional workers. Able to purchase land, housing, and consumer goods, many blacks became self-sufficient. However, this change substituted their dependence on agriculture for the vagaries of the market. Now bound to economic cycles of expansion and decline, black workers as well as whites relied on the possibilities and lapses of modern corporate capitalism. Learning a skill undoubtedly served workers best in the industrial order, but they grew detached from some of the rural habits that had long sustained them—family gardens, home production, and community interdependence. As Oliver showed students how to correctly set a dinner table, how to dress, how to speak, and how to act, she instructed them on assuming the palpable accoutrements of middle-class life. To her and to many other black and white educators, these actions allowed blacks and poor whites to establish themselves as future leaders and avoid the ridicule of poor pronunciation and manners. What counted was students' ability to enter respectable careers and demonstrate the potential for leadership in the black community.[96]

Yet properly setting a table and wearing nylon hose, a tie, or a slip under a dress required cash purchases from stores or catalogs. Consequently, African Americans had to modify what they construed as self-sufficiency. Throughout the 1920s and 1930s, with financial assistance from northern philanthropic agencies and New Deal programs such as the National Youth Administration, blacks accepted economic support attached to work. Like other Georgia residents, blacks again renegotiated the meaning of racial uplift and self-help in the 1940s as they began to draw on consumer culture for measures of respectability and leadership rather than moral values of temperance and duty. Rather than relying on their own labor, African Americans, like most whites, leaned on consumption for indications of self-accomplishment and racial improvement.

The next generation—black and white women who began teaching after World War II—replaced aspects of evangelical Protestantism with modernity by privileging individual rights over duties, secular patterns over religious practices, and replaceable commodities over inherited values. Still, women who fought for the respect and dignity of their profession in the 1940s clung to some traditional beliefs. Leona Clark Williams wondered why students who received free schoolbooks insisted on defacing them.[97] Whereas she saw books as precious and to be treated with care, her students saw books as replaceable goods.

Other teachers complained about the increasing amount of paperwork required by the state and national governments. Incorrect student attendance numbers could substantially decrease district funds; textbooks had to be checked out, returned, and evaluated; principals scrutinized lesson plans. Teachers had created a bureaucracy; now they had numerous forms to complete and send to county and state agencies.

Class, gender, and race tensions continued to pervade Georgia's social, economic, political, and cultural changes, and schools and education continued to galvanize supporters and detractors of change. Since Reconstruction, education had incited remarkable and even virulent debates about what education should accomplish, who should be educated, and who should teach. To communities, families, and churches across the state, schools constituted the fundamental cultural site in which the culture's past, present, and future were vested, the tangible illustrations of what a society should accomplish and hope to become. In 1950, Georgia's rural population had decreased almost 10 percent from 1940, while the state's urban population grew to more than 45 percent of the total. The populations of Augusta, Athens, Atlanta, Savannah, Gainesville, Valdosta, Marietta, and Rome increased from 10 to 28 percent of the state's residents. Sixty percent of white men worked at professional or wage-labor jobs, while 28 percent remained in farming. Seventy-four percent of white women worked for wages or in professions, while only slightly more than 10 percent worked on farms or as domestics. Forty-nine percent of black women and 32 percent of black men worked as domestics or farmhands, but more were entering the textile mills and poultry industries as well as professional work such as teaching. These industrial jobs paid poor wages but offered blacks a chance to escape farm labor.[98] The post–World War II rise of the Sunbelt's importance demographically and industrially began as factories and Americans left the Midwest and New England for the South.

Still, even the modest effects of the MFPE opened paths across the twisted course of Georgia's race, class, and gender hierarchy. Requiring a bachelor's degree for teacher certification meant that black teachers had to meet higher qualifications and black colleges had to offer better programs. Removing certification from local authorities forced counties to hire black teachers with education beyond the ninth grade and to increase their salaries. Although black school facilities still lagged behind those of white schools and black teachers earned less than white teachers, state improvements reached across racist boundaries and benefited black education.

By 1950 more than 80 percent of all students aged fourteen and fifteen attended school, an increase of more than 10 percent from 1940. Students remained in school longer, although class and race divisions remained. White urban children completed an average of 10.4 years of school, while black urban children averaged 5.6 years of education. Rural children still lagged, although their numbers had improved as well. White country children attended school for an average of more than 7 years, while black rural children attended for a little more than 4 years. Statewide, the shift over that ten-year period meant an increase of seven months of schooling for the average child of either race—an entire school year.[99]

Black and white teachers, most of them women, claimed a share of this shifting political terrain. They voted; they participated in teachers' organizations; they attended church and participated in church missionary societies and volunteer groups. Their educational organizations gained them respect and benefits in campaigns for better salaries, educational facilities, professional standards, and benefits. Belonging to the GTEA meant contributing to and often organizing local civil rights actions for equal education. These efforts did not result in a large grassroots movement, but without Jeanes teachers who were women organizing civic leagues and communities, without the GTEA's district meetings and contributions to the NAACP, without the GEA's and GTEA's advocacy for the MFPE, little would have been accomplished with school equalization after 1945. Black educators and business leaders provided leadership and organizational structure through the early 1950s in an effort to force local school districts to equalize facilities and teachers' salaries and provide transportation. They also sustained the call for voting rights and social justice.

This strategy failed at the state level and did not galvanize many working-class blacks. GTEA leaders sought middle-class professionals to protect teachers and the broader community. These individuals had the capital to fund equalization drives and could shield teachers from recrimination. Consequently, the GTEA's efforts benefited few blacks except in particular districts. Prior to the 1960s, Georgia's civil rights movement, whether led by the NAACP or the GTEA, registered most of its accomplishments at the county or city level. In the absence of other significant organizations, however, the GTEA preserved the momentum for civil rights, displaying courage and tenacity in a state that consistently resisted equalization efforts with violence, oppression, and even murder.

Black and white teachers believed that one of their greatest political acts and most significant contributions to the modern world was educating children, working for the MFPE, and raising professional standards. The calling to teach represented a gift to enrich Georgia children's lives by instructing them on ways to shed the beliefs that shackled children to poverty and ignorance. And this gift even allowed teachers concurrently to preserve their own families. Teaching children involved reshaping the next generation's hopes. Black and white children now sought wage labor that could help them purchase consumer goods. Migration to towns and cities increased. Teachers made much of this possible. By presenting themselves as professionals and representatives of the modern world, they taught students how to negotiate between traditions and change, how to keep what was best and discard what was not. To black teachers, this meant teaching equality, uplift, and God's salvation. To white teachers, it meant improving students' skills, reminding them of Christian redemption, and instructing them on surviving in a consumer society. As teachers did so, they unintentionally focused students on individual accomplishments that were often self-serving and were certainly subject to the whims of a capricious global market. Salvation became a political, economic, and Christian endeavor.

Epilogue

Freedom's Struggle Continues

IN 1955, the Atlanta Board of Education received a petition to desegregate its schools in accordance with the U.S. Supreme Court's 1954 decision in *Brown v. Board of Education, Topeka, Kansas*. Nine days later, on June 22, C. L. Harper died. For the next few years, the Georgia Teachers and Education Association (GTEA) lacked a leader with Harper's fortitude to spearhead the implementation of *Brown*. Some teachers nominated Horace Tate for the position of executive secretary, but he believed he was too young at the time. He taught for several more years at Fort Valley State College and received his doctorate at the University of Kentucky in 1961 before accepting the position a year later and returning verve to the group's efforts to equalize education. Tate served on Governor Carl Sanders's committee to improve education and was elected to Atlanta's Board of Education in 1965. In 1969 he became the first African American to run for mayor of Atlanta, and in 1974 he was elected a state senator. Georgia had changed.

Throughout the first decades of the twentieth century, Georgia reformers, northern philanthropists, and many African Americans had pushed for school reform. Withal, the school system remained segregated and unequal, its funding lagged most of the nation, and it continued to favor children in towns and cities. Some significant changes had nonetheless reshaped Georgia permanently. The many reforms included legislation that more equitably funded black and white education; teacher certification only for those with bachelor's degrees; a nine-month school year; state-provided schoolbooks; and compulsory attendance. Most Georgians came to perceive education as cultural capital vital for success and survival in the modern industrial state. Other changes underscored the professional status of teachers and different constructions of masculinity and femininity, notably in areas of family and community authority. Rather than relying on churches, households, and communities to determine who should attend school, what they should learn, and who should teach them, teachers became representatives of the state bureaucracy that set statewide guidelines for curriculum, hiring practices, and school terms. Black and white women created a public domain in which to articulate their authority and define their culture.

As other historians have remarked, these reforms clearly improved conditions in the state, not least in the areas of funding public education and implementing professional qualifications for teachers. Not all women hired by local trustees in the nineteenth and early twentieth centuries demonstrated the academic competency needed in modern schools. Inequities in funding allowed white students and teachers in cities and towns to use the best equipment, earn higher salaries, and obtain more education. Educational reforms undoubtedly lowered illiteracy rates and positioned a high school education as a necessary tool for the modern world—no small accomplishment for a state that relied primarily on its cotton crop until the New Deal and World War II. Students who improved their reading and math skills acquired jobs in industries that rapidly expanded after the war.

As central Georgia's farms mechanized, northern Georgia stopped raising cotton. As Sanford Byers, a former cotton grower in Hall County, noted, northern Georgia's hills prevented farmers from mechanizing cotton production, unlike farmers in the central and southern parts of the state. Northeast Georgia turned to livestock, primarily poultry, and became one of the South's poultry centers.[1] Sanford and Ruby Byers, like many who came of age during the Great Depression, heard of plans for the poultry industry in northeast Georgia and decided the new market called for eggs. They built henhouses and for twenty years raised about two thousand laying hens. The work never ended, but they earned enough to buy appliances their parents had never had. Their children finished high school, and three out of their four sons attended the University of Georgia. Like the Byers children, many youths who had been driven from farms during the Great Depression and World War II welcomed new jobs with guaranteed wages and benefits such as retirement plans. This generation earned the cash that allowed Georgians to participate in the corporate consumer society of the twentieth century, a society that other American regions had joined before the Great Depression.

At the same time, parents and churches lost authority to determine who should teach and what should be taught. As the state's educational bureaucracy grew in size and prominence, families and churches became less involved in decisions and policies. Rather than forming part of the traditional community structure, schools now represented the state and what the state deemed necessary for adulthood. Parents' and churches' voices, while never completely silenced, became less significant than state educational guidelines. What parents wanted for their children was less important than what the state defined as obligatory. Black and white teachers failed to combine their efforts to equalize education. Textile workers fought unsuccessfully to unionize. Local and state politicians vacillated between moderate reform and adherence to tradition. Worse still, the county unit system denied Georgians the simple democratic rule of one person, one vote until the U.S. Supreme Court ruled in favor of equal representation in *Baker v. Carr* in 1962.[2]

Although Georgia's earliest battles about this fundamental issue of education, which permeated every aspect of economic, social, and political life, began in the days of Reconstruction, the rapid pace of events between the New Deal and 1950 does not permit the identification of a particular point at which most white Georgians determined to change no further. White supremacy, the U.S. Department of Agriculture's Extension Service, northern philanthropy, expanding roles of black and white teachers, New Deal programs such as the National Youth Administration, industrialization during World War II, Eugene Talmadge's 1940 and 1946 campaigns, Ellis Arnall's moderation in the early 1940s, the campaigns by the National Association for the Advancement of Colored People and the GTEA between 1935 and 1950, political victories by the Georgia Education Association (GEA) and GTEA that resulted in educational reforms, including compulsory attendance, consolidation, and longer school terms—all of these factors combined in the spin of Georgia's social system by 1950. Easily recognized issues emerge—racism, the county unit system, the failure of labor organizations, the threat of communism. What is unmistakable is that education lay at the center of this swirl. Every dispute relied on improved schools or at some point intersected with educational reform. As some reformers realized at the turn of the century, education beckoned the disenfranchised—the poor, blacks, women. It promised hope and opportunities to those who wanted a better life, even if education alone could never enable them to reach those goals. It provided hundreds of women teachers with an opportunity for an independent, public life even if they remained in their original communities. Redefining gender roles, black and white teachers worked as agents of change.

At the same time, education reform by itself could never redeem society. It also carved a path for self-serving consumption and modern bureaucracies. By itself, education could not cut down the county unit system, register black and white voters, or bring economic equality. But during the first half of the twentieth century, education was blacks' and women's most useful tool for change. By the 1960s, when a new generation of southern blacks decided they had waited long enough and took action to tear down Jim Crow's rule once and for all, teachers all too often became targets of ridicule. Some civil rights workers regarded teachers as little more than accommodationists with white local authorities. For years, black teachers had fought to preserve and improve black schools. Now the call came to integrate schools. Teachers' past accomplishments no longer were recognized as political or even progressive.[3] In truth, however, few civil rights workers could have stood where they did had black teachers not for decades insisted that black children were the same as other children, fought for opportunities, and taught as best they could.

If Ellis Arnall and the coalition of blacks, white moderates, and workers who voted for him represented Georgia's potential to avoid the chaos of 1946, which set the path for the 1950s confrontations, it was at best a fragile coalition. No matter how well intentioned voters may have been, the county unit system pushed rural voters' choices to the forefront. These white Georgians tended to favor local authority, with its accompanying social hierarchy.[4] Some working-class whites turned to Eugene and Herman Talmadge because they felt betrayed by New Deal and World War II changes that had done little for them and more for the middle class. To make their voices heard, rural voters went back to someone who at least seemed to speak the language they knew and to appreciate their culture, even if the Talmadge rhetoric resembled the racist language that had divided working-class whites and blacks since the late nineteenth century.

Returning to Virginia in December 1939, Gay Bolling Shepperson must have watched these events with mixed emotions. Part of her legacy was the promotion of education and professional training for women and African Americans using Federal Emergency Relief Administration and Works Progress Administration funds. She demonstrated how federal money could benefit the state. Four years later, Georgia's politicians retrieved racist fears and communist monsters from their campaign chests and trounced reformers again and again for the next twenty years. In the traditional political sense, teachers did little as a group to stop Talmadge or the inequalities of Jim Crow. Yet when their actions are revisited through a lens of cultural activity, it becomes apparent that teachers acted to redefine their world. Through the GEA and GTEA, through their community work, and in their churches, they looked for solutions. The GTEA filled a gap in statewide civil rights organizations by promoting local campaigns against inequalities. This strategy taught a new generation about local struggles. In the wake of the public school crisis following the 1954 *Brown v. Board of Education* decision, white teachers' concern about children

Leona Clark Williams, ca. 1970.
(Courtesy of Leona Clark Williams.)

outweighed their fears about the races mixing. The GEA refused to support the anti-integration movement to close Georgia schools from 1955 to 1960.

In their own ways, some of the teachers interviewed for this work tried to find ways to ease the transition and understand what was happening. Charters Smith Embry, a white teacher, volunteered to teach at E. E. Butler High School, a black school built in Gainesville in the 1960s. Leona Clark Williams supervised a Head Start project in the 1960s. Unlike some teachers, she understood why some parents wanted school prayer abolished. In 1964, when the National Education Association called for integrated educational associations, the GEA and GTEA began negotiations for a merger. Ruth Smith Waters, Horace Tate, Leona Clark Williams, and Narvie Jordan Harris, among others, worked on this plan, which was finally approved by both associations in 1969, when the Georgia Association of Educators was formed. Horace Tate became the new group's associate executive secretary. In addition, Waters continued to teach after her class was integrated and contributed to local history talks at the Gainesville Public Library. Florrie Still worked as a visiting teacher for nine years before becoming state coordinator of visiting teachers from 1954 to 1969. After receiving numerous awards for her social welfare work, she retired. Still and her sister, Nelle Still Murphy, remain active in their Baptist church. Jimmie Kate Sams Cole taught in Fayette County for decades. Almost every white teacher interviewed still taught Sunday school. Although all of the women sympathized with integrating schools, although each remembered the injustices they had seen, they felt powerless to change state laws and local policies. Their contributions occurred at an individual level or through the GEA.

In 1947, the Reverend Byrd Oliver, Beulah Rucker Oliver's beloved husband, died. Over the next few years, Beulah began to have visions about building a new church at Sanders Chapel, where Byrd Oliver had preached. She had visions of an empty church and feared the decline of Protestant faith in the changing world. Beulah Oliver believed that evangelical Protestantism was vital to her race's future. So, just as she had in 1912, Oliver began to mobilize the community to build a church. Oliver donated a half acre to the congregation and worked with other church members to raise funds to buy additional land. After completion, the church was named Beulah Rucker Memorial Church. That the congregation chose to use Rucker's maiden name rather than her married name reminded the black community of what Rucker had accomplished as a black, Christian woman.

Dorothy Oliver Rucker, Laura Whelchel, and Charity Ector headed for the former white high school, Gainesville High School, in 1971, teaching there for the remainder of their careers. Rucker, Carrie Oliver Bailey, and Whelchel worked with a Gainesville committee to preserve Beulah Rucker's home that was funded in part by the Julius Rosenwald Foundation. In 1996, the Beulah Rucker Museum Project dedicated a new facility for local meetings and education courses. In the 1970s, Rosa Penson Anderson moved to Fayette County High School, where Jimmie Kate Sams Cole had taught for years. Narvie Jordan Harris worked as a Jeanes supervisor until 1969. She also organized and served as president of the local parent-teacher association. When Georgia schools integrated in 1971, she worked as an instructional coordinator for all schools in De Kalb County until her retirement in 1983. Susie Weems Wheeler received a six-year education specialist degree from the University of Kentucky in 1960 and a doctorate from the University of Georgia in 1978, writing a dissertation on school integration in Bartow County in 1968. She retired and formed a committee to preserve the Rosenwald school in Cartersville, and the facility opened in 1989 as a museum of black culture in northwest Georgia.

By 1971, black teachers worked with white teachers at what were formerly all-white schools. It took seventeen years for all of Georgia's school districts to comply with *Brown*. Still, little interaction occurred between teachers of different races—a polite smile, a nod of recognition, no more than was necessary

Beulah Rucker Oliver's home in Gainesville, Georgia, was restored in 1996. Celebrating the occasion from left to right, Laura Mosley Whelchel (a former teacher at Oliver's school), Florrie Still (Georgia's first visiting teacher), Dorothy Oliver Rucker (Beulah Rucker Oliver's daughter and a teacher at Oliver's school), and Nelle Still Murphy (a teacher and visual arts coordinator). (Courtesy of Nelle Still Murphy and Florrie Still.)

for good manners. Some teachers believed that much had been lost. Black principals quit rather than work as assistant principals.[5] Black teachers who had previously taught yearbook and journalism classes now taught English classes. Black athletes were welcomed on most sports teams, but few blacks became members of honor societies or student councils.

What was lost and what was gained as a result of *Brown* remain at the core of education debates today. Funded by property taxes, divided by neighborhood zoning and bedroom communities, education continues to illustrate our nation's weakest efforts to claim democratic opportunities. Yet teachers such as Rucker, Bailey, Williams, Waters, Embry, Still, Murphy, Anderson, Harris, Wheeler, Whelchel, and Cole continue their actions in church groups, Sunday school, or organizations for retired teachers. These women were among the last teachers to have taught in segregated Georgia. They watched their state move from its persistent hierarchy based on class, race, and gender to a different world. Women could now earn their own livings. People could change their class status by gaining more education, although that did not always occur. From Georgia came Dr. Martin Luther King Jr., Julian Bond, Horace Tate, Jo Ann Gibson Robinson, Bernice Johnson Reagon, and Andrew Young, the first black congressman elected from the South since Reconstruction—the new generation to whom the educational torch was passed.

Notes

Abbreviations

GDAH	Georgia Department of Archives and History, Atlanta
GEB Papers	General Education Board Papers, Rockefeller Archive Center, Pocantico Hills, N.Y.
JRF Archives	Julius Rosenwald Fund Archives, Fisk University Archives, Nashville, Tenn.
KSU	Kennesaw State University, Sturgis Library, Bentley Rare Book Room, Kennesaw State University, Kennesaw, Ga.
NAACP microfilm	National Association for the Advancement of Colored People Papers, Robert Woodruff Library, Emory University, Atlanta, and University of Georgia Main Library, Athens
NAACP Papers	National Association for the Advancement of Colored People Papers, Manuscript Division, Library of Congress, Washington, D.C.
NMAH	Oral History of Southern Agriculture, National Museum of American History, Smithsonian Institution, Washington, D.C.
NYA Records	National Youth Administration Records, RG 119, National Archives, Washington, D.C.
SBCHLA	Southern Baptist Convention Historical Library and Archives, Nashville, Tenn.
UGA	Hargrett Special Collections, University of Georgia Libraries, Athens
USDA Records	U.S. Department of Agriculture, Extension Service Records, RG 33, National Archives, College Park, Md.
WPA Collection	Works Progress Administration, Federal Writers' Project Collection, Georgia, Manuscript Division, Library of Congress, Washington, D.C.

Introduction

1. Dorothy Oliver Rucker and Carrie Oliver Bailey, interview by author, Gainesville, Ga., May 6, 19, September 14, 1993; Leona Clark Williams, interview by author, Buford, Ga., June 13, 1991.

2. For works on teachers during Reconstruction, see Butchart, *Northern Schools*; Jacqueline Jones, *Soldiers*. Studies on southern education include James Anderson, *Education*; Bond, *Education*; Link, *Hard Country*; Leloudis, *Schooling*; Fairclough, *Teaching Equality*.

3. Thomas, *Secret Eye*; Lines, *"To Raise Myself"*; Marsden, *Understanding Fundamentalism*, chaps. 1, 4, 5. On women and higher education, see Solomon, *In the Company*; McCandless, *Past in the Present*; Tyack and Hansot, *Managers*. Marsden distinguishes conservative evangelicals from fundamentalists because they rejected separatist strategies of fundamentalists while retaining antimodernist strategies. On southern women and religion, see Jean E. Friedman, *Enclosed Garden*; Higginbotham, *Righteous Discontent*; Fox-Genovese and Genovese, "Divine Sanction."

4. Rice, *He Included Me*, 68–94.

5. Fairclough, *Teaching Equality*; Hine, "Black Professionals"; Stephanie J. Shaw, *What a Woman Ought to Be*; Gilmore, *Gender and Jim Crow*.

6. Tuck, *Beyond Atlanta*, 14; see also Gilmore, *Gender and Jim Crow*; Hale, *Making Whiteness*; Litwack, *Trouble in Mind*; Daniel, *Standing*; Tera W. Hunter, *To 'Joy My Freedom*.

7. Leloudis, *Schooling*, xii.

8. See, for example, Ferguson, *Black Politics*, chap. 2.

9. Narvie Jordan Harris, interview by author, Atlanta, September 27, 2002.

10. Elsa Barkley Brown, "Negotiating"; Stephanie J. Shaw, "Black Club Women"; Hahn, *Nation*, chaps. 1–4.

11. Kelley, "'We Are Not What We Seem.'"

12. For the historiography on women's roles, see Kerber, "Separate Spheres." Among the many works on southern women, see Fox-Genovese, *Within the Plantation Household*; Joan E. Cashin, *Family Venture*; White, *Ar'n't I a Woman?*; Jacqueline Jones, *Labor*; Jacquelyn Dowd Hall et al., *Like a Family*; Tullos, *Habits*; Hagood, *Mothers*; Hine, *Black Women*; Stephanie J. Shaw, *What a Woman Ought to Be*; Higginbotham, *Righteous Discontent*; Mary E. Frederickson, "'Each One.'"

13. For examples of distinct gender constructions, see Deutsch, *No Separate Refuge*; Osterud, *Bonds*; McCurry, *Masters*; Sharpless, *Fertile Ground*.

14. See Hagood, *Mothers*; Tullos, *Habits*; Jacquelyn Dowd Hall et al., *Like a Family*; Sharpless, *Fertile Ground*; Stephanie J. Shaw, *What a Woman Ought to Be*; Terkel, *Hard Times*; Dittmer, *Local People*; Payne, *I've Got the Light*.

15. Thelen, *Memory*; Hobsbawm and Ranger, *Invention*; Stephanie J. Shaw, *What a Woman Ought to Be*, 1–10; Fox-Genovese, "My Statue, My Self"; W. Fitzhugh Brundage, "Introduction: No Deed but Memory," in *Where These Memories Grow*, ed. Brundage, 1–28; Halbwachs, *On Collective Memory*.

16. Kerber, "Separate Spheres"; Hine, *Black Women*; Fox-Genovese, *Within the Plantation Household*; Deutsch, *No Separate Refuge*; Glenn, *Daughters*; Fox-Genovese, "Women and Agriculture"; Stephanie J. Shaw, *What a Woman Ought to Be*; Wheeler, *New Women*; Elna C. Green, "'Ideals of Government.'"

17. In this book, women teachers are referred to by their full names—given, maiden, and, when appropriate, married.

18. The women interviewed were chosen in two ways: calls to women whose names appeared on retired teachers' lists, and recommendations from women contacted via the first method.

19. For discussions of modernity, see Joan E. Cashin, *Family Venture*, 146; Fox-Genovese, *Feminism*, chaps. 2, 5; Lyon, *Postmodernity*, 19, 21; Cobb, *Redefining*, 1–24; Daniel, *Lost Revolutions*, chap 1.

20. For autobiographical theory, see Benstock, "Authorizing"; Susan Stanford Friedman, "Women's Autobiographical Selves"; Fox-Genovese, "My Statue, My Self"; McKay, "Race, Gender, and Cultural Context"; Miller, "Writing Fictions"; Sidonie Smith, "Resisting the Gaze"; Heilbrun, *Writing*.

21. Bourdieu, *Distinction*; Raymond Williams, *Marxism*; Fox-Genovese, *Feminism*.

22. Oliver, *Rugged Pathway*, 3.

23. "Georgia Women's Christian Temperance Union," *Christian Index* 105 (February 12, 1925): 17, SBCHLA.

24. Gilmore, *Gender and Jim Crow*, chap. 6.

25. Egerton, *Speak Now*; Dittmer, *Local People*; Sullivan, *Days*; Tyson, *Radio Free Dixie*; Payne, *I've Got the Light*; Honey, *Southern Labor*; Korstad and Lichtenstein, "Opportunities Found and Lost"; Tuck, *Beyond Atlanta*.

1 · The Rugged Path

1. Oliver, *Rugged Pathway*, 9.

2. Ibid.

3. For African American religious beliefs, see Genovese, *Roll, Jordan, Roll*, bk. 1, pt. 1; Levine, *Black Culture*, chaps. 1–3; Frazier, *Negro Church*; Woodson, *History*; William E. Montgomery, *Under Their Own Vine*, chaps. 4–6; Higginbotham, *Righteous Discontent*, chaps. 1–3, 7; Lincoln and Mamiya, *Black Church*. For examples of southern African American women's visions, see Andrews, *Six Women's Slave Narratives*.

4. For African American women's activism, see Stephanie J. Shaw, "Black Club Women"; Elsa Barkley Brown, "Negotiating"; Morton, *Disfigured Images*; Neverdon-Morton, *Afro-American Women*, chaps. 2–4, 7; Rouse, *Lugenia Burns Hope*, 1–10; Giddings, *When and Where*; Higginbotham, *Righteous Discontent*; Hine, *Black Women*, chaps. 1–3. For white women, see Anne Firor Scott, *Southern Lady*; Jacquelyn Dowd Hall, *Revolt*; Wheeler, *New Women*; Hewitt and Lebsock, *Visible Women*; Bernhard et al., *Hidden Histories*. For works on southern Progressivism, see Link, *Paradox*; Grantham, *Southern Progressivism*; Woodward, *Origins*.

5. Leona Clark Williams, *We Remember*, 15; Leona Clark Williams, interview by author, Buford, Ga., June 13, 1991.

6. Brundage, "White Women"; Brundage, *Where These Memories Grow*; Halbwachs, *On Collective Memory*.

7. Ryan, *Women*, 4–17; see also Edwards, *Gendered Strife*; Elsa Barkley Brown, "Negotiating"; Gilmore, *Gender and Jim Crow*; Habermas, *Structural Transformation*. Georgians of both races defined themselves as self-sufficient concerning their ability to manage their economic, social, and political affairs. At the same time, these Georgians saw themselves as interdependent and relying on communities for preservation and sustenance.

8. Dorsey, *History*; Elrod, *Historical Notes*, chap. 2; Flanigan, *History*; Hahn, *Roots*, chap. 1; McCurry, *Masters*, 19–22; Keith, *Country People*, 12–25; Kirby, *Rural Worlds*; Daniel, *Breaking*; Woodward, *Origins*; Joan E. Cashin, "Structure"; Bardaglio, *Reconstructing*; Stanley, "Home Life"; Fox-Genovese, "Women and Agriculture."

9. Fox-Genovese, "Women and Agriculture"; Wright, *Old South*. For the differences between southern and northern households, see Fox-Genovese, *Within the Plantation Household*, 37–99; Genovese, *Political Economy*.

10. Flamming, *Creating*, chap. 1; Hahn, *Roots*; Bartley, *Creation*; Dorsey, *History*, 109.

11. Flamming, *Creating*, chap. 1; Hahn, *Roots*; Dorsey, *History*, 109.

12. Thomas, *Secret Eye*, pt. 4; Felton, *My Memoirs*; Felton, *Country Life*; Bartley, *Creation*, chap. 5; Friedlander, "A More Perfect Christian Womanhood," 47.

13. Noll, *History*, 170–80; Hatch, *Democratization*; Mathews, *Religion*; Ahlstrom, *Religious History*.

14. For example, Free Will Baptists sought to affirm the emphasis on an individual's free will as opposed to what they understood as an excessive emphasis on Calvinism's predestination. Others rejected the authority of a central convention as well as the belief in missionary work and became known as Primitive Baptists. Primitive Baptists rejected efforts at conversion outside the local congregation and refused to hold Sunday schools.

15. Wagner, *Profiles*, chaps. 4, 5; Cheeks-Collins, *Gwinnett County*, 48; Grant, *Way It Was*, chap. 2; Mason, *African-American Life*; Lassiter, *Generations*. Savannah's blacks founded the First African Baptist Church in 1832, and Gainesville's African American First Baptist Church was built in 1838.

16. Liberty Baptist Church, Lilburn, Georgia, Records, 1840–70, SBCHLA; Mount Zion Baptist Church, Snellville, Gwinnett County, Georgia, Records, 1853–1932, SBCHLA.

17. Leona Clark Williams, *We Remember*.

18. Wind and Lewis, *American Congregations*; Samuel S. Hill, *Varieties*; Eighmy, *Churches*; Loveland, *Southern Evangelicals*; Friedman, *Enclosed Garden*.

19. Marsden, *Fundamentalism and American Culture*, pt. 1; Link, *Paradox*, chap. 2; Ayers, *Promise*, chap. 7; Bartley, *Creation*, chap. 5; Minnix, *Laughter*.

20. Daniel, *Standing*; Ayers, *Promise*; Woodward, *Origins*; Tindall, *Emergence*; Link, *Paradox*; Kirby, *Darkness*; Tullos, *Habits*; Jacquelyn Dowd Hall et al., *Like a Family*.

21. McCandless, *Past in the Present*, chaps. 1, 2; Farnham, *Education*.

22. For similar views in other states, see Keith, *Country People*, 26–44; McCurry,

Masters, 171–207; Flamming, *Creating*, pt. 1; Leloudis, *Schooling*, 1–35; Link, *Hard Country*, 3–23; Orr, *History*, 19–180; Farnham, *Education*.

23. Prior to 1905, Georgia had 137 counties. The General Assembly agreed to allow more counties in 1904, and 9 counties were added. By 1918, the state had 155 counties, with 6 more added during the 1920s for a total of 161. In 1932, Milton and Campbell Counties merged with Fulton, leaving the state with 159 counties, second only to Texas.

24. Bartley, *Creation*, 16–44; Link, *Hard Country*, 3–23; Hahn, *Roots*, 50–133; Michael P. Johnson, *Toward a Patriarchal Republic*, 63–78; Wallenstein, *From Slave South to New South*, pt. 1.

25. Brattain, *Politics*, chap. 1; Flamming, *Creating*, chap. 1.

26. Kirby, *Rural Worlds*, chap. 7; Ruth Reed, *Negro Women*, 8–9; Bartley, *Creation*, chaps. 4, 5; Dittmer, *Black Georgia*; Dorsey, *History*; McRay, *Pictorial History*; Wright, *Old South*, chaps. 3, 6; Woodman, *King Cotton*.

27. Ruth Reed, *Negro Women*, 8, 9; Dittmer, *Black Georgia*; Drago, *Black Politicians*; Dorsey, *History*, 183, 230.

28. Phil Campbell, "Report of Farmers' Cooperative Demonstration Work in Georgia for Year Ending December 15, 1915," USDA Records, reel 1; U.S. Department of Commerce, Bureau of the Census, *Census of Agriculture*, 411, 507; Howard A. Turner and Howell, *Condition*.

29. Wagner, *Profiles*, 61–62.

30. Ruth Reed, *Negro Women*, 48.

31. Tera W. Hunter, *To 'Joy My Freedom*, chap. 2; Donaldson, "New Negroes."

32. Hattie Gaines Wilson, interview by Mary B. Cawley, Marietta, Ga., September 2, 1987, Cobb County Oral History Series, KSU; Hattie Gaines Wilson, interview by Kathryn A. Kelley, Gainesville, Ga., August 2, 17, 1994, Cobb County Oral History Series, KSU; members of Zion Baptist Church, interview by Thomas A. Scott, April 8, 24, 29, 1986, Marietta, Ga., Cobb County Oral History Series, KSU; Lassiter, *Generations*, 50.

33. Mason, *African-American Life*, 17.

34. Bartley, *Creation*, 79; Hahn, *Nation*, pts. 1–2; Schultz, *Unsolid South*.

35. Donaldson, "New Negroes," chap. 1; Grant, *Way It Was*, chaps. 4, 5; Bryant, *How Curious*; Lassiter, *Generations*, chap. 2; J. Douglas Smith, *Managing*, chap. 1.

36. Brundage, *Lynching*, 107, 121; Ayers, *Promise*, 156–59; Grant, *Way It Was*, 160–65; Donaldson, "New Negroes," 60–64; *Georgia Baptist*, April 27, 1899.

37. James D. Anderson, *Education*; Bond, *Education*; Woodson, *Mis-Education*; Frazier, *Negro Church*; William E. Montgomery, *Under Their Own Vine*; Higginbotham, *Righteous Discontent*; Richardson, *Christian Reconstruction*; Drago, *Black Politicians*; Dittmer, *Black Georgia*.

38. Andrews, *Six Women's Slave Narratives*; William E. Montgomery, *Under Their Own Vine*, chap. 6; Genovese, *Roll, Jordan, Roll*, bk. 2, pt. 1; Lassiter, *Generations*, 22.

39. Genovese, *Roll, Jordan, Roll*, bk. 2, pt. 1, pp. 209–55; Levine, *Black Culture*,

chaps. 1, 3; William E. Montgomery, *Under Their Own Vine*, chaps. 4, 6; Higginbotham, *Righteous Discontent*; Woodson, *History*; Frazier, *Negro Church*.

40. Harvey, *Redeeming*.

41. Beulah Rucker, "A Word from the Colored Industrial Institute, Gainesville, Ga.," *Atlanta Independent*, July 5, 1911, 3.

42. Stephanie J. Shaw, *What a Woman Ought to Be*; Richardson, *Christian Reconstruction*; William E. Montgomery, *Under Their Own Vine*, chaps. 4, 6. John 9:4 reads, "I must work the works of him that sent me, while it is day; the night cometh when no man can work."

43. Saville, *Work*, 18–24, 102–10; William E. Montgomery, *Under Their Own Vine*, chaps. 4–6; James D. Anderson, *Education*, chap. 1; Butchart, *Northern Schools*; Jones, *Soldiers*.

44. *Georgia Baptist*, September 13, 1900.

45. Dorsey, *History*, 176.

46. Lassiter, *Generations*, chap. 2; Donaldson, "New Negroes," 28–30.

47. Members of Zion Baptist Church interview.

48. Susie Weems Wheeler, interview by author, Cartersville, Ga., August 3, 2002.

49. Butchart, "Mission Matters"; Butchart and Rolleri, "Iowa Teachers"; Jennifer Lund Smith, "'Twill Take Some Time to Study.'"

50. Dorothy Oliver Rucker and Carrie Oliver Bailey, interview by author, Gainesville, Ga., May 6, 19, September 14, 1993; Wilson, interview by Cawley; Wilson, interview by Kelley; James D. Anderson, *Education*, chap. 1; Butchart, *Northern Schools*, chaps. 1–3; Jacqueline Jones, *Soldiers*; William E. Montgomery, *Under Their Own Vine*, chaps. 4, 6; Richardson, *Christian Reconstruction*, chap. 13.

51. Meier, *Negro Thought*; Lewis, *Du Bois: Biography*; Harlan, *Washington: Wizard*.

52. Grant, *Way It Was*, 176–77; Woodward, *Strange Career*; Litwack, *Trouble in Mind*.

53. Grant, *Way It Was*, 177.

54. Bartley, *Creation*, 79.

55. Harlan, *Separate and Unequal*.

56. According to Peter Wallenstein, Georgians paid higher property taxes during the 1870s and 1880s than ever before. At least half of this money went to white public schools and to Confederate pensions. Two problems nonetheless existed. First, white small farmers saw little benefit in paying higher taxes for education. Second, African Americans received only one-sixth of the budget for schools. As Georgia increased property taxes, it did little to tax the expanding railroad industry or other new industries. See Wallenstein, *From Slave South to New South*, pt. 3; see also Drago, *Black Politicians*; Dittmer, *Black Georgia*, 141–62; Harlan, *Separate and Unequal*.

57. Jimmie Kate Sams Cole, interview by author, Fayetteville, Ga., October 6, 1989.

58. Ruth Smith Waters, interview by author, Flowery Branch, Ga., June 28, 1991, June 10, December 7, 1993.

59. Richardson, *Christian Reconstruction*; Wyatt-Brown, "Black Schooling"; Jacqueline Jones, *Soldiers*; Butchart, *Northern Schools*.

60. James D. Anderson, *Education*; Grant, *Way It Was*, chaps. 3–5; Leslie, "No Middle Ground"; Chirhart, "Gardens"; Donaldson, "New Negroes," chap. 1; Jennifer Lund Smith, "Ties That Bind"; Bacote, *Story*, 91–105.

61. William E. Montgomery, *Under Their Own Vine*; Jennifer Lund Smith, "Ties That Bind"; Stephanie J. Shaw, *What a Woman Ought to Be*, 14–16.

62. For the link between Populism and education, see Hahn, *Roots*; Barton Shaw, *Wool-Hat Boys*; Bartley, *Creation*; Woodward, *Origins*. For the argument that whites increased their educational reform efforts because of the proliferation of black schools, see James D. Anderson, *Education*. For the concerns of specific white Georgia educators, see Orr, *History*; Bartley, *Creation*. For educational reform in the South from the late nineteenth to early twentieth century, see Ayers, *Promise*; Woodward, *Origins*; Link, *Paradox*; Grantham, *Southern Progressivism*; Leloudis, *Schooling*; Link, *Hard Country*.

63. Rebecca Latimer Felton, "The Industrial School for Girls," 72, MSS 81, microfilm roll 11, Rebecca Latimer Felton Papers, UGA.

64. Thomas, *Secret Eye*, 321.

65. Tolnay, *Bottom Rung*, 55, 75–80, 107.

66. Mary Ellen Allgood, interview by Barbara M. Wiley, Cobb County, Ga., July 20, 1984, Cobb County Oral History Series, KSU; Waters interview; Florrie Still and Nelle Still Murphy, interview by author, Gainesville, Ga., May 9, June 7, 1997; Orr, *History*, chaps. 10, 11; Duggan, *Educational Survey*; Dorsey, *History*, chap. 8; Elrod, *Historical Notes*, chap. 8; Flanigan, *History*, chap. 16.

67. Leona Clark Williams, *We Remember*, 11.

68. Mixon, "Georgia," 297–99; see also Ownby, *Subduing Satan*.

69. Liberty Baptist Church Records; Mount Zion Baptist Church Records; First Baptist Church, Commerce, Georgia, Records, 1874–1983, microfilm roll 1, SBCHLA.

70. M. E. Dodd, "Three Questions Concerning Modernism," *Christian Index*, January 22, 1925, 7, SBCHLA.

71. W. H. Faust, "The Supreme Work of the Church Today," *Christian Index*, January 21, 1915, 4, SBCHLA; see also "Another Challenge for Georgia Baptists," *Christian Index*, January 14, 1914, 2, SBCHLA.

72. Friedman, *Enclosed Garden*, chaps. 5, 6; Samuel S. Hill, *Varieties*; Wind and Lewis, *American Congregations*; Marsden, *Fundamentalism and American Culture*, pt. 1; see also McCurry, *Masters*, chaps. 4, 5; Keith, *Country People*, 45–57; Pope, *Millhands*.

73. "Resolution from Yellow River Primitive Baptist Association," n.d., box 1, folder 10, "Handbill to Voters of Gwinnett County, 1888," box 1, folder 11, John Riley Hopkins Papers, GDAH.

74. Leloudis, *Schooling*, 13–17; Waters interview; Leona Clark Williams interview; Still and Murphy interview.

75. Annie Mae Horne to E. C. Branson, July 28, 1903, ser. 1.1, box 48, folder 431, GEB Papers; see also "Religious, Civic, and Social Forces in Georgia," Citizens' Fact Finding Movement, Atlanta, 1938, box 203, folder 8, JRF Archives.

76. Dyer, *University of Georgia*, 37–38, 44; McCandless, *Past in the Present*, chap. 1.

77. Tolnay, *Bottom Rung*, 55, 75–80, 107.

78. Dorsey, *History*, 267–71.

79. Ibid.; Wallenstein, *From Slave South to New South*.

80. Waters interview; Rucker and Bailey interview; Leona Clark Williams interview; Wilson, interview by Cawley; Wilson, interview by Kelley; members of Zion Baptist Church interview; Allgood interview. See chap. 3 for a further discussion of the structure and evolution of the Georgia State Department of Education and of the county school systems.

81. *Augusta Chronicle*, June 9, 1897, April 28, 1899; Kousser, "Separate," 24–27; Donaldson, "New Negroes," 46–52; George M. Frederickson, *Black Image*, 210–21.

82. Edward J. Cashin, *Story*; Edward J. Cashin, *Quest*; Kousser, "Separate"; Donaldson, "New Negroes," 49; *Augusta Chronicle*, September 22, 1897; John C. Ladeveze to Booker T. Washington, July 4, 1898, in Washington, *Papers*, 4:437.

83. Grant, *Way It Was*, 195–204.

84. Donaldson, "New Negroes," 64–66; Lewis, *Du Bois: Biography*; Grant, *Way It Was*, chaps. 5, 6; *Georgia Baptist*, May 31, 1900.

85. *Georgia Baptist*, May 31, 1900.

86. Donaldson, "New Negroes," 66–73.

87. Grant, *Way It Was*, 205–7.

88. Donaldson, "New Negroes," 77.

89. Grant, *Way It Was*, 195–209.

90. Hale, *Making Whiteness*, chap. 1; Barbara Jeanne Fields, "Ideology and Race"; Bryant, *How Curious*; J. Douglas Smith, *Managing*, chap. 1; Ayers, *Promise*; Woodward, *Origins*; Gilmore, *Gender and Jim Crow*, chaps. 4, 5.

91. Lewis, *Du Bois: Biography*.

92. Key, *Southern Politics*, 119–21; Bartley, *Creation*; Dittmer, *Black Georgia*; Grant, *Way It Was*, chap. 5.

93. Moore, *Leading*; Leslie, "No Middle Ground," 124; J. Douglas Smith, *Managing*, chap. 1.

94. Harvey, *Redeeming*, chap. 7; Link, *Paradox*, chap. 4.

95. Higginbotham, *Righteous Discontent*; Richardson, *Christian Reconstruction*; William E. Montgomery, *Under Their Own Vine*; Bond, *Education*; Saville, *Work*; Scott, *Southern Lady*; Fox-Genovese, "Women and Agriculture"; Tyack and Hansot, *Managers*; Woodson, *Mis-Education*; James D. Anderson, *Education*; Leloudis, *Schooling*; Link, *Paradox*; Ayers, *Promise*; Giddings, *When and Where*. According to the 1870 census, women outnumbered men in Georgia by 36,000 (Scott, *Southern Lady*, 93).

96. Scott, *Southern Lady*, chap. 5; Faust, "Altars"; Whites, *Civil War*; Rable, *Civil*

Wars; Georgia Department of Education, *Thirty-ninth Annual Report*, 443; Georgia Department of Education, *Twenty-ninth Annual Report*.

97. Brundage, *Lynching*, 122.

98. C. B. Hackworth, "Rape, Lynchings Left Mark on Forsyth and Dawson," *Gainesville Times*, April 13, 1980, 1e; C. B. Hackworth, "Reminders of Events of 1912 Remain in Forsyth, Dawson," *Gainesville Times*, April 14, 1980, 1e.

99. T. P. Grissom, interview by author, Atlanta, December 10, 1993; Rucker and Bailey interview.

100. Rucker and Bailey interview; Nancy Stephens, interview by author, June 8, 1993, Gainesville, Ga.; Grissom interview.

101. Oliver, *Rugged Pathway*, 10.

102. Rucker and Bailey interview; see also Higginbotham, *Righteous Discontent*.

103. McCluskey, "'Most Sacrificing Service'"; Elaine M. Smith, "Mary McLeod Bethune," in *Black Women*, ed. Hine, Brown, and Terborg-Penn, 113–27; Littlefield, "Moving Quietly"; Williams-May, "Lucy Craft Laney"; Leslie, "No Middle Ground"; Berkeley, "Sage"; Gilmore, *Gender and Jim Crow*, chap. 6. Because few farm families could spare their sons' labor, women continued to serve as leading educators. Florida's Mary McLeod Bethune, North Carolina's Annie Holland, and Georgia's Lucy Craft Laney all established private schools to educate blacks.

104. County records no longer exist for black schools, so the precise date of construction is difficult to determine, but evidence from available sources suggests that Rucker's school was completed by 1919 or 1920. See "Negro School Building Fund," n.d., box 337, folder 10, JRF Archives; Georgia Department of Education, *Forty-ninth Annual Report*, 448; Grissom interview; see also "Annual Report 1921–22 of Field Secretary J. O. Martin," 1922, ser. 1.1, box 68, folder 593, GEB Papers; George Godard to county superintendents, January 1, 1919, ser. 1.1, box 212, folder 2038, GEB Papers.

105. "Rosenwald Schools, Georgia, 1931," box 337, folder 10, JRF Archives; "Community School Plans, Bulletin No. 3," 1924, 8, ser. 1.2, box 213, folder 2047, GEB Papers. For a comparison of the school types in other Georgia counties, see "Negro School Building Programs," n.d., box 337, folder 10, JRF Archives.

106. James D. Anderson, *Education*, chap. 5. Oliver's school became one of Georgia's first recipients of a Rosenwald grant.

107. "Rosenwald Schools, Georgia, 1931," box 337, folder 10, JRF Archives; "Community School Plans, Bulletin No. 3," 1924, 8, ser. 1.2, box 213, folder 2047, GEB Papers; see also "Statement of Receipts and Disbursements of Rosenwald Fund, July 1, 1924 to June 20, 1925," box 337, folder 10, JRF Archives; S. L. Smith to Georgia State School Superintendent Fort Land, March 10, 1927, box 337, folder 10, JRF Archives; Georgia Department of Education, *Fifty-fourth and Fifty-fifth Annual Reports*, 41.

108. Rucker and Bailey interview.

109. Gilmore, *Gender and Jim Crow*, chaps. 1, 2.

110. Dorsey, *History*, 292, quoting *Gainesville Eagle*, August 22, 1895.

2 · We Learned from Our Mothers' Knees

1. Oliver, *Rugged Pathway*, 9; Stephanie J. Shaw, *What a Woman Ought to Be*, 1–10.

2. Ownby, *Subduing Satan*; Melissa Walker, *All We Knew*, chap. 1; Ownby, *American Dreams*, 1–6, chap. 3; Ayers, *Promise*, chap. 4; Laird, *Advertising Progress*, pt. 3; Goodson, *Highbrows*; Cobb, *Redefining*; Garvey, *Adman*, 3–15, chap. 1; Damon-Moore, *Magazines*, chaps. 4, 7.

3. Some historians use the term *whiteness* to describe the social construction of identity and race. Relying on W. E. B. Du Bois's writings about the color line and how racism divided working-class people, scholars have explored how various immigrant groups and some African Americans attempted to become "white," a standard by which satisfactory Americans were measured. Because of the slippery meanings and avoidance of power issues that affect African Americans, I avoid using the term *whiteness* in this work. See Arnesen, "Whiteness"; James R. Barrett, "Whiteness Studies"; Brody, "Charismatic History"; Barbara Jeanne Fields, "Whiteness"; Foner, "Response"; Hattam, "Whiteness"; Adolph Reed Jr., "Response"; Arnesen, "Assessing"; see also Roediger, *Wages*; Hale, *Making Whiteness*; Barbara Jeanne Fields, "Ideology and Race"; Du Bois, *Black Reconstruction*.

4. Stephanie J. Shaw, "Black Club Women"; Stephanie J. Shaw, *What a Woman Ought to Be*; Elsa Barkley Brown, "Negotiating"; Gilmore, *Gender and Jim Crow*.

5. Jimmie Kate Sams Cole, interview by author, Fayetteville, Ga., October 6, November 18, 1989.

6. For the transformation of the antebellum countryside, see Hahn and Prude, *Countryside*; Henretta, "Families and Farms"; Fox-Genovese and Genovese, *Fruits*. On the southern postbellum transformation, see Woodward, *Origins*; Ayers, *Promise*; Link, *Paradox*; Tullos, *Habits*; Hahn, *Roots*; Jacquelyn Dowd Hall et al., *Like a Family*; Woodman, "Sequel."

7. Wells, *Revolutions*, 5, 159–60.

8. Among the many sources on southern families, see Genovese, *Roll, Jordan, Roll*; Fox-Genovese, *Within the Plantation Household*; Joan E. Cashin, *Family Venture*; White, *Ar'n't I a Woman?* Gutman, *Black Family*; Burton, *In My Father's House*; Walter J. Fraser Jr., Saunders, and Wakelyn, *Web*.

9. Wells, *Revolutions*, 163.

10. For examples of women's work in various American ethnic groups, see Pleck, "A Mother's Wages"; Dublin, "Women"; Yans-McLaughlin, "Patterns"; Tentler, *Wage-Earning Women*; Orlick, *Common Sense*; Glenn, *Daughters*; Linda Gordon, *Pitied*; Mintz, *Prison*; Anker, "Family"; Yung, *Unbound Feet*; Matsumoto, *Farming*; Ruiz, *From Out of the Shadows*.

11. Lu Ann Jones, *Mama*, 1–25; Melissa Walker, *All We Knew*; Sharpless, *Fertile Ground*.

12. Tolnay, *Bottom Rung*, 55, 107.

13. Ibid., 75–80; Wells, *Revolutions*, chaps. 5, 6.

14. Tolnay, *Bottom Rung*, 55, 78.

15. Anne Firor Scott, *Southern Lady*; Elna C. Green, *Southern Strategies*; Wheeler, *New Women*; Sharpless, *Fertile Ground*; Elizabeth Hayes Turner, *Women*.

16. Orr, *History*, chap. 11; Bartley, *Creation*, chaps. 5, 6; Joiner, *History*.

17. Georgia Department of Education, *Thirty-eighth Annual Report*, 499–503.

18. Georgia Department of Education, *Sixtieth and Sixty-first Annual Reports*, 211.

19. Georgia Department of Education, *Thirty-ninth Annual Report*, 255, 387–88; Georgia Department of Education, *Sixtieth and Sixty-first Annual Reports*, 148, 179.

20. Cindy Wright, interview by Grace McGune, December 13, 1938, WPA Collection.

21. Tolnay, *Bottom Rung*, 40–47; Hagood, *Mothers*, 211–12; Schultz, "Unsolid South," 376–85; see also Litwack, *Trouble in Mind*, 53–61.

22. Schultz, "Unsolid South," 375–81; Mrs. Louie D. Bradley, interview by Leola T. Bradley, September 27, 1939, WPA Collection; Inez Dennis, interview by Ada Radford, April 4, 1940, WPA Collection; Josephine Wood, interview by Grace McCune, January 13, 1939, WPA Collection.

23. Schultz, "Unsolid South," 379.

24. Donaldson, "New Negroes," chap. 4; Williams-May, "Lucy Craft Laney," chap. 2.

25. Ibid.; Leslie, "No Middle Ground."

26. Lucy Craft Laney, "The Burden of the Educated Colored Woman," *Southern Workman* 29 (September 1899): 341–44.

27. McCluskey, "'Most Sacrificing Service,'" 194; Leslie, "No Middle Ground," 128–29; Williams-May, "Lucy Craft Laney," 167–69; Donaldson, "New Negroes," 2 40–51.

28. *Georgia Baptist*, August 26, 1909.

29. Stephanie J. Shaw, *What a Woman Ought to Be*, 10.

30. Gaines, *Uplifting*; Stephanie J. Shaw, *What a Woman Ought to Be*; Donaldson, "New Negroes"; Leslie, "No Middle Ground"; Elsa Barkley Brown, "Negotiating"; J. Douglas Smith, *Managing*.

31. Oliver, *Rugged Pathway*, 1–2.

32. Ibid., 5. On the Georgia white education campaign, see Orr, *History*; Bartley, *Creation*, chaps. 5, 6. For education campaigns in other southern states, see Leloudis, *Schooling*; Link, *Hard Country*; Link, *Paradox*; Ayers, *Promise*; Grantham, *Southern Progressivism*; Woodward, *Origins*.

33. Walter B. Hill, *Rural Survey*, 28; Woofter, *Negroes*; Jacqueline Jones, *Soldiers*; Butchart, *Northern Schools*.

34. Oliver, *Rugged Pathway*, 8; Dorothy Oliver Rucker and Carrie Oliver Bailey, interview by author, Gainesville, Ga., May 6, 19, September 14, 1993.

35. Rucker, *Rugged Pathway*, 9, 7.

36. Rucker and Bailey interview.

37. Stephanie J. Shaw, *What a Woman Ought to Be*, 14–16.

38. Laura Mosley Whelchel, interview by author, Gainesville, Ga., June 18, 1993.

39. Rosa Penson Anderson, interview by author, Fayetteville, Ga., March 24, 1992.

40. Nancy Stephens, interview by author, Gainesville, Ga., June 8, 1993.

41. Susie Weems Wheeler, interview by Thomas A. Scott, Cartersville, Ga., March 3, 2000, North Georgia Oral History Series, KSU.

42. Whelchel interview.

43. Rosa Penson Anderson interview.

44. Georgia Department of Education, *Sixtieth and Sixty-first Annual Reports*, 148, 184.

45. Stephanie J. Shaw, *What a Woman Ought to Be*, chap. 1. For African American women's lives during slavery, see Jacqueline Jones, *Labor*.

46. Rucker and Bailey interview; Dorothy Oliver Rucker, Carrie Oliver Bailey, and Nancy Stephens, interview by author, Gainesville, Ga., June 10, 1993.

47. Whelchel interview.

48. Rosa Penson Anderson interview.

49. Rucker, Bailey, and Stephens interview.

50. Goodson, *Highbrows*, chap. 5; Stephanie J. Shaw, *What a Woman Ought to Be*.

51. Lewis, *Du Bois: Biography*, chap. 11; Daryl Michael Scott, *Contempt and Pity*, chap. 4.

52. Goodson, *Highbrows*, chaps. 5, 6; Hunter, *To 'Joy My Freedom*, chap. 8.

53. Hunter, *To 'Joy My Freedom*, 168–70; Goodson, *Highbrows*, 149–60.

54. Hahn, *Nation*, chap. 9; Schultz, "Unsolid South," 128–35; Litwack, *Trouble in Mind*, chap. 6.

55. Rucker, Bailey, and Stephens interview.

56. Oliver, *Rugged Pathway*, 10.

57. Beulah Rucker, "A Word from the Colored Industrial Institute, Gainesville, Ga.," *Atlanta Independent*, July 5, 1911, 3.

58. Stephanie J. Shaw, *What a Woman Ought to Be*, chaps. 1–2. Some historians have seen rules eschewing gambling, dancing, or drinking alcohol as examples of social control or the middle class's imposition of its morals on other classes; see esp. Katz, *Irony*. Grantham uses social control to explain the rise of Jim Crow legislation; see Grantham, *Southern Progressivism*, xx, chap. 7. Recent studies have moved away from a social control analysis of reform: see Link, *Paradox*, chaps. 3 and 5; Leloudis, *Schooling*, preface; James D. Anderson, *Education*, chap. 1; Higginbotham, *Righteous Discontent*, chap. 1; Stephanie J. Shaw, *What a Woman Ought to Be*, intro.

59. Members of Zion Baptist Church, interview by Thomas A. Scott, April 8, 24, 29, 1986, Cobb County Oral History Series, KSU.

60. Rucker and Bailey interview.

61. Rucker, Bailey, and Stephens interview.

62. Rosa Penson Anderson interview; Whelchel interview; Wheeler interview by author.

63. Georgia Department of Education, *Fifty-fourth and Fifty-fifth Annual Reports*, 241; Georgia Department of Education, *Sixtieth and Sixty-first Annual Reports*, 218; see also Jacqueline Jones, *Labor*; Miriam Cohen, "Italian American Women"; Neverdon-Morton, *Afro-American Women*; Giddings, *When and Where*; Leloudis, *Schooling*; James D. Anderson, *Education*; Ayers, *Promise*; Woodward, *Origins*. It is impossible to determine the exact numbers of male and female students at Rucker's school because records are no longer extant. According to Dorothy Oliver Rucker, Carrie Oliver Bailey, Laura Mosley Whelchel, and Nancy Stephens, more girls than boys attended Rucker's school (Rucker and Bailey interview; Whelchel interview; Stephens interview).

64. Rucker and Bailey interview.

65. Ibid.

66. For the impact of slavery on the black family and community, see Genovese, *Roll, Jordan, Roll*; Fox-Genovese, *Within the Plantation Household*, chaps. 1, 3, 4, 6; White, *Ar'n't I a Woman?* Jacqueline Jones, *Labor*, chap. 1; Gutman, *Black Family*; Cashin, *Family Venture*. For the renegotiation of collective ties in the postbellum South, notably among black women, see Stephanie J. Shaw, *What a Woman Ought to Be*, pt. 1; Saville, *Work*; Neverdon-Morton, *Afro-American Women*; Hine, *Black Women*; Higginbotham, *Righteous Discontent*, chap. 1; Giddings, *When and Where*.

67. Ruth Smith Waters, interview by author, Flowery Branch, Ga., June 28, 1991, June 10, December 7, 1993.

68. Leona Clark Williams, interview by author, Buford, Ga., June 13, 24, 1991; Leona Clark Williams, *We Remember*, 5, 11. The Clarks had moved to Ellijay, Georgia, in 1913 but returned to the Ellijay Creek area of North Carolina later that year. The land in North Carolina had been in the Clark family since the 1840s, and when the family returned, Robin Clark built a new log cabin for his growing family. In 1915, the Clarks moved back to his parents' home to care for his mother.

69. Jane Thigpen Alexander, interview by author, Lawrenceville, Ga., June 18, 1991.

70. Martha Breedlove Buice, interview by author, Buford, Ga., June 20, 1991.

71. Howard and Bunice Waldrip Reed, interview by Lu Ann Jones, Gainesville, Ga., April 23, 1987, NMAH.

72. Tom and Velva Blackstock, interview by Lu Ann Jones, Talmo, Ga., April 22, 1987, NMAH.

73. Sanford and Ruby Smith Byers, interview by Lu Ann Jones, Gainesville, Ga., April 20, 1987, NMAH.

74. Ruby Smith Byers, interview by Lu Ann Jones, Gainesville, Ga., April 23, 1987, NMAH.

75. Inez Dennis, interview by Ada Radford, April 4, 1940, Augusta, Ga., Josephine Wood, interview by Grace McGune, January 13, 1939, Mrs. Louis D. Bradley, interview by Leola T. Bradley, September 27, 1939, WPA Collection.

76. Leona Clark Williams interview.

77. Ibid.

78. Leona Clark Williams, *We Remember*, 16.

79. Waters interview.

80. Ibid.

81. Link, *Paradox*; Minnix, *Laughter*; Ayers, *Promise*; Pope, *Millhands*; Jacquelyn Dowd Hall, "Disorderly Women."

82. Goodson, *Highbrows*, 84–85.

83. Leona Clark Williams, *We Remember*, 13–74.

84. Waters interview.

85. Florrie Still and Nelle Still Murphy, interview by author, Gainesville, Ga., May 9, June 7, 1997.

86. Leona Clark Williams interview; Leona Clark Williams, *We Remember*, 18–19.

87. Waters interview.

88. Mrs. Luther Crawford, interview by Ina B. Hawkes, August 28, 1939, Works Progress Administration, Federal Writers' Project, Georgia, Manuscript Division, Library of Congress; Tolnay, *Bottom Rung*, chaps. 2, 5; Litwack, *Trouble in Mind*, chap. 7; Beardsley, *History*, pt. 1; U.S. Department of Commerce, *Thirteenth Census*, 336–92; U.S. Department of Commerce, *Fourteenth Census*, 202–15; see also Leona Clark Williams, *We Remember*; Rucker and Bailey interview; Waters interview.

89. Hattie Gaines Wilson, interview by Mary B. Cawley, Marietta, Ga., September 2, 1987, Cobb County Oral History Series, KSU; Hattie Gaines Wilson, interview by Kathryn A. Kelley, August 2, 17, 1994, Cobb County Oral History Series, KSU.

90. Aubrey and Ina Belle Benton, interview by Lu Ann Jones, Commerce, Ga., April 28, 1987, NMAH.

91. Faulkner, *Light*, 159.

92. Ruby Smith Byers interview; Blackstock interview.

93. Leona Clark Williams interview.

94. Alexander interview.

95. Sanford and Ruby Smith Byers interview. The use of feed sacks for clothing was common, and dealers began to sell sacks designed to appeal to women (Lu Ann Jones, "Gender").

96. Waters interview.

97. Leona Clark Williams interview; Leona Clark Williams, *We Remember*, 20–21.

98. Spurgeon Wellborn, interview by Lu Ann Jones, Jefferson, Ga., April 27, 1987, NMAH.

99. Jensen, *Promise*; Deborah Fink, *Agrarian Women*; Osterud, *Bonds*; Sharpless, *Fertile Ground*.

100. Sanford and Ruby Smith Byers interview.

101. Leona Clark Williams interview; Leona Clark Williams, *We Remember*, 21.

102. Sanford and Ruby Smith Byers interview.

103. Leona Clark Williams, *We Remember*.

104. See, for example, Georgia Department of Education, *Sixtieth and Sixty-first Annual Reports*, 210; see also Tolnay, *Bottom Rung*, chap. 2.

105. Waters interview; Cole interview; Buice interview; Leona Clark Williams interview.

106. Women's Missionary Union of the First Baptist Church, Gainesville, Ga., Records, 1900–1950, SBCHLA; see also Mary E. Frederickson, "'Each One.'"

107. Charters Smith Embry, interview by author, Gainesville, Ga., June 17, August 5, 1993; Cole interview; Waters interview; Leona Clark Williams interview.

108. Stephanie J. Shaw, *What a Woman Ought to Be*; Higginbotham, *Righteous Discontent*; Gilmore, *Gender and Jim Crow*; see also Cashin, *Our Common Affairs*.

109. Sam De Vincent Collection of Illustrated American Sheet Music, ser. 3.3, 3.4, boxes 73–76; ser. 3.1, box 70, Witmark Minstrel Folios, National Museum of American History, Smithsonian Institution, Washington, D.C.

110. Lillian Smith, *Killers*, 27; Lumpkin, *Making*, 99–147.

111. Lillian Smith, *Killers*, 29.

112. Leona Clark Williams interview; Waters interview; Cole interview.

113. Leona Clark Williams interview.

114. Waters interview.

115. Cole interview.

116. Wilson, interview by Kelley.

117. Blackstock interview.

118. Reed interview.

119. Mary Ellen Simpson Allgood, interview by Barbara M. Wiley, July 20, 1984, Cobb County Oral History Series, KSU.

120. Dorothy Oliver Rucker, telephone interview by author, Gainesville, Ga., July 14, 1995.

121. Rucker, Bailey, and Stephens interview.

122. Clara Belle McCrary, letter to author, June 18, 1994; Stephens interview; Wagner, *Profiles*, 48–67, 82–86.

123. Rucker and Bailey interview.

124. Leona Clark Williams interview.

125. Waters interview.

126. Leona Clark Williams interview.

127. Waters interview.

128. Leona Clark Williams, *We Remember*, 179.

129. Numerous examples of hearing God's call to action exist in African American narratives; see Molly Kensey, interview by Geneva Tonsill, December 1, 1939, WPA Collection.

130. Waters interview; Buice interview; Still and Murphy interview.

3 · Holding the Torch

1. Leona Clark Williams, interview by author, Buford, Ga., June 13, 24, 1991; Leona Clark Williams, *We Remember*, 24–26; Dorothy Oliver Rucker and Carrie Oliver Bailey, interview by author, May 6, 19, Gainesville, Ga., September 14, 1993.

2. Leloudis, *Schooling*, 1–36; Stephanie J. Shaw, *What a Woman Ought to Be*, 68–103.

3. Susie Weems Wheeler, interview by author, Cartersville, Ga., August 3, 2002; "Georgia—Monthly Report of Rosenwald Building Agent for Month of July 1931," Division of Negro Education Records, RG 12–6-62, box 1, folder "Vincent Harris Reports," GDAH.

4. In some areas, white moderates contributed to building projects for what became known as Rosenwald schools. For example, in Cartersville, Acworth, Jackson County, Hall County, and Hancock County, some whites raised between two hundred and a thousand dollars for black schools ("Rural School Program Negro Schools Georgia, 1921–34," box 337, folder 10, JRF Archives; Schultz, "Unsolid South," chap. 5; Wheeler, interview by author).

5. Orr, *History*, 280–83; Joiner, *History*, 194–99, 234–36, 281–83, 334–57.

6. Gilmore, *Gender and Jim Crow*, chap. 3.

7. Orr, *History*, 344–55; Joiner, *History*, 117–30; see also Dyer, *University of Georgia*; McCandless, *Past in the Present*.

8. Orr, *History*, 349; Joiner, *History*, chap. 2; Bartley, *Creation*, chap. 4; James D. Anderson, *Education*.

9. Orr, *History*, 353.

10. E. C. Branson, "Scholarships State Normal School," n.d., ser. 1.1, box 48, folder 431, GEB Papers. North Carolina and Virginia experienced similar problems; see Leloudis, *Schooling*; Link, *Hard Country*.

11. E. C. Branson to Wallace Buttrick, August 11, 1903, ser. 1.1, box 48, folder 431, GEB Papers.

12. Orr, *History*, 243–45; Joiner, *History*, chap. 2.

13. Orr, *History*, 252–53.

14. Dyer, *University of Georgia*, chaps. 6, 7.

15. Orr, *History*, 260–61; Bartley, *Creation*, chap. 7; Joiner, *History*, chap. 3.

16. The county unit system was used throughout the South and remained unchallenged until the U.S. Supreme Court's March 1962 *Baker v. Carr* decision, which dramatically altered southern politics; see Jimmy Carter, *Turning Point*, xxii–xxiii, 9–12; Bartley, *Creation*, 161.

17. Georgia Department of Education, *Thirty-ninth Annual Report*, 25–27.

18. Ruth Smith Waters, interview by author, Flowery Branch, Ga., June 28, 1991, June 10, December 7, 1993.

19. "Biography and Genealogy," box 1, folder 1, Walter B. Hill Papers, UGA.

20. Ibid.; Dennis, *Lessons*, 118–19.

21. "Biography and Genealogy," box 1, folder 1; box 18, folder "Letters July 11–15, 1905"; box 22, folders 1–3, Hill Papers; see also Dyer, *University of Georgia*, chap. 7.

22. Dennis, *Lessons*, chap. 5.

23. Box 22, folder 3, "November 1907," Hill Papers.

24. "Report of the Year's Progress of School Improvement Associations and Leagues

in the Southern States, December 28, 1909," box 22, folder 12, "December 1909," Hill Papers.

25. Ibid.

26. Georgia Department of Education, *Thirty-ninth Annual Report*, 25, 26.

27. Georgia Department of Education, *Forty-fourth Annual Report*, 7–8.

28. Dennis, *Lessons*, 127.

29. Orr, *History*, 263.

30. For more on the language of Progressivism, see Wiebe, *Search*; Rodgers, "In Search"; Grantham, *Southern Progressivism*; Link, *Paradox*; Woodward, *Origins*; for the bureaucratization of education, see Tyack, *One Best System*; Cremin, *Transformation*.

31. Orr, *History*, chap. 11; Joiner, *History*, chaps. 2, 3; Bartley, *Creation*, chap. 7; for how teachers were chosen in other southern states, see Leloudis, *Schooling*, chaps. 1, 4; Link, *Hard Country*; Link, *Paradox*, chap. 5; Woodward, *Origins*.

32. Joseph S. Stewart to Wallace Buttrick, December 28, 1903, ser. 1.1, box 55, folder 492, GEB Papers; see also Annie Mae Horne to E. C. Branson, July 28, 1903, ser. 1.1, box 48, folder 431, GEB Papers.

33. George Godard to Wallace Buttrick, December 9, 1914, ser. 1.1, box 68, folder 596, GEB Papers.

34. George Foster Peabody to Wickliffe Rose, June 25, 1925, ser. 1.1, box 55, folder 494, GEB Papers; see also T. J. Woofter to Frank Bachman, September 30, 1925, ser. 1.1, box 55, folder 494, GEB Papers.

35. Corra Mae White Harris, "Education," box 76, folder 3, Corra Mae White Harris Papers, UGA.

36. "Another Challenge to Georgia Baptists," *Christian Index*, January 14, 1915, 2, SBCHLA.

37. W. H. Faust, "The Supreme Work of the Church Today," *Christian Index*, January 21, 1915, 5, SBCHLA.

38. Joseph Stewart to Wallace Buttrick, August 28, 1906, ser. 1.1, box 56, folder 502, GEB Papers.

39. Joseph Stewart, "Relation of the Church to the Secondary School, Conference on Education of the Methodist Church South," April 7, 1911, ser. 1.1, box 57, folder 509, GEB Papers.

40. Georgia Department of Education, *Thirty-ninth Annual Report*, 17–18, 15–16.

41. M. L. Brittain, "The Rural School Awakening," *World's Work*, November 1903, 41, 45–46, UGA.

42. Correspondence between M. L. Brittain and Abraham Flexner, July–August 1914, ser. 1.1, box 69, folder 601, GEB Papers; correspondence and reports of rural school agent George Godard to Abraham Flexner, 1913–15, ser. 1.1, box 67, folder 591, GEB Papers.

43. George D. Godard to Wallace Buttrick, April 1, 1914, ser. 1.1, box 67, folder 591, GEB Papers. For more on industrial training as a hierarchical means to educate

students, see Cremin, *Transformation*; Tyack, *One Best System*; Butchart, "'Outthinking'"; James D. Anderson, *Education*; Leloudis, "'More Certain Means'"; Link, *Hard Country*; Link, *Paradox*; Ayers, *Promise*; Woodward, *Origins*; Grantham, *Southern Progressivism*.

44. Orr, *History*, chaps. 10–13.

45. Joiner, *History*, 193; Orr, *History*, 270–72.

46. Orr, *History*, 280; Joiner, *History*, 194.

47. Frank Bachman to Abraham Flexner, March 1, 1924, ser. 1.1, box 313, folder 3264, GEB Papers.

48. George Godard to Wallace Buttrick, December 24, 1913, ser. 1.1, box 67, folder 591, GEB Papers.

49. McCandless, *Past in the Present*, chap. 2.

50. Waters interview.

51. Martha Breedlove Buice, interview by author, Buford, Ga., June 20, 1991.

52. *Georgia State Teachers College Bulletin*, 1930, 19, UGA.

53. *University of Georgia Bulletin*, 1913–14, 14, UGA.

54. Buice interview.

55. Waters interview.

56. Mary Hall Swain, interview by H. G. Pennington, April 27, 1979, Kennesaw College Oral History Series, KSU.

57. Fanny B. McClure, interview by Thomas A. Scott, March 21, 2000, Cobb County Oral History Series, KSU.

58. Orr, *History*, 265–67; Joiner, *History*, 162–65.

59. Waters interview.

60. Ibid.

61. Jane Thigpen Alexander, interview by author, Lawrenceville, Ga., June 18, 1991.

62. Ibid.

63. Leona Clark Williams interview.

64. Woofter, *Teaching*, 26–30.

65. Georgia Department of Education, *Thirty-ninth Annual Report*, 48–56.

66. James D. Anderson, *Education*; see also Butchart, "'Outthinking'"; Bond, *Education*; Woodson, *Mis-Education*; Harlan, *Separate and Unequal*.

67. James D. Anderson, *Education*; see also Butchart, "'Outthinking'"; Bond, *Education*; Woodson, *Mis-Education*; Harlan, *Separate and Unequal*.

68. The African Methodist Episcopal Church founded the Agricultural and Mechanical School in Forsyth in 1902. In 1916, the school became known as State Teachers and Agricultural High School. In 1931, it received yet another moniker, State Teachers and Agricultural College. Finally, in 1939, the school merged with Fort Valley State College with the assistance of a grant from the Rosenwald Fund.

69. Georgia Department of Education, *Forty-ninth Annual Report*, 49–87. The General Education Board funded these programs; see James D. Anderson, *Education*.

70. Richardson, *Christian Reconstruction*; Stephanie J. Shaw, *What a Woman Ought to Be*, 71–78.

71. Bacote, *Story*, 75, 76, 90, chap. 3.

72. Clyde W. Hall, *One Hundred Years*, 20.

73. Haynes, *Black Boy*, chap. 4; Elmore, *Richard R. Wright*, chap. 2; Clyde W. Hall, *One Hundred Years*.

74. Haynes, *Black Boy*, chap. 4; Elmore, *Richard R. Wright*, chap. 2; James D. Anderson, *Education*, 122–23.

75. Box 7, folder 3, "July 11–31, 1896 Clippings," Hill Papers.

76. Box 33, folder 3, "Notes on Negro Problem," Hill Papers.

77. Dennis, *Lessons*, 17. The Blair Bill allocated funds based on the percentage of illiteracy in each state. Southern states would have benefited more than any other region, but southern congressmen opposed the bill because it provided funds for liberal arts education for African Americans.

78. Leroy Davis, *Clashing*, chaps. 5–6; Torrence, *Story*, chaps. 9, 11; Rouse, *Lugenia Burns Hope*; Lasch-Quinn, *Black Neighbors*.

79. "Land Grant Colleges Folders—Fort Valley, Georgia," Office of Historical Resources, National Museum of American History, Smithsonian Institution, Washington, D.C.

80. James D. Anderson, *Education*, 124–25.

81. H. A. Hunt to George Foster Peabody, April 12, 1904, ser. 1.1, box 45, folder 400, "Fort Valley State College 1903," GEB Papers.

82. Mary E. Frederickson, "'Each One.'"

83. Wagner, *Profiles*, 64.

84. Clyde W. Hall, *One Hundred Years*, 9, 22.

85. Harlan, *Separate and Unequal*, chap. 7.

86. "Statistical Reports on Rural School Construction Program," box 331, folder 2, JRF Archives; James D. Anderson, *Education*, 153–85; Litwack, *Trouble in Mind*, chap. 2; Dittmer, *Black Georgia*, 141–62.

87. Georgia Department of Education, *Forty-ninth Annual Report*, 87.

88. M. L. Brittain to Wallace Buttrick, May 5, 1913, ser. 1.1, box 67, folder 585, GEB Papers.

89. George D. Godard to M. L. Brittain, June 13, 1913, ser. 1.1, box 67, folder 585, GEB Papers.

90. George D. Godard to Wallace Buttrick, December 23, 1913, October 20, 1913, ser. 1.1, box 67, folder 585, GEB Papers.

91. George D. Godard to Wallace Buttrick, October 20, 1913, December 20, 1913, ser. 1.1, box 67, folder 585, GEB Papers; George D. Godard to Wallace Buttrick, December 24, 1913, ser. 1.1, box 67, folder 591, GEB Papers.

92. See Godard correspondence and reports, ser. 1.1, box 67, folder 591, GEB Papers.

93. Georgia Department of Education, *Thirty-ninth Annual Report;* Georgia Department of Education, *Forty-ninth Annual Report.*

94. For more on early-twentieth-century industrial training, see Cremin, *Transformation;* James D. Anderson, *Education;* Tyack, *One Best System.*

95. M. L. Brittain, untitled paper on Negro education, ca. 1913, ser. 1.1, box 67, folder 585, GEB Papers.

96. George D. Godard to Abraham Flexner, July 1915, ser. 1.1, box 67, folder 591, GEB Papers. Additional reports from Godard to Flexner reiterate these considerations.

97. Georgia Department of Education, *Forty-sixth Annual Report,* 34; see also Georgia Department of Education, *Thirty-ninth Annual Report,* 25–27.

98. Georgia Department of Education, *Forty-ninth Annual Report,* 36; see also reports from George D. Godard, January 1915, April 30, 1914, ser. 1.1, box 67, folder 591, GEB Papers.

99. George D. Godard to Wallace Buttrick, December 13, 1913, ser. 1.1, box 67, folder 591, GEB Papers. Similar statements from Godard are in the same folder in other correspondence.

100. "Notes on Negro Problem" and "Uncle Tom without a Cabin," 12–15, box 33, folder 3, Hill Papers.

101. Georgia Department of Education, *Forty-ninth Annual Report,* 36–44.

102. "Annual Report of George D. Godard to Dr. Abraham Flexner, May 19, 1915," 2, ser. 1.1, box 67, folder 591, GEB Papers; see also "To the County School Superintendent from George Godard," September 15, 1917, ser. 1.1, box 67, folder 591, GEB Papers.

103. George D. Godard to Wallace Buttrick, June 1, 1914, ser. 1.1, box 67, folder 591, GEB Papers; George D. Godard to M. L. Brittain, "March Report, 1917," ser. 1.1, box 67, folder 592, GEB Papers. Godard later contended that blacks did not migrate because of poor Georgia schools (George D. Godard to Abraham Flexner, September 17, 1917, ser. 1.1, box 67, folder 592, GEB Papers).

104. Walter B. Hill Jr. to General Education Board, May 25, 1923, ser. 1.2, box 275, folder 2861, GEB Papers; see also Fisk University Report to General Education Board, May 25, 1923, ser. 1.2, box 275, folder 2861, GEB Papers.

105. Walter B. Hill Jr., "Progress in Negro Education," in *Home, School, and Community,* 8, ser. 1.1, box 68, folder 593, GEB Papers.

106. Ibid.; see also Jackson Davis, "Recent Developments in Negro Schools and Colleges," May 25, 1927, 6, ser. 1.2, box 315, folder 3296, GEB Papers.

107. "Conference of State Agents for Negro Schools Held at Hampton Institute, Hampton, Virginia, May 6–9, 1923," box 88, folder 4, JRF Archives; for additional comments from Hill on black education, see "Discussion of Rosenwald Schools at Conference of State Agents," Nashville, Tenn., January 5, 6, 1921, and "Conference of State Agents of Rural Schools for Negroes," June 4, 5, 1929, Atlantic City, N.J., box 88, folder 4, JRF Archives.

108. U.S. Department of Commerce, Bureau of the Census, *Fourteenth Census*, vol. 3, *Composition and Characteristics of the Population by States*, 213; Jackson Davis, "State Normal Schools and Agricultural and Mechanical Colleges for Negroes 1912–1922," September 1924, 10–11, ser. 1.2, box 313, folder 3267, GEB Papers; see also "General Education Board Negro Education Meeting," November 17, 1927, 22–25, ser. 1.2, box 315, folder 3295, GEB Papers; Leo M. Favrot, "Negro Public Education in the South," 1927, 3–10, ser. 1.2, box 315, folder 3297, GEB Papers; McCuistion, *Higher Education*, 1–18.

109. Orr, *History*, 327; Clyde W. Hall, *One Hundred Years*, 22.

110. Georgia Association, *Jeanes Supervision*, 33–35.

111. Clyde W. Hall, *One Hundred Years*, 29–31; Georgia State Department of Education, "The Hill Affair," September 5, 1924, box 337, folder 10, JRF Archives; see also Walter B. Hill Jr. to Jackson Davis, March 24, 1924, ser. 1.1, box 67, folder 587, Jackson Davis to H. J. Thorkelson, March 19, 1924, ser. 1.1, box 67, folder 587, Jackson Davis, "State Normal Schools and Agricultural and Mechanical Colleges for Negroes 1912–1922," September 1924, 10–11, ser. 1.2, box 313, folder 3267, GEB Papers.

112. Mary Hill Brown to Parna Hill, June 1, 1924, box 26, folder 1, "Letters January–June 1924," Hill Papers.

113. Clyde W. Hall, *One Hundred Years*, 30.

114. Jackson Davis to H. J. Thorkelson, March 19, 1924, Jackson Davis to W. W. Brierly, June 23, 1925, ser. 1.1, box 67, folder 587, GEB Papers.

115. Rucker and Bailey interview.

116. Rosa Penson Anderson, interview by author, Fayetteville, Ga., March 24, 1992.

117. Haynes, *Black Boy*, 73–76.

118. Bacote, *Story*, chap. 9.

119. George D. Godard to Wallace Buttrick, April 30, 1914, ser. 1.1, box 67, folder 591, GEB Papers.

120. Clyde W. Hall, *One Hundred Years*, 8; Donaldson, "New Negroes," chap. 4; Williams-May, "Lucy Craft Laney," chap. 7.

121. Chirhart, "Gardens"; Littlefield, "Moving Quietly"; Berkeley, "Sage."

122. Laura Mosley Whelchel, interview by author, Gainesville, Ga., June 18, 1993.

123. See George D. Godard reports, ser. 1.1, box 67, folder 591, GEB Papers.

124. See, for example, James D. Anderson's discussion of the institute at Ben Hill in *Education*, chap. 4.

125. George D. Godard to M. L. Brittain, February 1916, ser. 1.1, box 67, folder 591, GEB Papers.

126. Sealander, *Private Wealth*, chaps. 3, 4.

127. J. Douglas Smith, *Managing*, chap. 2; Jacquelyn Dowd Hall, *Revolt*.

128. Daryl Michael Scott, *Contempt and Pity*, chap. 1.

129. S. L. Smith, "A Decade of Progress in Schoolhouse Construction: Fifteen Southern States, 1920–1930," October 14, 1931, box 331, folder 2, JRF Archives.

130. Outlaw, "State Normal School," chap. 1.

131. Georgia Department of Education, *Fifty-fourth and Fifty-fifth Annual Reports*, 93.

132. "Reorganization Follows Georgia Survey," October 15, 1939, ser. 1.1, box 69, folder 610, T. J. Woofter to Frank Bachman, September 30, 1925, ser. 1.1, box 55, folder 491, GEB Papers; see also Orr, *History*, chap. 11; Joiner, *History*, chap. 3.

133. T. J. Woofter to Frank Bachman, September 30, 1925, ser. 1.1, box 55, folder 491, GEB Papers.

134. "General Education Board Negro Education Meeting," November 17, 1927, ser. 1.2, box 315, folder 3295, GEB Papers.

135. J. C. Dixon to Fred McCuistion, December 2, 1931, box 204, folder 1, JRF Archives.

136. Robert Cousins to Jackson Davis, March 15, 1941, ser. 1.1, box 67, folder 590, GEB Papers; see also Walter B. Hill Jr. to Philip Weltner, August 25, 1933, Department of Education Records, RG 33-1-51, box 44, GDAH.

137. Robert Cousins to General Education Board, 1937, 3, ser. 1.1, box 67, folder 589, GEB Papers.

138. Leona Clark Williams interview.

139. Leloudis, *Schooling*, chap. 6.

4 · Carrying the Torch

1. Dorothy Oliver Rucker and Carrie Oliver Bailey, interview by author, Gainesville, Ga., May 6, 19, September 14, 1993.

2. Leona Clark Williams, interview by author, Buford, Ga., June 13, 24, 1991.

3. Gilmore, *Gender and Jim Crow*; Harlan, *Separate and Unequal*; Leloudis, *Schooling*; Link, *Paradox*; Ayers, *Promise*; White, *Too Heavy a Load*; Terborg-Penn, *African-American Women*; Hine, "Black Professionals"; Morton, *Disfigured Images*; Elna C. Green, *Southern Strategies*; Elizabeth Hayes Turner, *Women*.

4. Elsa Barkley Brown, "Negotiating"; Stephanie J. Shaw, "Black Club Women."

5. Hale, *Making Whiteness*.

6. Lines, *To Raise Myself*.

7. Gilmore, *Gender and Jim Crow*; Stephanie J. Shaw, *What a Woman Ought to Be*; White, *Too Heavy a Load*; Terborg-Penn, *African-American Women*; Kelley, "'We Are Not What We Seem'"; Elsa Barkley Brown, "Negotiating."

8. Hine, "Black Professionals."

9. Muncy, *Creating*; Sklar, "Hull House"; Linda Gordon, *Heroes*; Walkowitz, "Making"; Rosenberg, *Beyond Separate Spheres*.

10. Bledstein, *Culture*; Blumin, *Emergence*; Rodgers, "In Search."

11. Melosh, *"Physician's Hand"*; Muncy, *Creating*; Hine, *Black Women*; Giddings, *When and Where*; Rosenberg, *Beyond Separate Spheres*; Reverby, *Ordered*; see also Blumin, *Emergence*.

12. Cobb, *Redefining.*

13. Stephanie J. Shaw, "Black Club Women"; Stephanie J. Shaw, *What a Woman Ought to Be*; Hine, *Black Women*; Neverdon-Morton, *Afro-American Women*; Rouse, *Lugenia Burns Hope*; Giddings, *When and Where.*

14. Gilmore, *Gender and Jim Crow,* 148.

15. Ryan, *Women,* chap. 2.

16. Wheeler, *New Women*; Gilmore, *Gender and Jim Crow*; Case, "Historical Ideology"; Elizabeth Gillespie McRae, "Caretakers"; Bartley, *Creation.*

17. Donaldson, "New Negroes"; White, *Too Heavy a Load*; Stephanie J. Shaw, *What a Woman Ought to Be*; Leloudis, *Schooling.*

18. Kessler-Harris, *Out to Work.*

19. Sklar, *Catharine Beecher*; Leloudis, *Schooling.*

20. Dean, "College Women"; Jane Hunter, *Gospel*; Leloudis, "School Reform"; Chirhart, "Gardens"; see also Solomon, *In the Company.*

21. Marsden, *Fundamentalism and American Culture,* 11–21; see also Mathews, *Religion*; William E. Montgomery, *Under Their Own Vine*; Higginbotham, *Righteous Discontent*; Dean, "College Women"; Leloudis, *Schooling*; Pope, *Millhands.* For examples of the links between southern Protestantism and work, see Jacquelyn Dowd Hall et al., *Like a Family*; Tullos, *Habits*; Mary E. Frederickson, "'Each One.'"

22. Marsden, *Fundamentalism and American Culture,* 55–62, 102–8; see also William E. Montgomery, *Under Their Own Vine*; Woodson, *History*; Frazier, *Negro Church*; Mathews, *Religion*; Genovese, *Roll, Jordan, Roll.*

23. Sklar, *Catharine Beecher*; Chambers-Schiller, *Liberty*; Katz, *Irony*; Tyack, *One Best System.*

24. Bourdieu, *Distinction*; Raymond Williams, *Marxism*; Fox-Genovese, *Feminism*; Fox-Genovese, "Women and Agriculture"; Gilmore, *Gender and Jim Crow,* chap. 6.

25. Rouse, *Lugenia Burns Hope*; Polansky, "'I Certainly Hope.'"

26. Barbara Jeanne Fields, "Ideology and Race"; Dailey, Gilmore, and Simon, *Jumpin' Jim Crow.*

27. Laura Mosley Whelchel, interview by author, Gainesville, Ga., June 18, 1993.

28. Narvie J. Harris and Taylor, *African-American Education,* 14.

29. Whelchel interview.

30. Higginbotham, *Righteous Discontent*; Elsa Barkley Brown, "Negotiating"; Stephanie J. Shaw, *What a Woman Ought to Be.*

31. White, *Too Heavy a Load,* 57, 24, 63.

32. Ibid., chap. 2; Gaines, *Uplifting,* chap. 5; Donaldson, "New Negroes," chap. 4.

33. White, *Too Heavy a Load,* 67.

34. Lucy Craft Laney, "The Burden of the Educated Colored Woman," *Southern Workman* 28 (September 1899): 341–44.

35. McCluskey, "'Most Sacrificing Service,'" 194; Leslie, "No Middle Ground," 128–29; Williams-May, "Lucy Craft Laney," 167–69; Donaldson, "New Negroes," chap. 4.

36. Rouse, *Lugenia Burns Hope*, chap. 4; Donaldson, "New Negroes," chap. 4; Leslie, "No Middle Ground"; McCluskey, "'Most Sacrificing Service.'"

37. Susie Weems Wheeler, interview by author, Cartersville, Ga., August 3, 2002.

38. Rucker and Bailey interview. On the curriculum at the Haines Institute, see Williams-May, "Lucy Craft Laney"; Donaldson, "New Negroes," chap. 4; Clyde W. Hall, *One Hundred Years*.

39. Whelchel interview.

40. Rucker and Bailey interview; Williams-May, "Lucy Craft Laney"; Donaldson, "New Negroes," chap. 4; Wheeler, interview by author.

41. Wheeler, interview by author.

42. Narvie Jordan Harris, interview by author, Atlanta, Ga., September 27, 2003; Narvie J. Harris and Taylor, *African-American Education*, 12–14.

43. Gilmore, *Gender and Jim Crow*, chap. 7; Charlotte Hawkins Brown, *Correct Thing*.

44. Rucker and Bailey interview.

45. Stephanie J. Shaw, *What a Woman Ought to Be*, chaps. 3, 4; Leloudis, *Schooling*; Gilmore, *Gender and Jim Crow*.

46. Gilmore, *Gender and Jim Crow*, 186.

47. White, *Too Heavy a Load*, chap. 2; Donaldson, "New Negroes," chap. 4; Litwack, *Trouble in Mind*. In Hall County, Rucker seems to have encountered more opposition from the black middle class than from the working class, perhaps because she was dark skinned and practiced shouting and call-and-response in her church.

48. L. C. Teasley Sr., interview by author, Gainesville, Ga., June 8, 1994.

49. For other black women, see Rouse, *Lugenia Burns Hope*; Littlefield, "Moving Quietly"; Berkeley, "Sage."

50. Nancy Stephens, interview by author, Gainesville, Ga., June 8, 1993.

51. Wheeler, interview by author; Clyde W. Hall, *One Hundred Years*, chap. 2.

52. Rucker and Bailey interview; Williams-May, "Lucy Craft Laney"; Donaldson, "New Negroes," chap. 4.

53. Rucker and Bailey interview; see also Williams-May, "Lucy Craft Laney"; Gilmore, *Gender and Jim Crow*, chap. 6; Stephanie J. Shaw, *What a Woman Ought to Be*.

54. Rucker and Bailey interview; Whelchel interview; Teasley interview; Cleophus Allgood, telephone interview by author, Fort Valley, Ga., February, 14, 1995; Trummi Evans, interview by author, Gainesville, Ga., February 16, 1995.

55. Teasley interview.

56. Christine Rucker, interview by author, Gainesville, Ga., June 12, 1994.

57. Litwack, *Trouble in Mind*, 68.

58. Stephanie J. Shaw, *What a Woman Ought to Be*, chap. 4; Hine, *Black Women*.

59. Allgood interview.

60. Donaldson, "New Negroes," chaps. 1, 4; Williams-May, "Lucy Craft Laney," 189–215; McCluskey, "'Most Sacrificing Service.'"

61. Haynes, *Black Boy*, chap. 4; Georgia Teachers and Education Association, *Rising*, 23–25.

62. *Atlanta Independent*, June 16, 1913, 41.

63. Georgia Teachers and Education Association, *Rising*, 26.

64. Grant, *Way It Was*, 311–13.

65. Tuck, *Beyond Atlanta*, chap. 1; Mason, *African-American Life*, 31. Tuck and Mason state that United Negro Improvement Association's membership consisted primarily of black tenant farmers; see also Hahn, *Nation*, 468–73.

66. Georgia Teachers and Education Association, *Rising*, 45.

67. Eugene S. Williams, "Report from Georgia State Industrial College, Savannah," June 4, 1916, USDA Records, reel 1, 1909–16 (Floyd County).

68. "Home Demonstration Work in Georgia—1917," USDA Records, reel 2, Extension Service Annual Reports, Georgia, 1909–1944, 1916 (Gordon County)—Director 1918.

69. Haynes, *Black Boy*, chap. 4; Clyde W. Hall, *One Hundred Years*, 12–13.

70. Clyde W. Hall, *One Hundred Years*, 34.

71. "1919 Extension Service Annual Report," USDA Records, reel 3, Extension Service Annual Reports, Georgia, 1909–1944, 1918 (Home Demonstration Leader)—1920 (Veterinary).

72. Georgia Association, *Jeanes Supervision*, chap. 2.

73. Ibid.

74. "Hall County Home Demonstration Agent Report, 1921," USDA Records, reel 7, 1921 (Cobb-Johnson Counties).

75. Clyde W. Hall, *One Hundred Years*, 39.

76. P. H. Stone, "Annual Narrative Report, Negro Work, December 1, 1927–December 1, 1928," USDA Records, reel 30, 1927, Troup County—1928 State Club Leader; Camilla Weems, "Home Demonstration Annual Report—Negro Demonstration Work," reel 64 (1934 Horticulture—Carroll County), USDA Records.

77. Lu Ann Jones, *Mama*, 140; see also Melissa Walker, *All We Knew*.

78. Stephanie J. Shaw, *What a Woman Ought to Be*.

79. Allgood interview.

80. Woodson, *Mis-Education*; Tyack, *One Best System*.

81. See also Kelley, "'We Are Not What We Seem'"; Neverdon-Morton, *Afro-American Women*; Giddings, *When and Where*; Stephanie J. Shaw, *What a Woman Ought to Be*.

82. Neverdon-Morton, *Afro-American Women*, chap. 4; Rouse, *Lugenia Burns Hope*; Giddings, *When and Where*, pt. 2; Stephanie J. Shaw, *What a Woman Ought to Be*, chaps. 4–6; Berkeley, "Sage."

83. Littlefield, "Moving Quietly"; Berkeley, "Sage"; Leloudis, *Schooling*; James D. Anderson, *Education*; Stephanie J. Shaw, *What a Woman Ought to Be*.

84. *Georgia State College for Women Bulletin*, 1929, 44, 1939–40, 25, Georgia Room, University of Georgia Libraries, Athens.

85. Moina Belle Michael, Federal Writers' Project, 1936–40, Life Histories, February 8–9, 1939, WPA Collection.

86. Katherine Dozier to Wickliffe Rose, February 1, 1926, ser. 1.1, box 55, folder 495, GEB Papers; Emory Wells, interview by author, Savannah, Ga., June 30, 1994; Florrie Still and Nelle Still Murphy, interview by author, Gainesville, Ga., May 9, 1997.

87. Wells interview.

88. Katherine Dozier, "Curriculum Making in Elementary Grades," *Georgia Education Journal* 20 (January 1928): 9–14.

89. Atkins, "Philanthropy."

90. Case, "Historical Ideology."

91. Ruth Smith Waters, interview by author, Flowery Branch, Ga., June 28, 1991, June 10, December 7, 1993; Still and Murphy interview; Mary Hall Swain, interview by H. G. Pennington, April 27, 1979, Kennesaw College Oral History Series, KSU; Fanny B. McClure, interview by Thomas A. Scott, March 31, 2000, Cobb County Oral History Series, KSU.

92. Leona Clark Williams interview; Waters interview.

93. For the propensity of members of the southern labor force to remain in the same region, see Wright, *Old South*; Kirby, *Rural Worlds*; Daniel, *Standing*; see also Rosengarten, *All God's Dangers*.

94. Leona Clark Williams interview; Waters interview.

95. Jacquelyn Dowd Hall, "O. Delight Smith's Progressive Era"; Polansky, "'I Certainly Hope.'"

96. Leona Clark Williams interview; Waters interview.

97. Waters interview. For examples of dating and other leisure activities, see Tullos, *Habits*, chap. 6; Jacquelyn Dowd Hall et al., *Like a Family*, chap. 5.

98. McClure interview; Leona Clark Williams interview; Still and Murphy interview.

99. Leona Clark Williams interview.

100. Waters interview.

101. Brittain, *Manual*; Woofter, *Teaching*; Leona Clark Williams interview; McClure interview; Cole interview; Waters interview.

102. Leona Clark Williams interview.

103. On the relationship between Sunday school and education, see Boylan, *Sunday School*.

104. Waters interview.

105. Hagood, *Mothers*; Jacquelyn Dowd Hall et al., *Like a Family*; Tullos, *Habits*; Deborah Fink, *Agrarian Women*; Keith, *Country People*; Sharpless, *Fertile Ground*; Melissa Walker, *All We Knew*.

106. Jimmie Kate Sams Cole, interview by author, Fayetteville, Ga., October 6, 1989; Leona Clark Williams interview; Swain interview.

107. Thomas Early to J. Phil Campbell, October 24, 1910, USDA Records, reel 1, Extension Service Annual Reports, Georgia, 1909–44, 1910–16 (Floyd County); Extension Service Annual Reports, 1919, USDA Records, reel 3, Extension Service An-

nual Reports, Georgia 1909–44, 1918 (Home Demonstration Leader)–1920 (Veterinary).

108. "Home Demonstration Work in Georgia—1917," USDA Records, reel 2, Extension Service Annual Reports, Georgia, 1909–1944, 1916 (Gordon County)—Director 1918.

109. Lu Ann Jones, *Mama*, chaps. 3, 4; Walker, *All We Knew*, chap. 4.

110. Walker, *All We Knew*, 103.

111. "Jackson County, 1919, Lurline Collier" [annual report of home demonstration work], USDA Records, reel 3.

112. Laura Blackshear, "Showing the Way" [annual narrative report for Georgia], 1925 USDA Records, reel 19, 1924 (Wilcox County)–1925 (Chatham County).

113. As stated, Laura cuts her long hair and shortens her skirts, but these changes bore little resemblance to the notorious bobbed hair and above-the-knee skirts that were fashionable for flappers in the 1920s and which many Georgians found scandalous. Laura's hair remained below her ears, without all the curls, and her skirts were perhaps four to six inches above her ankles—modern yet not as glamorous as Hollywood star Gloria Swanson or writer Zelda Fitzgerald. Nationally, the shortest hair and highest hemlines appeared in 1926; hemlines subsequently lowered, again reaching midcalf in 1930.

114. Laura Blackshear, "Showing the Way" [annual narrative report for Georgia], 1925, USDA Records, reel 19, 1924 (Wilcox County)–1925 (Chatham County).

115. Blanche Whelchell, "Report of Home Demonstration Agent, Hall County," 1925, USDA Records, reel 20, Chatham County–Houston County.

116. Brittain, *Manual*, 7.

117. Woofter, *Teaching*, chap. 7.

118. Douglas G. McRae, "Georgia Education Association," esp. 16; Georgia Teachers and Education Association, *Rising*, 22.

119. Georgia Department of Education, *Thirty-ninth Annual Report*, 9–10.

120. Georgia Department of Education, *Forty-sixth Annual Report*, 8–9.

121. Georgia Department of Education, *Forty-ninth Annual Report*, 17–18.

122. Georgia Department of Education, *Fifty-eighth and Fifty-ninth Annual Reports*, 6–8.

123. Georgia Department of Education, *Sixtieth and Sixty-first Annual Reports*, 19–20.

124. H. A. Hunt to George Foster Peabody, July 5, 1913, H. A. Hunt to GEB, October 19, 1917, ser. 1.1, box 45, folder 402, GEB Papers.

125. Frank Bachman to Abraham Flexner, March 1, 1924, ser 1.2, box 313, folder 3264, GEB Papers; Tyack, *One Best System*; Tyack and Hansot, *Managers*; Cordier, *Schoolwomen*; Solomon, *In the Company*; Frank Bachman, "Memo re. Teacher Training in Southern State Universities," December 30, 1924, ser. 1.2, box 313, folder 3263, GEB Papers.

126. E. A. Pound to Frank Bachman, May 7, 1925, ser. 1.1, box 43, folder 380, GEB

Papers; Georgia Department of Education, *Fifty-fourth and Fifty-fifth Annual Reports*, 45–53, 93–100.

127. Jackson Davis, "State Normal Schools and Agricultural and Mechanical Colleges for Negroes, 1912–1922," 1924, ser. 1.2, box 313, folder 3267, GEB Papers.

128. T. J. Woofter to Frank Bachman, September 30, 1925, Harry Hodgson and David Barrow, "Statement Submitted by the Endowment Campaign Committee of the University of Georgia in Connection with Their Application to the General Education Board for a Gift to the Fund," n.d., 3–5, T. J. Woofter to Frank Bachman, November 8, 1928, ser. 1.1, box 55, folder 494, GEB Papers.

129. "General Education Board, Negro Education Meeting, November 17, 1927," ser. 1.2, box 315, folder 3295, GEB Papers; see also Leo Favrot, "Public Education—Negro, April 27, 1927," ser. 1.2, box 315, folder 3295, GEB Papers.

130. "Discussion of Rosenwald Schools at Conference of State Agents Assembled at Nashville, January 5 and 6, 1921," and "Conference of State Agents of Rural Schools for Negroes, June 4 and 5, 1929, Atlantic City, New Jersey," box 188, folder 4, JRF Archives; Leo M. Favrot, "Negro Public Education in the South," 1927, 3, ser. 1.2, box 315, folder 3297, GEB Papers; McCuistion, *Higher Education*, 18; see also Harlan, *Separate and Unequal*; Bartley, *Creation*; James D. Anderson, *Education*.

131. "Conference of State Agents of Rural Schools for Negroes, June 8 and 9, 1928, Signal Mountain, Tennessee," and "Conference of State Agents of Rural Schools for Negroes, June 4 and 5, 1929, Atlantic City, New Jersey," box 188, folder 4, JRF Archives.

132. J. C. Dixon to Fred McCuistion, December 2, 1931, box 204, folder 1, JRF Archives.

133. See correspondence to Edwin Embree, "Georgia University System 1937–1940," box 206, folder 3, JRF Archives; Jackson Davis and H. A. Hunt, "Interview, October 22, 1936," ser. 1.1, box 45, folder 407, GEB Papers; Leo Favrot to James Dillard, June 21, 1937, ser. 1.1, box 45, folder 407, GEB Papers; J. C. Dixon to Steadman Sanford, August 19, 1937, Department of Education Records, RG 33–1-51, box 52, "Julius Rosenwald Fund 1936–1938," GDAH.

134. Georgia Department of Education, *Sixtieth and Sixty-first Annual Reports*, 6; see also Walter Hill Jr. to S. L. Smith, March 16, 1929, box 337, folder 10, JRF Archives.

135. Ibid., 17–20.

136. Bartley, *Creation*; William Anderson, *Wild Man*.

5 · Passing the Torch

1. Oliver, *Rugged Pathway*, 11.

2. Leona Clark Williams, interview by author, Buford, Ga., June 13, 24, 1991; Leona Clark Williams, *We Remember*, 30–33.

3. Daniel, *Breaking*; Kirby, *Rural Worlds*; Simon, *Fabric*; Bartley, *Creation*; Cobb

and Namorato, *New Deal*; Ferguson, *Black Politics*; Korstad, *Civil Rights Unionism*; Tindall, *Emergence*; Brattain, *Politics*; Sullivan, *Days*.

4. Daniel, "Going."

5. For an analysis of the New Deal in Georgia, see Holmes, *New Deal*; Bartley, *Creation*, chaps. 7, 8; Corley, "National Youth Administration"; for general studies of the New Deal in the South, see Daniel, *Breaking*; Cobb, *Industrialization*; Cobb, *Selling*; Kirby, *Rural Worlds*; Biles, *South*; for the national impact of the New Deal, see Badger, *New Deal*; Leuchtenburg, *Franklin Delano Roosevelt*.

6. Daniel, "Going"; Kirby, *Rural Worlds*; Tindall, *Emergence*; Cobb and Namorato, *New Deal*; Bartley, *Creation*; Jacquelyn Dowd Hall et al., *Like a Family*; Simon, *Fabric*; Sullivan, *Days*; Bartley, *New South*.

7. Martin, *Brown*, 13.

8. For the mixed results of school reform, see Link, *Hard Country*; Leloudis, *Schooling*.

9. U.S. Department of Commerce, Bureau of the Census, *Fifteenth Census*, vol. 3, pt. 1, pp. 395, 83, 455, 1266.

10. Ibid., 459.

11. Ibid.; Leona Clark Williams interview; Ruth Smith Waters, interview by author, Flowery Branch, Ga., June 28, 1991, June 10, December 7, 1993; Dorothy Oliver Rucker and Carrie Oliver Bailey, interview by author, Gainesville, Ga., May 6, 19, September 14, 1993; Sanford Byers, interview by Lu Ann Jones, April 20, 1987, Gainesville, Ga., NMAH; Hattie Gaines Wilson, interview by Mary B. Cawley, Marietta, Ga., September 2, 1987, Cobb County Oral History Series, KSU; Hattie Gaines Wilson, interview by Kathryn Kelley, Marietta, Ga., August 2, 17, 1994, Cobb County Oral History Series, KSU; Cocking, *Report*; Georgia Fact-Finding Committee, "Georgia—Education," 2–3, box 203, folder 8, JRF Archives; Bartley, *Creation*, chaps. 6, 8; Georgia Department of Education, *Sixtieth and Sixty-first Annual Reports*, 113–203; "A History of the Georgia Civil Works Administration, 1933–34," 2–3, MSS 522, box 1, folder 1, Gay Bolling Shepperson Papers, Atlanta History Center, Atlanta.

12. Sanford Byers interview; Aubrey and Ina Belle Benton, interview by Lu Ann Jones, Commerce, Ga., April 28, 1987, NMAH; Mason, *African-American Life*, 26.

13. Georgia Department of Education, *Thirty-ninth Annual Report*, 443; Georgia Department of Education, *Sixtieth and Sixty-first Annual Reports*, 6; Leo M. Favrot, "Negro Public Education in the South," 1927, 3, ser. 1.2, box 315, folder 3297, GEB Papers; McCuistion, *Higher Education*, 18; "Average Annual Salaries of White and Negro Teachers, Principals, and Supervisors, 1933–34," Campaign for Educational Equality, 1913–50, ser. A, pt. 3, reel 3, NAACP microfilm; see also Harlan, *Separate and Unequal*; Bartley, *Creation*; James D. Anderson, *Education*.

14. Georgia Department of Education, *Sixtieth and Sixty-first Annual Reports*, 113–203.

15. "Average Annual Salaries of White and Negro Teachers, Principals, and Super-

visors, 1933–34," and "Inequalities in Expenditures for Public Schools," 3, Campaign for Educational Equality, 1913–50, ser. A, pt. 3, reel 3, NAACP microfilm; Georgia Department of Education, *Sixtieth and Sixty-first Annual Reports*, 6.

16. Lorena Hickok to Harry Hopkins, January 11, 1934, group 24, box 57, folder Georgia—Field Reports, Harry Hopkins Papers, Franklin Delano Roosevelt Library, Hyde Park, N.Y.

17. Lorena Hickok to Harry Hopkins, January 23, 1934, group 24, box 57, folder Georgia—Field Reports, Hopkins Papers.

18. Fairclough, "'Being'"; Leloudis, *Schooling*, 228; James D. Anderson, *Education*, 279–85.

19. "Report of Negro Home Demonstration Agent Camilla Weems," 1928, and Annual Report of Negro Agent P. H. Stone, 1928, reel 31, Georgia 1909–44, 1928 (County Agent Leader—Chatham County), USDA Records.

20. J. G. Oliver, "Annual Narrative Report for 1928," reel 31, Georgia 1909–44, 1928 (County Agent Leader—Chatham County), USDA Records; Tom and Velva Blackstock, interview by Lu Ann Jones, Talmo, Ga., April 22, 1987, NMAH; Sanford Byers interview; Ruby Byers, interview by Lu Ann Jones, Gainesville, Ga., April 23, 1987, NMAH.

21. Warren, "Progress," 74–83; Mrs. Moore, "How Many Days Have I Regretted . . . !" n.d., and Sadie Hornsby, "Life History of Ann Waldrop," January 12, 1939, 12, box 64, Works Progress Administration, Georgia Writers' Project Papers, UGA; Dykeman and Stokely, *Seeds*, 191–92; Molly Kensey, "I Got a Record," interview by Geneva Tonsill, December 1, 1939, and Mary Willingham, "I Ain't No Midwife," interview by Sadie Hornsby, March 14, May 29, 1939, WPA Collection; see also Stephanie J. Shaw, "Using the WPA Ex-Slave Narratives."

22. Mary Wright Hill, "Principal of Grammar School," interview by Sadie Hornsby, July 17, 1939, WPA Collection.

23. Leila Bramblett, interview by Sylvia Hornsby, June 17, 1938, WPA Collection; Ferguson, *Black Politics*, esp. 34; Narvie J. Harris and Taylor, *African-American Education*, 14; Narvie Jordan Harris, interview by author, Atlanta, September 27, 2002; Hine, "Black Professionals"; Stephanie J. Shaw, *What a Woman Ought to Be*.

24. Spurgeon L. Wellborn, interview by Lu Ann Jones, Jefferson, Ga., April 27, 1987, NMAH; Blanche Whelchell, report, Hall County, 1925, reel 20 (Chatham County–Houston County), USDA Records.

25. "The Club Girls' Own Room 16," December 1927, reel 30 (1927 Troup County–1928 State Club Leader, USDA Records.

26. "Clothing Program 19," August 1931, reel 45 (1930 Telfair County–1931 Director), USDA Records; Grace Adams, annual report, Hall County, 1944, reel 138 (1944 Greene–Oconee Counties), Leila Mize, "Marketing Miscellaneous Home Products 1939," reel 103 (1939 Home Improvement—Home Demonstration Leaders), USDA Records; Stephanie J. Shaw, "Using the WPA Ex-Slave Narratives"; "Annual Narrative

Report—Negro Home Demonstration Work," reel 64 (1934 Horticulture—Carroll County), USDA Records.

27. Mary Wright Hill, "Principal of Grammar School," interview by Sadie Hornsby, July 17, 1939, WPA Collection; Rucker and Bailey interview.

28. Georgia Department of Education, *Sixtieth and Sixty-first Annual Reports*, 24–69.

29. Citizens' Fact Finding Movement, "Religious, Civic, and Social Forces in Georgia," 1938, 3–6, box 203, folder 8, JRF Archives; Mixon, "Georgia," 300.

30. According to Baptist church minutes, Liberty Baptist Church was one of the last up-country congregations to stop disciplinary measures against congregants; see Still, *History and Memories*; see also Citizens' Fact Finding Movement, "Religious, Civic, and Social Forces in Georgia," 6, box 203, folder 8, JRF Archives; Doak Campbell, "Report of the Progress of the Study of the Southern Rural Schools of the South," January 3, 1939, 1–11, box 323, folder 11, JRF Archives.

31. E. Brooks Holifield, "Toward a History of American Congregations," in *American Congregations*, edited by Wind and Lewis, 23–53.

32. Mary E. Frederickson, "'Each One'"; Women's Missionary Union of the First Baptist Church, Gainesville, Ga., Records, 1900–1960, SBCHLA; Rucker and Bailey interview; Charters Smith Embry, interview by author, Gainesville, Ga., June 17, August 5, 1993.

33. Women's Missionary Union of the First Baptist Church, Gainesville, Ga., Records, 1900–1960, SBCHLA.

34. Embry interview.

35. Mixon, "Georgia," 300–302; for more on southern churchwomen, see Mary E. Frederickson, "'Each One.'"

36. J. C. Dixon to Walter Jones, May 9, 1932, box 3 "GTEA 1933–1939," ser. 012-06–071, Division of Negro Education Records, GDAH.

37. Ferguson, *Black Politics*, 54–56.

38. For an alternative interpretation, see Ferguson, *Black Politics*, 60.

39. Hine, "Black Professionals."

40. A. T. Walden to Robert Wagnall, March 22, 1932, "Membership Report Blank, February 1, 1932–March 1932," ser. A, pt. 12, reel 10, NAACP microfilm; Harris interview; Horace Tate, interview by author, Atlanta, June 21, 25, 29, July 23, August 2, 2002; Kari Frederickson, *Dixiecrat Revolt*, chap. 1; Tuck, *Beyond Atlanta*, chap. 1; Ferguson, *Black Politics*, 65.

41. William Anderson, *Wild Man*, chap. 5; for examples of this tension in other southern states, see Simon, *Fabric*; Carlton, *Mill and Town*; Bartley, *Creation*.

42. William Anderson, *Wild Man*, chaps. 5, 8; Bartley, *Creation*; Kytle and Mackay, *Who Runs Georgia?*; Kari Frederickson, *Dixiecrat Revolt*; Ferguson, *Black Politics*; Brattain, *Politics*, chap. 2; Tindall, *Emergence*, 615–19. For more on white southern masculinity, see Ownby, *Subduing Satan*; Simon, *Fabric*.

43. Holmes, *New Deal*, chap. 1.

44. "Gay Shepperson Papers—Summary," Shepperson Papers; see also Hickey, "'Lowest Form'"; Ferguson, Black Politics.

45. Biles, South, 64; "Federal Emergency Relief Administration," September 29, 1933, signed by Eugene Talmadge and Alan Johnstone; Alan Johnstone to Harry Hopkins, September 18, 1933, group 24, Confidential Political File, 1933–38, box 40, folder T, Hopkins Papers; Holmes, New Deal, chap. 1.

46. Alan Johnstone to Harry Hopkins, September 18, 1933, group 24, Confidential Political File, 1933–38, box 40, folder T, Hopkins Papers; Harry Hopkins and Gay Shepperson, transcript of telephone conversation, May 8, 1934, group 24, FERA-WPA Transcripts of Telephone Conversations, boxes 71–74, folder Transcripts of Telephone Conversations, Georgia–Illinois, Hopkins Papers; see also Daniel, Breaking.

47. Eugene Talmadge to Franklin Delano Roosevelt, January 10, 1934, group 24, Confidential Political File, 1933–38, box 40, folder T, Hopkins Papers. Because Talmadge destroyed his personal papers, these letters are some of the few extant documents that contain his direct statements about FERA and WPA work.

48. Alan Johnstone to Harry Hopkins, September 18, 1933, Shepperson Papers; William Anderson, Wild Man, 95.

49. "A History of the Georgia Civil Works Administration, 1933–34," 58, MSS 522, box 1, folder 1, Shepperson Papers.

50. Walter B. Hill Jr. to Clark Foreman, February 15, 1934, box 44, Department of Education Records, RG 33-1-51, GDAH; William Anderson, Wild Man, 209.

51. Ser. 150, Material Assistance Requested, boxes 2180–99, 2200–2219, Eleanor Roosevelt Papers, Franklin Delano Roosevelt Library, Hyde Park, N.Y.; see also Robert Cohen, "Public Schools."

52. Mrs. J. W. Sharp to Eleanor Roosevelt, March 9, 1934, ser. 150, Material Assistance Requested, boxes 2202–03, 1934, folder Sh–Sn, Eleanor Roosevelt Papers; "A History of the Georgia Civil Works Administration, 1933–34," 58, MSS 522, box 1, folder 1, Shepperson Papers; Maude Garrett to Eleanor Roosevelt, April 30, 1934, ser. 150, Material Assistance Requested, boxes 2202–03, 1934, Ga–Gi, Eleanor Roosevelt Papers; Agnes Macrae to Eleanor Roosevelt, June 30, 1934, ser. 150, Material Assistance Requested, boxes 2197–99, 1934, Lu–Ma, Eleanor Roosevelt Papers.

53. Varina Edwards to Eleanor Roosevelt, June 11, 1934, ser. 150, Material Assistance Requested, boxes 2192–94, E–Ha, Eleanor Roosevelt Papers.

54. Alan Johnstone to Harry Hopkins, January 19, 1934, group 24, Confidential Political File, 1933–38, box 40, folder T, Hopkins Papers; Holmes, New Deal, 22–23. Hopkins also federalized relief efforts in Oklahoma and Louisiana; see Biles, South, 64–65.

55. Harry Hopkins and Gay Shepperson, transcript of telephone conversation, April 22, 1935, group 24, FERA-WPA Transcripts of Telephone Conversations, boxes 71–74, folder Transcripts of Telephone Conversations, Georgia–Illinois, Hopkins Papers.

56. Florene Huddleston Adams, interview by author, Fayetteville, Ga., November 14, 1989; Lema Agnes Peebles, interview by author, Fayetteville, Ga., October 27, 1989.

57. "Relief in Georgia Hit in Resolution Offered in House," box 1, folder 4, "News Clipping Notebook," Shepperson Papers; Alan Johnstone to Harry Hopkins, March 6, 1935, group 24, box 22, folder FERA Procedural Issuances 1933–35, Hopkins Papers; "Relief in Georgia Hit in Resolution Offered in House," *Atlanta Journal*, February 10, 1935, n.p.

58. Polansky, "'I Certainly Hope'"; Florrie Still and Nelle Still Murphy, interview by author, Gainesville, Ga., May 9, June 7, 1997; Tarleton Collier, "Behind Headlines: The GERA and State Politics: Some Facts for the Probe," *Atlanta Georgian*, February 20, 1935, box 1, folder 4, "News Clippings Notebook," Shepperson Papers.

59. Alan Johnstone to Harry Hopkins, March 6, 1935, group 24, Confidential Political File, 1933–38, box 40, folder T, Hopkins Papers.

60. See Georgia Department of Education, *Sixtieth and Sixty-first Annual Reports*, 6; see also Walter B. Hill Jr. to S. L. Smith, March 16, 1929, box 337, folder 10, JRF Archives.

61. Georgia Fact-Finding Committee, "Georgia—Education," 1938, 4, box 203, folder 8, JRF Archives.

62. Jimmie Kate Sams Cole, interview by author, Fayetteville, Ga., October 6, November 18, 1989; Bartley, *Creation*, chap. 8.

63. Badger, *New Deal*; Kennedy, *Freedom*, 368–80; Hickey, "'Lowest Form'"; Ferguson, *Black Politics*, chaps. 2, 3; Andrew Johnson, "A Good Investment," interview by Leola Bradley, October 12, 1939, WPA Collection; Eugenia Martin, "I Managed to Carry On," interview by Geneva Tonsill, November 1939, WPA Collection.

64. Brattain, *Politics*, chap. 2; Bartley, *Creation*, 174–75.

65. Kari Frederickson, *Dixiecrat Revolt*; Grant, *Way It Was*, 350; Sitkoff, *New Deal*; Sullivan, *Days*; Egerton, *Speak Now*.

66. Walter B. Hill Jr. to Clark Foreman, February 15, 1934, box 44, Department of Education Records; Dillard Lasseter, "Report on the National Youth Administration in Georgia, June 26, 1935, to December 31, 1938," box 55, NYA Records; William Shell, "The Negro and the National Youth Administration in Georgia, Bulletin 13, 1939," box 35, NYA Records; see also Corley, "National Youth Administration."

67. Inez Oliveros, "Final Report, National Youth Administration for the State of Georgia, June 1935–July 1943," 14, box 1, "Final Reports of Forty-six States with NYA Offices," NYA Records; Dillard Lasseter, "Report on the National Youth Administration in Georgia, June 26, 1935, to December 31, 1938," 23, box 55, NYA Records; "National Youth Administration of Georgia Monthly Narrative for Month ending October 31, 1937," "Final Report," 28, Final Reports of the Division, 1936–39, box 1, Georgia 1936–37, NYA Records.

68. Palladino, *Teenagers*, 38–46.

69. Dillard Lasseter, "Youth Case Histories from Georgia," October 25, 1939, 5, 14, 15, 30, 81, group 58, National Youth Administration, box 15, Miscellaneous NYA Reports (Printed) and Final Reports, folder "Georgia Youth—Lasseter," Aubrey Williams Papers, Franklin Delano Roosevelt Library, Hyde Park, N.Y.

70. Sullivan, *Days*, 42–44.

71. Jerome Robinson, Alton Childs II, J. Garfield Dashiell, and Charles Lawrence, "A Comparative Study of Teacher Salary Differentials in Georgia, Tennessee, and North Carolina," 1939, 1–4, Campaign for Educational Equality, ser. A, pt. 3, reel 3, NAACP microfilm.

72. Ferguson, *Black Politics*.

73. "Amend or Defeat the Harrison-Black Bill," and "House Committee on Education Holds Hearing on Twice-Amended Federal Aid to Education Bill," April 2, 1937, 2, Campaign for Educational Equality, 1913–50, ser. A, pt. 3, reel 3, NAACP microfilm; Lewis, *Du Bois: Fight*, chap. 9.

74. "Opinion," *Georgia Education Journal*, November 1941, 10; Daniel, *Lost Revolutions*, chap. 1.

75. For an analysis of the *Gaines* decision, see Tushnet, *NAACP's Legal Strategy*, chap. 5; see also Tindall, *Emergence*, chap. 16; Franklin and Moss, *From Slavery to Freedom*, chap. 20.

76. Horace Mann Bond to Karl Bigelow, August 31, 1939, and Horace Mann Bond to Fred McCuistion, October 3, 1939, ser. 1.1, box 45, folder 407, GEB Papers; Tuck, *Beyond Atlanta*, chap. 1.

77. L. R. Siebert to Walter B. Hill Jr., March 19, 1936, box 43, Department of Education Records; see also chap. 3.

78. Steadman Sanford to Edwin Embree, March 18, 1939, Horace Mann Bond to Steadman Sanford, June 17, 1939, J. C. Dixon to Steadman Sanford, June 20, 1939, box 52, Department of Education Records; folder "Julius Rosenwald Fund 1939," box 52, Department of Education Records; "Fort Valley State College 1940–41," ser. 1.1, box 45, folder 408, GEB Papers; Robert Cousins to Jackson Davis, March 14, 1941, ser. 1.1, box 67, folder 590, GEB Papers; see also "Proposals for a Long Term Program of Teacher Education for Rural Teachers in Georgia and Suggestions for Implementing It," October 1, 1939, box 206, folder 3, "Rural School Program 1937–38, 1944–45," and box 323, folders 7, 10, JRF Archives.

79. Georgia Department of Education, *Sixty-sixth and Sixty-seventh Annual Reports*, 1–4, 15, 24; Georgia Department of Education, *Sixty-eighth and Sixty-ninth Annual Reports*, 14–21.

80. M. L. Duggan, "Brief Statement of M. L. Duggan," n.d., 3, Georgia Room, University of Georgia Libraries, Athens; Doak S. Campbell, "The Preparation of Teachers in the University System of Georgia," 1943, 1–3, RG 33–1-51, box 50, Department of Education Records.

81. Still and Murphy interview; Wellborn interview; Susie Weems Wheeler, interview by author, Cartersville, Ga., August 3, 2002; Blackstock interview.

82. Box 204, folder 2, JRF Archives; ser. 1.1, box 56, folder 497, GEB Papers; "Controversy over Dismissal of Dr. Walter D. Cocking, 1941" box 42, Department of Education Records; Ramsey, "University System Controversy"; William Anderson, *Wild Man*, chaps. 16 and 17.

83. See documents in ser. 1.1, box 56, folder 497, GEB Papers; Dorothy A. Elvidge to J. R. McCain, August 11, 1942, box 204, folder 2, JRF Archives.

84. Box 204, folder 2, JRF Archives; ser. 1.1, box 56, folder 497, GEB Papers; "Controversy over Dismissal of Dr. Walter D. Cocking, 1941," box 42, Department of Education Records; Ramsey, "University System Controversy"; William Anderson, *Wild Man*, chaps. 16 and 17.

85. For a discussion of Arnall as a pivotal figure in Georgia politics, see Harold Paulk Henderson and Roberts, *Georgia Governors*, 1–39; Bartley, *Creation*, chap. 8; Harold Paulk Henderson, *Politics*, chaps. 2–4; Patton, "Southern Liberal."

86. See "White Rural Schools of Georgia," November 23, 1937, 3, box 323, folder 10, JRF Archives; see also Georgia Department of Education, *Fifty-second Annual Report*, 1–3. Records regarding many challenges to school consolidations are located in the Georgia Department of Education Records. These proceedings, however, are sealed and unavailable at present.

87. As quoted in William Anderson, *Wild Man*, 200.

88. Mrs. Leonard Morey to Steadman Sanford, June 19, 1941, and Mrs. E. Stewart to Eugene Talmadge, June 19, 1941, box 42, "Controversy over the Dismissal of Dr. Walter D. Cocking 1941," Department of Education Records; William Anderson, *Wild Man*, 197; "Facts in the Cocking Case," 1942, box 204, folder 2, JRF Archives.

89. "Governor Says Dr. Holley Has Right Idea," *Atlanta Daily World*, July 25, 1941, 1; "Study Needs of Race Colleges," *Atlanta Daily World*, August 21, 1941, 1; Ramsey, "University System Controversy," 190–203.

90. William A. Fowlkes, "Seeing and Saying," *Atlanta Daily World*, July 15, 1941, 6; Walter D. Cocking, "A Chronological Record of the Case of Walter D. Cocking in His Ousting from the University of Georgia," 13–14, ser. 1.1, box 56, folder 497, GEB Papers; Ralph McGill to Edwin R. Embree, July 17, 1941, box 204, folder 2, JRF Archives.

91. *Georgia Education Journal*, August 1942, 12–13.

92. Steadman Sanford to Edwin Embree, March 18, 1939, box 52, folder "Julius Rosenwald Fund 1939," Department of Education Records; "A Digest of a Report of a Survey of the University System of Georgia," 138, box 1, Department of Education Records.

93. "A Month of Progress in Georgia," *Georgia Observer*, September 1941, 2, box 203, folder 9, JRF Archives; Waters interview.

94. Brattain, *Politics*, 105.

6 · A Brighter Light

1. The U.S. Congress passed the Servicemen's Readjustment Act, popularly known as the G.I. Bill, on June 22, 1944. The bill's benefits included provisions to enable returning service members to obtain education beyond high school.

2. Dorothy Oliver Rucker and Carrie Oliver Bailey, interview by author, Gaines-

ville, Ga., May 6, 19, September 14, 1993; Al Roper, interview by author, Gainesville, Ga., September 14, 1993.

3. Leona Clark Williams, interview by author, Buford, Ga., June 13, 24, 1991.

4. Patton, "Southern Liberal," 615; Brattain, *Politics*, chaps. 2, 3; Bartley, *Creation*, chap. 8; Harold Paulk Henderson, *Politics*; Egerton, *Speak Now*, pt. 2; Sullivan, *Days*; Tuck, *Beyond Atlanta*, chaps. 1, 2; Flamming, *Creating*, chaps. 9–12; Scranton, *Second Wave*; Eskew, *Labor*; Tindall, *Emergence*; Daniel, *Breaking*; Daniel, "Going"; Grant, *Way It Was*, chap. 9; Woodruff, "Mississippi Delta Planters."

5. Egerton, *Speak Now*; Dittmer, *Local People*, chaps. 1, 2; Sullivan, *Days*, chaps. 5, 6; Tyson, *Radio Free Dixie*, chaps. 2, 3; Payne, *I've Got the Light*, chaps. 1, 2; Honey, *Southern Labor*; Korstad and Lichtenstein, "Opportunities Found and Lost."

6. "Talmadge Is Right," *Atlanta Daily World*, September 6, 1942; "Support of NAACP Is Urged by 28 Leaders," *Atlanta Daily World*, April 8, 1941; "Special Conference with State Officials Set for Wednesday," *Atlanta Daily World*, April 8, 1941; "Democracy Wins," *Atlanta Daily World*, September 11, 1942; Joiner, *History*, chap. 4; Orr, *History*, chap. 12.

7. Harold Paulk Henderson, *Politics*, chap. 3; Harold Paulk Henderson and Roberts, *Georgia Governors*, 25–46; Bartley, *Creation*, chap. 8; Key, *Southern Politics*; Tindall, *Emergence*; Joiner, *History*, chaps. 4, 5.

8. Tuck, *Beyond Atlanta*, 23–24; Ferguson, *Black Politics*, pt. 2; Forrester B. Washington to Walter White, January 21, 1939, ser. A, pt. 12, reel 11, NAACP microfilm.

9. Ferguson, *Black Politics*, pt. 2; Tuck, *Beyond Atlanta*, 59; Brattain, *Politics*, chap. 3; Ferguson, "Politics of Exclusion."

10. Thurgood Marshall to Walter White, September 23, 1943, Campaign for Educational Equality, 1913–50, ser. B, pt. 3, reel 7, NAACP microfilm.

11. Eugene Martin to Walter White, January 13, 1941, Campaign for Educational Equality, 1913–50, ser. B, pt. 3, reel 11, NAACP microfilm; Hine, "Black Professionals."

12. Forrester B. Washington to Walter White, December 20, 1937, ser. A, pt. 12, reel 11, NAACP microfilm. Hubert later stated that black Georgia teachers completely supported the NAACP and its work (Benjamin F. Hubert to Walter White, September 10, 1940, Campaign for Educational Equality, 1913–50, ser. B, pt. 3, reel 7, NAACP microfilm).

13. "Booker T. Washington High School History Class of 1934," 2–4, Narvie Jordan Harris Papers; Georgia Teachers and Education Association, *Rising*, 161; Susie Weems Wheeler, interview by author, Cartersville, Ga., August 3, 2002; Horace Tate, interview by author, Atlanta, June 21, 25, 29, July 23, August 2, 2002.

14. S. Grace Bradley, "GSTEA Executives in Atlanta Session," *Atlanta Daily World*, May 5, 1941.

15. Georgia Teachers and Education Association, *Rising*, 112; S. Grace Bradley, "GSTEA Executives in Atlanta Session," *Atlanta Daily World*, May 5, 1941; Wheeler,

interview by author; Tate interview; *Herald* 9 (May 1945), Horace Mann Bond Papers (microfilm), Robert Woodruff Library, Emory University, Atlanta. On problems within the Atlanta branch of the NAACP, see Ferguson, *Black Politics*; Tuck, *Beyond Atlanta*, chaps. 1, 2.

16. Tate interview.

17. Ibid.; Tuck, *Beyond Atlanta*, chap. 2; see also Ferguson, "Politics of Exclusion"; "Constitution Proposed for Civicle National, 1943," *Civicle*, July 12, 1943–January 1945, pt. 2, Subject Files, reel 16, Horace Mann Bond Papers, Emory University, Atlanta.

18. Narvie Jordan Harris, interview by author, Atlanta, September 27, 2002; Wheeler, interview by author; Georgia Association, *Jeanes Supervision*, chap. 4.

19. Harris interview; Wheeler, interview by author; Georgia Association, *Jeanes Supervision*, 89.

20. Wheeler, interview by author; Susie Weems Wheeler, interview by Thomas A. Scott, March 3, 2000, North Georgia Oral History Series, KSU.

21. Wheeler, interview by author.

22. Harris interview; see also Narvie J. Harris and Taylor, *African-American Education*.

23. Harris interview; see also Narvie J. Harris and Taylor, *African-American Education*.

24. Sullivan, *Days*, 164.

25. Tuck, *Beyond Atlanta*, 62.

26. A. T. Walden to W. A. Sutton and Atlanta Board of Education, November 23, 1941, and "Attorney's Case Docket," n.d., Campaign for Educational Equality, 1913–50, ser. B., pt. 3, reel 7, NAACP microfilm.

27. "Pay Increases on Minds as Teachers Meet," *Atlanta Constitution*, April 23, 1942; "Governor on U.S. School Aid," *Atlanta Constitution*, April 10, 1942; "Fear Gripping State Teachers, Educator Says," *Atlanta Constitution*, October 19, 1941; "Serious Shortage of Teachers for Georgia Schools Reported," *Atlanta Constitution*, August 30, 1941; "1,200 Teachers in State Have Quit," *Atlanta Constitution*, September 4, 1941, all in ser. 1, reel 17, Commission on Interracial Cooperation Papers, Atlanta University, Robert W. Woodruff Library, Atlanta.

28. Jimmie Kate Sams Cole, interview by author, Fayetteville, Ga., October 6, November 18, 1989.

29. *Georgia Education Journal* 38 (October 1944); "Decisions of the Supreme Court of the U.S. Affecting Status of the Negro," ser. 1, reel 1, Commission on Interracial Cooperation Papers; "From the Editor's Desk," *Georgia Education Journal* 35 (September 1941): 7; Knox Walker, "President's Message," *Georgia Education Journal* 35 (September 1941): 14; "Education in the South," *Georgia Education Journal* 36 (January 1942): 7; "Federal Aid," *Georgia Education Journal* 37 (September 1943): 11; John Paschall, "Which Will You Choose?" *Georgia Education Journal* 37 (October 1943): 8.

30. *Georgia Education Journal* 38 (October 1944); "Decisions of the Supreme Court of the U.S. Affecting Status of the Negro," ser. 1, reel 1, Commission on Interracial Cooperation Papers; Leona Clark Williams interview.

31. "Against Teachers Salary Appeal," *Atlanta Journal*, September 10, 1941; see also ser. 1, reel 1, Commission on Interracial Cooperation Papers.

32. Leona Clark Williams interview.

33. Harold Paulk Henderson, *Politics*, 102.

34. Ruth Smith Waters, interview by author, Flowery Branch, Ga., June 28, 1991, June 10, December 7, 1993.

35. Cole interview. For the importance of family care to wage-earning women, see Tentler, *Wage-Earning Women*; Wandersee, *Women's Work*; for a different perspective, see Kessler-Harris, *Out to Work*; for the impact of World War II on women's labor, see Chafe, *Paradox*; Ware, *Holding Their Own*; Kessler-Harris, *Out to Work*, chap. 10.

36. Harris interview; Tate interview; Florrie Still and Nelle Still Murphy, interview by author, Gainesville, Ga., May 9, June 7, 1997; Florrie Still, "Some of the High and Low Spots in the History of Social Service in Georgia School Systems," n.d., Florrie Still and Nelle Still Murphy Papers.

37. Still and Murphy interview.

38. Ibid.

39. Ibid.; Cole interview.

40. Waters interview.

41. Mrs. R. O. DeLoach, "Educational Tear Drops of Tattnall," *Georgia Education Journal* 39 (January 1946): 5.

42. Joiner, *History*, 334–59.

43. Laura Mosley Whelchel, interview by author, Gainesville, Ga., June 18, 1993.

44. Ibid.

45. Nancy Stephens, interview by author, Gainesville, Ga., June 8, 1993.

46. Stephanie J. Shaw, *What a Woman Ought to Be*, chap. 4.

47. Hattie Gaines Wilson, interview by Mary B. Gawley and Kathryn A. Kelley, Marietta, Ga., September 2, 1987, August 2, 17, 1994, Cobb County Oral History Series, KSU.

48. Paschall, "Which Will You Choose?" 9; "Division of Teacher Education, Certification, and Curriculum," *Georgia Education Journal* 35 (April 1941): 82.

49. Sullivan, *Days*, 165; J. Douglas Smith, *Managing*, 280.

50. Tuck, *Beyond Atlanta*, 42–43; Grant, *Way It Was*, chaps. 9, 10; Spritzer and Bergmark, *Grace Towns Hamilton*, 110; Harold Paulk Henderson, *Politics*, esp. chap. 9; Ferguson, "Politics of Exclusion"; Brattain, *Politics*, chap. 3.

51. Spritzer and Bergmark, *Grace Towns Hamilton*, 103–4; Tuck, *Beyond Atlanta*, chap. 2.

52. Tuck, *Beyond Atlanta*, 63.

53. Ibid., 62–63; Spritzer and Bergmark, *Grace Towns Hamilton*, 103–8.

54. Tuck, *Beyond Atlanta*, chap. 2; Harold Paulk Henderson, *Politics*, chap. 9; Grant, *Way It Was*, 364–68; Bernd, "White Supremacy."

55. Tuck, *Beyond Atlanta*, 14; Sullivan, *Days*, 165; Grant, *Way It Was*, 280.

56. Harold Paulk Henderson, *Politics*, 166; undated clipping, group 2, ser. A, Georgia Crime, file 629, "Eugene Talmadge 1940–1948," NAACP Papers.

57. Patton, "Southern Liberal," 615–20; Harold Paulk Henderson, *Politics*, chap. 9; Kytle and Mackay, *Who Runs Georgia?* pt. 1; Brattain, *Politics*, chap. 4; "Talmadge Seems Winner in Governor's Race," *Atlanta Daily World*, July 19, 1946.

58. Tuck, *Beyond Atlanta*, 75; Jimmy Carter, *Turning Point*, xxii.

59. Grant, *Way It Was*, 364–68, 620; Sullivan, *Days*, 213; Bernd, "White Supremacy."

60. Tuck, *Beyond Atlanta*, 66–68; Grant, *Way It Was*, 364–65; Harold Paulk Henderson, *Politics*, 146.

61. Sullivan, *Days*, 213; Joel W. Smith, "Lynching Bee Staged at Monroe," *Atlanta Daily World*, July 27, 1946, 1; Wexler, *Fire*; William Anderson, *Wild Man*, 233; George Andrews, "Bullet Torn Bodies of Lynch Victims a Horrible Sight," *Atlanta Daily World*, July 27, 1946, 1; see also Harold Paulk Henderson, *Politics*, chap. 9; Bartley, *Creation*, chap. 8; "Notes on the Discussion at Conference of Georgians, August 8, 1946," box 188, folder 8, JRF Archives.

62. Patton, "Southern Liberal," 621; *Atlanta Daily World*, July–August 1946; Sullivan, *Days*.

63. "Notes on the Discussion at Conference of Georgians, August 8, 1946," 1, box 188, folder 8, JRF Archives; Kytle and Mackay, *Who Runs Georgia?* pt. 1.

64. Brattain, *Politics*, chap. 4, pp. 3–5.

65. Bartley, *Creation*, chap. 8; Harold Paulk Henderson, *Politics*, chap. 11; Kytle and Mackay, *Who Runs Georgia?* pt. 1.

66. Kytle and Mackay, *Who Runs Georgia?* 130.

67. Simon, "Racial Anxieties," 87; Blanche Wiesen Cook, *Eleanor Roosevelt*, 2:292.

68. Kari Frederickson, *Dixiecrat Revolt*, 56–57; Tuck, *Beyond Atlanta*, 42.

69. "The Facts of the Ingram Case," group 2, ser. A, Georgia Crime, 1948–55, NAACP Papers; Grant, *Way It Was*, 367–68.

70. Grant, *Way It Was*, 369.

71. "Membership and Financial Support Received from Georgia Branches," group 2, ser. C, folder 42, Georgia Branches, NAACP Papers; C. L. Harper to Gloster Current, February 22, 1949, ser. A, pt. 26, reel 9, NAACP microfilm; Armstead L. Robinson and Sullivan, *New Directions*, 99; see also Payne, *I've Got the Light*, chap. 2; Dittmer, *Local People*, chap. 2; Tyson, *Radio Free Dixie*.

72. Tate interview; Tuck, *Beyond Atlanta*, 60.

73. C. L. Harper to Madison Jones, October 27, 1945, ser. A, pt. 26, reel 9, NAACP microfilm; Robert Carter to Mr. White, "Georgia Teachers and Educational Association Conference," April 16, 1946, and C. L. Harper to Thurgood Marshall, August 3, 1947, ser. B, pt. 3, reel 1, NAACP microfilm.

74. C. L. Harper to Thurgood Marshall, August 3, 1947, ser. B, pt. 3, reel 1, NAACP microfilm; Georgia Teachers and Education Association, *Rising*, 112.

75. Tate interview.

76. Tate interview.

77. Tate interview.

78. Tate interview.

79. Tate interview

80. Tate interview.

81. Tate interview.

82. "Georgia State Conference of NAACP Branches: The Report of Policies and Objectives Committee Gainesville, Georgia, December 3, 1949," group 2, ser. C, pt. 42, NAACP Papers.

83. Clippings, Campaign for Educational Equality, 1913–50, ser. B, pt. 3, reel 1, NAACP microfilm; "We Can't Quarrel with Our Own Laws," *Atlanta Constitution*, August 12, 1949.

84. "Governor Talmadge's Radio Talk at 7:45 A.M., Saturday, October 22, 1949," 2, Campaign for Educational Equality, 1913–50, ser. B, pt. 3, reel 1, NAACP microfilm; Woodward, *Origins*, 398–99.

85. Robert Cousins, "Relationship of the GEA to Negro Education," *Georgia Education Journal* 39 (March 1946): 12.

86. Special Committee, *Survey*, 1, 44–45.

87. "The Best of Everything for Children Should Include Minimum Education," *Georgia Education Journal* 43 (January 1949): 27; "From the Editor's Desk: What We Want in the People, We Must Put in the Schools," *Georgia Education Journal* 42 (January 1948): 30; Tate interview; Harris interview.

88. O. C. Aderhold, "The Unfinished Task," *Georgia Education Journal* 43 (September 1949): 8.

89. Rucker and Bailey interview.

90. Leona Clark Williams interview; Still and Murphy interview.

91. M. J. Woods, interview by Thomas A. Scott, Kennesaw, Ga., October 12, 1978, Kennesaw College Oral History Series, KSU.

92. Leona Clark Williams interview.

93. Ibid.

94. Still and Murphy interview.

95. Cole interview.

96. Stephanie J. Shaw, *What a Woman Ought to Be*, chap. 3; Fairclough, "'Being.'"

97. Leona Clark Williams interview.

98. U.S. Department of Commerce, Bureau of the Census, *Seventeenth Census*, 11-6, 11-8, 11-51.

99. Ibid., 11-45-11-46.

Epilogue

1. Sanford Byers, interview by Lu Ann Jones, Gainesville, Ga., April 20, 1987, NMAH.

2. Carter, *Turning Point*, xxii–xxiii, 9–12.

3. Ulysses Byas, interview by author, Macon, Ga., September 18, 1993; Horace Tate, interview by author, Atlanta, June 21, 25, 29, July 23, August 2, 2002; Fairclough, *Teaching Equality*; Hine, "Black Professionals"; Patterson, *Brown*; Vanessa Siddle Walker, *Their Highest Potential*.

4. Brattain, *Politics*, 160–62; Bartley, *Creation*, 203.

5. Tate interview; Susie Weems Wheeler, interview by author, Cartersville, Ga., August 3, 2002; Narvie Jordan Harris, interview by author, Atlanta, September 27, 2002; Byas interview.

Bibliography

PRIMARY SOURCES

Oral History Interviews

Interviews conducted by author. All tape recordings and transcripts are in author's possession.

Florene Huddleston Adams, Jane Thigpen Alexander, Cleophus Allgood, Rosa Penson Anderson, Carrie Oliver Bailey, Dorothy Watkins Baylor, Martha Breedlove Buice, Ulysses S. Byas, Jimmie Kate Sams Cole, Rita Andrae Collins, Charity Honeycutt Ector, Charles Ector, Charters Smith Embry, Trummi Evans, T. P. Grissom, Narvie Jordan Harris, Eleanor Jones, Clara Belle McCrary, Arree Twitty Milner, Nelle Still Murphy, Lema Agnes Peebles, Lois Randolph, Al Roper, Christine Rucker, Dorothy Oliver Rucker, Nancy Stephens, Florrie Still, Horace Tate, Virginia Tate, L. C. Teasley Sr., Robert Threatt, Christine Walker, Ruth Smith Waters, Emory Wells, Ophelia Wharf, Susie Weems Wheeler, Laura Mosley Whelchel, Leona Clark Williams.

Kennesaw State University, Sturgis Library, Bentley Rare Book Room, Kennesaw, Ga.

Cobb County Oral History Series: Mary Ellen Simpson Allgood, Harvey E. Durham and Bessie H. Durham, Amos Durr, Evelyn Gragg, Alfred Jackson, Lex and LeoDelle Jolley, Fanny B. McClure, Ernestine Johnson Slade, Jessie Mae Spears Taylor, Louis C. Walker and Josetta O. Walker, Hattie Gaines Wilson, members of Zion Baptist Church.

Kennesaw College Oral History Series: Georgia Mae Adams, Joyce Ann Brown, Walter H. and Edith Barrett Cantrell, Cassie Wingo Chastain, Loyd C. Cox, Ione W. Johnson, Gail B. Meacham, Mary Hall Swain, Joe Mack Wilson, M. J. Woods.

North Georgia Oral History Series: Susie Weems Wheeler.

National Museum of American History, Smithsonian Institution, Washington, D.C.

"An Oral History of Southern Agriculture": Aubrey Benton, Ina Belle Benton, Tom Blackstock, Velva Blackstock, Ruby Smith Byers, Sanford Byers, Guy W. Castleberry, Arthur B. Fleming, Welchel Long, Bunice Waldrip Reed, Howard Reed, Spurgeon L. Wellborn.

Private Collection

Tate, Horace. Personal interview conducted by Tom and Molly O'Brien, Atlanta, August 31, 1995. Tape recording in author's possession.

Manuscript and Archive Material

Georgia

Atlanta History Center, Atlanta. Gay Bolling Shepperson Papers.

Atlanta University Center, Robert W. Woodruff Library, Atlanta. Commission on Interracial Cooperation Papers. Southern Education Foundation Records.

Emory University, Robert Woodruff Library, Atlanta. Horace Mann Bond Papers. National Association for the Advancement of Colored People Papers, microfilm.

Georgia Department of Archives and History, Atlanta. Department of Education Records. Director of Negro Education Subject Files. Division of Negro Education Records. John Riley Hopkins Papers.

Georgia Room, University of Georgia Libraries, Athens. Bulletins of the Georgia State College for Women. Bulletins of the State Normal School, Athens. *Christian Index. Georgia Education Journal.* Vertical files on Georgia counties.

Hargrett Special Collections, University of Georgia Libraries, Athens. *Bulletin of the University of Georgia,* 1895–96, 1913–14, 1922–23, 1930–31. Rebecca Latimer Felton Papers. Corra Mae White Harris Papers. Walter B. Hill Papers. May Irwin Talmadge Papers. Works Progress Administration (WPA) Federal Writers' Project Collection, Georgia. Yellow River Baptist Association Minutes.

University of Georgia Libraries, Athens. National Association for the Advancement of Colored People Papers, microfilm.

Maryland

National Archives, College Park. U.S. Department of Agriculture, Extension Service Records, RG 33.

New York

Franklin Delano Roosevelt Library, Hyde Park, New York. Harry Hopkins Papers. Eleanor Roosevelt Papers. Aubrey Williams Papers.

Rockefeller Archive Center, Pocantico Hills, New York. General Education Board Papers.

North Carolina

Southern Historical Collection, University of North Carolina, Chapel Hill. Howard Odum Papers.

Tennessee

Fisk University Archives, Nashville. Julius Rosenwald Fund Archives.
Southern Baptist Convention Historical Library and Archives, Nashville. *Christian Index*. First Baptist Church, Commerce, Georgia, Records (microfilm). First Baptist Church, Jefferson, Georgia, Records (microfilm). Una Roberts Lawrence Collection. Liberty Baptist Church, Lilburn, Georgia, Records (microfilm). Lithonia Baptist Church, Lithonia, Georgia, Records (microfilm). Mount Zion Baptist Church, Snellville, Georgia, Records (microfilm). *Royal Service*. Women's Missionary Union of the First Baptist Church, Gainesville, Georgia, Records. Zion Baptist Church, Buford, Georgia, Records (microfilm).

Washington, D.C.

Library of Congress, Division of Prints and Photographs. Farm Security Administration/Office of War Information Collection.
Library of Congress, Manuscript Division. National Association for the Advancement of Colored People Papers. Works Progress Administration (WPA) Federal Writers' Project Collection, Georgia.
National Archives. National Youth Administration Records, RG 119.
Smithsonian Institution, National Museum of American History. Collection on Historically Black Colleges. Sam De Vincent Collection of Illustrated American Sheet Music. Sears and Roebuck catalogs.

Private Collections

Narvie Jordan Harris Papers. Dorothy Oliver Rucker and Carrie Oliver Bailey Papers. Florrie Still and Nelle Still Murphy Papers. Dr. Horace Tate Papers. Dr. Robert Threatt Papers. Ruth Smith Waters Papers. Leona Clark Williams Papers.

Newspapers and Periodicals

Atlanta Constitution, 1915–20, 1930–50
Atlanta Daily World, 1930–50
Atlanta Herald, 1945–52
Atlanta Independent, 1900–1922
Atlanta Journal, 1930–50
Augusta Chronicle, 1897–1906
Gainesville Eagle, 1895
Gainesville Times, 1910–80
Georgia Baptist, 1898–1913
Georgia Education Journal, 1910–50

Published Primary Sources

Brittain, M. L. *Manual for Georgia Teachers*. Atlanta: Georgia Department of Education, 1916.

Brooks, R. P. *The Financial History of Georgia, 1732–1950*. Athens: Institute for the Study of Georgia Problems, University of Georgia, 1952.

Brown, H. A. *The Readjustment of a Rural High School to the Needs of the Community*. U.S. Bureau of Education Bulletin 20. Washington, D.C.: U.S. Government Printing Office, 1912.

Burnham, Ernest. *Rural Teacher Preparation in State Normal Schools*. U.S. Bureau of Education Bulletin 27. Washington, D.C.: U.S. Government Printing Office, 1918.

Caliver, Ambrose. *Availability of Education to Negroes in Rural Communities*. U.S. Bureau of Education Bulletin 12. Washington, D.C.: U.S. Government Printing Office, 1936.

———. *A Personnel Study of Negro College Students: A Study of the Relations between Certain Background Factors of Negro College Students and Their Subsequent Careers in College*. New York: Columbia University, 1931.

Cocking, Walter D. *Report of the Study on Higher Education of Negroes in Georgia*. Athens, Ga.: n.p., 1938.

Cook, Katherine M. *Constructive Tendencies in Rural Education*. U.S. Bureau of Education Bulletin 25. Washington, D.C.: U.S. Government Printing Office, 1925.

Davis, Jackson. *County Training Schools*. Hampton, Va.: Hampton Institute Press, 1918.

Duggan, M. L. *Educational Survey of Jackson County, Georgia*. Atlanta: State Department of Education, 1915.

Embree, Edwin R. *Brown America: The Story of a New Race*. New York: Viking, 1931.

Favrot, Leo M. *A Study of County Training Schools for Negroes in the South*. John F. Slater Fund Occasional Paper 23. Charlottesville, Va.: John F. Slater Fund, 1923.

Federal Writer's Project. *These Are Our Lives*. Chapel Hill: University of North Carolina Press, 1939.

Felton, Rebecca Latimer. *Country Life in Georgia in the Days of My Youth*. 1919; reprint, New York: Arno, 1980.

———. *My Memoirs of Georgia Politics*. Atlanta: Index Printing, 1911.

———. *The Romantic Story of Georgia's Women*. Atlanta: Atlanta Georgian and Sunday American, 1930.

Foght, H. W. *Rural Teacher Preparation in County Training Schools and High Schools*. U.S. Bureau of Education Bulletin 31. Washington, D.C.: U.S. Government Printing Office, 1917.

Georgia Department of Education. *Bulletin of the State Department of Education of the State of Georgia on Certification*. Atlanta: State Printing Office, 1935.

———. *Eightieth and Eighty-first Annual Reports of the Department of Education to the General Assembly of the State of Georgia for the Biennium Ending June 30, 1952*. Atlanta: State Printing Office, 1952.

————. *Fifty-eighth and Fifty-ninth Annual Reports of the Department of Education to the General Assembly of the State of Georgia for the Biennium Ending June 30, 1930.* Atlanta: State Printing Office, 1930.

————. *Fifty-fourth and Fifty-fifth Annual Reports of the Department of Education to the General Assembly of the State of Georgia for the Biennium Ending December 31, 1926.* Atlanta: State Printing Office, 1927.

————. *Fifty-second Annual Report of the Department of Education to the General Assembly of the State of Georgia for the School Year 1923–1924.* Atlanta: State Printing Office, 1924.

————. *Forty-fourth Annual Report of the Department of Education to the General Assembly of the State of Georgia for the School Year Ending December 31, 1915.* Atlanta: Charles Byrd, 1916.

————. *Forty-ninth Annual Report of the Department of Education to the General Assembly of Georgia for the School Year Ending December 31, 1920.* Atlanta: Charles Byrd, 1921.

————. *Forty-sixth Annual Report of the Department of Education to the General Assembly of the State of Georgia for the School Year Ending December 31, 1917.* Atlanta: Charles Byrd, 1918.

————. *Georgia Program for Improvement of Instruction: Preliminary Report of Procedures Committee on the Community as a Source of Materials for Instruction.* Atlanta: State Department of Education, 1936.

————. *Guide to Life-Related Teaching in the Negro High Schools of Georgia.* Bulletin 4A. Atlanta: State Department of Education, 1938.

————. *Health Manual for Georgia Schools.* Atlanta: State Department of Education, 1920.

————. *Manual for Georgia Teachers.* Atlanta: Department of Education, 1916.

————. *The Open Road: A Teacher's Study Guide for Child, Adult, and Community Development in Negro Elementary Schools of Georgia.* Bulletin 2A. Atlanta: State Department of Education, 1938.

————. *A Practice Book for Observation and Teaching in Small Rural Schools.* Bulletin 3A. Atlanta: State Department of Education, Division of Negro Education, 1938.

————. *Seventieth and Seventy-first Annual Reports of the Department of Education to the General Assembly of the State of Georgia for the Biennium Ending June 30, 1942.* Atlanta: State Printing Office, 1942.

————. *Sixtieth and Sixty-first Annual Reports of the Department of Education to the General Assembly of the State of Georgia for the Biennium Ending June 30, 1932.* Atlanta: State Printing Office, 1932.

————. *Sixty-eighth and Sixty-ninth Annual Reports of the Department of Education to the General Assembly of the State of Georgia for the Biennium Ending June 30, 1940.* Atlanta: State Printing Office, 1940.

————. *Sixty-sixth and Sixty-seventh Annual Reports of the State Department of Education to the Georgia General Assembly for the Biennium Ending June 30, 1938.* Atlanta: State Printing Office, 1938.

———. *Thirty-eighth Annual Report of the Department of Education to the General Assembly of the State of Georgia for the School Year Ending December 31, 1909.* Atlanta: Charles Byrd, 1910.

———. *Thirty-ninth Annual Report of the Department of Education to the General Assembly of the State of Georgia for the School Year Ending December 31, 1910.* Atlanta: Charles Byrd, 1911.

———. *Twenty-ninth Annual Report of the Department of Education to the General Assembly of the State of Georgia for the School Year Ending December 31, 1900.* Atlanta: Charles Byrd, 1901.

Hagood, Margaret Jarman. *Mothers of the South: Portraiture of the White Tenant Farm Woman.* Chapel Hill: University of North Carolina Press, 1939; reprint, New York: Norton, 1977.

Hanifan, L. J. *Problems of Rural Schools.* Washington, D.C.: U.S. Government Printing Office, 1913.

Hill, Walter B. *Rural Survey of Clarke County, Georgia, with Special Reference to the Negroes.* Phelps-Stokes Fellowship Studies 2. Athens: University of Georgia Press, 1915.

Hodges, W. T., comp. *Important Features in Rural School Improvement.* U.S. Bureau of Education Bulletin 25. Washington, D.C.: U.S. Government Printing Office, 1914.

Johnson, Charles S., Edwin R. Embree, and W. W. Alexander. *The Collapse of Cotton Tenancy.* Chapel Hill: University of North Carolina Press, 1935.

Johnson, Charles S., Lewis W. Jones, and Buford H. Junker. *Statistical Atlas of Southern Counties: Listing and Analysis of Socio-Economic Indices of 1104 Southern Economies.* Chapel Hill: University of North Carolina Press, 1941.

Johnson, D. B. *Education of Women in the Country.* U.S. Bureau of Education Bulletin 40–49. Washington, D.C.: U.S. Government Printing Office, 1913.

Long, David D., and Mark Baldwin. *Soil Survey of Jackson County, Georgia.* Athens: University of Georgia, 1914.

McCuistion, Fred. *Higher Education of Negroes (A Summary).* Nashville: Southern Association, Colleges and Secondary Schools, Committee on Approval of Negro Schools, 1933.

———. *The South's Negro Teaching Force.* Nashville: Julius Rosenwald Fund, 1931.

McKeever, William. *Farm Boys and Girls.* New York: Macmillan, 1912.

Miller, John T., Matthew Drosdoff, and G. L. Fuller. *Soil Survey of Hall County, Georgia.* Washington, D.C.: U.S. Department of Agriculture, 1941.

Odum, Howard. *Southern Regions of the United States.* Chapel Hill: University of North Carolina Press, 1936.

Oliver, Beulah Rucker. *The Rugged Pathway.* N.p., 1953.

Raper, Arthur F. *Preface to Peasantry: A Tale of Two Black Belt Counties.* Chapel Hill: University of North Carolina Press, 1936.

Reed, Ruth. *The Negro Women of Gainesville, Georgia.* Phelps-Stokes Studies 6. Athens: University of Georgia Press, 1921.

Rucker, Beulah. "A Word from the Colored Institute, Gainesville, Ga." *Atlanta Independent*, July 5, 1911.

Special Committee on Education. *A Survey of Public Education of Less than College Grade in Georgia*. Atlanta: State Department of Education, 1947.

Terrill, Tom E., and Jerrold Hirsch, eds. *Such as Us: Southern Voices of the Thirties*. Chapel Hill: University of North Carolina Press, 1978.

Trustees of the John F. Slater Fund. *Public Secondary Schools for Negroes in the Southern States of the United States*. Occasional Paper 29. Lynchburg, Va.: Bell, 1935.

———. *Reference List of Southern Colored Schools*. Occasional Paper 20. Lynchburg, Va.: Bell, 1921.

———. *A Suggested Course of Study for County Training Schools for Negroes in the South*. Lynchburg, Va.: Bell, 1917.

Turner, Howard A., and L. D. Howell. *Condition of Farmers in a White-Farmer Area of the Cotton Piedmont, 1924–1926*. Washington, D.C.: U.S. Department of Agriculture, 1929.

U.S. Department of Agriculture, Office of the Secretary. *Domestic Needs of Farm Women*. Report 104. Washington, D.C.: U.S. Government Printing Office, 1915.

———. *Economic Needs of Farm Women*. Report 105. Washington, D.C.: U.S. Government Printing Office, 1915.

———. *Social and Labor Needs of Farm Women*. Report 103. Washington, D.C.: U.S. Government Printing Office, 1915.

U.S. Department of Commerce, Bureau of the Census. *Census of Agriculture: 1924*. Pt. 2. Washington, D.C.: U.S. Government Printing Office, 1927.

———. *Fifteenth Census of the United States 1930: Population*. Washington, D.C.: U.S. Government Printing Office, 1932.

———. *Fourteenth Census of the United States, 1920: Population*. Washington, D.C.: U.S. Government Printing Office, 1921–22.

———. *Seventeenth Census of the United States, 1950*. Vol. 2. Washington, D.C.: U.S. Government Printing Office, 1952.

———. *Sixteenth Census of the United States, 1940: Population*. Vol. 2. Washington, D.C.: U.S. Government Printing Office, 1943.

———. *Thirteenth Census of the United States, 1910: Population*. Vol. 2, *Reports by States*. Washington, D.C.: U.S. Government Printing Office, 1913.

Vance, Rupert. *Human Geography of the South*. Chapel Hill: University of North Carolina Press, 1932.

Williams, Leona Clark. *We Remember*. N.p., 1976.

Woofter, Thomas Jackson. *The Negroes of Athens, Georgia*. Phelps-Stokes Fellowship Studies 1. Athens: University of Georgia Press, 1913.

———. *A Study of the Economic Status of the Negro*. N.p., 1930.

———. *Teaching in Rural Schools*. New York: Houghton Mifflin, 1917.

SECONDARY SOURCES

Abbott, Shirley. *The Bookmaker's Daughter: A Memory Unbound*. Boston: Ticknor and Fields, 1991.

Agee, James, and Walker Evans. *Let Us Now Praise Famous Men: Three Tenant Families*. Boston: Houghton Mifflin, 1941.

Ahlstrom, Sydney E. *A Religious History of the American People*. New Haven: Yale University Press, 1972.

"American Rural and Farm Women in Historical Perspective." *Agricultural History* 67 (spring 1993): 1–291.

Anderson, James D. *The Education of Blacks in the South, 1860–1935*. Chapel Hill: University of North Carolina Press, 1988.

Anderson, William. *The Wild Man from Sugar Creek: The Political Career of Eugene Talmadge*. Baton Rouge: Louisiana State University Press, 1975.

Andrews, William L. *To Tell a Free Story: The First Century of Afro-American Autobiography, 1760–1865*. Urbana: University of Illinois Press, 1986.

———, ed. *Sisters of the Spirit: Three Black Women's Autobiographies of the Nineteenth Century*. Bloomington: Indiana University Press, 1986.

———, ed. *Six Women's Slave Narratives*. New York: Oxford University Press, 1988.

Angelou, Maya. *I Know Why the Caged Bird Sings*. New York: Bantam, 1971.

Anker, Laura. "Family, Work, and Community: Southern and Eastern European Immigrant Women Speak from the Connecticut Federal Writer's Project." In *Gendered Domains: Rethinking Public and Private in Women's History*, edited by Dorothy O. Helly and Susan M. Reverby, 303–21. Ithaca: Cornell University Press, 1992.

Applebome, Peter. *Dixie Rising: How the South Is Shaping American Values, Politics, and Culture*. New York: Times Books, 1996.

Arnesen, Eric. "Assessing Whiteness Scholarship: A Response to James Barrett, et al." *International Labor and Working-Class History* 60 (fall 2001): 81–92.

———. "Whiteness and the Historians' Imagination." *International Labor and Working-Class History* 60 (fall 2001): 3–32.

Atkins, Jonathan M. "Philanthropy in the Mountains: Martha Berry and the Early Years of the Berry Schools." *Georgia Historical Quarterly* 72 (winter 1998): 856–76.

Ayers, Edward L. *The Promise of the New South: Life after Reconstruction*. New York: Oxford University Press, 1992.

Bacote, Clarence A. *The Story of Atlanta University: A Century of Service, 1865–1965*. Princeton: Princeton University Press, 1969.

Badger, Anthony J. *The New Deal: The Depression Years, 1933–1940*. New York: Farrar, Straus, and Giroux, 1989.

Baker, Houston A. *Workings of the Spirit: The Poetics of Afro-American Women's Writings*. Chicago: University of Chicago Press, 1991.

Baker, Paula. "The Domestication of Politics: Women and American Political Society, 1780–1920." *American Historical Review* 84 (June 1984): 620–47.

Bardaglio, Peter W. *Reconstructing the Household: Families, Sex, and the Law in the Nineteenth Century South.* Chapel Hill: University of North Carolina Press, 1995.

Barrett, James R. "Whiteness Studies: Anything Here for Historians of the Working Class?" *International Labor and Working-Class History* 60 (fall 2001): 33–42.

Barrett, Michele. "Ideology and the Cultural Production of Gender." In *Feminist Criticism and Social Change: Sex, Class, and Race in Literature and Culture,* edited by Judith Newton and Deborah Rosenfelt, 65–85. New York: Methuen, 1985.

Bartley, Numan V. *The Creation of Modern Georgia.* Athens: University of Georgia Press, 1990.

———. *The New South, 1945–1980: The Story of the South's Modernization.* Baton Rouge: Louisiana State University Press, 1995.

Bass, Jack, and Walter DeVries. *The Transformation of Southern Politics: Social Change and Political Consequences since 1945.* New York: Basic Books, 1976.

Bates, Daisy. *The Long Shadow of Little Rock.* Fayetteville: University of Arkansas Press, 1987.

Bayor, Ronald H. *Race and the Shaping of Twentieth-Century Atlanta.* Chapel Hill: University of North Carolina Press, 1996.

Beardsley, Edward H. *A History of Neglect: Health Care for Blacks and Mill Workers in the Twentieth-Century South.* Knoxville: University of Tennessee Press, 1987.

Bederman, Gail. *Manliness and Civilization: A Cultural History of Gender and Race in the United States, 1880–1917.* Chicago: University of Chicago Press, 1995.

Benson, Susan Porter. *Counter Cultures: Saleswomen, Managers, and Customers in American Department Stores, 1890–1940.* Urbana: University of Illinois Press, 1988.

Benstock, Shari. "Authorizing the Autobiographical." In *The Private Self: Theory and Practice of Women's Autobiographical Writings,* edited by Shari Benstock, 10–33. Chapel Hill: University of North Carolina Press, 1988.

Bercaw, Nancy. *Gender and the Southern Body Politic.* Jackson: University Press of Mississippi, 2000.

Berkeley, Kathleen C. "'Ladies Want to Bring about Reform in the Public Schools': Public Education and Women's Rights in the Post–Civil War South." *History of Education Quarterly* 24 (spring 1984): 45–58.

———. "The Sage of Sedalia: Education and Racial Uplift as Reflected in the Career of Charlotte Hawkins Brown, 1883–1961." Paper presented at the History of Education Society Meeting, Toronto, October 18, 1996.

Bernd, Joseph. "White Supremacy and the Disfranchisement of Blacks in Georgia, 1946." *Georgia Historical Quarterly* 66 (winter 1982): 493–513.

Bernhard, Virginia, Betty Brandon, Elizabeth Fox-Genovese, Theda Perdue, and Elizabeth H. Turner, eds. *Hidden Histories of Women in the New South.* Columbia: University of Missouri Press, 1994.

Biklen, Sari Knopp. *School Work: Gender and the Cultural Construction of Teaching*. New York: Teachers College Press, 1995.

Biles, Roger. *A New Deal for the American People*. De Kalb: Northern Illinois University Press, 1991.

———. *The South and the New Deal*. Lexington: University Press of Kentucky, 1994.

Blair, Karen J. *The Clubwoman as Feminist: True Womanhood Redefined, 1868–1914*. New York: Homes and Meier, 1980.

Bledstein, Burton J. *The Culture of Professionalism: The Middle Class and the Development of Higher Education in America*. New York: Norton, 1978.

Blee, Kathleen M. *Women of the Klan: Racism and Gender in the 1920s*. Berkeley: University of California Press, 1991.

Blumin, Stuart. *The Emergence of the Middle Class: Social Experience in the American City, 1760–1900*. New York: Cambridge University Press, 1989.

Boles, John B., and Evelyn Thomas Nolen, eds. *Interpreting Southern History: Historiographical Essays in Honor of Sanford W. Higginbotham*. Baton Rouge: Louisiana State University Press, 1987.

Bond, Horace Mann. *The Education of the Negro in the American Social Order*. New York: Prentice-Hall, 1934.

Bordin, Ruth. *Women and Temperance: The Quest for Power and Liberty, 1873–1900*. Philadelphia: Temple University Press, 1981.

Bourdieu, Pierre. *Distinction: A Social Critique of the Judgment of Taste*. Translated by Richard Nice. Cambridge: Harvard University Press, 1984.

Bowles, Samuel, and Herbert Gintis. *Schooling in Capitalist America: Educational Reform and the Contradictions of Economic Life*. New York: Basic Books, 1976.

Boydston, Jeanne, Mary Kelley, and Anne Margolis. *The Limits of Sisterhood: The Beecher Sisters on Women's Rights and Woman's Sphere*. Chapel Hill: University of North Carolina Press, 1988.

Boylan, Anne M. *Sunday School: The Formation of an American Institution, 1790–1880*. New Haven: Yale University Press, 1988.

Branch, Taylor. *Parting the Waters: America in the King Years, 1954–1963*. New York: Simon and Schuster, 1988.

Brattain, Michelle. *The Politics of Whiteness: Race, Workers, and Culture in the Modern South*. Princeton: Princeton University Press, 2001.

Brinkley, Alan. "The New Deal and Southern Politics." In *The New Deal and the South: Essays*, edited by James C. Cobb and Michael Namorato, 97–115. Jackson: University Press of Mississippi, 1984.

———. *Voices of Protest: Huey Long, Father Coughlin, and the Great Depression*. New York: Vintage, 1982.

Brody, David. "Charismatic History: Pros and Cons." *International Labor and Working-Class History* 60 (fall 2001): 43–47.

————. *Workers in Industrial America: Essays on the Twentieth-Century Struggle*. New York: Oxford University Press, 1981.

Brown, Charlotte Hawkins. *The Correct Thing to Do — to Say — to Wear*. Boston: Christopher, 1941.

Brown, Elsa Barkley. "Negotiating and Transforming the Public Sphere: African American Political Life in the Transition from Slavery to Freedom." In *Jumpin' Jim Crow: Southern Politics from Civil War to Civil Rights*, edited by Jane Dailey, Glenda Gilmore, and Bryant Simon, 28–66. Princeton: Princeton University Press, 2000.

————. "Womanist Consciousness: Maggie Lena Walker and the Independent Order of Saint Luke." In *Unequal Sisters: A Multicultural Reader in United States History*, edited by Ellen Carol DuBois and Vicki L. Ruiz, 208–23. New York: Routledge, Chapman, and Hall, 1990.

Brundage, W. Fitzhugh. *Lynching in the New South: Georgia and Virginia, 1880–1930*. Urbana: University of Illinois Press, 1993.

————. "White Women and the Politics of Historical Memory in the New South, 1880–1920." In *Jumpin' Jim Crow: Southern Politics from Civil War to Civil Rights*, edited by Jane Dailey, Glenda Gilmore, and Bryant Simon, 28–66. Princeton: Princeton University Press, 2000.

————, ed. *Up from Slavery by Booker T. Washington: With Related Documents*. Boston: Bedford/St. Martin's, 2003.

————, ed. *Where These Memories Grow: History, Memory, and Southern Identity*. Chapel Hill: University of North Carolina Press, 2000.

Bryant, Jonathan M. *How Curious a Land: Conflict and Change in Greene County, Georgia, 1850–1885*. Chapel Hill: University of North Carolina Press, 1996.

Burton, Orville Vernon. *In My Father's House Are Many Mansions: Family and Community in Edgefield, South Carolina*. Chapel Hill: University of North Carolina Press, 1985.

Butchart, Ronald E. "Mission Matters: Mount Holyoke, Oberlin, and the Schooling of Southern Blacks, 1861–1917." *History of Education Quarterly* 42 (spring 2002): 1–17.

————. *Northern Schools, Southern Blacks, and Reconstruction: Freedmen's Education, 1862–1875*. Westport, Conn.: Greenwood, 1980.

————. "'Outthinking and Outflanking the Owners of the World': A Historiography of the African American Struggle for Education." *History of Education Quarterly* 28 (fall 1988): 334–66.

Butchart, Ronald E., and Amy F. Rolleri. "Iowa Teachers among the Freedpeople of the South, 1862–1876." *Annals of Iowa* 62 (winter 2003): 1–29.

Campbell, D'Ann. *Women at War with America: Private Lives in a Patriotic Era*. Cambridge: Harvard University Press, 1984.

Cantor, Milton, and Bruce Laurie, eds. *Class, Sex, and the Woman Worker*. Westport, Conn.: Greenwood, 1977.

Carby, Hazel V. *Reconstructing Womanhood: The Emergence of the Afro-American Woman Novelist*. New York: Oxford University Press, 1987.

Carlton, David. *Mill and Town in South Carolina, 1880–1920*. Baton Rouge: Louisiana State University Press, 1982.

———. "The Revolution from Above: The National Market and the Beginnings of Industrialization in North Carolina." *Journal of American History* 77 (September 1990): 445–75.

Carter, Dan T. "From Segregation to Integration." In *Interpreting Southern History: Historiographical Essays in Honor of Sanford W. Higginbotham*, edited by John B. Boles and Evelyn Thomas Nolen, 408–33. Baton Rouge: Louisiana State University Press, 1987.

———. *The Politics of Rage: George Wallace, the Origins of the New Conservatism, and the Transformation of American Politics*. New York: Simon and Schuster, 1995.

———. *Scottsboro: A Tragedy of the American South*. Baton Rouge: Louisiana State University Press, 1979.

———. *When the War Was Over: The Failure of Self-Reconstruction in the South, 1865–1867*. Baton Rouge: Louisiana State University Press, 1985.

Carter, Jimmy. *Turning Point: A Candidate, a State, and a Nation Come of Age*. New York: Times Books, 1992.

Case, Sarah H. "The Historical Ideology of Mildred Lewis Rutherford: A Confederate Historian's New South Creed." *Journal of Southern History* 68 (August 2002): 599–628.

Cash, W. J. *The Mind of the South*. New York: Vintage, 1941.

Cashin, Edward J. *The Quest: A History of Public Education in Richmond County, Georgia*. Augusta, Ga.: Richmond County Board of Education, 1985.

———. *The Story of Augusta*. Augusta, Ga.: Richmond County Board of Education, 1980.

Cashin, Edward J., and Glenn T. Eskew. *Paternalism in a Southern City: Race, Religion, and Gender in Augusta, Georgia*. Athens: University of Georgia Press, 2001.

Cashin, Joan E. *A Family Venture: Men and Women on the Southern Frontier*. Baltimore: Johns Hopkins University Press, 1991.

———. *Our Common Affairs: Texts for Women in the Old South*. Baltimore, Md.: Johns Hopkins University Press, 1996.

———. "The Structure of Antebellum Families: 'The Ties That Bound Us Was Strong.'" *Journal of Southern History* 56 (February 1990): 55–70.

Cecelski, David S., and Timothy B. Tyson. *Democracy Betrayed: The Wilmington Race Riot of 1898 and Its Legacy*. Chapel Hill: University of North Carolina Press, 1998.

Chafe, William H. *The Paradox of Change: American Women in the Twentieth Century*. New York: Oxford University Press, 1981.

Chambers-Schiller, Lee. *Liberty, a Better Husband: Single Women in America, the Generations of 1790–1840*. New Haven: Yale University Press, 1984.

Cheeks-Collins, Jennifer E. *Gwinnett County, Georgia*. Charleston, S.C.: Arcadia, 2001.

Chirhart, Ann Short. "'Gardens of Education': Beulah Rucker and African-American Education in the Twentieth Century Georgia Upcountry." *Georgia Historical Quarterly* 82 (Winter 1998): 829–47.

———. "Gender, Jim Crow, and Eugene Talmadge: The Politics of Social Policy in Georgia." In *The New Deal and Beyond*, edited by Elna C. Green, 71–99. Athens: University of Georgia Press, 2003.

Christian, Barbara. *Black Feminist Criticism: Perspectives on Black Women Writers*. New York: Pergamon, 1985.

Cobb, James C. *Georgia Odyssey*. Athens: University of Georgia Press, 1997.

———. *Industrialization and Southern Society, 1877–1984*. Lexington: University Press of Kentucky, 1984.

———. *Redefining Southern Culture: Mind and Identity in the Modern South*. Athens: University of Georgia Press, 1999.

———. *The Selling of the South: The Southern Crusade for Industrial Development, 1936–1980*. Baton Rouge: Louisiana State University Press, 1982.

Cobb, James C., and Michael Namorato, eds. *The New Deal and the South: Essays*. Jackson: University Press of Mississippi, 1984.

Cohen, Lizabeth. *Making a New Deal: Industrial Workers in Chicago, 1919–1939*. New York: Cambridge University Press, 1990.

Cohen, Miriam. "Italian American Women in New York City, 1900–1950: Work and School." In *Class, Sex, and the Woman Worker*, edited by Milton Cantor and Bruce Laurie, 120–43. Westport, Conn.: Greenwood, 1977.

Cohen, Robert. "Public Schools in Hard Times: Letters from Georgia Educators and Students to Eleanor and Franklin Roosevelt, 1933–1940." *Georgia Historical Quarterly* 82 (spring 1998): 120–49.

Collins, Patricia Hill. "The Social Construction of Black Feminist Thought." *Signs* 14 (summer 1989): 745–73.

Cook, Blanche Wiesen. *Eleanor Roosevelt*. 2 vols. New York: Penguin, 1992–99.

Coon, Lynda L., Katherine J. Haldane, and Elisabeth W. Sommer, eds. *That Gentle Strength: Historical Perspectives on Women in Christianity*. Charlottesville: University Press of Virginia, 1990.

Cordier, Mary Hurlbut. *Schoolwomen of the Prairies and Plains: Personal Narratives from Iowa, Kansas, and Nebraska, 1860s–1920s*. Albuquerque: University of New Mexico Press, 1992.

Corley, Florence Fleming. "The National Youth Administration in Georgia: A New Deal for Young Blacks and Women." *Georgia Historical Quarterly* 77 (winter 1993): 728–56.

Cott, Nancy. *The Grounding of Modern Feminism*. New Haven: Yale University Press, 1987.

————. "What's in a Name? The Limits of 'Social Feminism'; or, Expanding the Vocabulary of Women's History." *Journal of American History* 76 (December 1989): 809–29.

Cowan, Ruth Schwartz. *More Work for Mother: The Ironies of Household Technology from the Open Hearth to the Microwave*. New York: Basic Books, 1983.

Cremin, Lawrence A. *The Transformation of the School: Progressivism in American Education, 1876–1957*. New York: Vintage, 1964.

Cubberly, Ellwood. *Public Education in the United States*. Boston: Houghton Mifflin, 1934.

Dabney, Charles William. *Universal Education in the South*. 2 vols. Chapel Hill: University of North Carolina Press, 1936.

Dailey, Jane. *Before Jim Crow: The Politics of Race in Postemancipation Virginia*. Chapel Hill: University of North Carolina Press, 2000.

Dailey, Jane, Glenda Elizabeth Gilmore, and Bryant Simon, eds. *Jumpin' Jim Crow: Southern Politics from Civil War to Civil Rights*. Princeton: Princeton University Press, 2000.

Damon-Moore, Helen. *Magazines for the Millions: Gender Commerce in the* Ladies' Home Journal *and the* Saturday Evening Post, *1880–1910*. Albany: State University of New York Press, 1994.

Daniel, Pete. *Breaking the Land: The Transformation of Cotton, Tobacco, and Rice Cultures since 1880*. Urbana: University of Illinois Press, 1985.

————. "Going among Strangers: Southern Reactions to World War II." *Journal of American History* 77 (December 1990): 886–911.

————. *Lost Revolutions: The South in the 1950s*. Chapel Hill: University of North Carolina Press, 2000.

————. *Standing at the Crossroads: Southern Life in the Twentieth Century*. New York: Hill and Wang, 1986.

Davis, Angela Y. *Women, Race, and Class*. New York: Random House, 1981.

Davis, Charles T., and Henry Louis Gates Jr., eds. *The Slave's Narrative*. New York: Oxford University Press, 1985.

Davis, Leroy. *A Clashing of the Soul: John Hope and the Dilemma of African American Leadership and Black Higher Education in the Early Twentieth Century*. Athens: University of Georgia Press, 1998.

Dean, Pamela. "College Women and Class Formation in the New South." Paper presented at the Southern Conference on Women's History, Chapel Hill, North Carolina, June 1991.

————. "Learning to Be New Women: Campus Culture at the North Carolina Normal and Industrial College." *North Carolina Historical Review* 68 (July 1991): 286–306.

Degler, Carl N. *At Odds: Women and the Family in America from the Revolution to the Present*. New York: Oxford University Press, 1980.

Dennis, Michael. *Lessons in Progress: State Universities and Progressivism in the New South, 1880–1920*. Urbana: University of Illinois Press, 2002.

Deutsch, Sarah. *No Separate Refuge: Culture, Class, and Gender on an Anglo-Hispanic Frontier in the American Southwest, 1880–1940*. New York: Oxford University Press, 1987.

Diner, Stephen J. *A Very Different Age: Americans of the Progressive Era*. New York: Hill and Wang, 1998.

Dittmer, John. *Black Georgia in the Progressive Era, 1900–1920*. Urbana: University of Illinois Press, 1977.

———. *Local People: The Struggle for Civil Rights in Mississippi*. Urbana: University of Illinois Press, 1994.

Dollard, John. *Caste and Class in a Southern Town*. New York: Doubleday Anchor, 1957.

Donaldson, Bobby J. "New Negroes in the New South: Race, Power, and Ideology in Georgia, 1890–1925." Ph.D. diss., Emory University, 2002.

———. "Standing on a Volcano: The Leadership of William Jefferson White." In *Paternalism in a Southern City: Race, Religion, and Gender in Augusta, Georgia*, edited by Edward J. Cashin and Glenn T. Eskew, 135–76. Athens: University of Georgia Press, 2001.

Dorsey, James E. *The History of Hall County*. Vol. 1. Gainesville, Ga.: Magnolia, 1991.

Douglas, Ann. *The Feminization of American Culture*. New York: Knopf, 1977.

Drago, Edmund L. *Black Politicians and Reconstruction in Georgia: A Splendid Failure*. Athens: University of Georgia Press, 1992.

Dublin, Thomas. "Women, Work, and the Family: Female Operatives in the Lowell Mills, 1830–1860." *Feminist Studies* 3 (fall 1975): 30–39.

Du Bois, W. E. B. *Black Reconstruction in America, 1860–1880*. 1935; reprint, New York: Atheneum, 1992.

———. *The Souls of Black Folk*. New York: New American Library, 1969.

Durkheim, Emile. *On Morality and Society*. Translated by Robert Bellah. Chicago: University of Chicago Press, 1973.

Durr, Virginia Foster. *Outside the Magic Circle: The Autobiography of Virginia Foster Durr*. Edited by Hollinger F. Barnard. University: University of Alabama Press, 1985.

Dyer, Thomas G. *The University of Georgia, a Bicentennial History, 1785–1985*. Athens: University of Georgia Press, 1985.

Dykeman, Wilma, and James Stokely. *Seeds of Southern Change: The Life of Will Alexander*. Chicago: University of Chicago Press, 1962.

Eagles, Charles W., ed. *The Civil Rights Movement in America*. Jackson: University Press of Mississippi, 1986.

Easter, Opal V. *Nannie Helen Burroughs*. New York: Garland, 1995.

Edwards, Laura F. *Gendered Strife and Confusion: The Politics of Reconstruction*. Urbana: University of Illinois Press, 1996.

Egerton, John. *Speak Now against the Day: The Generation before the Civil Rights Movement in the South*. New York: Knopf, 1994.

Eighmy, John Lee. *Churches in Cultural Captivity: A History of the Social Attitudes of Southern Baptists*. Rev. ed. by Samuel S. Hill. Knoxville: University of Tennessee Press, 1987.

Elias, Norbert. *The Civilizing Process*. Translated by Edmund Jephcott. New York: Oxford University Press, 1994.

Elmore, Charles J. *Richard R. Wright, Sr. at GSIC, 1891–1921: A Protean Force for the Social Uplift and Higher Education of Black Americans*. Savannah, Ga.: Atlantic, 1996.

Elrod, Frary. *Historical Notes on Jackson County, Georgia*. Jefferson, Ga.: n.p., 1967.

Elshtain, Jean Bethke. *Public Man, Private Woman: Women in Social and Political Thought*. Princeton: Princeton University Press, 1981.

Epstein, Barbara Leslie. *The Politics of Domesticity: Women, Evangelism, and Temperance in Nineteenth-Century America*. Middletown, Conn.: Wesleyan University Press, 1981.

Epstein, Cynthia Fuchs. *Deceptive Distinctions: Sex, Gender, and the Social Order*. New Haven: Yale University Press, 1988.

Eskew, Glenn T. *But for Birmingham: The Local and National Movements in the Civil Rights Struggle*. Chapel Hill: University of North Carolina Press, 1997.

———, ed. *Labor in the Modern South*. Athens: University of Georgia Press, 2001.

Evans, Augusta J. *Beulah*. 1859; reprint, New York: Dillingham, 1887.

———. *St. Elmo*. New York: Caldwell, 1911.

Fairclough, Adam. "'Being in the Field of Education and Also Being a Negro . . . Seems . . . Tragic': Black Teachers in the Jim Crow South." *Journal of American History* 87 (June 2000): 13–38.

———. *Teaching Equality: Black Schools in the Age of Jim Crow*. Athens: University of Georgia Press, 2001.

Faragher, John Mack. *Sugar Creek: Life on the Illinois Prairie*. New Haven: Yale University Press, 1986.

Farnham, Christie Anne. *The Education of the Southern Belle: Higher Education and Student Socialization in the Antebellum South*. New York: New York University Press, 1994.

———, ed. *Women of the American South: A Multicultural Reader*. New York: New York University Press, 1997.

Fass, Paula. *The Damned and the Beautiful: American Youth in the 1920s*. New York: Oxford University Press, 1977.

Faulkner, William. *Absalom, Absalom!* New York: Random House, 1964.

———. *As I Lay Dying*. New York: Vintage, 1964.

———. *Light in August*. New York: Random House, 1959.

Faust, Drew Gilpin. "Altars of Sacrifice: Confederate Women and the Narratives of War." *Journal of American History* 76 (March 1990): 1200–1228.

———. *Mothers of Invention: Women of the Slaveholding South in the American Civil War*. Chapel Hill: University of North Carolina Press, 1998.

Ferguson, Karen. *Black Politics in New Deal Atlanta*. Chapel Hill: University of North Carolina Press, 2002.

———. "The Politics of Exclusion: Wartime Industrialization, Civil Rights Mobilization, and Black Politics in Atlanta, 1942–1946." In *The Second Wave: Southern Industrialization from the 1940s to the 1970s*, edited by Philip Scranton, 43–80. Athens: University of Georgia Press, 2001.

Fields, Barbara Jeanne. "Ideology and Race in American History." In *Region, Race, and Reconstruction: Essays in Honor of C. Vann Woodward*, edited by J. Morgan Kousser and James M. McPherson, 143–77. New York: Oxford University Press, 1982.

———. "Slavery, Race, and Ideology." *New Left Review* 181 (1990): 95–118.

———. "Whiteness, Racism, and Identity." *International Labor and Working-Class History* 60 (fall 2001): 48–56.

Fields, Mamie Garvin, and Karen Fields. *Lemon Swamp and Other Places: A Carolina Memoir*. New York: Free Press, 1983.

Fink, Deborah. *Agrarian Women: Wives and Mothers in Rural Nebraska, 1880–1940*. Chapel Hill: University of North Carolina Press, 1992.

Fink, Leon. *Workingmen's Democracy: The Knights of Labor and American Politics*. Urbana: University of Illinois Press, 1983.

Finkelstein, Barbara. "Dollars and Dreams: Classrooms as Fictitious Message Systems, 1790–1930." *History of Education Quarterly* 31 (winter 1991): 463–87.

Fite, Gilbert C. *Cotton Fields No More: Southern Agriculture, 1865–1980*. Lexington: University Press of Kentucky, 1984.

———. *Richard B. Russell, Jr., Senator from Georgia*. Chapel Hill: University of North Carolina Press, 1991.

Fitzpatrick, Ellen. *Endless Crusade: Women Social Scientists and Progressive Reform*. New York: Oxford University Press, 1990.

Flamming, Douglas. *Creating the Modern South: Millhands and Managers in Dalton, Georgia, 1884–1984*. Chapel Hill: University of North Carolina Press, 1992.

Flanigan, James C. *History of Gwinnett County, Georgia, 1818–1960*. Vol. 2. Hapeville, Ga.: Longino and Porter, 1959.

Flexner, Eleanor. *Century of Struggle: The Woman's Rights Movement in the United States*. Rev. ed. Cambridge: Harvard University Press, 1975.

Flynn, Charles L., Jr. *White Land, Black Labor: Caste and Class in Late Nineteenth-Century Georgia*. Baton Rouge: Louisiana State University Press, 1983.

Flynt, Wayne. *Poor but Proud: Alabama's Poor Whites*. Tuscaloosa: University of Alabama Press, 1989.

Foner, Eric. *Reconstruction: America's Unfinished Revolution, 1863–1877*. New York: Harper and Row, 1988.

———. "Response to Eric Arnesen." *International Labor and Working-Class History* 60 (fall 2001): 57–60.

Foster, Gaines. *Ghosts of the Confederacy: Defeat, the Lost Cause, and the Emergence of the New South*. New York: Oxford University Press, 1987.

Foster, Michele. *Black Teachers on Teaching*. New York: Norton, 1997.

Fox-Genovese, Elizabeth. "Between Individualism and Community: Autobiographies of Southern Women." In *Located Lives: Place and Idea in Southern Autobiography*, edited by J. Bill Berry, 20–38. Athens: University of Georgia Press, 1990.

———. *Feminism without Illusions: A Critique of Individualism*. Chapel Hill: University of North Carolina Press, 1991.

———. Introduction to *The Autobiography of Du Pont de Nemours*. Wilmington: Scholarly Resources, 1984.

———. "My Statue, My Self: Autobiographical Writings of Afro-American Women." In *The Private Self: Theory and Practice of Women's Autobiographical Writings*, edited by Shari Benstock, 63–89. Chapel Hill: University of North Carolina Press, 1988.

———. "Placing Women's History in History." *New Left Review* 133 (May–June 1982): 5–29.

———. "Socialist-Feminist American Women's History: A Review Essay." *Journal of Women's History* 1 (winter 1990): 181–210.

———. *Within the Plantation Household: Black and White Women of the Old South*. Chapel Hill: University of North Carolina Press, 1988.

———. "Women and Agriculture in the Nineteenth Century." In *Agriculture and National Development: Views on the Nineteenth Century*, edited by Louis Ferleger, 267–302. Ames: Iowa State University Press, 1990.

Fox-Genovese, Elizabeth, and Eugene D. Genovese. "The Divine Sanction of Social Order: Religious Foundations of the Southern Slaveholders' World View." *Journal of the American Academy of Religion* 55 (summer 1987): 211–33.

———. *Fruits of Merchant Capital: Slavery and Bourgeois Property in the Rise and Expansion of Capitalism*. New York: Oxford University Press, 1983.

Frankel, Noralee, and Nancy S. Dye, eds. *Gender, Class, Race, and Reform in the Progressive Era*. Lexington: University Press of Kentucky, 1991.

Franklin, John Hope, and August Meier, eds. *Black Leaders of the Twentieth Century*. Urbana: University of Illinois Press, 1982.

Franklin, John Hope, and Alfred A. Moss Jr. *From Slavery to Freedom: A History of African Americans*. 7th ed. New York: McGraw-Hill, 1994.

Fraser, Steve. "Labor Question." In *The Rise and Fall of the New Deal Order, 1930–1980*, edited by Steve Fraser and Gary Gerstle, 55–84. Princeton: Princeton University Press, 1989.

Fraser, Walter J., Jr., R. Frank Saunders Jr., and Jon L. Wakelyn, eds. *The Web of Southern Social Relations: Women, Family, and Education*. Athens: University of Georgia Press, 1985.

Frazier, E. Franklin. *The Negro Church in America*. New York: Schocken, 1974.

———. *The Negro in the United States*. New York: Macmillan, 1957.

Frederickson, George M. *The Black Image in the White Mind: The Debate on Afro-American Character and Destiny, 1817–1914*. New York: Harper and Row, 1971.

Frederickson, Kari. *The Dixiecrat Revolt and the End of the Solid South, 1932–1968*. Chapel Hill: University of North Carolina Press, 2001.

Frederickson, Mary E. "'Each One Is Dependent on the Other': Southern Churchwomen, Racial Reform, and the Process of Transformation, 1880–1940." In *Visible Women: New Essays on American Activism*, edited by Nancy A. Hewitt and Suzanne Lebsock, 296–324. Urbana: University of Illinois Press, 1993.

Freidel, Frank. *FDR and the South*. Baton Rouge: Louisiana State University Press, 1965.

———. *Franklin D. Roosevelt: A Rendezvous with Destiny*. New York: Little, Brown, 1990.

Friedlander, Amy. "A More Perfect Christian Womanhood: Higher Learning for a New South." In *Education and the Rise of the New South*, edited by Ronald K. Goodenow and Arthur O. White, 72–91. Boston: G. K. Hall, 1981.

Friedman, Jean E. *The Enclosed Garden: Women and Community in the Evangelical South*. Chapel Hill: University of North Carolina Press, 1985.

Friedman, Susan Stanford. "Women's Autobiographical Selves: Theory and Practice." In *The Private Self: Theory and Practice of Women's Autobiographical Writings*, edited by Shari Benstock, 34–62. Chapel Hill: University of North Carolina Press, 1988.

Gaines, Kevin K. *Uplifting the Race: Black Leadership, Politics, and Culture in the Twentieth Century*. Chapel Hill: University of North Carolina Press, 1996.

Garrow, David J. *Bearing the Cross: Martin Luther King and the Southern Christian Leadership Conference*. New York: Vintage, 1986.

Garvey, Ellen Gruber. *The Adman in the Parlor: Magazines and the Gendering of Consumer Culture, 1880s to 1910s*. New York: Oxford University Press, 1996.

Gaston, Paul M. *The New South Creed: A Study in Southern Mythmaking*. Baton Rouge: Louisiana State University Press, 1970.

Gates, Henry Louis, Jr. *Figures in Black: Words, Signs, and the "Racial" Self*. New York: Oxford University Press, 1987.

———. *The Signifying Monkey: A Theory of African-American Literary Criticism*. New York: Oxford University Press, 1988.

Gatewood, Willard B. *Aristocrats of Color: The Black Elite, 1880–1920*. Bloomington: Indiana University Press, 1990.

Gaventa, John. *Power and Powerlessness: Quiescence and Rebellion in an Appalachian Valley*. Urbana: University of Illinois Press, 1980.

Genovese, Eugene D. *The Political Economy of Slavery*. New York: Vintage, 1967.

———. *Roll, Jordan, Roll: The World the Slaves Made*. New York: Vintage, 1976.

Georgia Association of Jeanes Curriculum Directors. *Jeanes Supervision in Georgia Schools: A Guiding Light in Education: A History of the Program from 1908–1975*. Athens: Georgia Association, 1975.

Georgia Teachers and Education Association, History Committee and Consultants. *Rising in the Sun: A History of the Georgia Teachers and Education Association, 1918–1966*. Atlanta: Harris, 1966.

Giddings, Paula. *When and Where I Enter: The Impact of Black Women on Race and Sex in America*. New York: Bantam, 1985.

Gilmore, Glenda Elizabeth. *Gender and Jim Crow: Women and the Politics of White Supremacy in North Carolina, 1896–1920*. Chapel Hill: University of North Carolina Press, 1996.

Ginzberg, Lori. *Women and the Work of Benevolence: Morality, Politics, and Class in the Nineteenth-Century United States*. New Haven: Yale University Press, 1990.

Glasgow, Ellen. *Barren Ground*. New York: Harcourt, Brace, Jovanovich, 1985.

————. *The Sheltered Life*. New York: Harcourt, Brace, Jovanovich, 1985.

Glenn, Susan A. *Daughters of the Shtetl: Life and Labor in the Immigrant Generation*. Ithaca: Cornell University Press, 1990.

Glymph, Thavolia, Harold D. Woodman, Barbara Jean Fields, and Armstead L. Robinson, eds. *Essays on the Postbellum Southern Economy*. College Station: Texas A & M University Press, 1985.

Goldin, Claudia. *Understanding the Gender Gap: An Economic History of American Women*. New York: Oxford University Press, 1989.

Goodenow, Ronald K., and Arthur O. White. *Education and the Rise of the New South*. Boston: Hall, 1981.

Goodson, Steve. *Highbrows, Hillbillies, and Hellfire: Public Entertainment in Atlanta, 1880–1930*. Athens: University of Georgia Press, 2002.

Goodwin, Doris Kearns. *No Ordinary Time: Franklin and Eleanor Roosevelt: The Home Front in World War II*. New York: Simon and Schuster, 1994.

Goodwyn, Lawrence. *The Populist Moment: A Short History of the Agrarian Revolt in America*. New York: Oxford University Press, 1978.

Gordon, Caroline. *None Shall Look Back*. New York: Scribner's, 1937.

Gordon, Linda. "Family Violence, Feminism, and Social Control." In *Unequal Sisters: A Multicultural Reader in United States Women's History*, edited by Ellen Carol DuBois and Vicki L. Ruiz, 141–56. New York: Routledge, Chapman, and Hall, 1990.

————. *Heroes of Their Own Lives: The Politics and History of Family Violence*. New York: Penguin, 1988.

————. *Pitied but Not Entitled: Single Mothers and the History of Welfare*. New York: Free Press, 1994.

Gordon, Lynn. *Gender and Higher Education in the Progressive Era*. New Haven: Yale University Press, 1990.

Gordon, Michael, ed. *The American Family in Social-Historical Perspective*. 3d ed. New York: St. Martin's, 1983.

Grant, Donald L. *The Way It Was in the South: The Black Experience in Georgia*. Athens: University of Georgia Press, 1993.

Grantham, Dewey. *Southern Progressivism: The Reconciliation of Progress and Tradition*. Knoxville: University of Tennessee Press, 1983.

Green, Elna C. "'Ideals of Government, of Home, and of Women': The Ideology of Southern White Antisuffragism." In *Hidden Histories of Women in the New South*, edited by Virginia Bernhard, Betty Brandon, Elizabeth Fox-Genovese, Theda Perdue, and Elizabeth H. Turner, 96–113. Columbia: University of Missouri Press, 1994.

————. *Southern Strategies: Southern Women and the Woman Suffrage Question*. Chapel Hill: University of North Carolina Press, 1998.

————, ed. *Before the New Deal: Social Welfare in the South, 1830–1930*. Athens: University of Georgia Press, 1999.

————, ed. *The New Deal and Beyond: Social Welfare in the South since 1930*. Athens: University of Georgia Press, 2003.

Green, James R. *The World of the Worker: Labor in Twentieth-Century America.* New York: Hill and Wang, 1980.

Greenwald, Maurine Weiner. "Working-Class Feminism and the Family Wage Ideal: The Seattle Debate on Married Women's Right to Work, 1914–1920." *Journal of American History* 76 (June 1989): 118–49.

Groneman, Carol, and Mary Beth Norton, eds. *"To Toil the Livelong Day": America's Women at Work, 1780–1980.* Ithaca: Cornell University Press, 1987.

Grossman, James R. *Land of Hope: Chicago, Black Southerners, and the Great Migration.* Chicago: University of Chicago Press, 1989.

Grumet, Madeleine R. *Bitter Milk: Women and Teaching.* Amherst: University of Massachusetts Press, 1988.

Gutman, Herbert G. *The Black Family in Slavery and Freedom, 1750–1925.* New York: Pantheon, 1976.

———. *Work, Culture, and Society in Industrializing America.* New York: Vintage, 1977.

Guy-Sheftall, Beverly. "Black Women and Higher Education: Spelman and Bennett Colleges Revisited." *Journal of Negro Education* 51 (summer 1982): 278–87.

Habermas, Jürgen. *The Structural Transformation of the Public Sphere: An Inquiry into a Category of Bourgeois Society.* Cambridge: MIT Press, 1989.

Hackworth, C. B. "Rape, Lynchings Left Mark on Forsyth and Dawson." *Gainesville Times,* April 13, 1980, p. 1–E.

———. "Reminder of Events of 1912 Remain in Forsyth, Dawson." *Gainesville Times,* April 14, 1980, p. 1.

Hagood, Margaret. *Mothers of the South: Portraiture of the White Tenant Farm Women.* 1939; reprint, New York: Norton, 1977.

Hahn, Steven. *A Nation under Our Feet: Black Political Struggles in the Rural South from Slavery to the Great Migration.* Cambridge: Harvard University Press, 2003.

———. *The Roots of Southern Populism: Yeoman Farmers and the Transformation of the Georgia Upcountry, 1850–1890.* New York: Oxford University Press, 1983.

Hahn, Steven, and Jonathan Prude, eds. *The Countryside in the Age of Capitalist Transformation.* Chapel Hill: University of North Carolina Press, 1985.

Halbwachs, Maurice. *On Collective Memory.* Translated by Lewis A. Coser. Chicago: University of Chicago Press, 1992.

Hale, Grace Elizabeth. *Making Whiteness: The Culture of Segregation in the South, 1890–1940.* New York: Vintage, 1998.

Hall, Clyde W. *One Hundred Years of Educating at Savannah State College, 1890–1990.* Peoria, Ill.: Versa, 1991.

Hall, Jacquelyn Dowd. "Disorderly Women: Gender and Labor Militancy in the Appalachian South." *Journal of American History* 73 (September 1986): 354–82.

———. "O. Delight Smith's Progressive Era: Labor, Feminism, and Reform in the Urban South—Atlanta, Georgia, 1907–1915." In *Visible Women: New Essays on American Activism,* edited by Nancy Hewitt and Suzanne Lebsock, 166–98. Urbana: University of Illinois Press, 1993.

———. *Revolt against Chivalry: Jessie Daniel Ames and the Women's Campaign against Lynching*. New York: Columbia University Press, 1979.

———. "'You Must Remember This': Autobiography as Social Critique." *Journal of American History* 85 (September 1998): 439–65.

Hall, Jacquelyn Dowd, James Leloudis, Robert Korstad, Mary Murphy, Lu Ann Jones, and Christopher B. Daly. *Like a Family: The Making of a Southern Cotton Mill World*. New York: Norton, 1987.

Hamby, Alonzo. *The New Deal: Analysis and Interpretation*. New York: Longmans, 1981.

Hampton, Henry, and Steven Fayer. *Voices of Freedom: An Oral History of the Civil Rights Movement from the 1950s through the 1980s*. New York: Bantam, 1990.

Hanchett, Thomas W. "The Rosenwald Schools and Black Education in North Carolina." *North Carolina Historical Review* 64 (October 1988): 387–427.

Harding, Vincent. *There Is a River: The Black Struggle for Freedom in America*. New York: Harcourt Brace Jovanovich, 1981.

Harlan, Louis R. *Booker T. Washington: The Making of a Black Leader, 1856–1901*. New York: Oxford University Press, 1972.

———. *Booker T. Washington: The Wizard of Tuskegee, 1901–1915*. New York: Oxford University Press, 1983.

———. *Separate and Unequal: Southern School Campaigns and Racism in the Southern Seaboard States, 1901–1915*. New York: Atheneum, 1968.

Harley, Sharon. "For the Good of the Family and Race: Gender, Work, and Domestic Roles in the Black Community, 1880–1930." *Signs* 15 (winter 1990): 336–49.

———. "'When Your Work Is Not Who You Are': The Development of a Working-Class Consciousness among Afro-American Women." In *Gender, Class, Race, and Reform in the Progressive Era*, edited by Noralee Frankel and Nancy S. Dye, 42–55. Lexington: University Press of Kentucky, 1991.

Harper, Frances E. W. *Iola Leroy*. 1893; reprint, Boston: Beacon, 1987.

Harris, Barbara. *Beyond Her Sphere: Women and Professions in American History*. Westport, Conn.: Greenwood, 1978.

Harris, Corra. *A Circuit Rider's Wife*. New York: Doubleday, 1910.

———. *The Recording Angel*. New York: Doubleday, 1912.

Harris, J. William. *Plain Folk and Gentry in a Slave Society: White Liberty and Black Slavery in Augusta's Hinterlands*. Middletown, Conn.: Wesleyan University Press, 1985.

Harris, Narvie J., and Dee Taylor. *African-American Education in De Kalb County*. Charleston, S.C.: Arcadia, 1999.

Harvey, Paul. *Redeeming the South: Religious Cultures and Racial Identities among Southern Baptists, 1865–1924*. Chapel Hill: University of North Carolina Press, 1997.

Hatch, Nathan O. *The Democratization of American Christianity*. New Haven: Yale University Press, 1989.

Hattam, Victoria C. "Whiteness: Theorizing Race, Eliding Ethnicity." *International Labor and Working-Class History* 60 (fall 2001): 61–68.

Haynes, Elizabeth Ross. *The Black Boy of Atlanta*. Boston: House of Edinboro, 1952.

Heilbrun, Carolyn G. *Writing a Woman's Life*. New York: Ballantine, 1988.

Hemenway, Robert E. *Zora Neale Hurston: A Literary Biography*. Urbana: University of Illinois Press, 1977.

Henderson, Harold Paulk. *The Politics of Change in Georgia: A Political Biography of Ellis Arnall*. Athens: University of Georgia Press, 1991.

Henderson, Harold Paulk, and Gary L. Roberts, eds. *Georgia Governors in an Age of Change: From Ellis Arnall to George Busbee*. Athens: University of Georgia Press, 1988.

Henderson, Mae Gwendolyn. "Speaking in Tongues: Dialogics, Dialectics, and the Black Woman Writer's Literary Tradition." In *Changing Our Own Words: Essays on Criticism, Theory, and Writing by Black Women*, edited by Cheryl A. Wall, 16–37. New Brunswick: Rutgers University Press, 1989.

Henretta, James A. "Families and Farms: *Mentalité* in Preindustrial America." *William and Mary Quarterly* 35 (January 1978): 3–32.

Herbst, Jurgen. *And Sadly Teach: Teacher Education and Professionalization in American Culture*. Madison: University of Wisconsin Press, 1989.

Hewitt, Nancy A. "Beyond the Search for Sisterhood: American Women's History in the 1980s." *Social History* 10 (October 1985): 299–321.

———. *Women's Activism and Social Change: Rochester, New York, 1822–1872*. Ithaca: Cornell University Press, 1984.

Hewitt, Nancy A., and Suzanne Lebsock, eds. *Visible Women: New Essays on American Activism*. Urbana: University of Illinois Press, 1993.

Hickey, Georgina. "'The Lowest Form of Work Relief': Authority, Gender, and the State in Atlanta's WPA Sewing Rooms." In *The New Deal and Beyond: Social Welfare in the South since 1930*, edited by Elna C. Green, 3–29. Athens: University of Georgia Press, 2003.

Higginbotham, Evelyn Brooks. "African-American Women's History and the Metalanguage of Race." *Signs* 17 (winter 1992): 251–74.

———. "Beyond the Sound of Silence: Afro-American Women's History." *Gender and History* 1 (spring 1989): 50–67.

———. *Righteous Discontent: The Women's Movement in the Black Baptist Church, 1880–1920*. Cambridge: Harvard University Press, 1993.

Hill, Hines Lafayette. "Negro Education in Rural Georgia." Master's thesis, Emory University, 1939.

Hill, Samuel S. *Southern Churches in Crisis*. New York: Holt, Rinehart, and Winston, 1966.

———, ed. *Varieties of Southern Religious Experience*. Baton Rouge: Louisiana State University Press, 1988.

Hine, Darlene Clark. "Black Professionals and Race Consciousness: Origins of the Civil Rights Movement, 1890–1950." *Journal of American History* 89 (March 2003): 1279–94.

———. *Black Women in White: Racial Conflict and Cooperation in the Nursing Profession, 1890–1950*. Bloomington: Indiana University Press, 1989.

———. "Lifting the Veil, Shattering the Silence: Black Women's History in Slavery and Freedom." In *The State of Afro-American History*, edited by Darlene Clark Hine, 223–49. Baton Rouge: Louisiana State University Press, 1986.

———. "Rape and the Inner Lives of Black Women in the Middle West: Preliminary Thoughts on the Culture of Dissemblance." *Signs* 14 (summer 1989): 912–20.

Hine, Darlene Clark, Elsa Barkley Brown, and Rosalyn Terborg-Penn, eds. *Black Women in America: An Historical Encyclopedia*. Bloomington: Indiana University Press, 1994.

Hobsbawm, Eric J. *The Age of Capital, 1848–1875*. New York: Penguin, 1975.

———. *The Age of Empire, 1875–1914*. New York: Vintage, 1987.

———. *The Age of Extremes: A History of the World, 1914–1991*. New York: Pantheon, 1995.

Hobsbawm, Eric J., and Terrance Ranger, eds. *The Invention of Tradition*. Cambridge: Cambridge University Press, 1984.

Hobson, Fred. *Tell about the South: The Southern Rage to Explain*. Baton Rouge: Louisiana State University Press, 1983.

Hoffman, Nancy. *Women's "True" Profession: Voices from the History of Teaching*. Old Westbury, N.Y.: Feminist Press, 1981.

Hofstadter, Richard. *The Age of Reform*. New York: Vintage, 1955.

Holmes, Michael. *The New Deal in Georgia: An Administrative History*. Westport, Conn.: Greenwood, 1975.

Holt, Rackham. *Mary McLeod Bethune: A Biography*. Garden City, N.Y.: Doubleday, 1964.

Holt, Sharon Ann. "Making Freedom Pay: Freedpeople Working for Themselves—North Carolina, 1865–1900." *Journal of Southern History* 60 (May 1994): 229–62.

Homans, Margaret. *Bearing the Word: Language and Female Experience in Nineteenth-Century Women's Writing*. Chicago: University of Chicago Press, 1986.

Honey, Michael K. *Southern Labor and Black Civil Rights: Organizing Memphis Workers*. Urbana: University of Illinois Press, 1993.

hooks, bell. *Ain't I a Woman: Black Women and Feminism*. Boston: South End Press, 1984.

Hopkins, Pauline. *Contending Forces: A Romance Illustrative of Negro Life in the North and South*. New York: Oxford University Press, 1988.

Horowitz, Helen Lefkowitz. *Campus Life: Undergraduate Cultures from the End of the Eighteenth Century to the Present*. New York: Knopf, 1987.

Hunter, Jane. *The Gospel of Gentility: American Women Missionaries in Turn-of-the-Century China*. New Haven: Yale University Press, 1984.

Hunter, Tera W. *To 'Joy My Freedom*. Cambridge: Harvard University Press.

Hunter-Gault, Charlayne. *In My Place*. New York: Vintage, 1992.

Hurston, Zora Neale. *Dust Tracks on a Road*. New York: HarperCollins, 1991.

———. *Their Eyes Were Watching God*. Urbana: University of Illinois Press, 1978.

Inscoe, John C. *Mountain Masters, Slavery, and the Sectional Crisis in Western North Carolina*. Knoxville: University of Tennessee Press, 1989.

―――, ed. *Georgia Black and White: Exploration in the Race Relations of a Southern State, 1865–1950*. Athens: University of Georgia Press, 1994.

Janiewski, Delores. *Sisterhood Denied: Race, Gender, and Class in a New South Community*. Philadelphia: Temple University Press, 1985.

Jaynes, Gerald David. *Branches without Roots: Genesis of the Black Working Class in the American South, 1862–1882*. New York: Oxford University Press, 1986.

Jeffrey, Julie Roy. *Frontier Women: The Trans-Mississippi West, 1840–1880*. New York: Hill and Wang, 1979.

Jensen, Joan M. *Loosening the Bonds: Mid-Atlantic Farm Women, 1750–1850*. New Haven: Yale University Press, 1986.

―――. *Promise to the Land: Essays on Rural Women*. Albuquerque: University of New Mexico Press, 1991.

Johnson, Guion Griffis. "Southern Paternalism toward Negroes after Emancipation." *Journal of Southern History* 23 (November 1957): 483–509.

Johnson, Michael P. *Toward a Patriarchal Republic: The Secession of Georgia*. Baton Rouge: Louisiana State University Press, 1977.

Johnson, Miriam M. *Strong Mothers, Weak Wives: The Search for Gender Equality*. Berkeley: University of California Press, 1988.

Joiner, Oscar, ed. *A History of Public Education in Georgia, 1734–1976*. Columbia, S.C.: Bryan, 1979.

Jones, Anne Goodwyn. *Tomorrow Is Another Day: The Woman Writer in the South, 1859–1936*. Baton Rouge: Louisiana State University Press, 1981.

Jones, Jacqueline. "Encounters Likely and Unlikely between Blacks and Poor White Women in the Rural South, 1865–1940." *Georgia Historical Quarterly* 76 (summer 1992): 333–53.

―――. *Labor of Love, Labor of Sorrow: Black Women, Work, and the Family from Slavery to the Present*. New York: Vintage, 1985.

―――. *Soldiers of Light and Love: Northern Teachers and Georgia Blacks, 1865–1873*. Chapel Hill: University of North Carolina Press, 1980.

Jones, Lu Ann. "Gender, Race, and Itinerant Commerce in the Rural New South." *Journal of Southern History* 66 (May 2000): 297–320.

―――. "'If I Must Say So Myself': Oral Histories of Rural Women." *Oral History Review* (fall 1989): 1–23.

―――. *Mama Learned Us to Work: Farm Women in the New South*. Chapel Hill: University of North Carolina Press, 2002.

Kaledin, Eugenia. *Daily Life in the United States, 1940–1959: Shifting Worlds*. Westport, Conn.: Greenwood, 2000.

Kasson, John F. *Amusing the Millions: Coney Island at the Turn of the Century*. New York: Hill and Wang, 1978.

Katz, Michael B. *Class, Bureaucracy, and the Schools: The Illusion of Educational Change in America*. New York: Praeger, 1971.

———. *The Irony of Early School Reform: Educational Innovation in Mid–Nineteenth Century Massachusetts*. Cambridge: Harvard University Press, 1968.

Kaufman, Polly Welts. *Women Teachers on the Frontier*. New Haven: Yale University Press, 1984.

Keith, Jeanette. *Country People in the New South: Tennessee's Upper Cumberland*. Chapel Hill: University of North Carolina Press, 1995.

Kelley, Robin D. G. *Hammer and Hoe: Alabama Communists during the Great Depression*. Chapel Hill: University of North Carolina Press, 1990.

———. *Race Rebels: Culture, Politics, and the Black Working Class*. New York: Free Press, 1994.

———. "'We Are Not What We Seem': Rethinking Black Working-Class Opposition in the Jim Crow South." *Journal of American History* 80 (June 1993): 75–112.

Kennedy, David M. *Freedom from Fear: The American People in Depression and War, 1929–1945*. New York: Oxford University Press, 1999.

Kerber, Linda K. "Separate Spheres, Female Worlds, Woman's Place: The Rhetoric of Women's History." *Journal of American History* 75 (June 1988): 9–39.

———. *Women of the Republic: Intellect and Ideology in Revolutionary America*. Chapel Hill: University of North Carolina Press, 1980.

Kessler-Harris, Alice. *Out to Work: A History of Wage-Earning Women in the United States*. New York: Oxford University Press, 1982.

Key, V. O. *Southern Politics in State and Nation*. New York: Knopf, 1949.

Kirby, Jack Temple. *Darkness at the Dawning: Race and Reform in the Progressive South*. Philadelphia: Lippincott, 1972.

———. *Rural Worlds Lost: The American South, 1920–1960*. Baton Rouge: Louisiana State University Press, 1987.

Kleinberg, S. J. *Women in the United States, 1830–1945*. New Brunswick, N.J.: Rutgers University Press, 1999.

Kleinberg, Susan J. "The Systematic Study of Urban Women." In *Class, Sex, and the Woman Worker*, edited by Milton Cantor and Bruce Laurie, 20–42. Westport, Conn.: Greenwood, 1977

Kolchin, Peter. "Whiteness Studies: The New History of Race in America." *Journal of American History* 89 (June 2002): 154–73.

Korstad, Robert. *Civil Rights Unionism: Tobacco Workers and the Struggle for Democracy in the Mid–Twentieth Century South*. Chapel Hill: University of North Carolina Press, 2003.

Korstad, Robert, and Nelson Lichtenstein. "Opportunities Found and Lost: Labor, Radicals, and the Early Civil Rights Movement." *Journal of American History* 75 (December 1988): 786–811.

Kousser, J. Morgan. "Progressivism—For Middle-Class Whites Only: North Carolina Education, 1880–1910." *Journal of Southern History* 46 (May 1980): 168–94.

———. "Separate but *Not* Equal: The Supreme Court's First Decision on Racial Discrimination in Schools." *Journal of Southern History* 46 (February 1980): 17–44.

———. *The Shaping of Southern Politics: Suffrage Restriction and the Establishment of the One-Party South, 1880–1910.* New Haven: Yale University Press, 1974.

Kraditor, Aileen. *The Idea of the Woman Suffrage Movement, 1890–1920.* New York: Columbia University Press, 1965.

Kunzel, Regina G. *Fallen Women, Problem Girls: Unmarried Mothers and the Professionalization of Social Work, 1890–1945.* New Haven: Yale University Press, 1993.

Kytle, Calvin, and James A. MacKay. *Who Runs Georgia? A Contemporary Account of the 1947 Crisis That Set the Stage for Georgia's Political Transformation.* Athens: University of Georgia Press, 1998.

Laird, Pamela Walker. *Advertising Progress: American Business and the Rise of Consumer Marketing.* Baltimore: Johns Hopkins University Press, 1998.

Lasch-Quinn, Elisabeth. *Black Neighbors: Race and the Limits of Reform in the American Settlement House Movement, 1890–1945.* Chapel Hill: University of North Carolina Press, 1993.

Lassiter, Patrice Shelton. *Generations of Black Life in Kennesaw and Marietta, Georgia.* Charleston, S.C.: Arcadia, 1999.

Lawson, Steven F. *Black Ballots: Voting Rights in the South, 1944–1969.* New York: Columbia University Press, 1976.

———. "Freedom Then, Freedom Now: The Historiography of the Civil Rights Movement." *American Historical Review* 96 (April 1991): 456–71.

———, ed. *To Secure These Rights: The Report of President Harry S. Truman's Committee on Civil Rights.* Boston: Bedford/St. Martin's, 2004.

Lears, T. J. Jackson. *No Place of Grace: Antimodernism and the Transformation of American Culture, 1880–1920.* New York: Pantheon, 1981.

Lebsock, Suzanne. "Woman Suffrage and White Supremacy: A Virginia Case Study." In *Visible Women: New Essays on American Activism,* edited by Nancy Hewitt and Suzanne Lebsock, 62–100. Urbana: University of Illinois Press, 1993.

LeGuin, Charles A., ed. *A Home-Concealed Woman: The Diaries of Magnolia Wynn LeGuin, 1901–1913.* Athens: University of Georgia Press, 1990.

Leloudis, James. "'A More Certain Means of Grace': Pedagogy, Self, and Society in North Carolina, 1880–1920," Ph.D. diss., University of North Carolina at Chapel Hill, 1989.

———. *Schooling the New South: Pedagogy, Self, and Society in North Carolina, 1880–1920.* Chapel Hill: University of North Carolina Press, 1996.

———. "School Reform in the New South: The Women's Association for the Betterment of Public School Houses in North Carolina, 1902–1919." *Journal of American History* 69 (March 1983): 886–909.

Leslie, Kent Anderson. "No Middle Ground: Elite African Americans in Augusta and the Coming of Jim Crow." In *Paternalism in a Southern City: Race, Religion, and Gender in Augusta, Georgia,* edited by Edward J. Cashin and Glenn T. Eskew, 110–34. Athens: University of Georgia Press, 2001.

Leuchtenburg, William E. *The FDR Years: On Roosevelt and His Legacy*. New York: Columbia University Press, 1995.

———. *Franklin Delano Roosevelt and the New Deal*. New York: Harper Torchbooks, 1963.

Levine, Lawrence W. *Black Culture and Black Consciousness: Afro-American Folk Thought from Slavery to Freedom*. New York: Oxford University Press, 1977.

Lewis, David Levering. *W. E. B. Du Bois: A Biography of a Race, 1868–1919*. New York: Holt, 1993.

———. *W. E. B. Du Bois: The Fight for Equality and the American Century, 1919–1963*. New York: Holt, 2000.

Lichtenstein, Nelson. "From Corporatism to Collective Bargaining: Organized Labor and the Eclipse of Social Democracy in the Postwar Era." In *The Rise and Fall of the New Deal Order, 1930–1980*, edited by Steve Fraser and Gary Gerstle, 122–52. Princeton: Princeton University Press, 1989.

Lincoln, C. Eric, and Lawrence H. Mamiya. *The Black Church in the African American Experience*. Durham: Duke University Press, 1990.

Lines, Amelia Akehurst. *"To Raise Myself a Little": The Diaries and Letters of Jennie, a Georgia Teacher, 1851–1886*. Edited by Thomas Dyer. Athens: University of Georgia Press, 1982.

Link, William A. *A Hard Country and a Lonely Place: Schooling, Society, and Reform in Rural Virginia, 1870–1920*. Chapel Hill: University of North Carolina Press, 1986.

———. *The Paradox of Southern Progressivism, 1880–1930*. Chapel Hill: University of North Carolina Press, 1992.

———. "Privies, Progressivism, and Public Schools: Health Reform and Education in the Rural South, 1909–1920." *Journal of Southern History* 54 (November 1988): 623–42.

Littlefield, Valinda Rogers. "Moving Quietly but Forceably: Annie W. Holland and Education in North Carolina, 1911–1934." Unpublished paper. In possession of author.

Litwack, Leon. *Been in the Storm So Long: The Aftermath of Slavery*. New York: Knopf, 1979.

———. *Trouble in Mind: Black Southerners in the Age of Jim Crow*. New York: Knopf, 1998.

Loveland, Anne. *Southern Evangelicals and the Social Order, 1800–1860*. Baton Rouge: Louisiana State University Press, 1980.

Luker, Paul. *The Social Gospel in Black and White: American Racial Reform, 1885–1912*. Chapel Hill: University of North Carolina Press, 1991.

Lumpkin, Katherine DuPre. *The Making of a Southerner*. Athens: University of Georgia Press, 1981.

Lyon, David. *Postmodernity*. Minneapolis: University of Minnesota Press, 1994.

MacLean, Nancy. *Behind the Mask of Chivalry: The Making of the Second Ku Klux Klan*. New York: Oxford University Press, 1994.

———. "The Leo Frank Case Reconsidered: Gender and Sexual Politics in the Making of Reactionary Populism." *Journal of American History* 78 (December 1991): 917–48.

Maharidge, Dale, and Michael Williamson. *And Their Children after Them: The Legacy of "Let Us Now Praise Famous Men."* New York: Pantheon, 1989.

Margo, Robert A. *Race and Schooling in the South, 1880–1950: An Economic History.* Chicago: University of Chicago Press, 1990.

Mars, Florence. *Witness in Philadelphia.* Baton Rouge: Louisiana State University Press, 1977.

Marsden, George M. *Fundamentalism and American Culture: The Shaping of Twentieth-Century Evangelicalism, 1870–1925.* New York: Oxford University Press, 1980.

———. *Understanding Fundamentalism and Evangelicalism.* Grand Rapids, Mich.: Eerdmans, 1991.

Martin, Waldo E., Jr. *Brown v. Board of Education: A Brief History with Documents.* Boston: Bedford/St. Martin's, 1998.

Marty, Martin E., and R. Scott Appleby, eds. *Fundamentalisms Comprehended.* Chicago: University of Chicago Press, 1995.

Mason, Herman "Skip," Jr. *African-American Life in De Kalb County, 1823–1970.* Charleston, S.C.: Arcadia, 1998.

Mathews, Donald G. *Religion in the Old South.* Chicago: University of Chicago Press, 1977.

Matsumoto, Valerie. *Farming the Home Place: A Japanese American Community in California, 1919–1982.* Ithaca: Cornell University Press, 1993.

May, Elaine Tyler. "Cold War—Warm Hearth: Politics and the Family in Postwar America." In *The Rise and Fall of the New Deal Order 1930–1960,* edited by Steve Fraser and Gary Gerstle, 153–81. Princeton: Princeton University Press, 1989.

———. *Homeward Bound: American Families in the Cold War Era.* New York: Basic Books, 1988.

May, Martha. "The Historical Problem of the Family Wage: The Ford Motor Company and the Five Dollar Day." *Feminist Studies* 8 (summer 1982): 399–424.

McArthur, Judith N. *Creating the New Woman: The Rise of Southern Women's Progressive Culture in Texas, 1893–1918.* Urbana: University of Illinois Press, 1998.

McCandless, Amy Thompson. *The Past in the Present: Women's Higher Education in the Twentieth-Century American South.* Tuscaloosa: University of Alabama Press, 1999.

McCluskey, Audrey Thomas. *Mary McLeod Bethune: Building a Better World.* Bloomington: Indiana University Press, 1999.

———. "'The Most Sacrificing Service': The Educational Leadership of Lucy Craft Laney and Mary McLeod Bethune." In *Women of the American South,* edited by Christie Anne Farnham, 189–203. New York: New York University Press, 1997.

McCurry, Stephanie G. *Masters of Small Worlds: Yeoman Households, Gender Relations, and the Political Culture of the Antebellum South Carolina Low Country.* New York: Oxford University Press, 1995.

McDowell, John Patrick. *The Social Gospel in the South: The Women's Home Mission Movement in the Methodist Episcopal Church, South, 1886–1939*. Baton Rouge: Louisiana State University Press, 1982.

McElvaine, Robert. *The Great Depression*. New York: Times Books, 1984.

McGerr, Michael. "Political Style and Women's Power, 1830–1930." *Journal of American History* 77 (December 1990): 864–85.

McKay, Nellie Y. "Race, Gender, and Cultural Context in Zora Neale Hurston's *Dust Tracks on a Road*." In *Life/Lines: Theorizing Women's Autobiography*, edited by Bella Brodzki and Celeste Schenck, 175–88. Ithaca: Cornell University Press, 1988.

McMath, Robert C. *Populist Vanguard: A History of the Southern Farmers' Alliance*. Chapel Hill: University of North Carolina Press, 1976.

McMillen, Neil R. *Dark Journey: Black Mississippians in the Age of Jim Crow*. Urbana: University of Illinois Press, 1990.

McMillen, Sally G. *To Raise Up the South: Sunday Schools in Black and White Churches, 1865–1915*. Baton Rouge: Louisiana State University Press, 2001.

McRae, Douglas G. "The Georgia Education Association." *Georgia Education Journal* 35 (April 1941): 7–25.

McRae, Elizabeth Gillespie. "Caretakers of Southern Civilization: Georgia Women and the Anti-Suffrage Campaign, 1914–1920." *Georgia Historical Quarterly* 82 (winter 1998): 801–28.

McRay, Sybil. *Pictorial History of Hall County*. Dallas: Taylor, 1985.

Meier, August. "History of the Negro Upper Class in Atlanta, Georgia, 1890–1958." *Journal of Negro Education* 28 (spring 1959): 128–39.

———. *Negro Thought in America, 1880–1915: Racial Ideologies in the Age of Booker T. Washington*. Ann Arbor: University of Michigan Press, 1963.

Melosh, Barbara. *"The Physician's Hand": Work Culture and Conflict in American Nursing*. Philadelphia: Temple University Press, 1982.

Meyerowitz, Joanne, ed. *Not June Cleaver: Women and Gender in Postwar America, 1945–1960*. Philadelphia: Temple University Press, 1994.

———. *Women Adrift: Independent Wage-Earners in Chicago, 1880–1930*. Chicago: University of Chicago Press, 1988.

Milkman, Ruth. *Gender at Work: The Dynamics of Job Segregation by Sex during World War II*. Urbana: University of Illinois Press, 1987.

———, ed. *Women, Work, and Protest: A Century of U.S. Women's Labor History*. Boston: Routledge and Kegan Paul, 1985.

Miller, Nancy K. "Writing Fictions: Women's Autobiography in France." In *Life/Lines: Theorizing Women's Autobiography*, edited by Bella Brodzki and Celeste Schenck, 45–61. Ithaca: Cornell University Press, 1988.

Minnix, Kathleen. *Laughter in the Amen Corner: The Life of Evangelist Sam Jones*. Athens: University of Georgia Press, 1993.

Mintz, Stephen. *A Prison of Expectations: The Family in Victorian Culture*. New York: New York University Press, 1983.

Mixon, Wayne. "Georgia." In *Encyclopedia of Religion in the South*, edited by Samuel S. Hill, 289–304. Macon: Mercer University Press, 1984.

Montgomery, David. *Workers' Control in America*. New York: Cambridge University Press, 1979.

Montgomery, William E. *Under Their Own Vine and Fig Tree: The African-American Church in the South, 1865–1900*. Baton Rouge: Louisiana State University Press, 1993.

Moody, Anne. *Coming of Age in Mississippi*. New York: Dell, 1968.

Moore, Jacqueline M. *Leading the Race: The Transformation of the Black Elite in the Nation's Capital, 1880–1920*. Charlottesville: University Press of Virginia, 1999.

Morantz-Sanchez, Regina Markell. *Sympathy and Science: Women Physicians in American Medicine*. New York: Oxford University Press, 1985.

Morris, Robert C. *Reading, 'Riting, and Reconstruction: The Education of Freemen in the South, 1861–1870*. Chicago: University of Chicago Press, 1981.

Morrison, Toni. *Beloved*. New York: New American Library, 1987.

Morton, Patricia. *Disfigured Images: The Historical Assault on Afro-American Women*. Westport, Conn.: Praeger, 1991.

Muncy, Robin. *Creating a Female Dominion in American Reform*. New York: Oxford University Press, 1991.

Neth, Mary. "Gender and the Family Labor System: Defining Work in the Rural Midwest." *Journal of Social History* 27 (spring 1994): 563–77.

Neverdon-Morton, Cynthia. *Afro-American Women of the South and the Advancement of Race, 1895–1925*. Knoxville: University of Tennessee Press, 1989.

Newby, I. A. *Black Carolinians: A History of Blacks in South Carolina from 1865 to 1968*. Columbia: University of South Carolina Press, 1973.

———. *Plain Folk in the New South: Social Change and Cultural Persistence, 1880–1915*. Baton Rouge: Louisiana State University Press, 1989.

Newton, Judith, and Deborah Rosenfelt, eds. *Feminist Criticism and Social Change: Sex, Class, and Race in Literature and Culture*. New York: Methuen, 1985.

Nicholson, Linda J. *Gender and History: The Limits of Social Theory in the Age of the Family*. New York: Columbia University Press, 1986.

Noll, Mark A. *A History of Christianity in the United States and Canada*. Grand Rapids, Mich.: Eerdmans, 1992.

———. *The Scandal of the Evangelical Mind*. Grand Rapids, Mich.: Eerdmans, 1994.

Norrell, Robert. *Reaping the Whirlwind: The Civil Rights Movement in Tuskegee*. New York: Knopf, 1985.

O'Brien, Michael. *Rethinking the South: Essays in Intellectual History*. Baltimore: Johns Hopkins University Press, 1988.

Odem, Mary. *Delinquent Daughters: Protecting and Policing Adolescent Female Sexuality in the United States, 1885–1920*. Chapel Hill: University of North Carolina Press, 1995.

Odum, Howard. *Race and Rumors of Race: Challenge to the American Crisis*. Chapel Hill: University of North Carolina Press, 1943.

Olson, Lynne. *Freedom's Daughters: The Unsung Heroines of the Civil Rights Movement from 1830–1970*. New York: Touchstone, 2001.

Orlick, Annelise. *Common Sense and a Little Fire: Women and Working-Class Politics in the United States, 1900–1965*. Chapel Hill: University of North Carolina Press, 1995.

Orr, Dorothy. *A History of Education in Georgia*. Chapel Hill: University of North Carolina Press, 1950.

Osterud, Nancy Grey. *Bonds of Community: The Lives of Farm Women in Nineteenth-Century New York*. Ithaca: Cornell University Press, 1991.

Outlaw, Mary Elizabeth. "State Normal School to Georgia State Teachers College: The Transition of an Institution." Ph.D. diss., University of Georgia, 1990.

Ownby, Ted. *American Dreams in Mississippi: Consumers, Poverty, and Culture, 1830–1998*. Chapel Hill: University of North Carolina Press, 1999.

———. *Subduing Satan: Religion, Recreation, and Manhood in the Rural South, 1865–1920*. Chapel Hill: University of North Carolina Press, 1990.

Owsley, Frank Lawrence. *Plain Folk of the Old South*. Baton Rouge: Louisiana State University Press, 1949.

Painter, Nell Irvin. *Exodusters: Black Migration to Kansas after Reconstruction*. New York: Knopf, 1976.

———. *Standing at Armageddon: The United States, 1877–1919*. New York: Norton, 1987.

Palladino, Grace. *Teenagers: An American History*. New York: Basic Books, 1996.

Palmer, Bryan D. *Descent into Discourse: The Reification of Language and the Writing of Social History*. Philadelphia: Temple University Press, 1990.

———. *"Man over Money": The Southern Populist Critique of American Capitalism*. Chapel Hill: University of North Carolina Press, 1980.

Parrish, Michael E. *Anxious Decades: America in Prosperity and Depression, 1920–1941*. New York: Norton, 1992.

Pascoe, Peggy A. *Relations of Rescue: The Search for Female Authority in the American West, 1874–1939*. New York: Oxford University Press, 1990.

Patterson, James T. *Brown v. Board of Education: A Civil Rights Milestone and Its Troubling Legacy*. New York: Oxford University Press, 2001.

———. *Congressional Conservatism and the New Deal: The Growth of the Conservative Coalition in Congress, 1933–1939*. Lexington: University Press of Kentucky, 1967.

Patton, Randall L. "A Southern Liberal and the Politics of Anti-Colonialism: The Governorship of Ellis Arnall." *Georgia Historical Quarterly* 74 (winter 1990): 599–621.

Payne, Charles M. *I've Got the Light of Freedom: The Organizing Tradition and the Mississippi Freedom Struggle*. Berkeley: University of California Press, 1995.

Peacock, James L., and Ruel W. Tyson Jr. *Pilgrims of Paradox: Calvinism and Experience among the Primitive Baptists of the Blue Ridge*. Washington, D.C.: Smithsonian Institution Press, 1989.

Peare, Catherine Owens. *Mary McLeod Bethune*. New York: Vanguard, 1951.

Peiss, Kathy. *Cheap Amusements: Working Women and Leisure in Turn-of-the-Century New York*. Philadelphia: Temple University Press, 1986.

Perkins, Linda. "The Impact of the 'Cult of True Womanhood' on the Education of Black Women." *Journal of Social Issues* 39 (1983): 17–28.

Pleck, Elizabeth H. "A Mother's Wages: Income Earning among Married Italian and Black Women, 1896–1911." In *A Heritage of Her Own: Toward a New Social History of American Women*, edited by Nancy F. Cott and Elizabeth H. Pleck, 490–510. New York: Simon and Schuster, 1979.

Polansky, Lee S. "'I Certainly Hope That You Will Be Able to Train Her': Reformers and the Georgia Training School for Girls." In *Before the New Deal: Social Welfare in the South, 1830–1930*, edited by Elna C. Green, 138–59. Athens: University of Georgia Press, 1999.

Pope, Liston. *Millhands and Preachers: A Study of Gastonia*. New Haven: Yale University Press, 1942.

Powdermaker, Hortense. *After Freedom: A Cultural Study of the Deep South*. New York: Viking, 1939.

Prentice, Alison, and Marjorie R. Theobald. *Women Who Taught: Perspectives on the History of Women and Teaching*. Toronto: University of Toronto Press, 1991.

Rabinowitz, Howard N. *Race Relations in the Urban South, 1865–1890*. New York: Oxford University Press, 1978.

Rable, George C. *Civil Wars: Women and the Crisis of Southern Nationalism*. Urbana: University of Illinois Press, 1989.

Raboteau, Albert J. *Slave Religion: The "Invisible Institution" in the Antebellum South*. New York: Oxford University Press, 1978.

Raines, Howell. *My Soul Is Rested: The Story of the Civil Rights Movement in the Deep South*. New York: Penguin, 1977.

Ramsey, B. Carlyle. "The University System Controversy Reexamined: The Talmadge-Holley Connection." *Georgia Historical Quarterly* 64 (spring 1980): 190–203.

Range, Willard. *A Century of Georgia Agriculture, 1850–1950*. Athens: University of Georgia Press, 1954.

———. *The Rise and Progress of Negro Colleges in Georgia, 1865–1949*. Athens: University of Georgia Press, 1951.

Raper, Arthur F. *Preface to Peasantry*. Chapel Hill: University of North Carolina Press, 1933.

———. *The Tragedy of Lynching*. Chapel Hill: University of North Carolina Press, 1933.

Rawick, George P. *From Sundown to Sunup: The Making of the Black Community*. Westport, Conn.: Greenwood, 1972.

Reed, Adolph, Jr. "Response to Eric Arnesen." *International Labor and Working-Class History* 60 (fall 2001): 69–80.

Reverby, Susan M. *Ordered to Care: The Dilemma of American Nursing, 1850–1945*. Cambridge: Cambridge University Press, 1987.

Ribuffo, Leo P. "Why Is There So Much Conservatism in the United States and Why Do So Few Historians Know Anything about It?" *American Historical Review* 99 (April 1994): 438–49.

Rice, Sarah. *He Included Me: The Autobiography of Sarah Rice*. Transcribed and edited by Louise Westling. Athens: University of Georgia Press, 1989.

Richardson, Joe M. *Christian Reconstruction: The American Missionary Association and Southern Blacks, 1861–1890*. Athens: University of Georgia Press, 1986.

Riley, Glenda. *The Female Frontier: A Comparative View of Women on the Prairie and the Plains*. Lawrence: University of Kansas Press, 1988.

Robinson, Armstead L., and Patricia Sullivan, eds. *New Directions in Civil Rights Studies*. Charlottesville: University Press of Virginia, 1991.

Robinson, Jo Ann Gibson. *The Montgomery Bus Boycott and the Women Who Started It: The Memoir of Jo Ann Gibson Robinson*. Edited by David J. Garrow. Knoxville: University of Tennessee Press, 1987.

Rodgers, Daniel T. "In Search of Progressivism." *Reviews in American History* 10 (December 1982): 113–32.

———. *The Work Ethic in Industrial America, 1850–1920*. Chicago: University of Chicago Press, 1978.

Roediger, David R. *The Wages of Whiteness: Race and the Making of the American Working Class*. London: Verso, 1991.

Rosaldo, Michelle Zimbalist. "The Use and Abuse of Anthropology: Reflections on Feminism and Cross-Cultural Understanding." *Signs* 5 (spring 1980): 389–417.

Rose, Willie Lee. *Rehearsal for Reconstruction: The Port Royal Experiment*. 1964; reprint, New York: Vintage, 1967.

Rosenberg, Rosalind. *Beyond Separate Spheres: Intellectual Roots of Modern Feminism*. New Haven: Yale University Press, 1982.

———. *Divided Lives: American Women in the Twentieth Century*. New York: Hill and Wang, 1992.

Rosengarten, Theodore, ed. *All God's Dangers: The Life of Nate Shaw*. New York: Vintage, 1984.

Rosenzweig, Roy. *Eight Hours for What We Will: Workers and Leisure in an Industrial City, 1870–1920*. New York: Cambridge University Press, 1983.

Ross, B. Joyce. "Mary McLeod Bethune and the National Youth Administration: A Case Study of Power Relationships in the Black Cabinet of Franklin D. Roosevelt." In *Black Leaders of the Twentieth Century*, edited by John Hope Franklin and August Meier, 191–220. Urbana: University of Illinois Press, 1982.

Rouse, Jacqueline Anne. *Lugenia Burns Hope, Black Southern Reformer*. Athens: University of Georgia Press, 1989.

Ruddick, Sara. *Maternal Thinking: Toward a Politics of Peace*. Boston: Beacon, 1989.

Ruether, Rosemary Radford, and Eleanor McLaughlin, eds. *Women of Spirit: Female Leadership in the Jewish and Christian Traditions*. New York: Simon and Schuster, 1979.

Ruiz, Vicki. *From Out of the Shadows*. New York: Oxford University Press, 1998.

Ryan, Mary P. *Cradle of the Middle Class: The Family in Oneida County, New York, 1790–1865*. New York: Cambridge University Press, 1981.

———. *Women in Public: Between Banners and Ballots, 1825–1880*. Baltimore: Johns Hopkins University Press, 1990.

Saville, Julie. *The Work of Reconstruction: From Slave to Wage Laborer in South Carolina, 1860–1870*. New York: Cambridge University Press, 1994.

Schackel, Sandra. *Social Housekeepers: Women Shaping Public Policy in New Mexico, 1920–1940*. Albuquerque: University of New Mexico, 1992.

Scharf, Lois. *To Work and to Wed: Female Employment, Feminism, and the Great Depression*. Westport, Conn.: Greenwood, 1980.

Scharf, Lois, and Joan M. Jensen, eds. *Decades of Discontent: The Women's Movement, 1920–1940*. Boston: Northeastern University Press, 1983.

Schlesinger, Arthur M., Jr. *The Coming of the New Deal*. Vol. 2, *The Age of Roosevelt*. Boston: Houghton Mifflin, 1959.

Schultz, Mark Roman. "The Unsolid South: An Oral History of Race, Class, and Geography in Hancock County, Georgia, 1910–1950." Ph.D. diss., University of Chicago, 1999.

Schwalm, Leslie A. *A Hard Fight for We: Women's Transition from Slavery to Freedom in South Carolina*. Urbana: University of Illinois Press, 1997.

Scott, Anne Firor. *Natural Allies: Women's Associations in American History*. Urbana: University of Illinois Press, 1991.

———. *The Southern Lady: From Pedestal to Politics, 1830–1930*. Chicago: University of Chicago Press, 1970.

Scott, Daryl Michael. *Contempt and Pity: Social Policy and the Image of the Damaged Black Psyche, 1880–1996*. Chapel Hill: University of North Carolina Press, 1997.

Scott, Joan Wallach. *Gender and the Politics of History*. New York: Columbia University Press, 1988.

Scranton, Philip, ed. *The Second Wave: Southern Industrialization from the 1940s to the 1970s*. Athens: University of Georgia Press, 2001.

Sealander, Judith. *Private Wealth and Public Duty: Foundation Philanthropy and the Reshaping of American Social Policy from Progressivism to the New Deal*. Baltimore: Johns Hopkins University Press, 1997.

Sell, E. S. *History of the State Normal School, Athens, Georgia*. Athens: University of Georgia Press, 1923.

Sharpless, M. Rebecca. *Fertile Ground, Narrow Choices: Women on Texas Cotton Farms, 1900–1940*. Chapel Hill: University of North Carolina Press, 1999.

Shaw, Barton. *The Wool-Hat Boys: Georgia's Populist Party*. Baton Rouge: Louisiana State University Press, 1984.

Shaw, Stephanie J. "Black Club Women and the Creation of the National Association of Colored Women." *Journal of Women's History* 3 (fall 1991): 10–25.

———. "Using the WPA Ex-Slave Narratives to Study the Impact of the Great Depression." *Journal of Southern History* 69 (August 2003): 623–54.

———. *What a Woman Ought to Be and to Do: Black Professional Women Workers during the Jim Crow Era*. Chicago: University of Chicago Press, 1996.

Simon, Bryant. *A Fabric of Defeat: The Politics of South Carolina Millhands, 1910–1948*. Chapel Hill: University of North Carolina Press, 1998.

———. "Racial Anxieties and Wartime Rumors." In *Labor in the South*, edited by Glenn T. Eskew, 83–101. Athens: University of Georgia Press, 2001.

Singal, Daniel Joseph. *The War Within: From Victorian to Modernist Thought in the South, 1919–1945*. Chapel Hill: University of North Carolina Press, 1982.

Sitkoff, Harvard. *A New Deal for Blacks: The Emergence of Civil Rights as a National Issue*. New York: Oxford University Press, 1978.

Sklar, Kathryn Kish. *Catharine Beecher, a Study in Domesticity*. New Haven: Yale University Press, 1973.

———. *Florence Kelley and the Nation's Work: The Rise of Women's Political Culture*. New Haven: Yale University Press, 1995.

———. "Hull House as a Community of Women Reformers in the 1890s." *Signs* 10 (summer 1985): 657–77.

Sklar, Martin J. *The Corporate Reconstruction of American Capitalism, 1890–1916: The Market, the Law, and Politics*. Cambridge: Cambridge University Press, 1988.

Smith, J. Douglas. *Managing White Supremacy: Race, Politics, and Citizenship in Jim Crow Virginia*. Chapel Hill: University of North Carolina Press, 2002.

Smith, Jennifer Lund. "The Ties That Bind: Educated African American Women in Postemancipation Atlanta." In *Georgia Black and White: Explorations in the Race Relations of a Southern State, 1865–1950*, edited by John C. Inscoe, 91–105. Athens: University of Georgia Press, 1994.

———. "'Twill Take Some Time to Study When I Get Over': Varieties of African American Education in Reconstruction Georgia." Ph.D. diss., University of Georgia, 1997.

Smith, Lillian. *Killers of the Dream*. New York: Norton, 1978.

Smith, Sidonie. "Resisting the Gaze of Embodiment: Women's Autobiography in the Nineteenth Century." In *American Women's Autobiography: Fea(s)ts of Memory*, edited by Margo Culley, 75–110. Madison: University of Wisconsin Press, 1992.

Solomon, Barbara Miller. *In the Company of Educated Women: A History of Women and Higher Education in America*. New Haven: Yale University Press, 1985.

Sosna, Morton. *In Search of the Silent South: Southern Liberals and the Race Issue*. New York: Columbia University Press, 1977.

Spritzer, Lorraine Nelson, and Jean B. Bergmark. *Grace Towns Hamilton and the Politics of Southern Change*. Athens: University of Georgia Press, 1997.

Stanley, Amy Dru. "Home Life and the Morality of the Market." In *The Market Revolution in America: Social, Political, and Religious Expressions, 1800–1880*, edited by Melvyn Stokes and Stephen Conway, 74–91. Charlottesville: University Press of Virginia, 1996.

Stepto, Robert B. *From behind the Veil: A Study of Afro-American Narrative*. Urbana: University of Illinois Press, 1979.

Still, Betty P. *History and Memories of Liberty Baptist Church/First Baptist Church, Lilburn, 1840–1980*. Buchanan, Ga.: Haralson, 1980.

Strasser, Susan. *Never Done: A History of American Housework*. New York: Pantheon, 1982.

Strober, Myra, and David B. Tyack. "Why Do Women Teach and Men Manage?" *Signs* 5 (spring 1980): 494–503.

Sullivan, Patricia. *Days of Hope: Race and Democracy in the New Deal Era*. Chapel Hill: University of North Carolina Press, 1996.

Susman, Warren I. *Culture as History: The Transformation of American Society in the Twentieth Century*. New York: Pantheon, 1984.

Swain, Martha H. *Ellen S. Woodward: New Deal Advocate for Women*. Jackson: University Press of Mississippi, 1995.

Tentler, Leslie Woodcock. *Wage-Earning Women: Industrial Work and Family Life in the United States, 1900–1930*. New York: Oxford University Press, 1979.

Terborg-Penn, Rosalyn. *African-American Women in the Struggle for the Vote, 1850–1920*. Bloomington: Indiana University Press, 1998.

Terkel, Studs. *Hard Times: An Oral History of the Great Depression*. New York: Pantheon, 1970.

Terrill, Tom E., and Jerrold Hirsch, eds. *Such as Us: Southern Voices of the Thirties*. Chapel Hill: University of North Carolina Press, 1978.

Thelen, David, ed. *Memory and American History*. Bloomington: Indiana University Press, 1990.

Thomas, Ella Gertrude Clanton. *The Secret Eye: The Journal of Ella Gertrude Clanton Thomas*. Edited by Virginia Ingraham Burr. Chapel Hill: University of North Carolina Press, 1990.

Thurmond, Michael. *A Story Untold: Black Men and Women in Athens*. Athens: Clarke County School District, 1978.

Tindall, George B. *The Emergence of the New South, 1913–1945*. Baton Rouge: Louisiana State University Press, 1967.

Tolnay, Stewart E. *The Bottom Rung: African American Life on Southern Farms*. Urbana: University of Illinois Press, 1999.

Torrence, Ridgely. *The Story of John Hope*. New York: Macmillan, 1948.

Trachtenberg, Alan. *The Incorporation of America: Culture and Society in the Gilded Age*. New York: Hill and Wang, 1982.

Trillin, Calvin. *An Education in Georgia*. Athens: University of Georgia Press, 1991.

Tuck, Stephen G. N. *Beyond Atlanta: The Struggle for Racial Equality in Georgia, 1940–1980*. Athens: University of Georgia Press, 2001.

Tullos, Allen. *Habits of Industry: White Culture and the Transformation of the Piedmont*. Chapel Hill: University of North Carolina Press, 1990.

Turner, Elizabeth Hayes. "'White-Gloved Ladies' and 'New Women' in the Texas Woman Suffrage Movement." In *Southern Women: Histories and Identities*, edited by Virginia Bernhard, Betty Brandon, Elizabeth Fox-Genovese, and Theda Perdue, 129–56. Columbia: University of Missouri Press, 1992.

———. *Women, Culture, and Community: Religion and Reform in Galveston, 1880–1920*. New York: Oxford University Press, 1997.

Tushnet, Mark V. *The NAACP's Legal Strategy against Segregated Education, 1925–1950*. Chapel Hill: University of North Carolina Press, 1987.

Tyack, David B. *The One Best System: A History of American Urban Education*. Cambridge: Harvard University Press, 1974.

Tyack, David B., and Elisabeth Hansot. *Managers of Virtue: Public School Leadership in America, 1820–1980*. New York: Basic Books, 1982.

Tyson, Timothy B. *Radio Free Dixie: Robert F. Williams and the Roots of Black Power*. Chapel Hill: University of North Carolina Press, 1999.

Urban, Wayne T. *Black Scholar: Horace Mann Bond, 1904–1972*. Athens: University of Georgia Press, 1992.

Wadelington, Charles W., and Richard F. Knapp. *Charlotte Hawkins Brown and Palmer Memorial Institute: What One Young African American Woman Could Do*. Chapel Hill: University of North Carolina Press, 1999.

Wagner, Clarence M. *Profiles of Black Georgia Baptists: 200 Years of Georgia Baptist and 100 Years of National Baptist History*. Atlanta: Bennett Brothers, 1980.

Walker, Melissa. *All We Knew Was to Farm: Rural Women in the Upcountry South, 1919–1941*. Baltimore: Johns Hopkins University Press, 2000.

Walker, Vanessa Siddle. *Their Highest Potential: An African American School Community in the Segregated South*. Chapel Hill: University of North Carolina Press, 1996.

Walkowitz, Daniel J. "The Making of a Feminine Professional Identity: Social Workers in the 1920s." *American Historical Review* 95 (October 1990): 1051–75.

Wallenstein, Peter. *From Slave South to New South: Public Policy in Nineteenth-Century Georgia*. Chapel Hill: University of North Carolina Press, 1987.

Wandersee, Winifred. *Women's Work and Family Values, 1920–1940*. New York: Cambridge University Press, 1981.

Ware, Susan. *Beyond Suffrage: Women in the New Deal*. Cambridge: Harvard University Press, 1981.

———. *Holding Their Own: American Women in the 1930s*. Boston: Twayne, 1982.

———. *Partner and I: Molly Dewson, Feminism, and New Deal Politics*. New Haven: Yale University Press, 1987.

Warren, Wallace Hugh. "Progress and Its Discontents: The Transformation of the Georgia Foothills, 1920–1970." Master's thesis, University of Georgia, 1997.

Washington, Booker T. *Booker T. Washington Papers*. 14 vols. Edited by Louis R. Harlan. Urbana: University of Illinois Press, 1972–89.

———. *Up from Slavery: The Autobiography of Booker T. Washington*. New York: Carol, 1989.

Wells, Robert V. *Revolutions in Americans' Lives: A Demographic Perspective on the History of Americans, Their Families, and Their Society.* Westport, Conn.: Greenwood, 1982.

Wells-Barnett, Ida B.. *Crusade for Justice: The Autobiography of Ida B. Wells.* Edited by Alfreda Duster. Chicago: University of Chicago Press, 1970.

Welty, Eudora. *Losing Battles.* New York: Vintage, 1970.

Wexler, Laura. *Fire in a Canebrake: The Last Mass Lynching in America.* New York: Scribner, 2003.

Wheeler, Marjorie Spruill. *New Women of the New South: The Leaders of the Woman Suffrage Movement in the Southern United States.* New York: Oxford University Press, 1993.

White, Deborah Gray. *Ar'n't I a Woman?: Female Slaves in the Plantation South.* New York: Norton, 1985.

———. *Too Heavy a Load: Black Women in Defense of Themselves, 1894–1994.* New York: Norton, 1999.

Whites, LeeAnn. *The Civil War as a Crisis in Gender: Augusta, Georgia, 1860–1890.* Athens: University of Georgia Press, 1995.

———. "Love, Hate, Rape, Lynching: Rebecca Latimer Felton and the Gender Politics of Racial Violence." In *Democracy Betrayed: The Wilmington Race Riot of 1898 and Its Legacy,* edited by David S. Cecelski and Timothy B. Tyson, 143–62. Chapel Hill: University of North Carolina Press, 1998.

———. "Rebecca Latimer Felton and the Wife's Farm: The Class and Racial Politics of Gender Reform." *Georgia Historical Quarterly* 76 (summer 1992): 354–72.

Wiebe, Robert H. *The Search for Order, 1877–1920.* New York: Hill and Wang, 1967.

Wilkerson-Freeman, Sarah. "The Woman Who Beat the Governor: Gay Shepperson of the Georgia New Deal vs. Eugene Talmadge and the Old Order." Paper presented at the Southern Historical Association Meeting, New Orleans, November 1991.

Williams, Raymond. *Marxism and Literature.* New York: Oxford University Press, 1977.

Williams-May, Gloria T. "Lucy Craft Laney—The Mother of the Children of the People, Educator, Reformer, Social Activist." Ph.D. diss., University of South Carolina, 1998.

Williamson, Joel. *The Crucible of Race: Black-White Relations in the American South since Emancipation.* New York: Oxford University Press, 1984.

Willis, Susan. *Specifying: Black Women Writing the American Experience.* Madison: University of Wisconsin Press, 1987.

Wilson, Charles Reagan. *Baptized in Blood: The Religion of the Lost Cause, 1865–1920.* Athens: University of Georgia Press, 1980.

Wind, James P., and James W. Lewis, eds. *American Congregations: New Perspectives in the Study of Congregations.* Vol. 2. Chicago: University of Chicago Press, 1994.

Wolcott, Victoria W. "'Bible, Bath, and Broom': Nannie Helen Burroughs's National Training School and African-American Racial Uplift." *Journal of Women's History* 9 (spring 1997): 88–110.

Wolgast, Elizabeth H. *The Grammar of Justice*. Ithaca: Cornell University Press, 1987.

Woloch, Nancy. *Women and the American Experience*. New York: McGraw-Hill, 1994.

Woodman, Harold D. *King Cotton and His Retainers: Financing and Marketing the Cotton Crop of the South, 1800–1925*. Lexington: University Press of Kentucky, 1968.

———. "Sequel to Slavery: The New History Views the Postbellum South." *Journal of Southern History* 43 (November 1977): 523–54.

Woodruff, Nan Elizabeth. "Mississippi Delta Planters and Debates over Mechanization, Labor, and Civil Rights in the 1940s." *Journal of Southern History* 60 (May 1994): 263–84.

Woodson, Carter G. *The History of the Negro Church*. Washington, D.C.: Associated Press, 1921.

———. *The Mis-Education of the Negro*. Washington, D.C.: Associated Press, 1933.

Woodward, C. Vann. *The Burden of Southern History*. Baton Rouge: Louisiana State University Press, 1968.

———. *Origins of the New South, 1877–1913*. Baton Rouge: Louisiana State University Press, 1951.

———. *The Strange Career of Jim Crow*. 3d ed. New York: Oxford University Press, 1974.

Wright, Gavin. *Old South, New South: Revolutions in the Southern Economy since the Civil War*. New York: Basic Books, 1986.

Wyatt-Brown, Bertram. "Black Schooling during Reconstruction." In *The Web of Southern Social Relations: Women, Family, and Education*, edited by Walter J. Fraser Jr., R. Frank Saunders Jr., and Jon L. Wakelyn, 146–65. Athens: University of Georgia Press, 1985.

———. *Southern Honor: Ethics and Behavior in the Old South*. New York: Oxford University Press, 1982.

Yans-McLaughlin, Virginia. *Family and Community: Italian Immigrants in Buffalo, 1880–1930*. Ithaca: Cornell University Press, 1977.

———. "Patterns of Work and Family Organization: Buffalo's Italians." In *The American Family in Social-Historical Perspective*, edited by Michael Gordon, 136–51. New York: St. Martin's, 1973.

Yung, Judy. *Unbound Feet: A Social History of Chinese Women in San Francisco*. Berkeley: University of California Press, 1995.

Index

Adams, Ercelene, 52

African American Civic Leagues, 202, 224, 226, 228. *See also* Georgia Teachers and Education Association; Harper, Charles Lincoln; Tate, Horace E.

African American education: beginnings of, 22, 29; and curriculum, 120–22; and denominational colleges, 92; funding for, 24, 96–97, 151; limitations on, 74, 82, 92, 102, 111, 158; meaning of, 3, 33, 99, 124, 156; and moral instruction, 50, 104, 123; and teacher certification, 152; white reformers' attitudes toward, 94. *See also* African American religion; Public education

African American families: discipline in, 49–52; disease in, 61; gender roles in, 42, 53, 156; and marriage, 43; and rural labor, 42; significance of women's work to, 16, 41, 43, 48–49; size of, 43; support of, for education, 43, 103, 156, 238; and voter registration, 180, 184, 195–96, 216, 217–18, 223

African American migration: in Georgia, 21, 157, 163; and the Great Migration, 100

African American religion: community role of, 67, 68–69; and membership, 167; relationship of, to education, 22, 68, 92, 95, 121; and salvation, 22. *See also* Evangelical Protestantism

African American teachers: ambitions of, 44; civil rights work of, 2, 200, 224, 227; community role of, 41, 119; as cultural mediators, 2, 4, 123; definition of, 112; education of, 96; family role of, 43; financial restrictions on, 96, 160; membership of, in GTEA, 170; membership of, in NAACP, 170; reforms of, 2, 113–14, 124, 233

Agricultural and Mechanical School for Colored Youth (State Teachers and Agricultural High School; State Teachers and Agricultural College, Forsyth): funding for, 151; and industrial education, 92; name changes of, 262 (n. 68)

Agricultural and Mechanical Schools, 88, 89, 90

Alexander, Jane Thigpen: childhood of, 57; education of, 90; and household labor, 62, 63; parents of, 55

American Missionary Association (AMA), 25, 92, 93

Anderson, Rosa Penson: and discipline, 50; education of, 104, 117; as educator, 242; family of, 48; mother of, 49, 53

Arnall, Ellis: attitude of, toward African Americans, 190; attitude of, to white primary, 217; gubernatorial campaign of, in 1942, 188–92; and impact of New Deal, 155; as moderate, 192, 195; policies of, 11; support of, for

White, William Jefferson: and African
American education, 23; and African
American equality, 21, 31; and Ware
High School, 30

White families: discipline among, 56–58,
59, 60; education of, 64, 156, 182, 186,
211, 238; family size of, 43; gender roles
in, 42, 56, 59, 63, 139, 156, 165, 211;
and labor, 42, 62; migration of, 163;
mortality in, 61; religion of, 67, 69–71,
167–68; and respectability, 58–59

White supremacy: and definitions of
race, 32, 65; and fears about miscegenation, 218; and restrictions on
voting, 31, 218; and violence, 21, 35,
220, 222–23

White teachers: changes among,
during World War II, 207; as cultural
mediators, 2, 4, 40, 146, 233; definition of, 112, 113, 230–32; distinctions
of, from African American teachers,
111; reforms of, 2, 114

Williams, Leona Clark: ambition of, 39;
childhood of, 56–57; on class, 66;
education of, 64, 73, 80, 90–91, 142,
215; as educator, 138, 141, 143, 164,
166, 194, 232, 241; family of, 43, 138;
household labor of, 62, 63; parents of,
13–14, 55, 59, 67, 257 (n. 68); on
racism, 66; relationship of, to trustees,
71; relatives of, in education, 67, 71;
and religion, 69, 70; on teachers, 141,
230, 231; and teaching conditions, 1,
110, 139; and values, 140, 164, 194;
work of, during World War II, 207

Woofter, Thomas Jackson, 88, 91, 146,
147

World War II: impact of, on education,
155; impact of, on Georgia, 155

Wright, Richard R.: at Georgia State
Industrial College, 30, 93, 105; and
Negro Civic Improvement League, 93;
at Ware High School, 30